Prehistoric
Coastal
Adaptations

THE ECONOMY AND ECOLOGY
OF MARITIME MIDDLE AMERICA

This is a volume in

Studies in Archeology

A complete list of titles in this series appears at the end of this volume.

Prehistoric Coastal Adaptations

THE ECONOMY AND ECOLOGY OF MARITIME MIDDLE AMERICA

EDITED BY

BARBARA L. STARK
Department of Anthropology
Arizona State University
Tempe, Arizona

BARBARA VOORHIES
Department of Anthropology
University of California, Santa Barbara
Santa Barbara, California

ACADEMIC PRESS   New York   San Francisco   London   1978

A Subsidiary of Harcourt Brace Jovanovich, Publishers

ACADEMIC PRESS, INC.
111 Fifth Avenue, New York, New York 10003

United Kingdom Edition published by
ACADEMIC PRESS, INC. (LONDON) LTD.
24/28 Oval Road, London NW1 7DX

Library of Congress Cataloging in Publication Data

Main entry under title:

Prehistoric coastal adaptations.

(Studies in archaeology)
Includes bibliographies.
1. Indians of Central America--Addresses, essays,
lectures. 2. Indians of Mexico--Addresses, essays,
lectures. 3. Maritime anthropology--Addresses, essays,
lectures. 4. Central America--Antiquities--Addresses,
essays, lectures. 5. Mexico--Antiquities--Addresses,
essays, lectures. I. Stark, Barbara L. II. Voorhies,
Barbara.
F1434.P73   972   77-77245
ISBN 0-12-663250-2

PRINTED IN THE UNITED STATES OF AMERICA

For costeños *we have known*
and the
"Real Coastal Archaeologists"
Michael D. Coe
and
Kent V. Flannery

Contents

PART II
Procurement Patterns   23

PART III
Settlement Patterns   97

List of Figures

List of Contributors

Numbers in parentheses indicate the pages on which the authors' contributions begin.

David A. Freidel (239), Department of Anthropology, Southern Methodist University, University Park, Dallas, Texas 75275

Pat Hansell (43), Department of Anthropology, Temple University, Philadelphia, Pennsylvania 19122

Mary W. Helms (121), Department of Anthropology, Northwestern University, Evanston, Illinois 60201

Frederick W. Lange (101), Museo Nacional de Costa Rica, San José, Costa Rica, Central America

Richard Werner Magnus (61), Banco Central de Nicaragua, Managua, Nicaragua, Central America

Maricruz Paillés H. (81), Sección de Arqueología, Museo Nacional de Anthropología, Reforma y Gandhi, Mexico City 5, Mexico

Anthony J. Ranere (43), Department of Anthropology, Temple University, Philadelphia, Pennsylvania 19122

William T. Sanders (269), Department of Anthropology, Pennsylvania State University, University Park, Pennsylvania 16902

Barbara L. Stark (211, 275), Department of Anthropology, Arizona State University, Tempe, Arizona 85281

Barbara Voorhies (5, 275), Department of Anthropology, University of California, Santa Barbara, California 93106

Elizabeth S. Wing (29), Florida State Museum, University of Florida, Gainesville, Florida 32601

Judith Francis Zeitlin (151), Department of Anthropology, Yale University, New Haven, Connecticut 06520

Robert N. Zeitlin (183), Department of Anthropology, Yale University, New Haven, Connecticut 06520

Preface

In 1975 we discussed the need to draw together researchers currently investigating ancient coastal peoples in Middle America; individual scholars with similar interests were scattered widely in North and Central America, and, as a result, communication among us was less than ideal. It appeared to us that there would be a marked benefit if we could foster increased exchange of ideas among ourselves. The result was a symposium at the May 1976 meeting of the Society for American Archaeology in Saint Louis, Missouri. Participants were invited to present papers dealing with aspects of ecology, economy, settlement pattern, and demography. Some contributors reported on current fieldwork; others spoke from the perspective of final data analysis. Under meeting conditions, the symposium contributors did not have as great an opportunity for informal discussion as we all would have preferred, but the papers presented encouraged us to pursue publication of an edited collection dealing with Middle American coastal studies. Regrettably other commitments prevented some symposium contributors from meeting the scheduled deadlines for this volume. However, we were fortunate in being able to expand the repertoire of papers with those of three contributors who did not participate at Saint Louis.

This volume provides the first instance of a published attempt to focus on ancient Middle American coastal peoples and to synthesize Middle American coastal studies. It represents our effort to move from a phase of limited communication among ourselves to a phase in which we share with others some of our efforts in coastal research. It contains information of particular interest to Middle Americanists, principally to archaeologists but also to ethnohistorians. However, it also gives an introduction to the underlying research problems historically and currently important in Middle American precontact coastal studies as well as treatments of ecological and economic aspects of coastal prehistory that have theoretical interest for specialists in those topics. The volume is in fact organized topically rather than areally.

The contents of this volume by no means fully represent current projects dealing with ecological and economic topics in a coastal setting. However, we are pleased to assemble a topically and geographically wide-ranging collection that illustrates some of the kinds of research under way. To better achieve our original goals of comparison and discussion, we asked William Sanders to comment on the contents, and we have added a final section dealing with future research directions.

We thank our colleagues John Martin, James Schoenwetter, and Dennis Young for their constructive criticism on parts of this book. We wish to thank Susana Berdecio, Karin Harris, and Paul Heuston for assistance with illustrations. Sue Lewenstein provided an English translation of Paillés's article. Bunny Rothman expertly and cheerfully typed portions of the manuscript.

PART I

Introduction

The studies assembled in this volume report recent research on Middle American peoples who lived within coastal habitats. There are two reasons to adopt this focus. First, commonalities between the two coastal plains that border the Middle American land mass provide similar physical and biotic conditions to which humans have adjusted their lives. Because of the environmental similarities, the two coasts can be treated as a single broad analytical unit. By comparing them with those of people elsewhere, we can begin to identify common factors in coastal adaptations. Coastal environments present situations where subsistence and other economic pursuits may differ markedly from those prevailing elsewhere. And coastal waters facilitate transport in a manner more marked than in most other environments. Therefore, coastal peoples may reveal adaptations representing a distinctive element in Middle American sociocultural evolution.

A second reason for the present collection is that archaeological and historical studies of Middle American coastal peoples have lagged behind similar studies of peoples in other Middle American settings. As a result we know relatively little about coastal culture history. Consequently, the role of coastal peoples in major social transformations has been undervalued in Middle American studies. This volume begins to fill this research void. Most of the authors report primary research carried out recently, but only at limited coastal locations. Hence, most of the contributors tackle prehistoric data for a fairly small region and a restricted time period. They also consider what ecological or economic processes or models may account for the recovered evidence.

A broader perspective is adopted in the first chapter by Voorhies, by Sanders in his "Commentary" (Chapter 12), and by the editors in the concluding chapter, "Future Research Directions." In these discussions some of the long-standing debates about the sociocultural role of coastal lowland peoples in Middle America are rekindled. Two major recurrent issues are the "marginality" of coastal societies and the relative balance between local environmental factors and economic ones (especially trade) in determining the course of coastal lowland prehistory.

Chapter 1, "Previous Research on Coastal Adaptations in Middle America," was written by Voorhies to counterpoint the other research reported here by providing a historical review of coastal studies in Middle American archaeology. Although Voorhies seeks to make generalizations about coastal life, she restricts her discussion to those sites that are located sufficiently close to the marine environment to imply possible utilization of aquatic resources. Voorhies thus interprets the theme of coastal adaptation in a functional way to mean the direct involvement of humans within the saltwater ecosystem. Other contributors to this volume have interpreted the central theme in a geographic way, emphasizing the coastal plain as the unit of study.

Voorhies organizes her discussion around four subjects, and we have chosen to arrange the chapters of this volume under three headings adopted from her introductory chapter. Her first subject is the known chronology of nearshore midden sites, with particular emphasis placed on the earliest occupations. Although the topic of origins also is addressed by other contributors, we have not chosen to arrange the articles according to this theme.

The second topic advanced in Voorhies' chapter is resource procurement patterns. The study of procurement patterns is necessarily fundamental to the ecological analysis of any population. One concern of the author is to identify some major coastal biotic zones and their relation to site locations. Ecological patterns of procurement at these sites seem to be correlated with site location. Because procurement patterns must be addressed in ecological and economic studies, it is not surprising that many contributors to this book include discussions of this topic. We have grouped together four of these essays in Part II, "Procurement Patterns," because of their focus on this issue.

Another topic in the introductory essay is settlement patterns. In the archaeological literature, settlement pattern has come to deal with all aspects of the spatial distribution of human groups and their remains. In some instances demographic characteristics such as population size and density are also included under this rubric. Within the subject matter of settlement pattern is included locational analysis, a topic dealing with the interpretation of spatial relationships of archaeological data. Both the demographic and spatial emphases in settlement pattern studies are receiving increasing attention in current archaeological work, but they are not represented in earlier studies. Previous coastal research is even quite deficient in regional-scale settlement investigations; most studies have dealt with only one or a few sites. Consequently, Voorhies' discussion of settlement patterns focuses only on whether sedentarism occurred earlier in the coastal lowlands as compared with the uplands, as some previous investigators have suggested. Voorhies argues against this proposition, in part because of its restricted view of the role of exchange. Most contributors to the present volume are concerned, in some measure, with reconstructing the spatial distribution of people who once occupied the site or region under investigation. We have grouped together under "Settlement Patterns" three chapters in which this topic is particularly emphasized.

Voorhies' discussion of exchange patterns raises the issue of the role of coastal peoples as participants in interregional networks of resource exchange. For this topic there is a marked lack of evidence available in the published literature, which seriously hinders perception of general patterns. Exchange is currently receiving increasing and systematic archaeological attention. Consequently, resource exchange is a topic that is discussed by many of this volume's contributors. Part IV contains three chapters that have this topic as their primary focus.

We have selected the three topics of procurement, settlement, and exchange patterns as organizational devices because they not only work satisfactorily but also constitute important categories of data for the study of economy and ecology. We suspect that ecologic–economic factors ultimately will explain many kinds of variations in human behavioral systems. The three topics each offer slightly different kinds of variables with which we can model ecological and economic processes. The success of current and future research depends on identification of variables amenable to archaeological study as well as on development and testing of behavioral models that articulate variables to one another and spell out the effects of changes in them. As will become apparent from these contributions, we are at an early stage in the process of identifying variables, of developing and probing alternative models, and of assembling appropriate kinds of data with which to analyze them.

chapter 1

Previous Research on Nearshore Coastal Adaptations in Middle America

BARBARA VOORHIES
University of California, Santa Barbara

INTRODUCTION

The purpose of this chapter is to review some published research that focuses on the ecologies of prehistoric coastal peoples of Middle America. The review is intended primarily for the nonspecialist unfamiliar with these archaeological studies. Accordingly, it is an orientation device designed to enable the reader to formulate a more informed assessment of the current research reported in the present volume. In addition to my primary purpose of providing background information, I will discuss briefly some current research trends. These trends are discussed more fully in the last chapter of this book.

I am considering here only investigations of stratified deposits (middens) that occur in close proximity to the Middle American shorelines. The reasons for this narrow focus are that (a) habitats, and by implication the ecologies of prehistoric peoples responsible for these deposits, are approximately similar and therefore permit meaningful comparison; and (b) ecological problems frequently have been studied by investigators of this type of site (and often ignored at other site types). Although the considered sites (Table 1.1) do not exhaust the list of publications on Middle American coastal middens, they are among the studies that have had the greatest research impact. In addition, these studies can be considered representative of the type of work that has been carried out and published to date.

Sites that are located on the coastal plain but far from the shoreline and sites with large-scale public architecture are not treated in this discussion. The reason for the exclusion of the first class of sites is that the inland location initially suggests that inhabitants exhibited ecologies significantly different from (but not necessarily independent of) those of the peoples of the coastal margins. The inland situation of these sites suggests that direct ecological interactions with the biophysical environment would be primarily within the terrestrial ecosystem. In contrast, people occupying nearshore sites are expected to have participated more significantly within the saltwater ecosystem. I am also excluding from the present discussion sites with large-scale public architecture. This is because studies of such higher-order settlements usually have not been designed to produce ecological data and hence cannot be used in ecological comparisons.

The coastal plains of Middle America have been the foci of archaeological research for only a comparatively short time. In the early part of this century, coastal midden sites were generally ignored in favor of civic–ceremonial centers. Because the majority of these sites are found in upland rather than coastal habitats, research interests were directed at noncoastal geographic regions. As late as the middle 1950s only a few coastal middens had been reported (e.g., Ekholm 1944; Drucker 1948). The few reported sites received scant attention other than their identification, so that the nature of coastal adaptations was obscure.

Most of the reports of coastal sites considered here have been published since the middle 1950s (Table 1.1). The geographic distribution of archaeological investigations at Middle American coastal locations is shown in Figure 1.1. The areas are widely separated and few in number. They are also more numerous on the west coast compared with the east coast of Middle America. The distributional disparity easily might be the result of vagaries of research, but possibly it is the indirect result of environmental differences between the two coastal zones. This possibility has not yet been investigated.

Some of the previous studies discussed here have involved subsurface sampling at a limited number of sites. None of the regional studies consulted, however, has reported results of an intensive archaeological study of a defined section of the coastal plain that combines environmental stratification, detailed surface survey, and subsurface sampling at a large number of sites. This lack means that at the present time no portion of the Middle

Figure 1.1. Coastal archaeological sites in Middle America that are mentioned in text. The location of Santa Luisa has not been plotted. It is on the Gulf Coast, north of Patarata 52 and south of the peninsula shown on the map.

American coastal plain has been thoroughly studied in such a way that its entire culture history is uniformly well known. Instead, available knowledge of the culture history of the Middle American coastal plains is effectively limited to some well-studied specific occupations that are widely separated in time and space.

The deficiency of information concerning the prehistory of Middle American coastal lowlands is in striking contrast with the relatively more abundant research available for several upland valleys. At least five upland valleys (i.e., the Central Depression of Chiapas, and the valleys of Oaxaca, Puebla, Tehuacán, and Teotihuacán) recently have been the foci of large-scale research projects that have no counterparts in the humid coastal lowlands. This previous research bias has produced a distorted view that necessarily deemphasizes the role of coastal peoples throughout Middle American culture history.

Sanders (1968), for example, views Mesoamerican coastal lowland peoples as not significantly involved in the processes leading to the de-

Table 1.1
COASTAL SITES MENTIONED IN TEXT

Site or regional names	Occupational phases	Dates	Locations	Sources
Pacific Coast				
Marismas Nacionales	related to those of Chametla and Amapa	A.D. 700–750 to 1300	southern Sinaloa and northern Nayarit	Scott 1974; Shenkel 1971,1974
San Blas 4	Matanchén	minimum age 1570 B.C. (1972) 1760 B.C. (1974)	San Blas, Nayarit	Mountjoy 1971,1972, 1974
Barra de Navidad	—	A.D. 600 to contact	Barra de Navidad, Jalisco	Nicholson and Meighan 1974; Long and Wire 1966
Puerto Marqués	Ostiones	2950–2450 B.C. (Brush)	Puerto Marqués, Guerrero	Brush 1965, 1969
Chantuto sites	Chantuto	3000–2000 B.C.	Chantuto zone, Chiapas	Drucker 1948; Lorenzo 1955; Voorhies 1975, 1976
Ocós Area				
La Victoria	Ocos Conchas 1–2 Cuadros Jocotal	1300–1100 B.C. (?) 800–300 B.C. 1000–850 B.C. 850–800 B.C. (?)	Ocós area, Guatemala	Coe 1961
Salinas La Blanca				Coe and Flannery 1967
IS-3, IS-7, IS-11	Chiriquí	A.D. 1100–1500	Gulf of Chiriquí, Panama	Linares de Sapir 1968

8

Cerro Mangote	—	4858 B.C. ± 100 years (Stone 1972:21)	Cerro Mangote, Panama	McGimsey 1956
Atlantic Coast Cancún midden	—	250 B.C.	Isla Cancún, Quintana Roo	Andrews IV 1969, 1975; Andrews IV et al. 1975; Wing 1975
Patarata 52	Camarón 1–3	A.D. 250–550	Lower Papaloapan drainage, Veracruz	Stark 1974
	Limón	A.D. 600–900		
Not reported	Viejón	undated	Central Veracruz	MacNeish 1967
Isla de Pithaya	—	Formative (?)	near Colonia de las Flores, Tampico	Ekholm 1944; Cook 1946
Santa Luisa	Palo Hueco, and many subsequent	3100–2600 B.C.; 1300 B.C. to present	Lower Tecolutla drainage, Veracruz	Wilkerson 1975; Wing, this volume

velopment of a state level of sociopolitical organization. This organization, which may have first occurred in the uplands of Central Mexico, was a result, Sanders believes, of the development of a symbiotic exchange system among upland communities located in distinct habitats. One alternative view is that the significant symbiosis was instead between peoples living in more fundamentally different environments, as, for example, in the upland valleys and the coastal plains. The paucity of information concerning the coastal zones makes it impossible to assess these alternative views.

There are several research problems that I consider to be pivotal in the ongoing study of Middle American coastal populations. These central problems concern the beginnings of coastal adaptation and diachronic attributes of the prehistoric systems of resource procurement, resource exchange, and human settlement. These topical issues will now be discussed in turn.

BEGINNINGS

Relative to other environmental zones in Middle America, the known chronology of the coastal plains is unusually short. This situation is illustrated by Figure 1.2, on which are plotted the dated occupations of the sites under consideration.

The earliest dated occupation of 5000 B.C. (from Cerro Mangote, Panama) is approximate (cited by Stone 1972:21; see also Ranere and Hansell, this volume). It derives from a single radiocarbon dated sample, and by virtue of this fact alone, it must be considered suspect. Nevertheless, it is consistent with the patterning of other known dated coastal occupations, which tend, however, to be younger in age. Accordingly, the date of 5000 B.C. provisionally can be accepted as the minimal age of human occupation along Middle American coasts. This minimal date falls within the Archaic Period in the general Mesoamerican chronology.

In addition to the Cerro Mangote material, three other early coastal occupations have been positively identified (Chantuto, Matanchén, Ostiones, Palo Hueco). These are represented by large accumulations of midden material in which ceramics are conspicuously lacking, although lithics are present. The volume of deposits indicates either a rapid rate of deposition over a short period of time or a slow rate of deposition over a long period of time. At the Chantuto sites (Voorhies 1976), which perhaps are the most thoroughly studied, radiocarbon dates bracket the occupation between 3000 and 2000 B.C. Other evidence indicates to me that a small resident population at these sites may have been seasonally augmented by temporary in-migrants. At the present time it is not justified to extend this pattern to all of the known Archaic Period occupations. The Ostiones and

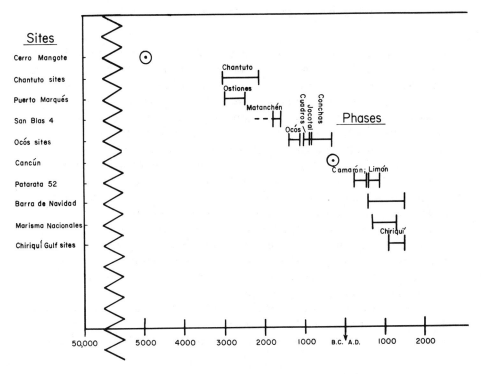

Figure 1.2. Chronology of coastal sites. Data on Santa Luisa have not been included. The earliest phase, Palo Hueco, is dated approximately between 3100 and 2600 B.C. (Wilkerson 1975:121).

Matanchén occupations are insufficiently studied, the Palo Hueco occupation has been reported only briefly, and at Cerro Mangote a different sort of occupation is indicated by the high density of lithic tools in comparison to their low density at the Chantuto sites.

It is also unwarranted to conclude that known occupations represent the earliest human sites on Middle American coasts. It seems to me quite possible that these deposits could postdate occupations by earlier peoples who sporadically procured small amounts of coastal resources as part of a procurement cycle that involved habitat shifts on a regular basis. Such deposits presumably will be difficult to locate because rates of midden accumulation would have been slow, and might have been equaled by rates of erosion or sedimentation by natural agents. In addition, rising sea level could conceal early short-term sites. Perhaps such early remains will be identified when systematic and persistent reconnaissance is carried out in coastal regions.

PROCUREMENT PATTERNS

The single paramount factor of coastal adaptation is that a human population forms an integral component of *both* the terrestrial and the coastal aquatic ecosystems. The way in which humans fit into these two interlocking systems can and does vary widely among present-day peoples. Another way of saying this is that among coastal peoples, specific ecological niches differ considerably. It is reasonable, therefore, to expect to find a variety of ecological patterns manifested in the archaeological record.

A cursory examination of reconstructed procurement patterns for the coastal sites considered here reveals that diets (as represented by studied remains) have varied considerably. Direct comparison of these procurement patterns is very difficult because of variations in research methods. These include a lack of uniformity in the recovery and reporting of data and the use of noncomparable methods in assessing contributions of food from invertebrate, vertebrate, and plant sources. Because it is not possible to make precise comparisons of previously reported procurement patterns, I will restrict this discussion to some general observations.

The studied sites are located within different biotic zones which can be illustrated by a transection through a generalized tropical coast (Figure 1.3). A comparison of the reconstructed procurement patterns shows that a site's

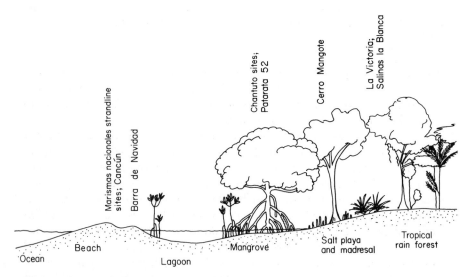

Figure 1.3. Transection of a generalized tropical coast, with sites considered in text plotted by habitat. The Santa Luisa site is omitted.

position in relation to these biotic zones predicts the relative contribution of organisms from the aquatic zone as compared with the terrestrial zone (Voorhies 1976).

For example, the most seaward sites in this sample, Cancún and strandline sites from the Marismas Nacionales, yielded food remains that were almost entirely from aquatic species. The strandline Marismas Nacionales sites were almost entirely composed of remains of shellfish (Shenkel 1971). This fact, plus the scarcity of tools and low diversity of tool types, suggests that only a part of the total prehistoric procurement pattern is represented by these deposits. At Cancún the faunal remains include both vertebrate and invertebrate species. Wing (1975) reports that with the exception of one fragment, all vertebrate remains derived from species of the inshore aquatic zone.

The prehistoric location of Barra de Navidad is thought to have been at the seaside margin of a lagoon (Long and Wire 1966:3). The recovered food remains indicate a primary emphasis on shellfish. Most of these mollusks were from a single species of intertidal clam. Vertebrate bones were rare, but included terrestrial as well as aquatic species.

Mangrove zone sites include the Chantuto sites and Patarata 52. The reconstructed procurement patterns for wild species in each of these study areas suggest a primary emphasis on aquatic organisms, with important supplements from the terrestrial environment. In both study areas most invertebrate and vertebrate remains are from species that are common in the lagoon–estuary habitat. Deep-water species are not represented. Both investigators recognize the difficulties of weighing the contribution of plants against that of animals in dietary reconstruction, but despite this limitation both consider that plant foods played a lesser role compared to animal foodstuffs than has been assumed to be typical of inland sites (Stark 1974; Voorhies 1976).

The present-day location of Cerro Mangote is landward of both a tidal grassland zone and a coastal mangrove zone (McGimsey 1956:151–153). The site's former location relative to biotic zones has not been determined. Possibly it was located on the landward side of the former mangrove zone, and I have placed it in this position in the generalized transection (Figure 1.3). The food remains of animals recovered from the site suggest a mixed procurement pattern based on a variety of molluscan, crustacean, and vertebrate fauna from both terrestrial and aquatic habitats. The abundance of grinding tools at the site could be interpreted as evidence for utilization of plant resources, although these artifacts might have had other functions. McGimsey (1956:156) has suggested that they were associated with the processing of shellfish.

It is difficult to place the location of the Santa Luisa site on the schematic transection of a tropical coast. The site is located on a river terrace, and during the preceramic Palo Hueco phase it was close to the margin of a shallow bay (Wilkerson 1975:111). Mangrove formation may or may not have been present between the site and the bay. Analysis of the vertebrate faunal remains is not reported in detail for the preceramic component (cf. Wing, this volume), but vertebrates from both terrestrial and aquatic habitats are represented (Wilkerson 1975:113). In addition, shellfish were utilized. Oysters were the most popular mollusk, but several other estuarine species are represented in the collections (Wilkerson 1975:113). The contribution of plants has not been assessed, but Wilkerson notes the absence of manos and metates, or any tools clearly associated with agriculture.

The most landward of the coastal sites considered here are those found in the Ocós region. Both La Victoria and Salinas La Blanca are located above the stormtide level within the tropical forest zone. At these sites the reconstructed food patterns indicate primary emphasis on terrestrial food items, especially those derived from agriculture. These foods were supplemented by both terrestrial and aquatic animals.

In the studies considered here the habitat location of a site provides a strong indicator of the habitats of organisms that were preferred foods for the former human inhabitants. However, exceptions to this correlation should be expected to occur, and this relationship should not be assumed. In addition, there are at least two major obstacles in comparing procurement patterns of ancient coastal peoples. The first is methodological. No standard methods have been used to recover and to report the quantities of each class of food remains represented at sites, thus making impossible direct comparisons among sites. In addition, the remains of the plant and animal components are not usually directly comparable and have the possible effect of exaggerating the importance of faunal constituents. The second difficulty concerns the scattered and scanty research on coastal sites. Lack of evidence prevents the determination of possible shifts in the human ecology of Middle American coastal habitats over the entire period of occupation. Although I expect that eventually we will be able to detect certain trends in the record of human adaptation to the coastal zones, such trends are not yet readily apparent. When archaeological studies of sequences of occupations within biotic zones of several coastal segments become available, it may be possible to assess patterns of change in human coastal adaptations through time.

EXCHANGE PATTERNS

The consideration of resource procurement leads to the question of interpopulational exchanges in foodstuffs and other goods. This issue has not been examined by most previous investigators, who have been concerned mainly with evidence for cultural contacts as demonstrated by the distribution of single classes of artifacts (e.g., ceramics). Little attention has been directed at the reciprocal or systemic nature of exchange systems (see Stark and Voorhies, this volume, for a discussion of problems associated with this research).

There are several questions that profitably could be pursued regarding the development of interregional exchanges. First, at what time and under what conditions did interregional resource exchange become a significant factor in integrating coastal and upland populations? Second, when, why, and how were these populations critically dependent on exchange for their well-being? Third, how developed was interregional exchange between coastal and inland groups during the Classic Period? I have posed this last question especially because of its relevance for the clarification of the operation of the complex societies that are characteristic of the Classic Period.

Although current studies (see especially Stark; Freidel; and R. Zeitlin, this volume) are making progress in this direction, these issues cannot be adequately pursued on the basis of current data. Previously published data only provide some tantalizing hints. For example, the presence of obsidian in the midden deposits at the Chantuto sites unambiguously demonstrates the presence of interregional resource exchange between coastal and inland populations as early as 3000 B.C. (Voorhies 1976). Wilkerson (1975:112), working at the coastal Veracruz site of Santa Luisa, has established that obsidian was received from Queretaro at approximately the same time. Insufficiency of evidence makes it impossible to determine the beginnings of these particular systems or the representativeness of the indicated exchange for coeval populations. However, this early inception of exchange in what may have been an "everyday" commodity raises the possibility that exchange systems knitting together local populations could have contributed to a spiral of development in economic production, distribution, and consumption in the evolution of societies.

Some limited information is also available concerning the degree of interpopulational exchange between coastal and upland peoples during the Classic Period. This bears on one traditional view of the Classic Maya, a group often explicitly described as living in a uniform environment (e.g., Rathje 1971; Tourtellot and Sabloff 1972; Voorhies 1973) and implicitly as politically and economically isolated (but see Freidel, this volume). Stark (1974) has suggested that the Early Classic inhabitants of the mangrove swamp in the Lower Papaloapan Basin may have provided economic goods and transshipment services to inland peoples. This view of a lively system of exchange in Classic times is a compelling one that deserves careful testing at coastal sites, as well as at sites in significantly different habitats.

SETTLEMENT PATTERNS

As I noted before, we lack intensive surveys combined with an excavation sampling strategy that would permit diachronic characterization of a specific coastal zone. Consequently two potentially critical settlement pattern topics are not amenable to discussion on the basis of published research: (a) the density and distribution patterns of coastal sites and populations; and (b) functional and hierarchical differentiation among sites.

Most previously studied coastal sites in Middle America fall into two categories: temporary food extraction stations and permanent settlements. The sites interpreted by their investigators as single-activity food extraction stations include Barra de Navidad, the Matanchén occupation at San Blas 4, and the strandline deposits at Marismas Nacionales. Single-activity sites represent one facet of total prehistoric community patterns. The inhabitants may have been primarily settled village farmers, but this is difficult to verify due to the lack of investigation at the presumed sites of permanent residence. The failure to research sites systematically on a regional basis thus has resulted in biased descriptions of community life.

Continuous habitation has been reconstructed for La Victoria, Salinas La Blanca, Cerro Mangote, Puerto Marqués, supratidal sites in the Marismas Nacionales, Patarata 52, and Santa Luisa. Andrews IV (1975:158) has speculated that Isla Cancún was a residence site, but duration of habitation was not determined. La Victoria and Salinas La Blanca have been reconstructed by their investigators as hamlets. The Cerro Mangote site is interpreted as representing a community "larger than a single extended family [McGimsey 1956:161]" and thus also may be provisionally considered a hamlet. The Ostiones deposits at Puerto Marqués are interpreted by the investigator as the remains of a former village. Because this assignment was based only on the large volume of unstratified deposits (Brush 1969:97), I believe that its designation as a village is equivocal. Residence type was not determined at the supratidal sites in the Marismas Nacionales. In the absence of data, the investigator (Shenkel 1971) calculated a range of possible population sizes based on assumptions about the location of the consumers. Stark (personal communication) has not yet determined the spatial limits of the prehistoric occupation of Patarata 52 and, therefore, is not able to assign it to a settlement type. Wilkerson (1975) interprets the Palo Hueco Phase deposits as remains of a village, but direct evidence was unavailable to test this proposition. He believes that the nearby site of La Conchita (Wilkerson 1975:113–114) may have served as a hunting station for the villagers during Palo Hueco times, but this possibility requires additional confirmation.

My research in the Chantuto zone has produced data suggesting that the sites investigated were loci of both permanent and periodic occupations.

The permanent occupation is indicated by an artificial stratum, containing a human burial, that I interpret as a house floor. I have not yet determined whether the presumed structure was an isolated household or part of a larger settlement. The evidence for periodic occupation derives from various analyses of the bedded deposits that comprise the middens (Voorhies 1976:98–100). The periodic occupations, I believe, were due to in-migrations of mainlanders who collected clams, fish, and possibly shrimp (Voorhies 1976). These products may have been consumed inland of the littoral zone, but this possibility has not yet been investigated.

It is significant that none of the previously studied coastal sites has been interpreted as a seasonal station in an annual circuit of varied habitats. El Viejón, which contained Coxcatlan projectile points, might be such a site since the Coxcatlan people in the Tehuacán Valley were seasonally mobile. (Excavations at El Viejón [Meddellín Zenil 1960:183–189] apparently did not encounter the early material reported subsequently by MacNeish [1967].) I predict that when adequate research has been carried out, the settlement patterns of the coast will show an overall developmental sequence from (a) an earlier stage with temporary collecting sites only and minimal interpopulational resource exchange to (b) a later stage with permanent habitation sites, some temporary collecting sites, and increased interpopulational exchange.

One previously expressed view regarding the nature and process of change in coastal settlement patterns is that permanent occupation took place along water bodies prior to its inception in other regions. The primacy of sedentarism in such environments has been suggested or implied by Sauer (1952:23–24), Coe and Flannery (1964), Reichel-Dolmatoff (1965), Mac-Neish (1967:311), and Binford (1968) among others. It seems to me possible that this view has been conditioned at least in part by the belief that aquatic food resources are in some way either significantly more stationary, abundant, nonseasonal, or predictable than terrestrial resources. In other words, aquatic resources, including nearshore coastal ones, have been viewed as relatively nonfluctuating in availability to humans and, where sufficiently abundant, capable of supporting localized human population aggregates either without agriculture or when plant domestication was in its early stages. This view may be an accurate one, but its assessment requires more detailed resource characterization of both coastal and upland environments than has been assembled to date.

Some evidence indicates to me, however, that the model just described concerning the primacy of coastal sedentarism will not be validated by future research. First, the model may be based on implicit assumptions about the relationship between human foragers and their animal resources without full assessment of the role of plant resources. This is apparently an effect of the poor preservation of plant remains compared with animal remains (but see Coe and Flannery 1962, 1967). This widely recognized reality of the archaeological data base perhaps has not been fully assessed at the level of interpretation (but see Flannery 1968). Foraging populations living at either low or middle altitudes in the tropics might have had access to localized, abundant, and nonseasonal plant resources that would allow sedentarism as early as was possible for coastal populations. I am not questioning here whether sedentarism occurred early on the coasts but only whether this situation was restricted to water-rich environments.

A second reason for doubting the primacy of coastal settlement is hypothetical. It is my expectation that sedentarism is concomitant with habitat specialization. Spatial restriction and economic specialization may be critically dependent on the presence of mechanisms for exchanging resources. Resource exchange is a form of mutualism, that is, it requires the interaction of two or more groups. According to this reasoning the development of habitat reduction in one region, for example, the uplands, might stimulate a similar development in another region, such as the lowlands. If this parallel development did not occur in approximately synchronous fashion, interregional exchange would be severely limited in developmental potential.

The third reason for questioning the proposed primacy of coastal settlement is that the available archaeological evidence does not support this view. The two earliest Middle American architectural remains come from the Tehuacán Valley, a highland region, and the Chantuto zone, a coastal lowland area. The remains are approximately the same age. The highland feature, called the Chilac house, occurs in Abejas Phase deposits (3400–2300 B.C.) and is believed to have been occupied approximately at 3000 B.C. (MacNeish and García Cook 1972:160; see also Flannery 1972). In the lowlands, the artificially constructed clay stratum within the Chantuto Phase (3000–2000 B.C.) deposits at Tlacuachero has bracketing dates of 2860–2570 B.C. (Voorhies 1976:43). Accordingly, the meager evidence presently available supports the hypothesis that upland and lowland populations experienced sedentarism concurrently rather than sequentially.

In this chapter I have briefly summarized the status of archaeological research on coastal sites as determined through some published reports. I also have discussed some central problems around which current and future research might be profitably oriented. Coastal sites today are receiving more attention than they have in the past. A happy consequence of this increased interest is that the problems of common interest to researchers working in coastal zones can be approached best not only through regional-scale research, but also through the concentrated and cooperative effort of investigators. This volume is one such effort toward reaching that ultimate goal.

ACKNOWLEDGMENTS

I received constructive comments on this chapter from Sally Simon, Barbara L. Stark, Jack Mallory, and Phillip L. Walker. Paul E. Heuston drafted the figures.

REFERENCES

Andrews, E. Wyllys, IV
   1969   The archaeological use and distribution of Mollusca in the Maya Lowlands. *Middle American Research Institute* Publication 34. Tulane University.
   1975   Excavation of shell midden at Isla Cancún, Quintana Roo. In Progress report on the 1960–1964 field seasons, National Geographic Society-Tulane University, Dzibilchaltún Program. *Middle American Research Institute* Publication 31. Tulane University. Pp. 42–45.
Andrews, E. Wyllys, IV, Michael P. Simmons, Elizabeth S. Wing, and E. Wyllys Andrews V
   1975   Excavation on an early shell midden on Isla Cancún, Quintana Roo, Mexico. *Middle American Research Institute* Publication 31. Tulane University. Pp. 147–197.
Binford, Lewis R.
   1968   Post-Pleistocene adaptations. In *New perspectives in archaeology*, edited by Sally R. Binford and Lewis R. Binford. Chicago: Aldine. Pp. 313–341.
Brush, C. F.
   1965   Pox pottery: Earliest identified Mexican ceramic. *Science* **149**:194–195.
   1969   A contribution to the archaeology of coastal Guerrero, Mexico. Ph.D. dissertation, Anthropology Department, Columbia University.
Coe, Michael D.
   1961   La Victoria: An early site on the Pacific Coast of Guatemala. *Papers of the Peabody Museum of Archaeology and Ethnology* Vol. 53. Harvard University.
Coe, Michael D., and Kent V. Flannery
   1964   Microenvironments and Mesoamerican prehistory. *Science* **143** (3607):650–654.
   1967   Early cultures and human ecology in south coastal Guatemala. *Smithsonian Contributions to Anthropology* Vol. 3.
Cook, S. F.
   1964   A reconsideration of shell mounds with respect to population and nutrition. *American Antiquity* **12** (1):50–51.
Drucker, Philip
   1948   Preliminary notes on an archaeological survey of the Chiapas coast. In *Middle American research records* Vol. 1. Tulane University. Pp. 151–169.
Ekholm, Gordon F.
   1944   Excavations at Tampico and Panuco in the Huasteca, Mexico. *Anthropological Papers of the American Museum of Natural History* Vol. 38, Part 5.
Flannery, Kent V.
   1968   Archaeological systems theory and early Mesoamerica. In *Anthropological archeology in the Americas*, edited by Betty J. Meggers, Washington, D.C.: The Anthropological Society of Washington. Pp. 67–87.
   1972   The origins of the village as a settlement type in Mesoamerica and the Near East: A comparative study. In *Man, settlement, and urbanism*, edited by P. J. Ucko, R. Tringham, and G. W. Dimbleby. London: Duckworth. Pp. 23–53.

Linares de Sapir, Olga
    1968   Cultural chronology of the Gulf of Chiriquí, Panama. *Smithsonian Contributions to Anthropology* Vol. 8.
Long, Stanley, and Marcia V. V. Wire
    1966   Excavations at Barra de Navidad, Jalisco. *Antropológica* **18:**3–81. Caracas.
Lorenzo, José L.
    1955   Los concheros de la costa de Chiapas. *Anales del Instituto Nacional de Antropología e Historia* Vol. 7. Mexico. Pp. 41–50.
MacNeish, Richard S.
    1967   Mesoamerican archaeology. In *Biennial review of anthropology,* edited by Bernard Siegel and Alan Beals. Stanford: Stanford University Press. Pp. 306–331.
MacNeish, Richard S., and Angel García Cook
    1972   Excavations in the San Marcos locality in the travertine slopes. In *Excavations and reconnaissance,* edited by Richard S. MacNeish et al. *The Prehistory of the Tehuacán Valley* Vol. 5. Austin: University of Texas Press. Pp. 137–160.
Medellín Zenil, Alfonso
    1960   *Cerámicas del Totonacapan: Exploraciones arqueológicas en el centro de Veracruz.* Xalapa: Universidad Veracruzana.
McGimsey, Charles R., III
    1956   Cerro Mangote: A preceramic site in Panama. *American Antiquity* **22:**151–161.
Mountjoy, Joseph B.
    1971   Prehispanic culture history and cultural contact on the southern coast of Nayarit, Mexico. Ph.D. dissertation, Anthropology Department, Southern Illinois University.
    1972   Matanchén Complex: New radiocarbon dates on early coastal adaptation in West Mexico. *Science* **175:**1242–1243.
    1974   San Blas Complex ecology. In *The archaeology of West Mexico,* edited by Betty Bell. Ajijic, Mexico: Sociedad de Estudios Avanzados del Occidente de México. Pp. 106–119.
Nicholson, H. B., and Clement W. Meighan
    1974   The UCLA Department of Anthropology Program in West Mexican Archaeology–Ethnohistory 1956–1970. In *The archaeology of West Mexico,* edited by Betty Bell. Ajijic, Mexico: Sociedad de Estudios Avanzados del Occidente de Mexico. Pp. 6–18.
Rathje, William L.
    1971   The origin and development of Lowland Classic Maya civilization. *American Antiquity* **36:**275–285.
Reichel-Dolmatoff, Gerard
    1965   *Columbia.* New York: Praeger.
Sauer, Carl O.
    1952   *Agricultural origins and dispersals.* New York: The American Geographic Society.
Sanders, William T.
    1968   Hydraulic agriculture, economic symbiosis, and the evolution of states in Central Mexico. In *Anthropological archaeology in the Americas,* edited by B. G. Meggers, Washington, D.C.: The Anthropological Society of Washington. Pp. 88–107.
Scott, Stuart D.
    1974   Archaeology and estuary: Researching prehistory and paleoecology in the Marismas Nacionales, Sinaloa and Nayarit, Mexico. In *The archaeology of West Mexico,* edited by Betty Bell. Ajijic, Mexico: Sociedad de Estudios Avanzados del Occidente de Mexico. Pp. 51–56.
Shenkel, J. Richard
    1971   Cultural adaptation to the mollusk: A methodological survey of shellmound ar-

chaeology and a consideration of the shellmounds of the Marismas Nacionales, West Mexico. Ph.D. dissertation, Anthropology Department, University of New York at Buffalo.

1974 Quantitative analysis and population estimates of the shell mounds of the Marismas Nacionales, West Mexico. In *The archaeology of West Mexico,* edited by Betty Bell. Ajijic, Mexico: Sociedad de Estudios Avanzados del Occidente de Mexico. Pp. 57–67.

Stark, Barbara Louise
1974 Patarata Island, Veracruz, Mexico and the role of estuarine mangrove swamps in ancient Mesoamerica. Ph.D. dissertation, Anthropology Department, Yale University.

Stone, Doris
1972 *Pre-Columbian man finds Central America: The archaeological bridge.* Cambridge: Peabody Museum Press.

Tourtellot, Gair, and Jeremy A. Sabloff
1972 Exchange systems among the ancient Maya. *American Antiquity* **37:**126–135.

Voorhies, Barbara
1973 Possible social factors in the exchange system of the Prehistoric Maya. *American Antiquity* **38:**486–489.

1975 Los conchales de la Zona Chantuto, Chiapas, México. Sociedad Mexicana de Antropología, 13th Mesa Redonda, Arqueología II. México. Pp. 1–10.

1976 The Chantuto people: An Archaic Period society of the Chiapas littoral, Mexico. *Papers of the New World Archaeological Foundation* No. 41. Provo, Utah: Brigham Young University.

Wilkerson, S. Jeffrey K.
1975 Pre-agricultural village life: The late Preceramic Period in Veracruz. In *Studies in ancient Mesoamerica, II. Contributions of the University of California Archaeological Research Facility* No. 27, edited by John A. Graham. Pp. 111–122.

Wing, Elizabeth S.
1975 Vertebrate faunal remains. In *Archaeological investigations on the Yucatan Peninsula. Middle American Research Institute* Publication 31. Tulane University. Pp. 186–188.

PART II

Procurement Patterns

The term *procurement pattern* apparently was first introduced into the vocabulary of archaeologists by Kent V. Flannery (1968). Flannery used the term to indicate a people's patterned activities that are directly involved in obtaining resources from their habitat. The term is akin to that of subsistence patterns in the anthropological literature, but it is not necessarily restricted to a consideration of basic food necessities, as is true for subsistence patterns. For example, in some localities procurement patterns might encompass extraction of stone or mineral resources. This term is also similar to the concept of production in economics but lacks the strong connotation of human manipulation of resources by farming or manufacture that is inherent in that term.

Flannery points out in his article that a people's adaptation may not be to specific biotic zones but rather to a more limited assemblage of plant and animals whose ranges crosscut several biotopes. In coastal habitats subsistence is striking in that the plants and animals used by humans for food are commonly derived from aquatic as well as terrestrial biotopes. Many estuarine species may crosscut both brackish and freshwater habitats. We must confront, therefore, both biotope and genus–species orientations in coastal procurement patterns.

The identification of the particular assemblage of food items that is utilized by each group of coastal people is now a routine concern of most investigators. The chapters we have grouped as studies of coastal procurement patterns vary in their objectives and in their methods. Wing's chapter, "Use of Dogs for Food: An Adaptation to the Coastal Environment," compares coeval vertebrate faunal remains from four sites located within the state of Veracruz, Mexico. Three of these sites are quite near the Gulf Coast, whereas the fourth is a riverine site. Wing has determined the numbers of individual animals represented for each species; by then converting this information to edible biomass, she has been able to calculate the relative contribution of each species to the total vertebrate diet of the human consumers. Wing's results demonstrate that, at the sites studied, the relative contribution of terrestrial animals is substantial and is most accurately perceived with interspecific comparisons of usable meat rather than with numbers of individuals. Wing's analysis also demonstrates that dog was a highly preferred terrestrial food item. These findings are unexpected in that they reveal a much greater reliance for food on game and on a domesticated species by these Late Formative coastal and riverine peoples than is indicated when less complete analyses are performed.

Wing's findings suggest that an important factor in the utilization of dog meat in the communities studied may have been the constant availability of this source of protein. The factor of continuous availability is a characteristic advantage of all domestic animals that provide food or other materials for humans. In addition, because dogs are scavengers they neither compete directly with humans for food nor require large investments of human energy for their maintenance. It is possible that in analogous modern communities the functional role of dogs in prehispanic times has been usurped by an Old World domesticate, the pig.

The chapters by Ranere and Hansell and by Magnus are similar in that, in each case reported, procurement patterns are reconstructed for coeval populations in contrastive coastal and interior habitats. In each case the reconstruction of subsistence patterns on a broad regional scale at a number of sites leads the investigators into issues involving settlement–subsistence systems (Struever 1971). In Ranere and Hansell's research report, "Early Subsistence Patterns along the Pacific Coast of Central Panama," resource procurement patterns are compared between coastal and interior occupations during late preceramic and early ceramic periods. The authors interpret the interior sites as stations for hunting and wild plant collection. In contrast, the investigators found that all nearshore sites yielded deposits in which aquatic resources contributed substantial amounts of food to the diet of prehistoric site inhabitants. However, terrestrial faunal remains are also reported as frequent, which appears to correspond to Wing's general findings. When biomass conversions become available, it will be possible to discover if the terrestrial dietary component actually exceeds that of the aquatic component, as in Wing's study of the assemblages from Veracruz.

According to Ranere and Hansell, there is no evidence that maize agriculture was practiced during any of the early Panamanian occupations considered; it is possible that its eventual introduction stimulated the relocation of communities to river plains away from both the shoreline and piedmont locations which appear to have been favored previously. Whether or not early coastal and interior sites were linked in a transhumant hunting and gathering system is unknown, although some coastal food resources have been found in inland sites. The possibility of early manioc cultivation is another issue Ranere and Hansell raise but cannot yet resolve. Despite the fact that the final results of Ranere and Hansell's investigations are not yet available, their chapter provides a good illustration of the necessity of pursuing archaeological studies on a broad regional rather than on a limited basis.

In his chapter, "The Prehistoric and Modern Subsistence of the Atlantic Coast of Nicaragua: A Comparison," Magnus analyzes modern and prehistoric procurement and settlement patterns on the Atlantic coast of Nicaragua. He contends that three modern villages exhibit important variations in subsistence and that this variation is due to differential continuity with pre-European traditions and to different responses to changes in the nature of European contacts. He compares the habitats and procurement patterns of the villages and concludes that location is not an accurate predictor of aquatic procurement patterns in one of the three cases (although it is an accurate predictor for agricultural pursuits in all cases). It could be argued, however, that this exception is not sufficiently documented in view of the broad habitat classification that Magnus employs. Magnus also generates descriptions of the archaeological remains that he expects will be produced by these modern settlements.

Turning to the archaeological data, the author then discusses subsistence data from four different cultural assemblages. Most of these data are not quantified and do not permit detailed comparisons with the modern villages. Magnus believes, however, that there is sufficient evidence to indicate a significant contrast in prehispanic and posthispanic times. His interpretation is that in prehispanic times regional settlement consisted of central villages, possibly located in riverine habitats, which were linked to coastal fishing stations. In posthispanic times settlement patterns shifted to coastal villages with inland agricultural stations. Like the variation in modern village subsistence, Magnus argues that this shift is in large part due to the impact of European economic activities centered on the coast. A very similar interpretation of settlement and subsistence change in Nicaragua and Panama is presented by Helms in Part III of this book.

Paillés reports the results of excavations at a coastal site in Chiapas, Mexico, in "The Process of Transformation at Pajón: A Preclassic Society Located in an Estuary in Chiapas, Mexico." This chapter furnishes a good example of new data being obtained from recent coastal investigations. It includes basic information about changes at a single site during a 1600-year period. The author is concerned with reconstructing all aspects of prehistoric life including patterns of procurement, settlement, and exchange. The Pajón population seems to have been principally engaged in estuarine fishing and shellfishing, combined with collection of wild plants such as *Setaria*. There is no direct evidence of agriculture practiced by the site inhabitants. Paillés attributes the social changes recorded in the sequence (indicated by the onset of construction of artificial, presumably public, platforms at Pajón) to local factors because there is little evidence for long-distance trade and contacts. However, she hypothesizes that there may have been exchange of estuarine foods with neighboring peoples in different biotopes, who possibly were levee agriculturalists. This exchange is the one factor the author isolates as possibly contributing to the social changes manifested at Pajón.

In the four chapters of Part II, we can observe three issues regarding coastal procurement patterns. First, we must confront several instances of documented contemporaneous variations in coastal resource procurement. For example, both Magnus and Paillés contend that contemporaneous oc-cupations at different coastal localities may exhibit markedly different sub-sistence orientations in regard to the balance between aquatic foods and agriculture. Magnus bases his assertion on observation of modern Nicara-guan villagers. Paillés implies a similar variation for the Soconusco coast in the Preclassic Period. The Pajón practice of estuarine fishing combined with wild plant collection was coeval with occupations in the Ocós area in which agriculture was combined with estuarine exploitation (Coe 1961; Coe and Flannery 1967). Voorhies's chapter pointed to site locations in different coastal habitats as one factor that can help explain variations in coastal subsistence practices. In addition, Paillés and Voorhies both suspect that exchange patterns also may be closely related to procurement patterns at individual sites.

Second, we see clear evidence in Ranere and Hansell's and in Magnus's discussions that marked shifts over time in the use of coastal resources have occurred in a number of areas (see also Lange in Part III). These findings echo those of Coe and Flannery (1967) for the Ocós region of Guatemala and those of Voorhies (1976) for Chantuto sites on the Soconusco coast.

These notable shifts over time would appear to demand a regional framework for explanation.

Third, Wing's and Ranere and Hansell's chapters indicate that methods applied to data collection, such as screening or flotation, and those applied to data analysis can materially change or even reverse our understanding of what resources figured significantly in prehistoric subsistence. Although all of these discussions are concerned with food items, the same issue holds for our understanding of the procurement of nonfood resources. For example, R. Zeitlin's chapter in the section on exchange patterns employs an index of usage intensity of shell and other products to gauge fluctuations in resource exploitation rather than raw counts or percentages of types of items in these categories. In this manner, some control is achieved for differences in volume of excavation and in population size. Obviously such scaling methods have pitfalls, such as the unwitting comparison of remains from contrastive activity loci, but they warrant further examination and experimentation.

REFERENCES

Coe, M. D.
    1961   La Victoria, an early site on the Pacific Coast of Guatemala. *Papers of the Peabody Museum of Anthropology and Ethnology* Vol. 53. Harvard University.

Coe, M. D., and K. V. Flannery
    1967   Early cultures and human ecology in South Coastal Guatemala. *Smithsonian Contributions to Anthropology* Vol. 3. Smithsonian Institution.

Flannery, K. V.
    1968   Archaeological systems theory and early Mesoamerica. In *Anthropological archaeology in the Americas,* edited by Betty J. Meggers, Washington, D.C.: The Anthropological Society of Washington. Pp. 67–87.

Struever, S.
    1971   Comments on archaeological data requirements and research strategy. *American Antiquity* **36:**9–19.

Voorhies, Barbara
    1976   The Chantuto people: An Archaic Period society of the Chiapas littoral. *Papers of the New World Archaeological Foundation* No. 41. Provo, Utah: Brigham Young University.

chapter 2

Use of Dogs for Food: An Adaptation to the Coastal Environment

ELIZABETH S. WING

University of Florida

INTRODUCTION

"To primitive collector and modern naturalist alike, the borders of the sea are richly rewarding. Between high and low tide a wide assemblage of life forms useful to man is to be had for the taking [Sauer 1962:45]." Sea beaches and cliffs may indeed harbor concentrations of breeding sea mammals, shore birds, and sea turtles, and inshore, reef, and pelagic waters can abound with fishes, mollusks, and crustaceans. However, obtaining these sources of food may be more difficult than Sauer suggests. For example, rookeries are located sporadically along the coast. Where rookeries are established, the reproducing animals are available only during a particular time of year. The harvest of marine resources requires both skill and luck to avoid the unpredictable currents, wind, and waves that may destroy boats and fishing equipment. In contrast, waters in the more protected river mouths tend to be calmer than those of the exposed coast, but they are subject to changes in salinity during seasonal flooding, which results in fluctuating abundances of estuarine organisms. This fluctuation in aquatic species would require an adjustment in scheduling by people who use them for their subsistence.

Peoples who live in the coastal ecosystem may depend primarily on coastal resources or may insulate themselves somewhat from the vagaries of these resources by introducing and managing the major portion of their food supply. The objective of this analysis is to determine the extent to which the vertebrate remains excavated from three sites in coastal Veracruz reflect these two opposed hypothetic strategies. Only vertebrate remains are considered in the present analysis because of the lack of other potential remains such as eggshells, shrimp exoskeletons, and seaweed in the archaeological deposits I have studied.

The sites on which this study are based (Figure 2.1) are Santa Luisa, excavated by S. Jeffrey K. Wilkerson (1973); Chalahuites, excavated by the late James A. Ford (field notes in Florida State Museum); and Patarata, excavated by Barbara Stark (1977). These were chosen for analysis as they are similar in several respects. All are located in Veracruz within 10 km of the coast. For this analysis only the fauna associated with Late Formative to Early Classic levels dating from about 300 B.C. to A.D. 300 are considered.

Figure 2.1 Archaeological sites in Veracruz from which fauna have been analyzed.

The vertebrate remains from the coastal sites also will be compared with the faunal assemblage from the site of San Lorenzo, excavated by Michael D. Coe (1968). This site is located on the Coatzacoalcos River approximately 62 km inland from the coast but also in Veracruz. This site was occupied earlier (1200–900 B.C.) than the other sites analyzed here.

MATERIALS AND METHODS

Analysis is based on a conversion of the data to minimum numbers of individuals of each vertebrate species in a cultural unit (White 1953). These conversions were then used in estimation of the biomass and usable meat the various animals could have provided. Body weight estimates were obtained by the technique advocated by Casteel (1974). This technique is based on correlations between a linear dimension in the skeleton and live body weight using a least squares regression analysis. The general formula used is $y = bx^m$, where y is body weight, x is the chosen linear dimension, m is the slope, and b the y-axis intercept of a log–log plot. By transforming the data to common logarithms, one can use the formula $\log y = m(\log x) + \log b$.

In order to establish a predictive formula to estimate body weight of a particular species, a linear dimension that is both practical to measure and closely correlated with body weight must be chosen. Such a measurement that is successful in estimating weight of dogs is the height of the jaw taken at the middle of the first molar (see Table 2.1 for the regression formula). Other formulas for estimating body weight of dogs, based on the length of the premolar tooth row and the molar tooth row, must be used with caution as crowding of the teeth in the jaw will give a misleading estimate. In this study I used the first formula whenever possible.

A correlation was similarly established between body weight and the length of the lower diastema in deer. This measurement is taken along the superior surface of the mandible from the posterior alveolus of the third incisor to the anterior alveolus of the first premolar.

The body weight was estimated from the linear measurement of the cheek tooth row of rabbits. This measurement is taken from the anterior margin of the alveolus of the first premolar to the posterior margin of the alveolus of the last molar in the cheek tooth row of any species of the order Lagomorpha (rabbits or hares).

In order to estimate the body weight of fishes from a linear measurement, a structure must be chosen that is conservative and not readily modified by particular swimming or feeding adaptations. A linear measurement that correlates well with the body weight of catfishes is the width of the

Table 2.1
REGRESSION FORMULAS USED IN ESTIMATING LIVE WEIGHTS OF ANIMALS REPRESENTED IN FAUNAL STUDIES

Animals	Measurement	Number	Formula[a]	Correlation coefficient
Canis familiaris				
Domestic dog	Height of jaw at M,	8	$\log y = 2.2574(\log x) + 1.1164$	.9808
Domestic dog	length of lower premolar tooth row	8	$\log y = 3.0691(\log x) - .7307$	.948
Domestic dog	Length of lower molar tooth row	8	$\log y = 3.2735(\log x) - .8873$	.934
Odocoileus virginianus White-tailed deer	length of the diastema in the lower jaw	12	$\log y = 2.9737(\log x) - .8001$	.98
Lagomorpha rabbits and hares	Length of the lower cheek tooth row	10	$\log y = 3.8430(\log x) - .1452$	.95
Siluriformes catfishes	Width of posterior face of cervical centrum	6	$\log y = 3.0195(\log x) + .1458$	.9845
Percomorpha percomorph fishes	Anterior face of centrum of any cervical vertebra	6	$\log y = 2.6810(\log x) + .726$	.9918

[a] y = body weight, x = linear dimension.

posterior face of the cervical centrum. Similarly, the width of the anterior face of the centrum of any cervical vertebra of a percomorph or spiny rayed fish correlates well with body weight.

The formulas presented in Table 2.1 are more accurate in estimating body weight than other methods that are in use (Wing 1976). The formulas are based on only a few specimens, but special effort has been made to use specimens ranging widely in size, for example, the percomorph fishes used range in size from .45 to 118 kg total body weight. The aims of continuing research are to enlarge the sample of accurately weighed and measured specimens to improve these formulas and derive others for different animal groups.

At the present state of research, I do not have correlations established by which I can estimate the weight of all of the species represented in the sites. In the case of the species for which correlations have not been determined, I have directly compared the size of the bone from the faunal remains with a skeleton of comparable size from our reference collection. By means of linear regression or direct comparison I have attempted to estimate the biomass represented by the individuals of the vertebrate species in each of the archaeological faunal samples.

Usable meat is clearly only a portion of the total body weight. The proportion of usable meat to body weight differs in different types of animals. Turtles have a relatively small proportion of usable meat compared to their body weight because of the heaviness of their shell. Fish, on the other hand, have a much higher proportion of usable meat weight to body weight. The percentages of usable meat potentially provided by each species are based on averages computed from the Florida State Museum comparative collection. Tables 2.2–2.5 summarize these biomass and usable meat calculations.

DISCUSSION

As one can see in the comparative tables, the relative abundance of the species represented in each faunal sample does not necessarily correspond to their estimated biomass or to the projected amount of meat they could provide. This difference is related to the size of the animals used. For example, few deer may have been caught, but each could potentially provide the same amount of meat as 64 rabbits. For the three coastal sites under consideration, the percentage of the numbers of terrestrial animals represented is relatively smaller than the percentage of their estimated biomass or amount of usable meat. In other words, terrestrial animals provided as much or more meat than aquatic forms, although aquatic forms are abundant in each faunal assemblage.

Table 2.2
SUMMARY OF THE FAUNA ASSEMBLAGE FROM THE PATARATA SITE, CAMARON I SUBPHASE, AND ESTIMATE OF BIOMASS AND USABLE MEAT

	Minimum number of individuals[a] (MNI)	Percentage MNI	Individual body weight (gm)	Body weight × MNI	Percentage contribution to biomass	Percentage usable meat	Total meat yield (gm)	Percentage meat contribution to diet
Didelphis (opossum)	1	2.1	3,168	3,168	1.4	65	2,028	1.5
Canis (dog)	11	22.9	11,746	129,203	57.8	58	74,938	53.4
Meleagris (turkey)	3	6.3	5,150	15,450	6.9	60	9,270	6.6
Total terrestrial animals	15	31.3		147,821	66.2		86,236	61.5
Dermatemys (river turtle)	2	4.2	≈3,000	6,000	2.7	35	2,100	1.5
Chelydra (snapping turtle)	1	2.1	≈3,000	3,000	1.3	35	1,050	.8
Kinosternon (musk turtle)	11	22.9	212	2,332	1.0	35	816	.6
Claudius (musk turtle)	1	2.1	≈100	100	.05	35	35	.02
Staurotypus (musk turtle)	4	8.3	450	1,800	.8	35	630	.5
Chrysemys (pond turtle)	4	8.3	3,008	12,032	5.4	35	4,211	3.0
Ictalurus (catfish)	2	4.2	346	692	.3	77	533	.4
Arius (sea catfish)	1	2.1	346	346	.2	77	266	.2
Centropomus (snook)	7	14.6	7,038	49,268	22.1	90	44,341	31.6
Total aquatic animals	33	68.8		75,570	33.8		53,982	38.5
Total vertebrates	48			223,391			140,218	

[a]Data from Wing (1977).

Table 2.3
SUMMARY OF THE FAUNA ASSEMBLAGE FROM THE SANTA LUISA SITE AND ESTIMATES OF BIOMASS AND USABLE MEAT

	Minimum number of individuals (MNI)	Percentage MNI	Individual body weight (gm)	Body weight × MNI	Percentage contribution to biomass	Percentage usable meat	Total meat yield (gm)	Percentage meat contribution to diet
Sylvilagus (rabbit)	1	1.5	1,159	1,159	.2	63	730	.2
Procyon (raccoon)	1	1.5	3,480	3,480	.5	65	2,262	.5
Canis (dog)	8	11.6	11,053	88,424	12.9	58	51,286	10.7
Tayassu (peccary)	1	1.5	16,556	16,556	2.4	70	11,589	2.4
Odocoileus (deer)	6	8.7	44,452	266,712	38.9	62	165,361	34.4
Meleagris (turkey)	3	4.4	5,150	15,450	2.3	60	9,270	1.9
Anatidae (duck)	1	1.5	1,225	1,225	.2	77	943	.2
Ardeidae (heron)	1	1.5	310	310	.05	70	217	.05
Total terrestrial animals	22	31.9		393,316	57.5		241,658	50.3
Kinosternon (musk turtle)	1	1.5	212	212	.03	35	74	.02
Dermatemys (river turtle)	1	1.5	≈3,000	3,000	.4	35	1,050	.2
Iguana (iguana)	1	1.5	4,536	4,536	.7	60	2,722	.6
Cheloniidae (sea turtle)	1	1.5	45,000	45,000	6.6	47	21,150	4.4
Pristis (sawfish)	1	1.5	23,177	23,177	3.4	90	20,859	4.3
Shark	2	2.9	4,069	8,138	1.2	90	7,324	1.5
Ariidae (sea catfish)	6	8.7	346	2,076	.3	77	1,599	.3
Centropomus (snook)	17	24.6	9,353	159,001	32.2	90	143,101	29.8
Lutjanus (snapper)	2	2.9	≈3,000	6,000	.9	90	5,400	1.1
Caranx (jack)	2	2.9	2,936	5,873	.9	90	5,286	1.1
Sciaenidae (trout)	3	4.4	≈3,000	9,000	1.3	90	8,100	1.7
Cynoscion (sea trout)	3	4.4	≈3,000	9,000	1.3	90	8,100	1.7
Archosargus (sheephead)	5	7.3	≈3,000	15,000	2.2	90	13,500	2.8
Gobiomorus (sleeper)	2	2.9	±346	692	.1	90	623	.1
Total aquatic animals	47	68.1		290,705	34.8		238,888	49.7
Total vertebrates	69			684,021			480,546	

Table 2.4
SUMMARY OF THE FAUNA ASSEMBLAGE FROM THE CHALAHUITES SITE AND ESTIMATES OF BIOMASS AND USABLE MEAT

	Minimum number of individuals (MNI)	Percentage MNI	Individual body weight (gm)	Body weight × MNI	Percentage contribution to biomass	Percentage usable meat	Total meat yield (gm)	Percentage meat contribution to diet
Didelphis (opossum)	2	7.1	3,168	6,336	3.4	64	4,055	3.5
Dasypus (armadillo)	1	3.6	5,897	5,897	3.4	54	3,184	2.7
Sylvilagus (rabbit)	2	7.1	811	1,621	.9	63	1,021	.9
Orthogeomys (pocket gopher)	3	10.7	226	678	.4	60	407	.4
Canis (dog)	8	28.6	11,303	90,426	47.9	58	52,447	44.7
Tayassu (peccary)	1	3.6	16,556	16,556	8.8	70	11,589	9.9
Odocoileus (deer)	1	3.6	44,452	44,452	23.6	62	27,560	23.5
Total terrestrial animals	18	64.3		165,966	87.9		100,263	85.4
Iguanid (iguana)	1	3.6	4,536	4,536	2.4	60	2,722	2.3
Snake	1	3.6	125	125	.07	85	160	.1
Kinosternon (musk turtle)	1	3.6	212	212	.1	35	74	.06
Staurotypus (musk turtle)	1	3.6	450	450	.2	35	158	.1
Chrysemys (pond turtle)	1	3.6	3,008	3,008	1.6	35	1,053	.9
Shark	1	3.6	1,407	1,407	.7	90	1,266	1.1
Centropomus (snook)	1	3.6	7,252	7,252	3.8	90	6,527	5.6
Epinephelus (grouper)	1	3.6	3,097	3,097	1.6	90	2,787	2.4
Pogonias (drum)	1	3.6	909	909	.5	90	818	.7
Mugil (mullet)	1	3.6	1,741	1,741	.9	90	1,567	1.3
Total aquatic animals	10	35.7		22,737	12.1		17,132	14.6
Total vertebrates	28			188,703			117,395	

Table 2.5
SUMMARY OF THE FAUNAL ASSEMBLAGE FROM THE SAN LORENZO SITE AND ESTIMATES OF BIOMASS AND USABLE MEAT

	Minimum number of individuals (MNI)	Percentage MNI	Individual body weight (gm)	Body weight × MNI	Percentage contribution to biomass	Percentage usable meat	Total meat yield (gm)	Percentage meat contribution to diet
Sylvilagus (rabbit)	1	.8	811	811	.1	63	511	.1
Orthogeomys (pocket gopher)	3	2.3	226	678	.1	60	407	.1
Canis (dog)	18	13.4	9,931	178,758	31.0	58	103,670	26
Procyon (raccoon)	2	1.5	3,480	6,960	1.2	65	4,524	1.1
Tayassu (peccary)	1	.7	16,556	16,556	2.9	70	11,589	2.9
Odocoileus (deer)	1	.8	444,452	44,452	7.7	62	27,560	6.9
Bird	2	1.5	1,000	2,000	.4	77	1,540	.4
Anatidae (duck)	2	1.5	1,225	2,450	.4	77	1,887	.5
Anas (duck)	2	1.5	1,225	2,450	.4	77	1,887	.5
Aythya (pochard)	1	.8	1,225	1,225	.2	77	943	.2
Buteogallus (black hawk)	1	.8	936	936	.2	70	655	.2
Total terrestrial animals	34	25.6		257,276	44.7		155,183	38.9
Dermatemys (river turtle)	14	10.5	≈3,000	42,000	7.3	35	14,700	3.7
Chelydra (snapping turtle)	3	2.3	≈3,000	9,000	1.6	35	3,150	.8
Claudius (musk turtle)	28	21.1	≈100	2,800	.5	35	980	.3
Kinosternon (musk turtle)	3	2.7	212	636	.1	35	223	.06
Staurotypus (musk turtle)	8	6.0	450	3,600	.6	35	1,260	.3
Geomyda (turtle)	1	.8	≈1,000	1,000	.2	35	350	.9
Chrysemys (pond turtle)	6	4.5	3,008	18,048	3.1	35	6,317	1.6
Megalops (tarpon)	1	.7	1,626	1,626	.3	90	1,463	.4
Arius (sea catfish)	2	1.5	320	640	.1	77	493	.1
Rhamdia (freshwater catfish)	1	.8	165	165	.03	77	127	.03
Centropomus (snook)	28	21.1	8,063	225,764	39.2	90	203,188	50.9
Lutjanus (snapper)	2	1.5	5,000	10,000	1.7	90	9,000	2.3
Caranx (jack)	1	.8	3,096	3,096	.5	90	2,786	.7
Cichlasoma (mojarra)	1	.8	165	165	.03	90	149	.04
Total aquatic animals	99	74.4		318,540	55.3		244,186	61.1
Total vertebrates	133			575,816			399,369	

The most abundant species of the terrestrial component of each of the sites is the domestic dog. Dog burials, so frequently encountered in West Mexican sites and in a late horizon at Santa Luisa, are typically several associated parts of a single skeleton and found in relation to a human burial or a prominent architectural structure. The dog remains analyzed here are clearly not burials but fragmentary remains associated with other refuse materials. At the Santa Luisa site some of the dog bones bear scars typically seen on bones gnawed by dogs. Similar scars are also evident on some of the deer bone from this site, suggesting that dogs indiscriminately gnawed bone from the refuse. Only a few bones are burned in these three sites, but some of these are also dog remains. The associations and condition of the dog remains suggest that dogs were used for food during the time period under consideration at these sites. If they were used for food, they could have provided a substantial amount of meat in the Formative Period diet. They could, in fact, have contributed 45% of the meat at Chalahuites, 53% at Patarata, 26% at San Lorenzo, and 11% at Santa Luisa.

Although the estimates indicate that the bulk of the meat was provided by game and dogs, fish also accounted for a substantial contribution to the diet. The single most important fish, both in terms of numbers of individuals and amount of meat each provided, is snook (*Centropomus*). Snook contributed approximately 50% of the usable meat at San Lorenzo, 30% at Santa Luisa and Patarata, and 6% at Chalahuites.

Snook are typically estuarine fishes. They breed in inshore waters but otherwise live in the shallow brackish waters of estuaries. They will migrate upstream into fresh water during high water. Snook are caught today by a number of different techniques. They are a prized game fish for the sports fisherman using hook and line. Commercial enterprises operate in Veracruz using seines to catch snook as they migrate upstream when the rivers are in flood stage. In West Mexico, snook are speared at night from platforms that are set up over an opening in a segment of a weir. They may also be caught in traps. Clearly snook may be caught using a wide variety of fishing techniques but always in rivers or estuaries. The other species represented, such as mullet, catfish, and snapper, also tend to inhabit estuaries. Only at Chalahuites, which is not located next to a river, are the aquatic forms of little importance.

Inasmuch as the faunal remains excavated from these sites reflect use of animal resources, these data indicate aspects of the adaptation of populations to their environments. When the faunal data are considered in terms of the estimated contribution of each animal or groups of animals to the prehistoric diet, it becomes evident that terrestrial animals, that is, game and the domestic dog, provided the bulk of the animal protein in the diet. Some support for this interpretation of the importance of dog is derived from the often-repeated historical accounts describing the importance of dog meat in the Indian diet. Fray Diego Durán (1967:218–219), writing during the sixteenth century, describes dogs being sold for food in the market at Alcoman. He reports seeing more than 400 dogs being offered for sale at one time and was told that generally more were available. Dog meat was evidently highly esteemed, selling for higher prices than beef during Colonial times.

Clearly, to produce as many dogs as Durán described or as appear in the archaeological faunal remains, care must have been taken in their nurture. Evidence from strontium analysis of dog bone suggests that dogs' diets were composed of the same, or perhaps greater, proportion of plant foods as their masters' diets (Brown, personal communication). Several examples exist of Colima dogs holding an ear of corn in their mouths (Figure 2.2). This possibly indicates a diet based on corn, which may have originated when dogs were first raised for food. In addition, dogs probably scavenged the waste material of the community as they do now. In this capacity of waste removers they would doubly benefit the community.

The degree of human dependence on dogs for food (Table 2.6) as reflected by these data is quite comparable to the dependence on domestic animals throughout Neolithic and even up to Medieval times in Europe and the Near East (Bökönyi 1975). In early Western European subsistence patterns, the protein provided by domesticated animals constituted between a quarter and a half of the animal protein consumed. In some cases domesticated animals constituted only 10% of the total. This production of protein was augmented by hunting and fishing for wild animals. In coastal Veracruz, meat from the domestic animal was supplemented primarily by deer at Chalahuites, which is not close to a river, and by snook at the other three sites, all located close to rivers or estuaries. Dog may be considered the basic animal protein, supplemented by snook, a seasonally available aquatic resource.

Accordingly, my analysis does not indicate that Late Formative coastal peoples of Veracruz were primarily using marine resources. Rather, the

Figure 2.2. A representation of a dog with an ear of corn in its mouth (reproduction of a Colima dog).

Table 2.6
COMPARISON OF THE RELATIVE ABUNDANCE OF DOG AND SNOOK AND OF TERRESTRIAL AND AQUATIC ELEMENTS OF THE FAUNAS

	Percentage	Chalahuites	Patarata	Santa Luisa	San Lorenzo
Dog	MNI[a]	29	23	12	11
	biomass	48	58	13	31
	contribution to diet	45	53	11	26
Terrestrial fauna	MNI	64	31	32	26
	biomass	88	66	58	45
	contribution to diet	85	62	50	39
Snook	MNI	4	15	25	17
	biomass	4	22	32	39
	contribution to diet	6	32	30	51
Aquatic fauna	MNI	36	69	68	74
	biomass	12	34	35	55
	contribution to diet	15	39	50	61
Total	MNI	28	48	69	133
	biomass	188,703	223,391	684,021	575,816
	usable meat	117,395	140,218	480,546	399,369

[a]MNI = Minimum number of individuals.

evidence indicates that much of the animal protein was derived from a domestic species and that this food source was supplemented by animals obtained by hunting or riverine–estuarine fishing.

ACKNOWLEDGMENTS

I am most grateful to Jeffrey Wilkerson, James Ford, Barbara Stark, and Michael Coe for the opportunity to study the faunal samples they have excavated. Thanks are also due to my many associates who have provided and prepared comparative specimens used in this analysis.

REFERENCES

Bökönyi, S.
    1974 *History of domestic mammals in Central and Western Europe.* Budapest, Hungary: Adamemiai Kiado.
Casteel, Richard W.
    1974 A method for estimation of live weight of fish from the size of skeletal elements. *American Antiquity* **39** (1):94–98.
Coe, Michael D.
    1968 *America's first civilization.* New York: American Heritage Publishing Co.
Durán, Fray Diego
    1967 *Historia de las Indias de Nueva España e Islas de Tierra Firma México.* Introduction by J. F. Ramirez. México: Editora Nacional.
Sauer, C. O.
    1962 Seashore—primitive home of man? *Proceedings of the American Philosophical Society* **106** (1):41–47.
Stark, Barbara L.
    1977 Adaptation to the mangrove swamp. In *Prehistoric ecology at Patarata 52, Veracruz, Mexico,* edited by B. L. Stark. Vanderbilt University Publications in Anthropology, No. 18.
White, Theodore
    1953 A method of calculating the dietary percentage of various food animals utilized by aboriginal peoples. *American Antiquity* **18**:396–398.
Wilkerson, S. Jeffrey K.
    1973 An archaeological sequence from Santa Luisa, Veracruz, Mexico. *Contributions of the University of California Archaeological Research Facility* No. 18. Pp. 37–50.
Wing, E. S.
    1976 Ways of going from a sliver of bone to a calorie. Paper presented at the 41st Annual Meeting of the Society for American Archaeology, St. Louis, May 1976.
    1977 Floral and faunal analysis: Vertebrates. In *Prehistoric ecology at Patarata 52, Veracruz, Mexico,* edited by B. L. Stark. Vanderbilt University Publications in Anthropology, No. 18. Pp. 204–212.

chapter 3

Early Subsistence Patterns along the Pacific Coast of Central Panama

ANTHONY J. RANERE AND PAT HANSELL

Temple University

INTRODUCTION

Research pioneered by Stirling, Willey, and McGimsey in the late 1940s and the 1950s revealed the presence of an old and stable adaptation to littoral resources in central Panama. At the time of excavation, Cerro Mangote (McGimsey 1956) and the Monagrillo Phase sites (Willey and McGimsey 1954) were the only preceramic and early ceramic sites known from Lower Central America. Because this was still true at the time Willey (1971) wrote his comprehensive volume on South American archaeology, these sites figured importantly in his formulation of the Northwest South American Littoral Tradition. Subsequently, however, in Panama alone a number of sites contemporary with those mentioned above have been excavated. In addition to the investigation of four preceramic rockshelters, located just south of the continental divide in western Panama (Linares and Ranere 1971; Ranere 1972, 1975a, 1976), two rockshelters in the interior of central Panama containing cultural components similar to those found at Cerro

43

Mangote and Monagrillo have been excavated (Bird and Cooke 1974; Ranere and McCarty 1976). The discovery of these latter materials in non-coastal contexts suggests that a reassessment of the subsistence–settlement system of the late preceramic and early ceramic periods in central Panama is in order.

In addition to a reexamination of the previous excavation reports of the Monagrillo Phase sites and Cerro Mangote, this chapter draws on preliminary results from the excavation of the two inland sites, the Aguadulce Shelter and La Cueva de los Ladrones, and from reexcavation of the Monagrillo site (Ranere 1975b).

THE ENVIRONMENTAL SETTING

The central Pacific region of Panama includes the most favorable agricultural zone in the country (FAO 1971) and the most productive seacoast. Parita Bay is a shallow, silt-filled embayment forming the northwest corner of the Gulf of Panama. Strong offshore winds that accompany the December to April dry season displace surface water in the Gulf of Panama and initiate upwelling (Glynn 1972). The combination of the upwelling and the extensive mud flats around the head of Parita Bay accounts for large populations of mollusks, crustaceans, and fish today and, judging from the archaeological record, for the past 7000 years as well. The mangrove-fringed shoreline of the bay is backed by a zone of low-lying swamps, marshes, and salt flats. Beyond this zone, plains or *llanos* encircle Parita Bay and extend inland 20 to 30 km (Figure 3.1). Several major rivers with broad alluvial floodplains cross the *llanos* and empty into the bay. Rising rather abruptly behind the *llanos* are the foothills of the Cordillera Central. The continental divide is approximately 45 km from the Pacific coast and varies in elevation from approximately 1400 m in the west to 400 m in the east. In this region just to the east of the Azuero Peninsula, the width of the Isthmus does not exceed 100 km.

Annual rainfall in the region varies from less than 1000 mm along the coast to 1600 mm on the *llanos* to well over 3000 mm near the continental divide. Approximately 90 to 95% of this precipitation occurs during the May to November wet season (FAO 1971). The Parita Bay shoreline and the adjacent plains make up the driest region in Panama. Natural vegetation for this zone has been reconstructed by Tosi (FAO 1971) as dry tropical forest and dry premontane forest for elevations below 100 m and moist tropical forest and moist premontane forest for elevations between 100 and 600 m above sea level. Today, this vegetation exists only in small isolated pockets in and around rocky outcrops in the *llanos* and in somewhat modified form

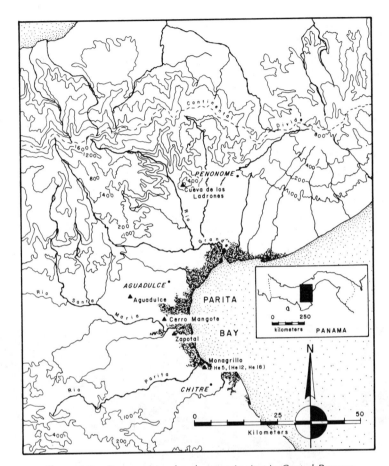

Figure 3.1. Preceramic and early ceramic sites in Central Panama.

as gallery forests along some of the major rivers (Bennett 1968). The present-day vegetation is primarily savanna, maintained by fire and used for grazing cattle. Fire-resistant tree or shrub species—particularly *chumico* (*Curatella americana*), *marañon* (*Anacardium occidentale*), and *nance* (*Byrsonima crassifolia*)—are numerous and widespread, indicating that the fire-maintained savannas are of some antiquity in this part of Panama.

MONAGRILLO

The Monagrillo site (He-5) is located 1.5 km south of the Parita River on a narrow neck of land jutting out into what is today an *alvina* or salt flat

(Figure 3.2). The site is 5 km northeast of Chitre, the capital city of Herrera province. The site, which measures approximately 210 by 85 m, consists of two low, parallel ridges separated by a central trough. The ridges contain culture-bearing deposits of sand and shell layers that average nearly 2 m in thickness along the main axis. Willey and McGimsey conducted major excavations at the site in 1952 and tested two other sites in the immediate vicinity (He-12 and He-18) with similar ceramic components (Willey and McGimsey 1954). Monagrillo had been previously discovered and tested by Stirling in 1948. Approximately 435 m² of the site were excavated in 1948 and 1952. Our excavations in 1975 were limited to one 1- by 2-m cut and one 2- by 2-m cut excavated into the south and north ridges, respectively (Figures 3.3 and 3.4).

The 1975 excavations support the conclusion of Willey and McGimsey that, at the time of initial occupation, the site was on the active shoreline of the Parita Bay. Occupation was temporary since both ridges were subject to inundation during spring tides (potsherds in the lowest layers are

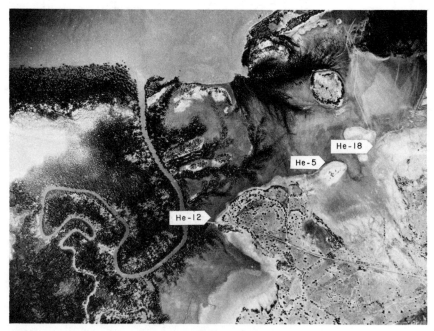

Figure 3.2. The location of three early ceramic sites, Monagrillo (He-5), He-12, and He-18, on the old shoreline of Parita Bay, south of the Parita River. (The photograph was provided by the Instituto Geográfico Nacional "Tommy Guardia," Panama.)

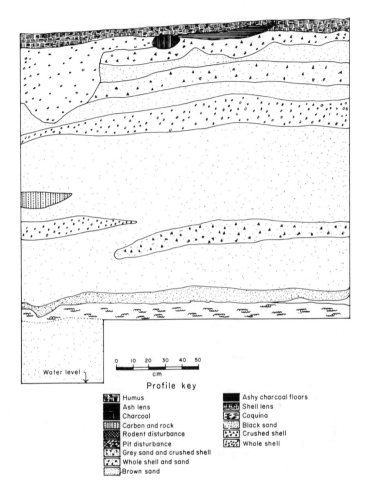

Profile key

Humus
Ash lens
Charcoal
Carbon and rock
Rodent disturbance
Pit disturbance
Grey sand and crushed shell
Whole shell and sand
Brown sand

Ashy charcoal floors
Shell lens
Coquina
Black sand
Crushed shell
Whole shell

Figure 3.3. Profile of the 1975 excavation on the south ridge of the Monagrillo site (He-5), Block 2E, east wall.

waterworn). Later during the occupation, it seems clear that the present coastline was established through the buildup of an offshore bar and that the environment around the site was transformed into a lagoon. With the ridges of the site no longer subject to inundation, occupation seems to have been on a more permanent basis. Features such as hearths, postholes, and pits became common, and concentrations of shell, bone, pottery, charcoal, and stone tools increase. The silting-in of the lagoon and its conversion into a salt flat appear to coincide with the abandonment of the site by the Monagrillo Phase inhabitants. The location, however, continues to receive sporadic use

Figure 3.4 Profile of the 1975 excavation on the north ridge of the Monagrillo site (He-5), Block 1W, east wall. See Figure 3.3 for key.

by groups of people who add some subsurface features and cultural remains to the site.

During the 1975 excavations natural or cultural stratigraphic units were removed by small hand tools. All materials were sifted through a set of graduated screens (from 13-mm to 1-mm mesh) and the fractions retained for water separation and chemical flotation. Although only a preliminary sorting of some of the collections has been completed, we can suggest certain additions and corrections to the published description of the site (Willey and McGimsey 1954).

By far the most numerous faunal component in our collections was fish. Literally thousands of small sardine-sized vertebrae were recovered, as well as appreciable numbers of elements from larger species. This contrasts markedly with the published figure of only 37 vertebrae from fish for the entire site. Similarly, hundreds upon hundreds of crab claws were recovered in our small excavations, in contrast to the 50 specimens previously listed for the entire site.

Shell occurred in large quantities, and all such remains represent mud flat and/or sandy, shallow-water species. The bulk of the shell, however, tended to occur in concentrated lenses rather than in an evenly distributed fashion. Qualitative and quantitative analysis suggests that quantity alone is not sufficient to indicate shellfish as a dietary staple (Parmalee and Klippel 1974). Further analysis of the fish and crab remains may indicate that these sources of food were of equal or greater importance than mollusks.

White-tailed deer (*Odocoileus*) was the most common terrestrial species at the site, accounting for 70% of the 97 identifiable mammal bones recovered in the 1975 excavations. Other mammals present include collared peccary (*Tayassu tajacu*), agouti (*Dasyprocta punctata*), cottontail rabbit (*Sivilagus*), and armadillo (*Dayspus*) (Burnston 1977). Given the quantity of fish, crab, and mollusks represented at the site, it seems fair to state that animal protein was primarily supplied by the sea, with a lesser but still significant amount provided by deer.

Considerable amounts of wood charcoal were recovered from Monagrillo deposits, but very little else in the way of plant remains was found. Preliminary examination of the charred remains revealed a few fragments of palm nuts, but no carbonized remains of maize were encountered, even though we specifically looked for it. We must now hope that closer scrutiny of the charred plant remains and the analysis of pollen samples from the site will provide some clarification of the collecting and/or cultivating of plants by the Monagrillo inhabitants. The presence of edge-ground cobbles, presumably used with boulder milling stones, suggests that processing of plant foods did take place on the site. Thus, while we are probably on safe ground in suggesting that plants provided an important portion of the diet, we cannot identify which plants they might have been or whether any were domesticated.

ZAPOTAL

The Zapotal site occupies a slight rise of ground that extends out into the floodplain of the Santa Maria River about 6 km from its mouth. Cerro Mangote is 4 km farther upstream. Although new data cannot be added for this site, its salient components are being reviewed for comparison. Cultural deposits averaging 1 to 1.5 m in depth extend for an estimated 200 m along the ridge and down 20 m on either side (Willey and McGimsey 1954:91–100). Six 3-m² test pits were excavated at the site. Beach deposits on the eastern side of the site underlying the cultural strata corroborate the fact that the location was once on the shoreline of Parita Bay. Occupation of the ridge is thought to have occurred at a time when an active lagoon was nearby. Shell was observed crushed and scattered throughout the midden deposit, but no identifiable bone was recovered. Nonetheless, Willey and McGimsey infer from the old coastline location that Zapotal was a station for fishing as well as for shellfish collecting.

The pottery at the site was for the most part similar to that recovered at the Monagrillo site. Slight differences in the pottery types and their frequencies led Willey and McGimsey to suggest that the Zapotal site may date to a somewhat later time period than the Monagrillo site. Also recovered at Zapotal were a few utilized chert flakes, three pebble choppers (or edge-battered cobbles), and four round pebble hammers, all characteristic also of the Monagrillo site.

CERRO MANGOTE

The Cerro Mangote shell midden is located near the crest of a hill that rises 45 m above the coastal plain on the north bank of the Santa Maria River (McGimsey 1956). The mouth of the river is presently 10 km downstream from the site, but evidence suggests that when the midden was formed the coastline was near the base of the hill from which Cerro Mangote takes its name. McGimsey (1956) describes the site as shaped like an hourglass with a length of 55 m and a maximum width of about 25 m. The site was extensively excavated by McGimsey during the middle 1950s (McGimsey 1956; McGimsey, Collin, and McKern 1966) with particular attention paid to numerous human burials encountered at the site. A single charcoal sample has yielded the date of 6810 ± 100 radiocarbon years: 4860 ± 100 B.C. (Deevey, Gralenski, and Hoffren 1959:142–172). Because we were unable to reexcavate the site in 1975 as originally planned, we must rely on the original reports for information on plant and animal remains.

McGimsey (1956:154) reports that "deer constituted approximately 40% of the bone present, small mammals 25%, turtle 15%, bird 10%, fish 5% and other forms 5%." However, in light of the revisions necessary in the Monagrillo faunal assemblage, we would do well to heed McGimsey's warning that the fish remains at the site were not adequately represented in his excavated sample. Adding the mollusk and crab remains to the presumably large quantity of fish remains, we must conclude that at Cerro Mangote, as at Monagrillo, the sea provided the greater portion of animal protein consumed at the site, with terrestrial fauna (principally deer) providing a significant amount in addition.

Although no plant remains were reported from the site, the plant-processing tools—for example, edge-ground cobbles, pebble milling stones, and boulder milling-stone bases—were present in some quantities. Again, we can do no more than suggest that plants provided a significant amount of food in the diet of the Cerro Mangote inhabitants, without being able to specify which plants or whether any of them were cultivated.

AGUADULCE SHELTER

A group of low hills rise out of the *llanos* near the small community of El Roble, 13 km west of the town of Aguadulce. On the southernmost hill between two enormous boulders is a habitation site containing both pre-ceramic and early ceramic components. Site dimensions are approximately 12 by 10 m, with a portion of the area protected by one of the boulders that looms above it. The present coastline is 18 km distant, although at the time the site was occupied the active coastline was several kilometers closer.

The site was discovered and tested by Ranere and McCarty in 1973. At that time, one 1- by 1-m test pit and two 1- by 2-m test pits were excavated (Ranere and McCarty 1976). In 1975 two additional 1- by 2-m blocks were excavated. The cultural deposits, which reached a maximum depth of 85 cm, contain a preceramic as well as an early ceramic component (Figure 3.5). The pottery is similar to that recovered at the Monagrillo site. Like Monagrillo, a number of edge-ground cobbles were recovered at the Aguadulce Shelter, as well as some boulder milling-stone bases. Unlike Monagrillo, thousands of chipped-stone tools and flakes were recovered.

Of the 529 bones identified from the 1973 excavations, 51% were land turtle, 32% were fish, and 9% were deer (White 1974). Also represented in the collections were rodents, birds, rabbit, armadillo, amphibian, lizard, raccoon, snake, crocodile, and shark. Although modest quantities of crab and shellfish were also present, it is interesting to note that the latter category were all of the mud flat and/or sandy, shallow-water species, as they were at Monagrillo.

The site produced very little charcoal in spite of the use of fine screens and water-separation recovery procedures. Nonetheless, numerous palm nut fragments were recovered in the 1975 excavations.

Given the difference in size between deer and turtle and the fact that 30% of the unidentified bone was almost certainly that of deer, it seems

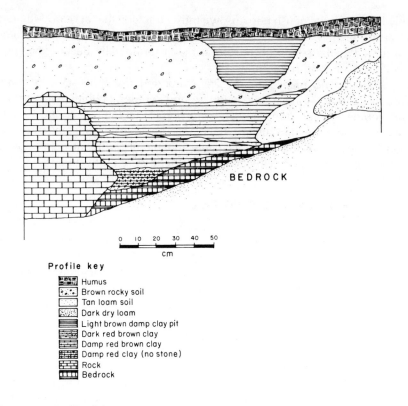

BEDROCK

0   10   20   30   40   50
cm

Profile key

Humus
Brown rocky soil
Tan loam soil
Dark dry loam
Light brown damp clay pit
Dark red brown clay
Damp red brown clay
Damp red clay (no stone)
Rock
Bedrock

Figure 3.5. Profile of the 1975 excavation at the Aguadulce Shelter, Blocks 4 and 5, west wall.

clear that the bulk of the animal protein consumed at the site was provided by deer, with turtle being second in importance. Fish, crab, and shellfish provided a smaller but not negligible amount of protein. This pattern persists throughout the occupation of the site.

We have not yet obtained dates for the Aguadulce deposits, but the similarities between the preceramic component and the Cerro Mangote assemblage (McGimsey 1956) and between the ceramic component and the Monagrillo site materials suggest that the Aguadulce Shelter was occupied between the fifth and the first millennium B.C.

We should note here that fragmentary remains of five individuals were recovered in two small shallow pits associated with the preceramic layers at the Aguadulce Shelter. The manner of disposal and the obvious butchering (all long bones were broken and the marrow extracted) suggests cannibalism.

LA CUEVA DE LOS LADRONES

This rockshelter is located at an elevation of 400 m above sea level in a region of broken topography between the Central Llanos and the continental divide. From the site, one can see Parita Bay some 25 km to the southeast. La Cueva de los Ladrones was excavated in 1974 by J. Bird with the assistance of R. Cooke (Bird and Cooke 1974). Like the Aguadulce Shelter, Ladrones contained both a preceramic and an early ceramic component with Monagrillo pottery. No charred plant remains other than wood charcoal were recovered in the excavations. Cooke's preliminary analysis of the faunal remains indicate that white-tailed deer is by far the most common species. Collared peccary and armadillo are also common. Small amounts of rodent, bird, and lizard bone are present. Also recovered were 2.5 kg of marine shells and three crab claws.

Bird and Cooke make a good case for considering this site to be primarily a hunting station. No agriculture is practiced today within the immediate vicinity of the shelter. The land is poor, the topography broken, and the streams deeply entrenched. While some milling stones were recovered at the site, mainly from the early ceramic layers, none of the edge-ground cobbles so common at Monagrillo, Cerro Mangote, and Aguadulce are present at Ladrones. Thus, the most important subsistence activity at Ladrones appears to be the hunting of terrestrial fauna, with some gathering and processing of plant foods.

DISCUSSION

What evidence we have on settlement patterns during the preceramic and early ceramic periods, 5000 to 1000 B.C., suggests continuity and stability. The Aguadulce and Ladrones sites continue to be utilized in both periods. Cerro Mangote is abandoned before the early ceramic period begins, but Zapotal, 4 km downstream, is then occupied. This shift in site location may simply reflect a shift in the location of active lagoons as silt deposition pushed the Santa Maria River delta farther out into Parita Bay. The Cerro Mangote site, the Zapotal site, and the three Monagrillo phase sites south of the Parita River are in similar topographic positions. That is, all are located on the ends of peninsulas that, at the time each was occupied, extended out into Parita Bay and/or into active estuary–lagoon systems. It does not take a catchment analysis to realize that site placement maximizes access to aquatic, not terrestrial, resources. Access to terrestrial resources was gained by establishing small camp sites inland on the *llanos* (e.g., the Aguadulce Shelter) or in the foothills (e.g., La Cueva de los Ladrones).

It is instructive to compare the location of settlements during the pre-ceramic and early ceramic periods with those of later periods when the presence of maize agriculture is well documented (see Cooke 1976 for a summary of the evidence). These later settlements are concentrated along major river courses where fertile alluvial soils are readily accessible. Sitio Sierra, a village in the Santa Maria River valley just 3 km upriver from Cerro Mangote, is a case in point (Cooke 1975). The site was occupied for most of the first millennium A.D. Although the enormous quantity of fish remains recovered in Cooke's excavation documents the continued importance of aquatic resources, the site was located 13 km upriver from the coast and 1 km back from the river bank on ground high enough to escape inundation during wet season flooding. Clearly, access to the rich alluvial soils of the Santa Maria River floodplain was the determining factor in site location. Recovery of charred fragments of maize along with the manos and metates used in preparing flour documents the presence of a maize agricultural complex at Sitio Sierra.

Given the time period during which the early sites were occupied, 5000 to 1000 B.C., the most obvious question about subsistence patterns is whether or not agriculture was practiced during all or part of the period. Since initial dates for plant domestication are being pushed back into, and perhaps beyond, the eighth millennium B.C. both in highland Mexico and the Andes, the presence of agriculture at the beginning of the occupations of Cerro Mangote and Aguadulce is not unreasonable. However, we cannot yet answer the question concerning the presence or absence of food production during any of the time period under consideration, although the unanalyzed samples of charcoal and pollen from Monagrillo and the Aguadulce Shelter may eventually permit us to do so.

We can, however, say with some confidence that maize agriculture was *not* a part of these early subsistence systems. The following lines of evidence suggest this to be true. First, as we noted above, sites that demonstrably have maize agriculture complexes, for example, Sitio Sierra, are located in differ-ent environmental contexts than those of preceramic and early ceramic sites. Second, although there are abundant remains of maize found in these later habitation sites in central Panama (Cooke 1975, 1976), maize is absent from the Monagrillo site in spite of the fact that charcoal is abundant and well preserved. Maize is also absent from the Aguadulce Shelter and La Cueva de los Ladrones. A similar situation exists in western Panama. Maize has been recovered from sites that are less than 2500 years old (Linares, Sheets, and Rosenthal 1975; Einhaus 1976) but is absent from four excavated pre-ceramic rockshelters. These sites, located within 5 km of each other in the Chiriquí River canyon, were occupied during the fifth through the first millennium B.C. (4610 ± 120 B.C. to 350 ± 75 B.C. is the range for the radiocarbon determinations from the sites). Hundreds of charred fragments of palm nuts, tree legumes, and *nance* seeds were recovered in the rockshelter deposits, but not one maize kernel or cob fragment (Ranere 1972, 1976). Like the central Panama sites 150 km to the east, the Chiriquí shelters contained the edge-ground cobble–boulder milling-stone complex and a technologically simple chipped-stone tool complex (Ranere 1975a). Monagrillo pottery is, however, absent from the Río Chiriquí sites, which remain preceramic at least until 350 B.C.

Bartlett, Barghoorn, and Berger (1969) have reported the presence of pollen from wild maize in cores from Gatun Lake, just east of the Panama Canal, at levels dated at 5350 ± 130 B.C. and 4280 ± 80 B.C. The earliest unequivocal date for pollen from cultivated maize in the Gatun Lake sequence is 1200 ± 60 B.C., where it occurs with finely divided charcoal and greatly increased percentages of Gramineae and Compositae.

If not maize, then what plants were being used during this period from 5000 to 1000 B.C.? The most common plant remains found in preceramic and early ceramic contexts in Panama are those of trees. Palm nuts are the most common, with lesser amounts of tree legumes and pits from the fruit of the nance. These trees are all common elements in secondary growth and probably belong to dry tropical forest formations. Today these trees are protected. Protection or cultivation in the past is not inconceivable but is difficult to demonstrate (Earle Smith, personal communication).

Missing from the discussion thus far and from our preceramic and early ceramic samples are root crops. A number of researchers (Sauer 1952; Harris 1972; and many more) have suggested that root crop agriculture is extremely ancient in the New World tropics. Given the importance of root crops historically, their widespread distribution in the Americas, and the archaeological evidence for their use during the first millennium B.C. in highland Mexico and coastal Peru (see Lathrap 1973 for a summary of the evidence), such suggestions seem warranted. It is our feeling that root crop agriculture was practiced in central Panama at least by the end of the third millennium B.C., and perhaps even earlier (cf. Ranere 1972, 1976). We can only hope that analysis of the pollen samples from Monagrillo and Aguadulce will provide some information about root crop cultivation in central Panama.

CONCLUSION

What seems clear at this stage of analysis is the relative dependence of the preceramic and early ceramic site occupants on broadly defined resource zones. Cerro Mangote and Monagrillo are unquestionably oriented toward aquatic resources for procurement of animal protein. The other early ceramic sites of Zapotal, He-12, and He-18 are in topographic positions along the coast similar to those occupied by Cerro Mangote and Monagrillo (see Willey and McGimsey 1954) and share their orientation to aquatic resources. The large sample of white-tailed deer remains (and lesser amounts of other land animals) from Cerro Mangote and Monagrillo indicates that terrestrial resources provide important, albeit smaller, amounts of protein in the diet.

The emphasis on aquatic and terrestrial resources is reversed at the Aguadulce Shelter, which was at the time of its occupation about 12 km from the coast. The terrestrial faunal assemblage at Aguadulce appears, on the basis of the preliminary examination, quite similar to assemblages at Cerro Mangote and Monagrillo in spite of the fact that at Aguadulce it accounts for a much larger proportion of the total fauna. Remains of shellfish, crabs, and fish, though represented at the Aguadulce Shelter, are present in modest amounts.

La Cueva de los Ladrones is understandably dependent almost entirely on terrestrial resources for animal protein. Though the coast of Parita Bay is visible from the site, it is nearly 25 km away. Given the site's remoteness from the coast, it is somewhat surprising that shellfish and crab are represented at all in the deposits. They must, however, be considered a negligible component of the food consumed at the site.

As might be expected when most of the sites under discussion have recently been excavated or reexcavated and the data incompletely analyzed, a large number of questions remain unanswered. Of considerable importance is the dating of these sites. Regrettably, no radiometric dates are available for Zapotal, He-12, and He-18, nor have any been obtained as yet from the Aguadulce Shelter or La Cueva de los Ladrones. Single radiocarbon determinations have been published for Cerro Mangote, 6810 ± 100 radiocarbon years: 4860 ± 110 B.C., and for Monagrillo, 4090 ± 70 radiocarbon years: 2140 ± 70 B.C. (Deevey, Gralenski, and Hoffren 1959:142–172). We can now add a series of eight radiocarbon determinations on charcoal collected in the 1975 excavations at Monagrillo (Table 3.1).

These dates are not easily interpreted. Given their inconsistencies, the dates for Block 1 are perhaps best ignored. However, they do serve to emphasize the complicated stratigraphy in Block 1 (see Figure 3.4) and, taken together, suggest a time span for the Monagrillo occupation of approximately 1000 years. In Block 2 (Figure 3.3), where the stratigraphy was not disturbed by numerous pits, the first three dates provide an internally consistent series. The fourth date from Block 2 is inexplicably early. At this stage in the analysis, we tentatively suggest that the Monagrillo occupation at the site

Table 3.1
MONAGRILLO RADIOCARBON DETERMINATIONS

Block	Number	"Level" (centimeters below surface)	Radiocarbon years	
Block 1	SI-2842	20–30	4405 ± 75 B.P.	2455 ± 75 B.C.
	SI-2843	50–56	3245 ± 100 B.P.	1295 ± 100 B.C.
	SI-2844	97–100	4135 ± 80 B.P.	2185 ± 80 B.C.
	I-9384	150–160	3325 ± 85 B.P.	1375 ± 85 B.C.
Block 2	SI-2838	20–30	3385 ± 75 B.P.	1435 ± 75 B.C.
	SI-2839	50–60	3485 ± 100 B.P.	1535 ± 100 B.C.
	SI-2840	95–100	3615 ± 80 B.P.	1665 ± 80 B.C.
	SI-2841	110–120	5385 ± 95 B.P.	3435 ± 95 B.C.

began around 2500–2300 B.C. and ended around 1300 B.C. Additional radiocarbon dates from Monagrillo will be needed in order to provide us with a clearer understanding of the site's chronology.

The completion of the faunal and shell analysis for the sites of Aguadulce, Monagrillo, and La Cueva de los Ladrones will provide information on a number of problems, among them the relative importance of individual species in the diet, the specific habitats exploited by the sites' inhabitants, and the seasonality or permanency of occupation. Analysis of the stone and ceramic assemblages should allow us to better assess the proposition that the coastal sites, inland *llanos* sites, and the foothill sites are (are not) products of a single population utilizing a transhumant adaptive strategy. Finally, the question of the presence of agriculture and the nature of the agricultural system (if present) can perhaps be answered through the analysis of charred plant remains and pollen.

ACKNOWLEDGMENTS

The research on which much of this chapter is based was funded by the American Philosophical Society (Grant 7393, Penrose Fund), the Smithsonian Tropical Research Institute, and Temple University (Faculty Grant-in-Aid). Seven radiocarbon dates from the Monagrillo site were provided by the Smithsonian Institution's Radiocarbon Laboratory, Robert Stuckenrath, Director. The project was carried out in cooperation with the Patrimonio Histórico de Panamá, Reina Torres de Arauz, Director.

We wish to thank O. F. Linares, codirector of the project, and R. G. Cooke, C. S. Einhaus, R. L. McCarty, E. J. Rosenthal, K. Sargeant, and R. White, all of whom participated in the 1975 excavations of Monagrillo and the Aguadulce Shelter. We also thank H. Hansell and M. Kirkpatrick for preparing the figures.

REFERENCES

Bartlett, A., E. Barghoorn, and R. Berger
1969 Fossil maize fron Panama. *Science* **165** (3891):389–390.

Bird, Junius, and Richard G. Cooke
1974 Excavaciones arqueológicas en la cueva de los Ladrones, Districto de La Pintada, Provincia de Coclé, Panamá. Report submitted to the Patrimonio Histórico del I.N.A.C., Panamá.

Bennett, Charles
1968 *Human influences on the zoogeography of Panama.* Berkeley: University of California Press.

Burnston, Sharon
1977 A preliminary report on the Monagrillo mammal and bird remains. Manuscript on file, Department of Anthropology, Temple University, Philadelphia.

Cooke, Richard G.
1975 La Excavación de una Aldea Agrícola Precolombina. In *Dominical,* El Panama-Americana, 6 de Julio.
1976 El hombre y la tierra en el Panamá prehistórico. *Revista Nacional de Cultura* **2:**17–38. Panamá.

Deevey, E. S., L. J. Gralenski, and V. Hoffren
1959 Yale natural radiocarbon measurements IV. *American Journal of Science,* Radiocarbon Supplement **1**:142–172.

Einhaus, Catherine Shelton
1976 A technological and functional analysis of stone tools from Isla Palenque, Panama. Master's thesis, Department of Anthropology, Temple University, Philadelphia.

FAO (Food and Agriculture Organization of the United Nations)
1971 Inventariación y demostraciones forestales, Panamá. Zonas de vida. Based on the work of Joseph A. Tosi. Rome. FO:SF Pan 6. Technical Report 2.

Glynn, Peter W.
1972 Observations on the ecology of the Caribbean and Pacific coasts of Panama. *Biological Society of Washington* Bulletin No. 2. Pp. 13–30.

Harris, David
1972 The origins of agriculture in the tropics. *American Scientist* **60** (2):180–193.

Lathrap, Donald
1973 The antiquity and importance of long-distance trade relationships in the moist tropics of Pre-Colombian South America. *World Archaeology* **5**(2):170–186.

Linares, Olga, and Anthony Ranere
1971 Human adaptation to the tropical forests of Western Panama. *Archaeology* **24**(4):346–355.

Linares, O., P. Sheets, and E. J. Rosenthal
1975 Preceramic agriculture in tropical highlands. *Science* **187:**137–145.

McGimsey, Charles
1956 Cerro Mangote: A Preceramic site in Panama. *American Antiquity* **22**(2):151–161.

McGimsey, Charles, M. Collin, and T. McKern
1966 Cerro Mangote and its population. Paper presented at the 37th International Congress of Americanists, Mar de Plata, Argentina.

Parmalee, P., and E. Klippel
1974 Freshwater mussels as a prehistoric food resource. *American Antiquity* **39**(3):421–434.

Ranere, Anthony
    1972   Early human adaptations to New World tropical forests: The view from Panama. Ph.D. dissertation, Department of Anthropology, University of California, Davis.
    1975a   Toolmaking and tool use among the Preceramic peoples of Panama. In *Lithic technology. Making and using stone tools*. The Hague: Mouton. Pp. 173–209.
    1975b   Report on the 1975 archaeological investigations at Monagrillo and the Aguadulce Shelter, Central Panama. Report to the Patrimonio Historico del I.N.A.C., Panama. Unpublished manuscript.
    1976   The Preceramic of Panama: The view from the interior. In *Proceedings of the First Puerto Rican Symposium on archàeology*. San Juan. Pp. 103–137.
Ranere, Anthony, and Richard McCarty
    1976   Informe preliminar sobre excavación de un sitio preceramico en Coclé. In *Actas del IV Simposio de Antropología*. Panama.
Sauer, Carl
    1952   *Agricultural origins and dispersals*. New York: American Geographical Society.
White, Richard
    1974   Preliminary notes on the vertebrate fauna from Aguadulce Shelter. Manuscript on file, Department of Anthropology, Temple University, Philadelphia.
Willey, Gordon
    1971   *An introduction to American archaeology, Vol. 2: South America*. Englewood Cliffs: Prentice-Hall.
Willey, Gordon, and Charles McGimsey
    1954   The Monagrillo culture of Panama. *Papers of the Peabody Museum of Archaeology and Ethnology*, Vol. 49, No. 2. Harvard University.

chapter 4

The Prehistoric and Modern Subsistence Patterns of the Atlantic Coast of Nicaragua: A Comparison

RICHARD WERNER MAGNUS

Banco Central de Nicaragua

INTRODUCTION

The purpose of this chapter is twofold. The principal goal is to develop a working model of prehistoric subsistence patterns on the Atlantic coast of Nicaragua by means of an investigation of a portion of the southern sector (Figure 4.1). To do this, various modern villages and their subsistence patterns will be described. The archaeological remains that these villages could produce will be outlined and compared with available prehistoric data. These comparisons should then indicate either similarities or differences between the prehistoric subsistence of a site and that of modern villages. A model for prehistory can then be tentatively developed using the elements of similarity between post- and precontact settlements. The second purpose of this study is to illustrate and explain the degree of continuity of prehistoric subsistence with that of later times. This goal is interrelated with hypotheses about the development of the Miskito as a distinct ethnic group.

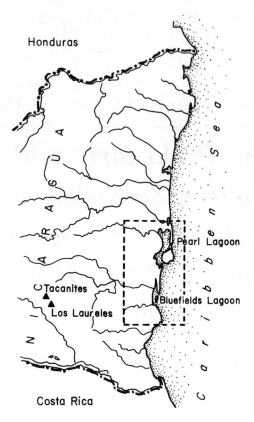

Figure 4.1. Atlantic lowlands of Nicaragua. Inset shows location of area in Figures 4.2 and 4.3.

The archaeological and prehistoric data relevant to ecological studies of the Atlantic coast of Nicaragua are far from complete. The archaeological work discussed has been carried out over the last 5 years under grants from the National Science Foundation and the Banco Central de Nicaragua. Detailed information on excavation methodology as well as site descriptions and ceramic data can be found elsewhere (Magnus 1974, 1975, 1976). More field research is planned, as well as additional analyses of existing collections.

Survey of the zone, important to many of the problems at hand, is all but impossible. There are vast tropical forests and swamps that are almost impossible to penetrate, let alone to search thoroughly for archaeological sites. The heavy bush obscures even very large mounds. Therefore, I prefer to consider this a working report rather than a final presentation of data and their interpretation.

MODERN SUBSISTENCE PATTERNS OF
THE ATLANTIC COAST

Since the majority of excavated sites are either on large lagoons or on rivers close to the seashore, only villages that are in similar settings will be discussed. Furthermore, I emphasize that I will describe village subsistence systems because it is invalid to assume any one to be representative of a given ethnic group. For example, Tasbapauni and Kakabila have quite different subsistence patterns although they are both Miskito settlements. The projection of the kinds of archaeological remains these villages could produce will be done in general terms because many technological differences between prehistoric and modern times make a detailed, specific description useless for my purposes.

Tasbapauni

The modern village of Tasbapauni is located on a very narrow haulover that separates Pearl Lagoon from the Caribbean Sea (Figure 4.2). It is this extremely advantageous position that gives the inhabitants access to a large number of different biotopes. They can exploit the sea with its turtles, fish, shellfish, and other animals as well as the lagoon, which affords another environment to broaden the subsistence base. Along the beaches it is possible to hunt as well as plant crops, including coconuts, dasheen (Colocasia esculenta), cassava (Manihot dulcis), duswa (Xanthosoma spp.), plantains, and bananas. Finally, along the rivers and creeks leading into Pearl Lagoon, good alluvial soils are found for plantations. In protecting the river farms, the villagers shoot deer (both white and brocket) and peccary (both white-lipped and collared) as well as other animals which form a significant part of the diet.

According to Nietschmann (1973:17), the village contains approximately 1000 people who live in about 200 houses distributed along half a mile of beachfront. The houses are generally made of wood which is either crudely sawed or found on the beach. Most are thatched although a few have zinc roofs. The floors are raised off the ground on stilts.

Present-day subsistence of the Miskito of Tasbapauni is a complex adaptation including agriculture, hunting, and fishing. These activities work in a complementary fashion in that fishing occurs during the dry season, hunting during the rainy season, and agriculture all year around. If the fishing and hunting fail, there is always agriculture to fall back upon, as disagreeable as a "so-so" (without meat) meal is to Miskito taste.

Nietschmann (1973:166) says that "the coastal Miskito have adapted much of their technology, lifeways, and internal and external economic patterns to predictable behavior patterns and relatively dependable catches of green turtle." His figures show that during the study period 70% of the meat brought into the village came from the green turtle (Nietschmann 1973: Table 21). Furthermore, 13% of the remaining meat came from marine sources. Hunting, although more favorable during the dry season, is primarily done in the rainy months so as not to divert energy from the exploitation of marine resources. Only 15% of the total meat needs are produced by hunting.

Agricultural activities occur as far as 25 or 30 miles up the rivers from the village. The Tasbapauni Miskito prefer the fluvial soils and work them whenever possible. Cassava grown provides 40% of the diet by weight (Nietschmann 1973:234). Bananas, plaintains, and other root crops likewise are important sources of energy.

Essentially, the Tasbapauni villagers are strongly marine-oriented people who practice agriculture and hunt to supply themselves with additional foods. The location of the village provides easy access to the marine resources but is distant from good plantation and hunting areas. These areas are only reached with the expense of much energy and time.

Projection of archaeological subsistence remains for the village of Tasbapauni is readily done. First, there will be a specialized tool inventory showing the marine adaptation. Nietschmann (1973:156) notes that "Miskito employ an array of different points and harpoons for striking fish, manatee, and turtle. Two types of fish lances with fixed points and a harpoon with detachable point are used for manatee." Second, abundant osteological remains of marine animals, particularly green turtle, will occur in butchering loci as well as house sites. Since turtle shell is very durable, there should be no problem with preservation. Third, if no major coastline change occurs, house mounds in a marine setting will remain, each containing a full range of the material culture of the inhabitants. Few architectural details will remain, since wood will not leave meaningful features in this climate. Fourth, auxiliary agricultural activity loci will be found along the rivers, primarily in the form of ranch remains. These loci will not exhibit the full range of the material culture since principally food storage is carried out at these sites. In addition, no specialized tool kits will be found because the multipurpose machete is the only tool used. The styles of recovered artifacts will correlate with those found in the principal habitation site.

Kakabila

The Miskito village of Kakabila is located on the southwestern shore of Pearl Lagoon on the first prominent point north of Pearl Lagoon City (Figure 4.2). This gives the villagers access to the resources of the lagoon and to

Figure 4.2. South Atlantic coast of Nicaragua with modern villages mentioned in text.

those of the sea, which are across the lagoon and outside the bar. Furthermore, plantations can be placed along the shore of the lagoon and up its creeks and rivers. The same inland areas contain terrestrial game.

Kakabila is quite small with perhaps 20 to 30 houses and between 100 and 200 inhabitants. The structures are usually made from thin saplings placed close to each other and nailed together with horizontal crossbars. They have dirt floors and thatched roofing. There is generally one living space, which may be partitioned off with inner walls. These habitations are much less complex than those of Tasbapauni and provide less convenient living conditions.

The subsistence of Kakabila is very different from that of Tasbapauni and does not reflect a particularly efficient adaptation to the resources available. One would expect there to be extensive use of marine and estuarine biotopes, especially those of the adjacent lagoon. However, this is not the case and, as nearly as I can determine, limited fishing is done. I spent 2 months in the village, and fish was rarely in the diet in the houses I visited.

This was particularly striking because my visit occurred during the dry months of March and April when fishing is at its height in other lagoon villages. In one house there was occasionally some shrimp and turtle, but this resulted from the family's cooperation with Tasbapauni turtlemen.

Apparently, agriculture is a full-time occupation of the inhabitants of Kakabila. They have plantations of cassava, *duswa*, plantains, and bananas directly behind the village and along the nearby shores. Few of the plantings are far from the houses, and most can be reached within an hour by boat. My impression is that the diet is primarily based on root crops, and even rice and beans are rare.

It is difficult to explain this adaptation synchronically in cultural or ecological terms. No one expresses any distaste at the idea of eating marine products. Furthermore, I have seen persons from other villages catching large quantities of fish at Kakabila Point. Rather than these explanations I prefer a historical one which I will present later.

Archaeological remains from Kakabila would be very limited. The houses will not produce many remains because the thin walls will rot and few nonperishable items occur inside. No specialized food preparation tools are used with the exception of graters for cassava and *duswa*. Agricultural equipment principally consists of the multipurpose machete. Agricultural growing and storage loci will not be found since *ranchos* are not constructed. Only the central habitation site will be discernible. Kakabila will give meager data on which to base ecological hypotheses. What is present is an agriculturally oriented village in a coastal setting.

Big Lagoon

In spite of its name, Big Lagoon is not on a lagoon but in a riverine setting located close to the Caribbean shore. It is southwest of Kukra Hill about midway between Bluefields and Pearl Lagoon (Figure 4.2). This zone has highly fertile agricultural soil now used for sugarcane production. The principal assets of the location are the excellent land for planting, rivers for fishing, and tropical forest for hunting. The sea and lagoons are still within easy reach. The settlement is highly dispersed and consists of approximately 40 houses for 100 to 150 people. Most of the houses are similar to those of Tasbapauni with walls of crudely sawed lumber.

As one might expect, the principal economic concentration is agricultural. Because of the excellent conditions, corn can be grown to supplement the Caribbean root crops. Apart from agriculture, some animals are hunted in nearby forests. Fishing is likewise limited, and no use is made of the sea and lagoon biotopes.

The archaeological remains for Big Lagoon would simply consist of dispersed house mounds containing very few artifacts. Metates and manos as well as comales would be found, which suggest the presence of maize cultivation. Cassava and *duswa* graters also would be present. However, botanical data will be limited due to poor preservation. Some bone remains from domestic and wild land animals as well as fish may be found in house mounds, but large amounts are unlikely. Since there are no *ranchos* or special activity loci, only the house mounds and associated outdoor work areas will be encountered. Essentially, subsistence is based on agriculture supplemented by hunting and fishing. Archaeological remains for such an economy will not be plentiful since most will perish with time.

Summary

Three different examples of subsistence on the Atlantic coast of Nicaragua have been presented. Tasbapauni depends primarily upon the marine biotopes and secondarily upon terrestrial ones. There is a central settlement with dispersed *ranchos* that are used for short stays in distant plantations. Kakabila's subsistence is almost entirely agriculturally oriented. Naturally, a small amount of marine products are included in the diet, but they are not very significant. Both Kakabila and Tasbapauni are in somewhat similar settings, and the difference in subsistence patterns is striking. Big Lagoon, in contrast, presents a dispersed village in a riverine location not far from the sea. Subsistence is almost entirely based on agriculture; little hunting and fishing are done. Big Lagoon differs from Kakabila in its access to exploitable biotopes; however, the agricultural subsistence patterns of the two villages are remarkably similar.

ARCHAEOLOGICAL SUBSISTENCE DATA

I will discuss the evidence for the precontact subsistence systems first by complex and then by site or group of similar sites. As discussed earlier, the ethnographic data are not valid for a larger group than the community from which they were collected. Similarly, two archaeological sites can have the same cultural material but not share subsistence patterns. The only sites that will be discussed together are those that apparently have the same subsistence bases or represent a similar element in a larger exploitation system.

Siteia Complex

The Siteia complex is the only member to date of the polychrome Siteioid tradition (Magnus 1974). It has been found in three coastal shell

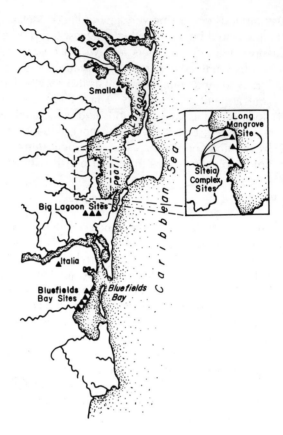

Figure 4.3. Archaeological sites on the south Atlantic coast of Nicaragua which are mentioned in text.

middens on Pearl Lagoon as well as in an inland shell heap at Italia behind Bluefields (Figure 4.3).

Coastal Sites

These shell middens are on the south end of Pearl Lagoon near the villages of Kakabila and Brown Bank. Although primarily excavated for cultural material, care was taken to recover biotic remains with ¼-in. screening. Only very small bits of animal and fish bones were found. The matrix of the sites was made of *Neocyrena* cf. *nicaraguana* and *Donax denticulatus* with a few *Strombus* sp. No macrobotanical remains resulted, and pollen was not collected.

A few celts, mano and metate fragments, and irregular flint tools were recovered. The function of the celts is unclear because there are no traces of wear. The manos and metates may have been used for grinding corn, but there is no way to test this interpretation. Finally, the irregular flints may have been general-use tools to skin animals, although once again this function cannot be confirmed. They have no retouching or edge wear which would substantiate a functional assignment. No hearths or other architectural features were found at these sites.

Italia Site

This site is located approximately 12 km west of Bluefields on a small creek leading into the bay. It consists of a group of shell mounds with associated habitational remains. The shells in the excavated mound were principally *Neocyrena* cf. *nicaraguana* and *Donax denticulatus* with a few *Strombus* sp. The site contained large quantities of bone material, and the kinds of fish, mammals, and reptiles identified to date are listed in Table 4.1 along with provisional counts of minimum numbers of individuals. Macrobotanical remains did not appear, although pollen might be found in the future. All material was ultimately floated after passing a ¼-in. screen.

Very large quantities of ceramics and stone artifacts were recovered. The stone material includes manos, metates, celts, and irregular flint tools. The manos and metates were probably used for grinding corn, but the function of the other tools is less certain. Although none have yet been excavated, it is almost certain that house remains could be found at this site. The range of material culture clearly indicates permanent dwellings. Large patches of burning found in the shell deposits excavated probably represent temporary hearths.

Nueva Guinea Complex

The data for this complex come from two sites belonging to the Smalloid tradition and located in Colonia Laureles and Tacanites in western Zelaya (Figure 4.1). They are approximately 160 km from the sea in a riverine setting. The excavation was effected primarily to establish the inland extent of the coastal traditions. Absolutely no bone material was recovered from either site, despite screening. This is remarkable in view of the midden nature of the deposits. Botanical data were not recovered and, apart from pollen perhaps, probably did not survive. Pollen might be found in some of the sites of this zone, but the soils do not favor its preservation. Architectural remains are likely to be found in other parts of the site.

Table 4.1

FAUNAL REMAINS FROM THE ITALIA SITE

Fauna	Provisional minimum number of individuals
Mammals	
Tayassu sp. (peccary)	4
Dasyprocta cf. *punctata richmondi* (agouti)	1
Trichechus manatus ssp. (manatee)	1
Didelphis sp. (opossum)	1
Tapirus cf. *bairdii* (tapir)	1
Mazama americana ssp. (deer)	1
Small rodents	8
Reptiles	
Constrictor contrictor (boa)	1
Crocodylus acutus (crocodile)	1
Kinosternon leucostomum (mud or musk turtle)	32
Rhinoclemmys sp. (hicatee turtle)	1
Chrysemys scripta (hicatee turtle)	1
Chelydra serpentina (snapper turtle)	1
Iguanidae (iguana)	1
Fish	
Carcharhinus leucas (bull shark)	1
Carcharhinus maculipinnis (spinner shark)	1
Negaprion brevirostris (lemon shark)	1
Sphyrna tiburo (bonnethead shark)	1
Pristis sp. (sawfish)	1
Dasyatis cf. *americana* (southern stingray)	1
Aetobatus narinari (spotted eagle ray)	1
Arius cf. *spixus* (catfish)	63
Bagre sp. (catfish)	11
Batracoides cf. *gilberti* (toadfish)	25
Centropomus sp. (snook)	24
Epinephelus sp. (jewfish)	2
Caranx sp. (jack)	28
Archosargus probatocephalus (sheepshead)	2
Conodon cf. *nobilis* (barred grunt)	1
Micropogonias sp. (croaker)	27
Bairdiella santaeluciae (striped croaker)	20
Menticirrhus sp. (kingfish)	3
Cynoscion virescens (corvina)	11

Smalla Complex

Temporally the Smalla complex follows the Nueva Guinea (Magnus 1974). It has been located only at one site, the Smalla site, on the north end of Pearl Lagoon. This site is directly west of the village of Tasbapauni and on a villager's plantation. The excavation was carried out with culture historical goals, and only ¼-in. screening was used for the recovery of biotic remains. However, a number of bones were found, including those of the white-lipped peccary (*Tayassu pecari*), brocket deer (*Mazama americana*), hicatee turtle (*Chrysemys* sp.), manatee (*Trichechus* sp.), and various kinds of fish. Although positive identification of the fish bones was not made, they include jack (*Caranx* sp.), snook (*Centropomus* sp.), and coppermouth (*Cynoscion* sp.). The actual site was made up of *Neocyrena* cf. *nicaraguana* and *Donax denticulatus*. No oyster shells were found. Unfortunately, most of the faunal data were lost in the Managua earthquake, which precludes their further study.

The cultural material includes numerous amorphous flint tools that are very similar to those from the Nueva Guinea sites. They seem to be multipurpose implements perhaps used for both skinning animals and cutting plant material. None shows any distinctive wear marks or retouching. There are likewise mano and metate fragments for grinding corn. No hearths or architectural features were found, but this is perhaps due to the small 2 m × 3 m cut effected.

Jarquin Complex

Long Mangrove Site

This site is a shell midden on the south end of Pearl Lagoon. It is directly on the shore of the lagoon and was extensively excavated to recover cultural remains. Practically no ceramics and virtually no stone tools resulted. Though the excavations were oriented toward culture history and used only ¼-in. screening, we were careful in our search for bone material, which seemed to be nonexistent. The only faunal remains were the *Donax denticulatus* and *Neocyrena* cf. *nicaraguana* shells from which the mound was made. No hearths or similar features were encountered. This absence is significant in view of the size of the excavations, which covered over 60% of the site.

Big Lagoon

Three sites were excavated in the Big Lagoon zone. All of these were earth mounds, some of which were surrounded by rings of stones. The excavations were aimed principally at the recovery of data for culture history studies, but ¼-in. screening should have yielded faunal data. In fact, no bones were located. This is strange since these mounds must represent house bases onto which trash was dumped during their use. No botanical remains were found, although with the use of flotation it is possible that some could be encountered. Generally, the same kinds of general-use, amorphous flint tools were found in all the Big Lagoon sites. These were similar to those from the previous complexes. A miniature metate, as well as full-sized manos and metates, was located. Little else found gives any indication of the subsistence methods used at the site.

Kukra Point Complex

Five sites along the west shore of Bluefields Bay were excavated and their cultural material classified in this complex. All of these sites were shell heaps, although one at Kukra Point is considerably larger than the rest. Despite the use of flotation, bone material from the Kukra Point site was not particularly abundant. A partial identification reveals the mammals, reptiles, and fish listed in Table 4.2, along with provisional minimum numbers of individuals. Furthermore, I have calculated that 1 m³ of midden contains over 250,000 shells of *Neocyrena* cf. *nicaraguana* and *Donax denticulatus*. In the cubic meter sample tabulated, 93.4% was *Neocyrena* and 6.5% *Donax*. A few *Strombus* sp. were also found.

In addition to shellfish and animal bones, the sites of Bluefields Bay yielded manos and metates and the same amorphous flint tools discussed previously. No architecture or other features have been defined at any of the sites.

A PRECONTACT SUBSISTENCE MODEL

Although the above archaeological data are very fragmentary, they suggest some working hypotheses for the prehistoric subsistence patterns of the Atlantic lowlands of Nicaragua. In this section, the sites will be treated in two major groups, those apparently relying principally on marine biotopes and those that were more terrestrial in their subsistence orientation. This division crosscuts the Siteia and Jarquin complexes which have both marine and terrestrial sites. However, the fact that the other complexes do not have both types of sites should not be considered significant. I consider it likely that a more comprehensive survey, were it possible, would reveal both terrestrial and marine sites for all complexes.

Table 4.2
FAUNAL REMAINS FROM THE KUKRA POINT SITE

Fauna	Provisional minimum number of individuals
Mammals	
Tayassu sp. (peccary)	1
Agouti paca (agouti)	1
Dasyprocta cf. *punctata richmondi* (agouti)	2
Sylvilagus cf. *brasiliensis* (rabbit)	1
Dasypus sp. (armadillo)	1
Nasua sp. (coati-mundi)	1
Trichechus manatus ssp. (manatee)	1
Reptiles	
Constrictor constrictor (boa)	1
Crocodylus acutus (crocodile)	1
Kinosternon leucostomum (mud or musk turtle)	1
Rhinoclemmys sp. (hicatee turtle)	1
Chelydra serpentina (snapper turtle)	1
Fish	
Carcharhinus maculipinnis (spinner shark)	1
Carcharhinus limbatus (blacktip shark)	1
Pristis sp. (sawfish)	4
Dasyatis cf. *americana* (southern stingray)	4
Aetobatus narinari (spotted eagle ray)	2
Arius cf. *spixus* (catfish)	205
Bagre sp. (catfish)	2
Batracoides cf. *gilberti* (toadfish)	31
Epinephelus sp. (jewfish)	2
Centropomus sp. (snook)	5
Micropogonias sp. (croaker)	3
Dormitator maculatus (fat sleeper)	1

Marine-Oriented Sites

Siteia Complex Pearl Lagoon Sites

These sites yielded very few fish or mammal bones, an indication that the people were not thoroughly utilizing all available biotopes. The occurrence of *Donax denticulatus* points to the presence of boats to carry the gatherers outside the bar to the seashore. Although *Neocyrena* cf. *nicaraguana* is found in the muddy lagoon, the *Donax denticulatus* only occurs in the sand of the Caribbean shore.

The only specialized tools, manos and metates, point toward corn agriculture. The unspecialized flint tools are not indicative of a marine adaptation, since it was noted that at the modern village of Tasbapauni an elaborate material culture is associated with the fishing and turtling activities. It must be kept in mind, however, that specialized tools could have been made of perishable material and thus not preserved. But coupled with the lack of bones, this interpretation is not strongly supported.

Also significant is the fact that no architectural remains, hearths, etc. were detected in the cuts. Although it is possible that they were missed because of the size of the excavations, this seems doubtful since the middens were not large and the cuts covered at least 50% of their surface. Rather, it is possible that no elaborate structure was ever present.

These sites' remains are, therefore, different from those projected for the modern villages described earlier because they probably represent elements in a different type of subsistence system. It might be hypothesized that the Siteia complex Pearl Lagoon sites are temporary hunting and fishing stations of a group whose permanent base was located elsewhere. The question remains whether this group was coastal or came from the "back," as the interior is called today. The latter seems more likely for one reason: The Siteia sites' positions do not offer any obvious benefits over the rest of the lagoon for hunting and fishing. Therefore, a coastal group would have no need to travel any distance for their subsistence activities and to establish fishing stations. Furthermore, the coast of Pearl Lagoon is a likely place to find people from the interior since the mouth of the Kuringwas River, a route for east–west travel, opens into the Lagoon's north end. Finally, though the presence of manos and metates in the site does not conclusively indicate whether a river or coastal people were present, agricultural groups generally prefer the alluvial river soils.

A working hypothesis might be, therefore, that these sites were the camps of an agriculturally oriented riverine people visiting coastal biotopes to supplement their diet. This general pattern is known elsewhere in Lower Central America and was established archaeologically, for example, by Claude Baudez (personal communication) in the Gulf of Fonseca, Honduras. Examination of more data from additional sites, including the inland Siteia complex site, supports this model. Accordingly, the coastline may not have been significantly inhabited until postconquest times.

Smalla Site

The Smalla site contained terrestrial mammal, fish, and reptile remains which indicate that its users hunted and fished. Furthermore, the range of the terrestrial mammal remains points to a familiarity with the forest, while the turtle, manatee, and fish show the same for the marine biotopes. Once again, the presence of *Donax denticulatus* is significant in that the collectors had to cross the lagoon, presumably by boat, to find the shellfish along the Caribbean shore.

The lack of any kind of developed stone tool kit which would have been useful in the exploitation of the marine environment is striking. This absence is significant in that it may demonstrate a familiarity with the marine biotopes but not a close adaptation to them. Countering this is the hypothesized presence of boats, but this need not show a coastal adaptation since watercraft are also found among river peoples.

As in the Siteia complex coastal sites, no architectural remains, hearths, etc. were found. Whether this results from sample size, use of perishable architecture, or the lack of architecture cannot be determined at present. It seems likely that this site was a temporary fishing and hunting camp of an inland agricultural people. In most ways, it is very similar to the Siteia complex marine sites and may have served the same function in a similar subsistence system.

Long Mangrove Site

Since this site contained almost no cultural material and only the shells as subsistence data, it cannot be considered a permanent habitation locus. Furthermore, it appears from the extremely limited range of biotopes exploited that the users of this site were not intensively utilizing either the forest or lagoon. On the other hand, they probably had boats since they had to cross the lagoon to reach the *Donax denticulatus* on the shore. Based on this data alone, one might expect that the group came from the interior, probably by river, and gathered shellfish that require minimal experience to find. The lack of architecture or other features would support this gathering station interpretation.

Further strength for this model is derived from the presence of sites belonging to this complex in interior, riverine settings. It would even seem possible that Long Mangrove could be a fishing station of some of the Big Lagoon sites which are not at a great distance. Again, the proposed model of temporary movement to the coast from permanent interior sites would explain the data. Nothing in the modern ethnography is parallel to this site, thus emphasizing the difference in subsistence between pre- and postcontact times.

Bluefields Bay Sites

From the relatively small amount of food remains apart from shellfish, it appears that the sites' users were not thoroughly exploiting their resources and may not have been well adapted to the coastal environment. The fish species represented are those generally caught from a shore zone without elaborate equipment. Exceptions to this are the *Carcharhinus limbatus* and the *Carcharhinus maculipinnis*. The latter species is not generally found in less than 6 to 9 m of water (Gilbert, personal communication). Both may have been caught, however, at the bay mouth since we know that the people went that far to gather *Donax denticulatus*. Particularly striking is that the majority of the fish represented are *Bagre, Arius, Batracoides,* and *Centropomus*.

The turtle present is chiefly of the genus *Kinosternon,* which is readily available in low, muddy areas. *Constrictor constrictor,* other snakes, and crocodile occur in very small quantities. The manatee is represented by only a few bones. Terrestrial faunal remains demonstrate familiarity with land resources, although once again their quantity is so small as to indicate that the animals were not killed routinely.

The largest amount of animal protein came from shellfish. Although no exact figures can be presented, I have calculated that approximately 1000 to 1250 meals could have been obtained from each cubic meter of deposit. This large quantity of shellfish remains is not present in any of the modern villages described and not even in Rama Key in Bluefields Bay, where shellfish form a major part of the diet.

The complete lack of architecture is most suprising in that all permanent modern villages will have such material in their archaeological remains. Rama Key even has houses built on top of shell middens. The temporary plantation sites of Tasbapauni provide the best model for these archaeological data. However, evidence for agriculture is lacking for the prehistoric sites.

The lack of a specialized chipped-stone tool kit suggests a relatively unspecialized adaptation since modern villages have very specific implements for fishing. Rather, the multipurpose tools of agricultural communities such as Kakabila and Big Lagoon may have their prehistoric counterparts here. Furthermore, the presence of manos and metates indicates the importance of agriculture in this subsistence system.

Summary

The most likely interpretation of these marine-oriented sites is that they were temporary fishing stations. The location of the respective permanent habitations is unknown, but the best speculation is that they are inland by the rivers. This explains the presence of boats, the limited use of coastal resources, the lack of a specialized flint tool inventory, the presence of agriculturally oriented ground stone tools, and the lack of architecture and other features.

Terrestrial Sites

Italia Site

This site shows the use of agriculture, hunting, and fishing to provide food. The range of fish is considerably larger, and mammals seem to have been numerically more significant than at coastal sites. Most of the fish represented are of the lagoon–estuary type, with the exception of *Carcharhinus maculipinnis* and *Negaprion breviorstris*. These do not usually occur in rivers, and people would have to move to the coast in order to catch them (Gilbert, personal communication).

Large manos and metates point to a dependence on agriculture, probably corn. The flint tools are the same as elsewhere. No clear function for them is evident, and they are perhaps similar to the multipurpose machete of today.

Clear signs of features are present. Although only temporary midden hearths were excavated, there is little doubt that house remains could be found nearby. This suggests a more permanent type settlement than seen in the marine oriented sites.

Ceramics at this site tie in with the coastal Siteia complex sites. Accordingly it is possible that the latter represent fishing stations of people living in inland sites such as this. However, it would seem doubtful that the Italia site was related to those in Pearl Lagoon because of the distance between them. There may be an inland site near Pearl Lagoon that would be Italia's functional counterpart.

Nueva Guinea Sites

The people of these sites seem to have been entirely oriented toward plant cultivation. Considerable numbers of manos and metates were found at both locations, and they seem to signal agriculture. The general-use, chipped-stone tools were what one might expect in this environmental context. The lack of animal bones points to plants as the principal basis of subsistence. Unfortunately, botanical data are not available to confirm this interpretation. The lack of architectural remains indicative of permanent habitations probably resulted from my limited excavations in midden deposits rather than in surrounding mounds.

Although the ceramics from these localities belong to the same tradition as some from the coastal sites, it is impossible to say whether their inhabitants traveled to the sea. The distance is not so great as to prevent this movement, and nearby rivers lead into coastal lagoons. However, until more thorough survey has revealed coastal sites of the same complex, this problem will remain unsolved.

The most important question is what crops were grown. The presence of manos and metates raises the possibility of corn agriculture, normally discounted in this zone. Corn actually grows very well in many parts of the Atlantic lowlands of Nicaragua, especially in the area around these two sites; it may have been a determining factor in their placement.

Big Lagoon Sites

These three sites reflect the same adaptation as those in the Nueva Guinea zone. No bone material was recovered. Manos and metates indicate possible agriculture. The chipped-stone tools are similar to those from Nueva Guinea and show little specialization. Stone rings around some of the mounds signal that they are probably house remains.

It seems very likely that the inhabitants of the Big Lagoon sites traveled to nearby Pearl Lagoon for fishing since the Long Mangrove site belongs to the same complex. As I have already noted, Long Mangrove even may have been a fishing station of the Big Lagoon sites. The exact relationship between the two sites may be resolved by thermoluminescence studies of the pottery. Should the two locales yield ceramics with similar glow curves and thus common clay sources, their interrelationship will be strongly suggested.

Summary

The Big Lagoon and Nueva Guinea sites are similar in subsistence base to the modern villages in the same places. Their primary focus is agriculture. If they alone had been excavated, I would not have suspected the possibility of temporary movement to the coast. Taking the coastal sites into account, however, this model seems most appropriate to explain the remains of the zone as a whole.

CHANGES IN SUBSISTENCE FROM PREHISTORIC TO MODERN TIMES

The final purpose of this chapter is to explain the discontinuity in subsistence from precontact to postcontact times. It is quite apparent that there have been some major changes over time in subsistence in the Atlantic lowlands of Nicaragua. In contrast to permanent inland habitations and coastal fishing stations of prehistoric times, today there are permanent shore habitations and inland agricultural stations. Other modern subsistence patterns include coastal agricultural villages such as Kakabila and inland farming communities like Big Lagoon. The residents of each do little hunting or fishing. I suspect that the Tasbapauni- and Kakabila-type settlements are variations on the prehistoric model brought about by postcontact economic forces.

Helms (1971:228) has speculated that the Miskito are a postcontact group made up of smaller units who accepted the Europeans and their material culture. It is obvious that if the Miskito wanted to make continued contact with trading and pirate ships, they had to live on the seacoast. Furthermore, they had to modify their subsistence pattern radically to fit this new way of life. In the Tasbapauni-type community, the major subsistence focus changed from agriculture to marine resources, and the plantations became only a secondary source of food. People now lived where they fished, and traveled to the farm instead of the opposite pattern of precontact times.

The Kakabila model is very different in that its adaptation is primarily agricultural. I suggest that this pattern is the result of continuity with precontact subsistence patterns. Instead of depending principally on the sea, people moved to its shores but still remained within easy access to good farmland, which continued to be the primary subsistence focus. Now that trade with foreign ships has ended, this type of village depends entirely on agriculture.

Big Lagoon is not an old community but represents a recent adaptation similar to the precontact one, with the exception of fishing. It is interesting to note that for a second time a riverine and agriculturally focused subsistence pattern is developing in the same zone. It seems likely that the precontact system was more suited to the zone's environment than were later developments, and so now it is returning at Big Lagoon and many other similar settlements.

In conclusion, it would seem reasonable to attribute to historical factors surrounding foreign trade the changes in subsistence on the Atlantic coast of Nicaragua. The interesting question is whether there will be a reversion to agriculture in the coastal villages now that continued presence on the shore is not necessary and fishing is more difficult due to overexploitation for commerce. It seems obvious that Tasbapauni, for one, will have to undergo a major change in its subsistence basis, and I suspect that it will be toward agriculture and partial resettlement in the interior, as in prehistory.

ACKNOWLEDGMENTS

I would like to thank Dr. Elizabeth Wing of the Florida State Museum for her help in faunal identification. I would also like to thank Dr. Carter Gilbert for the information he provided me on the fish identified.

REFERENCES

Helms, Mary Wallace
  1971   Asang: Adaptations to culture contact in a Miskito community. Gainesville: University of Florida Press.
Magnus, Richard W.
  1974   The prehistory of the Miskito Coast of Nicaragua: Study in cultural relationships. Ph.D. dissertation, Department of Anthropology, Yale University.
  1975   La Costa Atlantica de Nicaraqua. *Vínculos* **2**(1):67–74. San José.
  1976   The prehistoric cultural relationships of the Miskito Coast. *Actas del XLI Congreso Internacional de Americanistas* Vol. 1. Mexico, D.F. Pp. 568–578.
Nietschmann, Bernard
  1973   *Between land and water: The subsistence ecology of the Miskito Indians, Eastern Nicaragua.* New York: Seminar Press.

chapter 5

The Process of Transformation at Pajón: A Preclassic Society Located in an Estuary in Chiapas, Mexico

MARICRUZ PAILLÉS H.

Museo Nacional de Antropología, Instituto Nacional de Antropología e Historia, México

INTRODUCTION

This chapter discusses a series of investigations carried out at the Pajón site, which are detailed in another source (Paillés 1976). The Pajón site consists of several mounds located in an estuary on the coastal plain of Chiapas (Figure 5.1). The principal objective of this research was to obtain an understanding of the development of Early Preclassic Period cultures on the coast of Chiapas and in particular of a site established directly within the littoral zone.

The Pacific coastal plain is one of the most uniform physiographic regions in Chiapas. The region has an extensive fluvial network formed by numerous rivers that originate in the mountains and descend to empty directly into the sea or into coastal swamps, lagoons, and estuaries. The region is bounded on the northeast by the Sierra Madre de Chiapas and on the southwest by the sea. The physiographic landform continues west into the state of Oaxaca and east into Central America.

Figure 5.1. Map of Mexico featuring the state of Chiapas and the region in which the Pajón site is located.

According to Bassols Batalla (1974), the Pacific coast of Chiapas is divided into two subregions, each of which encompasses approximately one-half of the territory. One subregion, Soconusco, includes the southeastern portion of the plain, from the *municipio* of Mapastepec to beyond the Guatemalan border. The Pajón site lies in the remaining subregion, called the Chiapas coast, which takes in the rest of the plain from Mapastepec northwest to the Chiapas–Oaxaca boundary.

The subdivision described above was established on the basis of economic–geographic studies, taking into account certain climatic factors such as prevailing wind direction, mountain barriers affecting winds, degree of cloud cover, and humidity, each of which is a factor in the determination of resources and cultural development. The southeastern part of the coastal plain, the Soconusco subregion, is the more humid (De la Peña 1951), while the northwest, or Chiapas coast subregion, is drier, with aridity increasing as one approaches the Oaxacan border (Bataillon 1969).

SITE DESCRIPTION

The Pajón archaeological zone lies in an estuary known locally as the Pajón Pampa. The entire site consists of 18 mounds, 11 of which are concentrated within an area of approximately .5 km² (Figure 5.2). The other mounds are dispersed, five of them at a distance of 2 km to the west of the group already mentioned. Included in these five is the El Guacalito Mound. Only two mounds can be found in the old, now dry part of the southeastern estuary. One of these is El Encanto (Figure 5.3b), which is located 1.5 km to the east of the larger group of 11 mounds. Surrounding the mounds there is a midden area indicating prehispanic occupation.

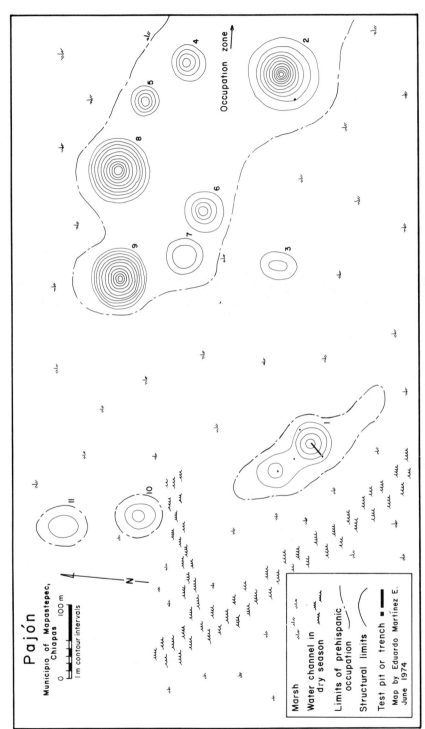

Figure 5.2. Topographic map of the Pajón site. Courtesy of The New World Archaeological Foundation.

83

There is a great deal of variation in mound size. The smallest ones measure approximately 50 m in length and 2–3 m in height. Medium-sized mounds are 60 m long and 4–5 m high. The largest vary between 80–100 m in length and 8–11 m in height. There is no definite alignment observable in mound placement (Figure 5.2).

The Pajón excavations consisted of several test pits and a trench into Mounds 1 and 2 (Figures 5.2, 5.3a) and into the El Encanto and El Guacalito mounds. In addition, a collection of surface materials was made at the site.

Figure 5.3a. The *pampa* in foreground and Mound 2 in the background.

Figure 5.3b. The southeastern zone of the *pampa,* now dry, and El Encanto mound.

This work will discuss social changes that may have taken place within this Early and Middle Preclassic Period community. During its occupation, Pajón seems to have been a fishing–gathering village. From 850–800 B.C. there was an increase in population in this locality; remains of monumental architecture and other factors suggest a change toward a more complex social structure. Possibly around 600 B.C. the site was abandoned. The change in social complexity postulated for Pajón society was perhaps the outgrowth of a self-sufficient local economy based on agriculture (an activity not yet detected in the area) or on an exchange or trade of surplus aquatic resources, both marine and estuarine, with other groups who inhabited different ecological zones. The basis for these interpretations will be detailed phase by phase.

CULTURAL AND CHRONOLOGICAL SEQUENCE

The cultural and chronological sequence at Pajón was developed as a result of research carried out during two field seasons, with subsequent study and analysis of the recovered materials. This scheme is tentative and subject to modification in light of future archaeological investigation at the site. The period of occupation established at Pajón extends from 1000 to 600 B.C. This period of just 400 years represents only the investigated portion of Pajón. In other areas of the site (not yet sampled), deposits from earlier or later times may exist.

The temporal sequence was set up on the basis of relative and absolute chronology. Analysis of the ceramics and their cultural affinities placed the site in the context of phases already established for other related sites in the area, such as Altamira (Green and Lowe 1967) and Izapa (Ekholm 1969) in Chiapas, and Salinas La Blanca (Coe and Flannery 1967) in Guatemala (Figure 5.4). A radiocarbon age determination corroborates this chronology: 2805 ± 280 radiocarbon years: 855 B.C. (I–8183) (Paillés 1976:53).

The Pajón occupation has been divided into two phases, Dunas and Encanto, the first of which was further broken down into two subphases. The occupational phases at the site will be discussed below, beginning with the earliest.

EARLY DUNAS SUBPHASE

The earliest occupation detected at Pajón is the Early Dunas Subphase, which is coeval with the Cuadros Phase known from the Pacific coast of

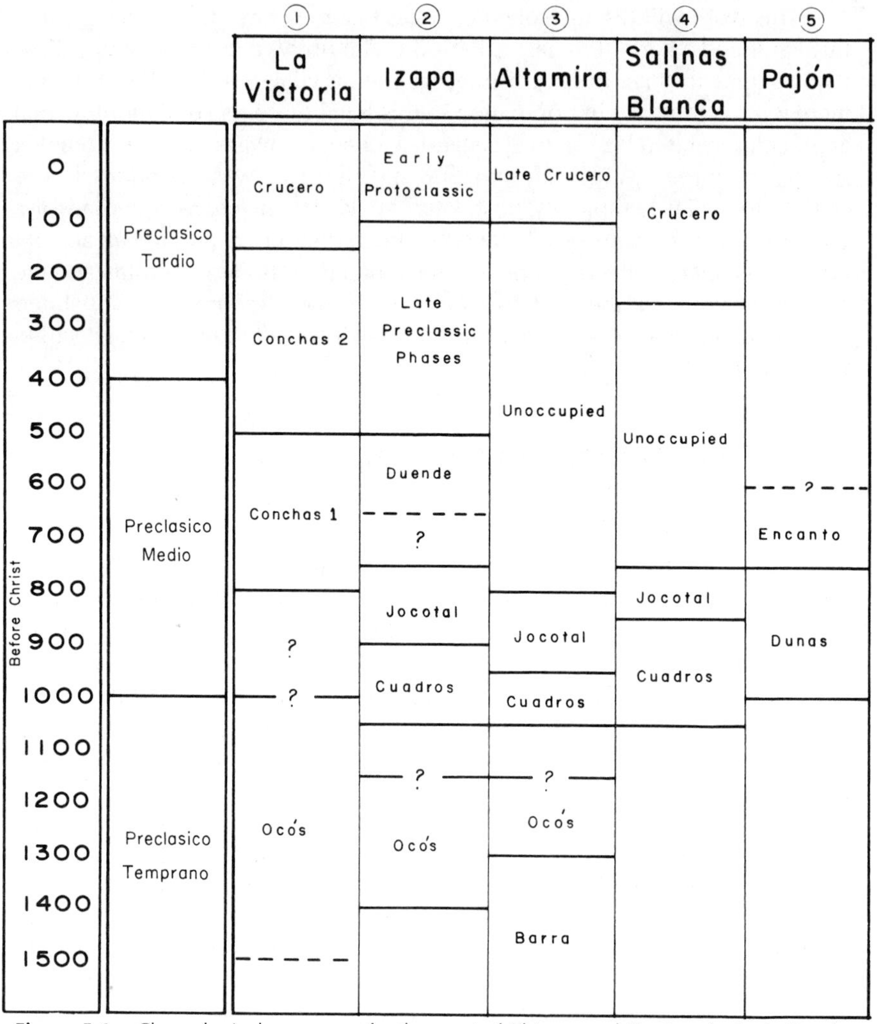

		① La Victoria	② Izapa	③ Altamira	④ Salinas la Blanca	⑤ Pajón
O		Crucero	Early Protoclassic	Late Crucero		
100	Preclasico Tardio				Crucero	
200						
300		Conchas 2	Late Preclassic Phases			
400						
500				Unoccupied	Unoccupied	
600			Duende			- - - ? - - -
700	Preclasico Medio	Conchas 1	- - - - - - ?			Encanto
800			Jocotal		Jocotal	
900		?		Jocotal		Dunas
1000		- ? -	Cuadros	Cuadros	Cuadros	
1100						
1200			- ? -	- ? -		
1300	Preclasico Temprano	Ocós	Ocós	Ocós		
1400						
1500		- - - - -		Barra		

(Left axis label: Before Christ)

Figure 5.4. Chronological sequences for the coast of Chiapas and Guatemala, including the new phases from the Pajón site. 1—Coe (1961); 2—Ekholm (1969); 3—Green and Lowe (1967); 4—Coe and Flannery (1967); 5—Paillés (1967).

Chiapas and Guatemala (Coe and Flannery 1967). This first Pajón period is limited to four zones at the site: (a) the lower levels of Mound 1; (b) a small rise located 58 m to the northeast on the same island as Mound 1; (c) the test pit at the foot of Mound 2; and (d) the lower levels of the test unit excavated at the base of El Encanto Mound. The earliest occupation of the site is associated with elevated areas not more than 1 m above water level. This elevation is the result of the gradual accumulation of occupational debris at the site.

For the Early Dunas Subphase, most of the data on subsistence come from the deposits from Mound 1, which was the area in which our investigation concentrated. These data include faunal and floral remains, and they will be discussed later. The contents of the deposit suggest that possibly economic activities were performed there. The mound structure was built up by the accumulation of strata, formed for the most part by burned earth, potsherds (many of them burned), and hearths. These latter features were made of vertically placed sherds arranged to form a circle. Several layers of the same material form the floor of the hearth (Figure 5.5a,b). The five excavated hearths were arranged in a straight line that corresponds to the length of a trench. These hearths measure between 60–97 cm in diameter; wall height varies between 22–34 cm.

It is possible that an activity requiring the intensive use of fire was associated with Mound 1. The various stratigraphic levels were, to a great extent, altered by the fire. The biologist Lauro González Quintero of the Department of Prehistory of Instituto Nacional de Antropología e Historia (I.N.A.H.) has identified ferrous clays, limonitic in nature, which were transformed by desiccation from their natural yellow to a reddish color (González Quintero 1976:164–168). He postulates alternative uses for fire in this context: the salting and smoking of self-replenishing marine resources, such as shrimp or fish, and pottery manufacture. Along with those possibilities, I include salt procurement.

Conclusive evidence for any of the four alternatives is lacking. Nevertheless, ethnographic analogy is most supportive of the hypothesized exploitation of edible fauna from the vicinity. The fishing and shrimp harvesting that are presently carried on in this area suggest a way of life that perhaps is not unlike the life-style of the ancient inhabitants of Pajón. An elaboration of this analogy will be presented below, followed by a discussion of the salt-making hypothesis, which is considered to be the second most likely explanation of the observed phenomena.

Today there are many techniques of shrimp procurement in this region. The practice of setting *tapas* involves the placement of fencelike enclosures in the shallow water of the estuary and the arrangement of nets as traps; this is done from January to May. During April and May it is customary to *candilear* (fish by light). Candles or lights are taken out at night in small boats or *cayucos* in order to attract the shrimp, which are then caught in nets.

A fisherman from the village of El Zapotal (Adolfo Ruíz) reports that there are places in the area where, instead of going out in *cayucos* with candles, the men light bonfires on the edge of the swamp in order to attract the shrimp, and then fishermen seize them in nets from the shore. This is a possible explanation for the evidence of extensive use of fire at Mound 1. That is, during certain months of the year the ancient inhabitants of Pajón were involved in shrimp fishing; in fact, they may have occupied the island in order to have easy access to this aquatic resource. In support of this interpretation the following information can be noted: According to the present inhabitants of Pajón, the *pampa* or lagoon was formerly saline. It is a common complaint among the old people of the area that in former times they were able to harvest shrimp in the shallow *pampa*, but that about 30 to 40 years ago a branch of the Río Novillero shifted its channel and entered the lagoon, resulting in the death of all the shrimp and other saltwater species. Thus, according to the hydrographic situation, shrimp fishing was possible in the Pajón area.

The possibility that fire was used in connection with salt manufacture can also be strengthened with relevant data. Baudez (1973:507–520) has reported groups of salt-procurement sites on the south coast of Honduras that date from A.D. 1000 to 1200. The primitive salt producers evaporated sea water in large hemispherical vessels which were placed in depressions dug into the earth. Fires were built in order to accelerate the evaporation of the liquid. Perhaps a similar procedure was carried out at Mound 1, where, it will be recalled, excavation uncovered areas of burned earth, possible hearths or ovens (Figure 5.5a,b), and great numbers of sherds from burned

Figure 5.5a. Feature 1, which constitutes one of a series of hearths found in Trench A. In this cut one can observe potsherds placed vertically to form the walls and in alternate layers to form the floor of the hearth.

Figure 5.5b. Floor plan of Feature 5. This feature is one of the hearths uncovered in Trench A; the circular form in which the sherds were placed is visible.

tecomates (neckless, globular vessels). All of this suggests an industrial activity similar to that described by Baudez for the production of salt.

Faunal remains recovered from Mound 1 were scarce, but sufficient to provide a general idea of prehistoric diet at Pajón. Included were mollusks, such as *Anadara smerarca, Chione lirophora, Agaronia propatula,* and *Cerithidea pulchra.* These are all brackish water species. Other faunal remains consisted of two bones from white-tailed deer (*Odocoileus virginianus*), a catfish fragment, and two pieces of turtle.

The almost total absence of fishbones and shrimp remains in the excavations would be explained if both products were exported whole. Such a practice would not leave material remains, since the entire animal would have been exported. Also it is possible that fish and shrimp remains have been destroyed by the acidity of the soil.

The floral remains do not seem to indicate that the inhabitants of Pajón were practicing agriculture. Floral analysis indicates that the lower levels of Mound 1 contained evidence of wild vegetation only. There is evidence of *Setaria* seeds; the seeds of this vertisolic grass can be used as human food. Callen (1967:266–268) mentions the use of *Setaria* in the diet of groups living in the Tehuacán Valley, Puebla, beginning with the El Riego Phase. Other vegetal remains found in Mound 1 that indicate plants probably eaten by the Pajón people are those of *Leucaena* and *Pithecellobium* or *huamuchil*. Lauro González Q. (personal communication) believes that *Leucaena* probably is a type of edible pod and that *Pithecellobium* contains a pod with edible fruit.

The stone tool sample for the Early Dunas Subphase is very meager, consisting of a grinding stone and two fragments of oval metates similar to those found at Altamira (Green and Lowe 1967:Fig. 36b) and at Salinas La Blanca (Coe and Flannery 1967:21). The function of these instruments is not known to me; probably grass seeds were ground on them. No traces of maize were found at Pajón. However, this grain was used by contemporaneous groups in the Soconusco. At Salinas La Blanca, Guatemala, mineralized corncobs have been recovered from Cuadros Phase deposits (Coe and Flannery 1967:127–128). At Pajón no obsidian chips were found, although they are common in Ocós Phase deposits at Altamira. Lowe (in Green and Lowe 1967, 1975) suggests that at Altamira obsidian chips were inserted in wooden blocks and used as grater teeth to produce flour from the root crop manioc, or *yuca*. Neither the artifacts nor the floral remains of Pajón yield conclusive evidence of agriculture, although preservation factors could mask this activity.

At present, I cannot determine whether the population at Pajón was economically specialized or diversified. Specifically, it is uncertain whether the people only fished and gathered wild resources or if they also were utilizing agricultural products.

The ceramic assemblage provides more concrete evidence for interchange with other groups. The most abundant material collected at the site, regardless of phase, was pottery. The sample is notable in that 79.75% of the ceramics consist of *tecomates*. Except for the 3.05% of the pottery that is imported, the ceramics are of local manufacture (Paillés 1976). For the Early Dunas Subphase a large number of sherds from locally made pottery were found, principally *tecomates* decorated using techniques such as brushing, corrugation or incision, rocker stamping, finger impression, red painting, and others.

It is evident that until the end of the subphase exchange with other areas resulted in the importation of few ceramic vessels. Among these are some established Soconusco types, such as Tilapa Red-on-white, Tacaná Incised, Cuchilla White, and Siltepec White (Coe and Flannery 1967; Green and Lowe 1967; Ekholm 1969). Others are very fine paste ceramics, in some cases pale orange and white in color; it has not been possible to identify the origin of these fine paste types. The latter were examined by Ing. Luis Torres (personal communication) of the Department of Restoration, Patrimonio

Cultural, I.N.A.H.; Torres indicated that the white clay of the paste is similar to some low-quality kaolins. Kaolin can be found in any region of Mesoamerica in which igneous rocks, especially tuff, occur. Such a general identification cannot of itself be diagnostic of source. Although aparrently derived from the Isthmus or Veracruz regions, the imported, very fine paste ceramics at Pajón must be subjected to more precise analysis or to ceramic classification in order for them to be assigned a definite geographic and cultural provenience.

For the Early Dunas Subphase there is no evidence for construction of high mounds. Apparently occupation occurred only on low elevations. I conclude that during this subphase Pajón was a village occupied by an egalitarian society in which subsistence activities may have been organized on the level of kinship. There is no concrete evidence of specialization or trade, although it is possible that the site was occupied by a group of specialized fishermen–gatherers who bartered or exchanged estuarine and marine products for agricultural produce and ceramics from other areas.

LATE DUNAS SUBPHASE

About 900 B.C. a series of changes took place at Pajón. This was a time of population increase, which is manifested by the increase in the size of Mound 1 and the construction of some of the highest mounds at the site. New local ceramics also appear. Nevertheless, major changes in subsistence or exchange patterns are not evident.

During the Late Dunas Subphase the extent of the known occupation was limited to the upper levels of Mound 1 and to the larger mounds, such as Mound 2 (Figure 5.2), El Guacalito, and El Encanto. This subphase corresponds in time with the Jocotal Phase at Salinas La Blanca, Guatemala (Coe and Flannery 1967).

During the course of excavation in El Encanto Mound, only Late Dunas ceramics were encountered in the lower levels. It was during that period that the El Encanto platform began to form by deliberate accumulation of clay and potsherds. It is probable that a similar construction history explains the beginnings of other large mounds at the site. Judging from their present conical shape, these large Pajón mounds were destined to become pyramidal platforms, erected higher and higher for sustaining a series of small summit structures. Such is surely the case for Mounds 2 (Figure 5.3a), 8,9 (Figure 5.2), El Guacalito, and El Encanto (Figure 5.3b). The construction of these large platforms certainly was the result of the combined effort of many persons. These structures suggest a considerable increase in the Pajón population and imply a transition to a more complex social structure, one that could organize and oversee the public works, thus leaving behind these massive architectural remains.

The transformation that occurred within early Pajón society was the result primarily of an internal process of local development. This conclusion is based on the lack of any sudden change in ceramic materials from one subphase to another at the site; in fact, the stylistic continuity is noteworthy. The ceramic types of the first subphase continue unchanged into the second. *Tecomates* continue to predominate over other local ceramic forms. Some innovations appear, however, such as the decrease in *tecomate* size and the presence of short necks on some of these forms. There is also continuity of decorative technique from the Early to the Late Dunas Subphase, but the brushing becomes very light, rocker stamping is absent, and finger impressions occur more frequently. In general, Late Dunas pottery is more simple in its decoration as compared to Early Dunas pottery.

Some imported pottery was also found, principally plates and bowls with flat bases and rims incised with the double line break. These imported, very fine paste ceramics also are copied in the local clay. In general, Late Dunas pottery is comparable to the Jocotal Phase (Coe and Flannery 1967).

The pattern of subsistence continued to be one of fishermen–gatherers. Among the faunal remains a great many mussels (*Mytilus*) were found, indicating an ecological shift, but we are not yet able to define its nature.

At present there is no evidence that the Late Dunas residents of Pajón practiced maize agriculture. Floral remains are very scarce; only some *Setaria* and *Spartina* seeds were identified. The use of grains or seeds in the diet is also suggested by the presence of 8 manos, 14 fragments of metates, and 3 pounding implements.

If primitive agriculture were practiced in the Pajón region, it is most likely that fertile levees along the rivers were selected for cultivation. These lands, which tend to be sandy and grass-free, offer certain advantages for farming: (a) they are elevated and well drained; (b) they are fertile as a result of seasonal deposition of muds and clays; and (c) they are easily cultivated with simple tools (Paillés 1976:145). These levee zones, apparently from the Preclassic Period to the present day, are found a short distance behind the old swamp that was the site of the Pajón occupation.

In the Late Dunas, as in the previous subphase, there is no evidence of large-scale commerce with other areas. At Pajón, materials such as obsidian, jade, pyrite, magnetite, and other minerals were not recovered, but there were a few imported ceramics that must have had a certain commercial value.

ENCANTO PHASE

The final period of occupation presently known for Pajón, the Encanto Phase, began between about 750 and 700 B.C., and came to a close with the possible abandonment of the site for unknown reasons around 600 B.C. Encanto Phase is coeval with Conchas I of la Victoria (Coe 1961), Duende of Izapa, and late Dili for the Central Basin of Chiapas (Ekholm 1969). For this phase there is no evidence of any major change in subsistence, level of trade, or in architecture.

The soil analysis did not show any change in subsistence practices. Among the floral remains, only *Spartina* seeds were found; there was no trace of maize. The few animal remains consist of some saltwater snails and fragments of myriapods (Paillés 1976:166).

During this phase certain pottery types associated with previous phases continued to be represented, but new ceramic forms appeared in addition to the *tecomates,* including flat-bottomed bowls and *ollas*. It is interesting to note that some Encanto Phase pottery, such as red-rimmed bowls, is similar to that excavated by Piña Chan at La Venta, Tabasco (collections of the Ceramoteca of the Museo Nacional de Antropología, México). Imported ceramics occur, but in very small numbers.

The Encanto Phase remains were confined to two pits excavated in the mound to the same name, but it is probable that they are also present in the upper levels of large mounds not yet tested. The stratigraphy of El Encanto Mound and that of the other large mounds, such as Mound 2 and El Guacalito, indicate that all of these constructions were formed by the simple accumulation of layers of earth and potsherds. Apparently a social organization capable of maintaining such constructions was still in existence, and probably intensified.

One of the most important findings during the second season of excavation was a burial of an individual who had been deposited in the upper part of El Encanto Mound. The remains were identified by Professor Arturo Romano and María Salas of the Physical Anthropology Department, I.N.A.H., as representing those of a 12-year-old individual, probably male. The most distinguishing characteristic observed was on the skull, which showed intentional deformation, of the fronto-occipital, tabular erect variety. The morphology of the cranial molding produced in this case is interesting because it recalls the intentional cephalic forms typical of Olmec culture (Paillés 1976:157–163).

The fact that a burial was found in the upper part of one of the largest mounds at the site indicates that the interred individual was buried in that spot because of his elevated social rank. In addition, a person with a cranial deformation similar to those observed on Olmec figurines of clay and stone suggests a religious or funerary ritual in which the person in question may have played the principal role.

SUMMARY

At Pajón there is evidence of a process of transformation from an egalitarian society with an economy organized along kinship lines to another stage associated with monumental architecture and other remains that indicate a greater social complexity. For the moment, it may be inferred that this process of transformation was partly the result of a self-sufficient economy on the community level. This society could have been based on either (a) agriculture (an activity that has not yet been detected in the area) or (b) the procurement of wild resources. Fishing–gathering could have been augmented by the exchange of surplus marine and estuarine harvests with groups living in other ecological zones. Inland areas, lacking equal ease of access to necessary protein sources, may have constituted eager markets for protein-rich estuarine produce, such as fish, shrimp, and mollusks, among others. It still is not known what products the inhabitants of Pajón might have received in exchange; the only available evidence of trade is imported pottery.

Obviously, this model of exchange between coastal zones and inland areas offers only a tentative explanation. It will be necessary to undertake research in the areas adjacent to Pajón to determine whether this site actually did specialize in the exploitation of aquatic resources. Such a hypothesis, however, is supported by the lack of evidence pointing to other factors having transformed Pajón society. The early processes of change were apparently internal ones, but larger external forces may have influenced first the Middle Preclassic expansion of Pajón, and then its early collapse and abandonment. Either modified environmental factors or changing patterns of procurement and distribution signaling the Late Preclassic era may explain this early demise of an unusually important estuarine center.

ACKNOWLEDGMENTS

The research carried out at the Pajón site was supported by the B.Y.U. New World Archaeological Foundation during 1973. The archaeological field work was completed during the course of two field seasons, the first of which was directed by Dr. Gareth W. Lowe, and the second by me.

I would like to express my appreciation for the help in editing and revising this manuscript that was given me by archaeologist Felipe Solis O., a researcher in the Sección de Arqueología of the Museo Nacional de Antropología, I.N.A.H., México and to thank Sue Lewenstein for providing the English translation.

REFERENCES

Bassols Batalla, Angel
    1974   Realidad y problemática general de la costa. In *La Costa de Chiapas,* edited by Angel Bassols Batalla. México, D.F.: Universidad Nacional Autónoma de México. Pp.11–93.
Bataillon, Claude
    1969   *Las regiones geográficas de México.* México, D.F.: Editorial Siglo XXI, S.A.
Baudez, Claude F.
    1973   Les camps de saliniers de la Côte Méridional du Honduras: Données archeologiques et documentes historiques. In *L'Homme, hier et aujourd'hui. Hommage à Andre Leroi Gourhan.* Paris: Editiones Cujas. Pp. 507–520.
Callen, Eric O.
    1967   Analysis of the Tehuácan coprolites. In *The prehistory of the Tehuácan Valley, Vol. 1,* edited by Douglas S. Byers. Austin: University of Texas Press. Pp. 261–289.
Coe, Michael D.
    1961   La Victoria: An early site on the Pacific Coast of Guatemala. *Papers of the Peabody Museum of Archaeology and History* Vol. 53. Harvard University.
Coe, Michael D., and Kent V. Flannery
    1967   Early cultures and human ecology in South Coastal Guatemala. *Smithsonian Contributions to Anthropology* Vol. 3.
De la Peña, Moisés T.
    1951   *Chiapas económico.* Vol. I, Tuxtla Gutiérrez, Chiapas.
Ekholm, Susanna M.
    1969   Mound 30a and the Early Preclassic ceramic sequence of Izapa, Chiapas, Mexico. *Papers of the New World Archeological Foundation* No. 25.
González Quintero, Lauro
    1976   Apéndice 2: Informe sobre el análisis de Muestras de Tierra, Procendentes de Pajón, Chiapas. In Pampa el Pajón, un sitio del Preclasico temprano-medio en la Costa de Chiapas, by Maricruz Paillés H. Master's thesis in Archaeology, Escuela Nacional de Antropología e Historia, México, D.F.
Green, Dee F., and Gareth W. Lowe
    1967   Altamira and Padre Piedra. Early Preclassic sites in Chiapas, Mexico. *Papers of the New World Archaeological Foundation* No. 20.
Lowe, Gareth W.
    1975   The Early Preclassic Barra phase of Altamira, Chiapas. *Papers of the New World Archaeological Foundation* No. 38.
Paillés, Maricruz
    1976   Pampa El Pajón, un sitio del Preclasico temprano-medio en la costa de Chiapas, Mexico. Master's thesis in Archaeology, Escuela Nacional de Antropología e Historia, México, D.F. (In press as *Papers of the New World Archeological Foundation,* No. 44.)

PART III

Settlement Patterns

The way in which humans arrange themselves spatially is one primary concern of anthropologists as well as of human geographers. This is because the spatial distribution of people and their remains directly reflects certain aspects of their social organization and behavior. The spatial aspects of human behavior can be studied at the level of interpersonal relations (proxemics), at the level of family (a basic social unit in all societies), at the community level, and on a regional or interregional basis at the intercommunity level. Archaeologists, limited in their research to material remains, are concerned only with the last three types of analysis. However, problems in inferring social units lead to archaeological analysis in terms of successive archaeological levels: activity areas, structures, clusters of structures and areas, settlements, and finally regions within which settlement systems can be defined (cf. Trigger 1967; Parsons 1972; Streuver 1971; Flannery 1976:5–6).

The systematic study of Mesoamerican prehistoric societies from a spatial perspective is currently in the developmental stage. As Voorhies points out, a systematic and rigorous spatial analysis of human settlements related to regional biotic zones has not been available for any Middle American coastal zone. Some settlement level and household level studies are available (see especially Flannery 1976).

Nevertheless, many previous archaeological studies have been concerned to some extent with settlement patterns. Streuver (1971) has noted the close interrelation of settlement and subsistence in situations involving seasonal movement of the population, spatially segregated procurement of resources, or exchange of critical resources among groups. Among the chapters in this volume, those by Magnus and Paillés (which we have placed in the section "Procurement Patterns") are concerned with settlement patterns almost as much as with procurement patterns. Magnus traces settlement pattern changes on a regional scale, whereas Paillés uses a site-level analysis. Three other chapters are more centrally concerned with spatial studies because of their regional focus, and we have grouped them under "Settlement Patterns."

In "Coastal Settlement in Northwestern Costa Rica" Frederick Lange provides an overview of settlement locations and subsistence evidence in the coastal and inland habitats of Costa Rica throughout the duration of known occupation. Using data collected by a number of investigators, Lange outlines a culture–historic framework of the region's prehistory, organized by period. Within each time division he describes available information on site locations, settlement types, and procurement patterns. Lange disputes the utility of previous explanations of culture changes; population growth, overexploitation of local fauna, local cultural preference, and local trade networks are noted as additional variables that may help us understand northwestern Costa Rican prehistory.

Mary Helms' chapter, "Coastal Adaptations as Contact Phenomena among Miskito and Cuna Indians of Lower Central America," is a good example of a documentary settlement and subsistence study on a regional basis. She examines the culture histories of two groups of people currently living in coastal habitats in lower Central America. Helms is able to reconstruct their earlier settlement patterns during early historic and prehispanic times. She demonstrates that in late prehispanic times both groups were riverine oriented and that the shift to a coastal habitat correlates with increased impingement of Euroamericans on the indigenous peoples. According to Helms' analysis, both coastal and riverine adaptations were part of an integrated native system. Although changing relative emphases on coastal and riverine exploitation appear to have been responsive to outside political and economic variables, at the same time these changes represent oscillations of emphasis within the native system. Although we have tended to stress the utility of a regional-scale analysis, it is clear in this study that an adequate temporal span is also required to define long-term cycles of emphasis in settlement–subsistence systems. Helms stresses that a short-term view of lower Central American coastal adaptations is an inadequate frame of reference with which to grasp the underlying nature of native adaptations.

In "Changing Patterns of Resource Exploitation, Settlement Distribution, and Demography in the Southern Isthmus of Tehuantepec, Mexico," Judith Zeitlin reports some results of investigations carried out jointly with Robert Zeitlin in the Pacific sector of the Isthmus of Tehuantepec. Her investigations, in conjunction with those of her coinvestigator, constitute one of the first systematic regional studies of part of the Mesoamerican coast. The project included systematic surface survey of a sample area stratified into three natural zones. Subsurface sampling was carried out at three sites. J. Zeitlin uses faunal remains recovered from these excavations in order to reconstruct a long sequence of procurement patterns. The diachronic analysis reveals significantly different Postclassic subsistence patterns, as compared to earlier phases. Ultimately this shift and a marked settlement change are related to extralocal events. For preceding periods, she emphasizes local factors within the study area.

In J. Zeitlin's diachronic analysis of settlement patterns, three variables are studied: (a) site locations; (b) population sizes; and (c) settlement ranks. Settlement pattern suggests additional information about procurement patterns, illustrating the close relation of settlement and subsistence study. The author then compares the archaeological settlement patterns with a classic central-place model developed in economic geography. Some variance between the real situation and this ideal model is explained. However, discrepancies with the classical model lead the author to a consideration of explicitly diachronic models. J. Zeitlin compares both a carrying-capacity model and a colonization–growth model with the Tehuantepec study area. By identifying the more appropriate model, she isolates some of the possible variables that contributed to the observed pattern of settlement growth. Zeitlin's chapter is an important contribution to the growing literature on locational analysis in archaeology.

REFERENCES

Flannery, K. V., ed.
   1976   *The Early Mesoamerican village.* New York: Academic Press
Parsons, J. R.
   1972   Archaeological settlement patterns. In *Annual review of anthropology*, Vol. 1, edited by B. J. Siegel, A. R. Beals, S. A. Tyler. Palo Alto, California: Annual Reviews. Pp. 127–150.

Struever, S.
    1971 Comments on archaeological data requirements and research strategy. *American Antiquity* **36:**9–19.
Trigger, B. G.
    1967 Settlement archaeology—Its goals and promise. *American Antiquity* **32**(2):149–160.

chapter 6

Coastal Settlement in Northwestern Costa Rica

FREDERICK W. LANGE
Museo Nacional de Costa Rica

The northwestern Costa Rican–southwestern Nicaraguan Pacific coastal area is part of a region with a common cultural tradition, indicated by the distribution of similar ceramic types. The area corresponds roughly to what Norweb (1961, 1964) defined as the Greater Nicoya Archaeological Subarea (Figure 6.1), stating that it "includes most of Pacific Nicaragua and regions in northwestern Costa Rica adjacent to the Gulf of Nicoya [p. 561]."

In northwestern Costa Rica, the first scientific research was conducted by Hartman (1901, 1907; see also Rowe 1959). It was not until the late 1950s and the early 1960s that further research was undertaken by M. D. Coe (1962a,b; more fully reported on by Sweeney 1975) and Baudez (1959, 1962, 1967). Baudez and Coe also published three joint articles (1962, 1966; Coe and Baudez 1961) detailing various aspects of their work, which primarily focused on establishing a regional cultural chronology. Minelli (1976) has distributed a preliminary report on work at the site of Barrahonda on the Nicoya Peninsula, and Murray and Jess (1976) have conducted as yet unpublished surveys of the Tilaran–Lake Arenal region and that of the Rio Sabalo. Finally, Finch (1977) has completed an intensive survey of Hacienda Jerico on the western slope of the Tenorio Volcano.

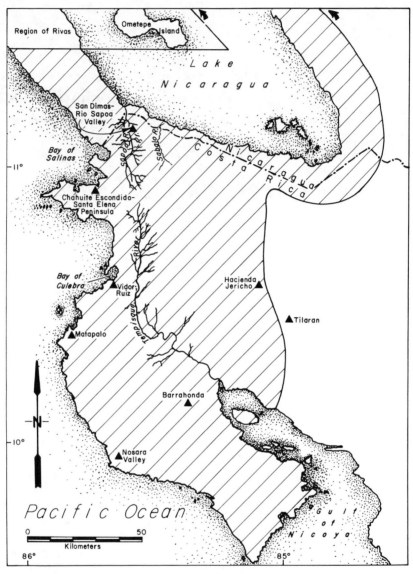

Figure 6.1. Locations of sites and research areas mentioned in text. The Greater Nicoya Archaeological Subarea is shown by hatching.

Research by the author since 1969 on the Pacific coast of Guanacaste Province, Costa Rica, has sought to develop a detailed picture of regional prehistoric cultural development (Lange 1969, 1970, 1971a,b, 1972, 1975, 1976a,b,c; Lange and Scheidenhelm 1972; Lange and Murray 1972; Lange and Rydberg 1972; Lange and Carty 1975; Lange, Bernstein, Siegel, and Tase 1976). Primary research focuses have been (a) to analyze settlement patterns and related subsistence data; (b) to determine the position of this area as a frontier or buffer between northern and southern influences; and (c) to analyze localized cultural differences between the northern Pacific coast with its many embayments and the straighter southern coast of the Nicoya Peninsula.

Regardless of emphases by various researchers, the typical field approach has been to survey randomly or selectively a geographically delimited area, to conduct subsurface testing at some sites, and on the basis of survey and testing results to conduct concentrated excavations (with vertical rather than horizontal emphasis) at a limited number of sites. Techniques of data recovery have differed, and there are consequent problems in comparability of all categories of data.

The following discussion broadly summarizes the published data and incorporates some unpublished data from continuing work at the Vidor site on the Bay of Culebra. This latter work factually contributes to new perspectives and elucidates particular methodological problems encountered in research in the area. The successes and shortcomings of the previous 20 years of research are discussed, and immediate needs for future research efforts outlined, particularly a closer alliance between archaeologists and natural scientists working in the same area. Recent volcanic eruptions, earthquakes, and floods in Central America have been forceful reminders that aspects of the cultural development of coastal Pacific Costa Rica were almost certainly closely related to its recent natural history.

Archaeologists have been poorly prepared to deal with many questions regarding marine biology, volcanic activity, and plate tectonics essential to integrating human and natural data. For example, we have extensive molluscan data from excavations but little marine biological data pertinent to the species involved. The bays of Salinas and Culebra, with their protected shores and seasonally substantial supply of inflowing water carrying nutrients and generating upwelling that increases marine production at the lower end of the food chain, were important to precolumbian Indians in a number of ways, but we are still woefully ignorant of the details of various coastal habitats.

Shorelines themselves are unstable, and the availability of various resources fluctuates in long- and short-term cycles. Plate tectonic movement has raised the Guanacaste coast (Frazier 1970) during the period of human occupation; Professor Ronald Chavez (personal communication) of the University of Costa Rica estimates a rate of 1 cm per century. Such uplift, with related settling of coastal sedimentary pockets, would have significant impact on the presence or absence of mangrove swamps and other productive zones.

Evidence from the Vidor site strongly suggests that the estuary near which the site is located was impounded by sandbars from time to time in the prehistoric past with resultant flooding and deposition of waterborne deposits. The site was also blanketed twice during periods of prehistoric occupation by sufficient quantities of volcanic ash (Figure 6.2) to have

Figure 6.2. Volcanic ash deposit, late Middle Polychrome Period, Vidor site.

caused at least temporary abandonment. Such observations, however, fall far short of the level of analysis necessary to incorporate such data with artifactual evidence for cultural interpretation.

CULTURE HISTORY OF THE COASTAL AREA

For the present discussion, the coastal parts of this region include the shoreline and any inland areas (or offshore areas such as islands) where evidence demonstrates that during all or part of the year people derived the majority of their subsistence from marine–estuary environments. Highly developed trade networks do not seem to have existed in this area, and the farthest inland such a definition of *coastal* would be extended is to shell middens of less than 2 full days' round-trip journey from the shore.

At present it is not known whether marine resources were procured directly through trips to the coast by inhabitants from inland sites or whether they were traded through numerous intermediary sites also reflecting extensive marine resource utilization (Finch and Swartz 1976). The exact relationship of sites on the coast to those inland sites using marine resources cannot be defined until more work is done at the latter.

Present chronometric data are inadequate for all but the bare skeleton of the regional sequence. Sweeney (1975:35–36) has summarized the bulk of the available data. There are currently 5 dates for the Zoned Bichrome Period (1500 B.C. to A.D. 300) from 3 Costa Rican sites; 6 dates for the Early Polychrome Period (300 to 800 A.D.) from 1 Nicaraguan and 2 Costa Rican sites; 17 dates from the Middle Polychrome Period (A.D. 800 to 1200) from 1 Nicaraguan and 4 Costa Rican sites; and 6 dates from the Late Polychrome Period (A.D. 1200 to 1600) from 4 Costa Rican sites. All of these dates are from geographically scattered contexts; in most cases they are single samples from an individual context and are often from shell midden strata susceptible to postdepositional disturbance. The limited number of dates and their widespread geographical distribution makes them difficult to apply to questions of cultural process.

Until the 1970s, the known culture history of the area "began" at the very late date of 300 B.C.   Minelli (1976) has reported dates of 3400 ± 1000 radiocarbon years: 1550 B.C. and 8230 ± 1000 radiocarbon years: 6280 B.C. from the site of Barrahonda, both single dates from separate contexts. The younger date is associated with Zoned Bichrome materials and offers promise of extending the regional sequence into the earlier parts of the Formative Period. Neither date can be fully accepted at present because details are lacking regarding the material being dated and the nature of the context. The oldest date definitely appears to be from mixed cultural and natural deposits.

Available chronometric and cultural data permit a general overview of the prehistoric development of the Northwestern Costa Rican coastal area, but, as will be seen, one lacking in many desirable specific details.

Zoned Bichrome Period (1500 B.C. to A.D. 300)

Zoned, painted bichrome pottery is a generalized Nuclear American Formative characteristic with a wide distribution. The presence of this trait in the study area indicates that northwestern Costa Rica participated in this widespread pattern. With the exception of Barrahonda, most known sites from this period are currently assumed to be from the very end of the Formative Period. Although a substantial time depth is indicated, sites from this period have lacked well-stratified material suitable for subdivision. Current work at the Vidor site has isolated two distinct Zoned Bichrome phases. Present excavations will secure a much larger sample, but the two phases appear to be contrasted by the presence of fine-incised zoning in the more recent phase and thick-line zoning in the earlier (Figures 6.3 and 6.4).

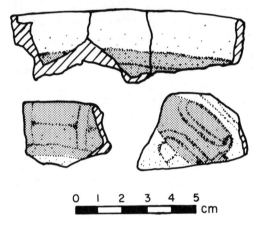

Figure 6.3.   Fine-lined Zoned Bichrome ceramics from upper Zoned Bichrome level at Vidor site.   Black painted areas are stippled; red painted areas are left white.

Figure 6.4.   Thick-lined Zoned Bichrome and bichrome ceramics from lower Zoned Bichrome level at Vidor site.

Zoned Bichrome Period components are found in single and multicomponent sites. In large shell-midden sites near the shore these are often deeply buried (up to 4.8 m), creating mechanical problems in excavating samples comparable in quantity to those of later periods that are closer to the surface and usually more extensively exploited archaeologically (Brown 1975; Lange 1971a; Sweeney 1975:37). For example, early attempts to reach Zoned Bichrome components at the Vidor site necessitated considerable effort to remove up to 5 m of midden material safely. Portions of the site later were mechanically leveled as much as 2 m, and Zoned Bichrome components are now proportionately closer to the new ground surface. This is permitting more extensive excavations at these levels and is providing evidence that the horizontal extent of the site during this period was much greater than previously suspected.

Zoned Bichrome components at the Vidor site contain concentrations of small adobe fragments indicating wattle-and-daub structures. Sweeney (1975:431–432) also reported wattle-and-daub concentrations with Zoned Bichrome components at Matapalo, although such evidence was absent from Chahuite Escondido. Baudez (1967) mentioned neither the presence nor absence of wattle-and-daub fragments, whereas Healy (1974:439) indicated that large quantities were found at sites in the Rivas area of Nicaragua.

With the tentative exception of one site briefly tested by Baudez (1967:48), all presently known Zoned Bichrome Period components are from nonshell-midden contexts. Subsistence data from this period are very limited, although absence of molluscan remains from coastal sites with immediate access to estuary and intertidal resources appears to be a clear case of cultural preference. This contrasts with M. D. Coe's initial working hypothesis that "the nature of the deeply indented coastline, with broad bays, estuaries, and rivers running through alluviated valleys would seem to have offered an inviting prospect to early farmers who yet retained an interest in older patterns of fishing and the collections of mollusks [1962a:358]." The earliest currently known occupations appear to have been based on procurement activities that excluded collection of mollusks, a subsistence practice that emerged slowly over time as populations increased.

The presence of Zoned Bichrome materials on Ometepe Island in Lake Nicaragua (Harberland 1963, 1966a,b, 1969) indicates that the skills necessary for constructing boats or rafts (and navigational skills necessary on the often-rough lake) had already been acquired. Ocean-going craft were probably used as well, although direct evidence is nonexistent.

Limited occurrences of materials with Olmec motifs (Balser 1959, 1969; Stone 1972:97; Lange et al. 1976) suggest at least tenuous connections to the north during this period. Pohorilenko (1976) has reviewed the

Olmecoid evidence from Costa Rica and has concluded that most portrayals on ceramics and jade represent local imitations and that very few are imports or the work of Olmec artisans.

The finely made ceramics, jade carvings, and formalized cemeteries (Lange and Scheidenhelm 1972) contrast with the apparent absence of large settlements. Deep burial of coastal components may partially explain this discrepancy, but inland Zoned Bichrome sites in the Tempisque and San Dimas valleys (Figure 6.1) have been shallow, single-component sites of limited horizontal extent, reflecting small populations and shifting residence.

The Linear Decorated Problem

In Baudez and Coe's original formulation of their Tempisque and Santa Elena Peninsula materials (1962) the Early Polychrome Period was divided into subperiods A and B, with A being the earlier and equivalent to the Linear Decorated Period (A.D. 300 to 500) in Baudez's (1967) refinement of the sequence. In Baudez's view, the Linear Decorated Period marked the transition from Zoned Bichrome designs and decorative techniques to true polychromes. That such a transition took place is not at issue; the question is whether it should be recognized as a separate period in the regional sequence. Linear Decorated materials are not associated as an assemblage with specific radiocarbon dates and are identified as a separate component at only two sites (Baudez 1967). It is increasingly doubtful as a distinct temporal period, and data currently being obtained from the Vidor site are expected to demonstrate that this transitional stage is best viewed as the final phase of a Zoned Bichrome Period, extending to A.D. 500. This view is strongly buttressed by as yet unpublished data from the Atlantic watershed of Costa Rica and the increasing evidence for temporally equivalent shared modes between the Pacific and the Atlantic (Snarskis 1977, personal communication). Snarskis' 1977 research produced a series of dates (UCLA 2113: A, B, D, M, N, O) clustered between 500 and 1000 B.C., the oldest securely dated archaeological contexts in Costa Rica. He has designated the associated ceramics, which share many modes with presently undated Guanacaste materials, as the La Montaña complex.

Many of the distinctive features of the Linear Decorated Period were supposed to have been derived from Mesoamerican areas to the north. The absence of a coeval period in Pacific Nicaragua (more heavily influenced by Mesoamerica than was Pacific Costa Rica; Healy 1974:474–475) is of comparative interest. Such interpretative difficulties are potentially present when culture histories are reconstructed only from ceramic complexes, rather than from changes in whole cultural complexes. This may be particularly true in a buffer zone–frontier area where various changes were not always evenly incorporated. Many archaeologists have looked north toward

Mexico for influence on northwestern Costa Rican ceramics during all temporal periods. This tendency to look for similarities has masked many internal features of precolumbian Costa Rican development, especially the seemingly general cultural unity between the Atlantic and Pacific watersheds. It is doubtful that prehistoric Costa Rican peoples were suffi- ciently influenced by external forces during the first five centuries A.D. to necessitate searching for such influences as major explanatory devices; if such evidence is sought, it is much more likely to be found to the east and south rather than to the northwest.

Early Polychrome Period (A.D. 500 to 800)

This period begins the evolution of the distinctive Nicoya Polychrome ceramic tradition. More importantly, this period reflects the completion of a settlement and subsistence transition (begun during the final phase of the Zoned Bichrome Period as it would be defined on the basis of the previously referred to new data) that was perhaps one of the most important events in the history of this coastal zone, that is, the utilization of mollusks and offshore fishing resources. Hunting continued to be of importance, but the precise role of agriculture is unknown.

Early Polychrome Period components are found in inland areas, with Finch (1977) reporting materials from the Hacienda Tenorio area, but the majority of such sites in Costa Rica are concentrated near coastal habitats. In Nicaragua, Healy (1974:517) described an expansion of the rich farming opportunities offered in the Isthmus of Rivas. The shift to molluscan exploita- tion in coastal Guanacaste is not reflected in Nicaragua, where settlements were instead located around freshwater Lake Nicaragua.

The 1977 excavations at the Vidor site encountered a large cemetery concentration which was partially excavated; additional work is anticipated for the immediate future. More than 60 complete or fragmentary individuals have been identified so far. The few adults are female, while the majority of the burials are infants, many in paired inverted jars; some foetus burials are suspected. Sweeney (1975:45) also reported child burials in inverted jars for Chahuite Escondido, but no large skeletal populations comparable to that from the Vidor site have been excavated in the Pacific coastal area. The potential importance of specialized female-infant burial areas within sites is clear, and restudy of other coastal sites (such as Chahuite Escondido, where some burials were encountered during preliminary testing) is urgently re- quired to develop comparative data. In a frontier zone, incursions by new cultural groups (or lack thereof) will very likely be reflected in the skeletal remains of the people themselves, or in mortuary practices.

Middle Polychrome Period
(A.D. 800 to 1200)

Components from this period are known from coastal and inland sites, but principal population concentration was again along the shore. It is not known whether these different Middle Polychrome components represent seasonal or permanent occupations, although at larger coastal shell middens some inhabitants were certainly there on a year-round basis. Finch (1977) reported no materials from this period from his survey of Hacienda Tenorio.

The main occupation in the Nosara Valley, on the southern coast of the Nicoya Peninsula, where the absence of shell middens contrasts strongly with dense midden concentrations to the north, occurred during this period. Middle Polychrome also marks the peak of the Nicoya Polychrome tradition, although influences from both highland Mexico and the Maya lowlands are evident. Faunal analysis from the Vidor site indicated a relative increase in fishing and decrease in hunting from the preceding period. This trend was not noted at Chahuite Escondido (Sweeney 1975:457), although perhaps as a result of poor recovery of materials. Agriculture was also practiced, with Healy (1974:521) noting its continued importance in Nicaragua, as well as hunting and fishing.

Nutting stones are an important part of the lithic assemblage on the Bay of Salinas but are less common at the Vidor site. They were probably employed to process acorns as well as other nuts and berries. Sweeney (1975:55) suggested that they may have been used to process *pejibaye*. Although this is a suitable possibility for eastern Costa Rica and Panama, the *pejibaye* palm does not grow naturally in drier Guanacaste, and no evidence suggests a climatic change since 800 A.D.

The Middle Polychrome Period also provides the first concrete evidence of shore–inland trade in the presence of shell middens up to 10 km inland. Dried fish, salt, and purple dye may have been traded inland along the same paths, with nonculinary pottery and perhaps agricultural products going to the shore zones.

If ceramics accurately reflect other aspects of culture, then widespread distribution of similar ceramic types and varieties during this period indicates an overall cultural unity. There is also a strong commonality between Pacific coastal Costa Rica and adjacent Nicaragua during this period, with the majority of ceramic types being found throughout the area.

Late Polychrome Period (A.D. 1200 to 1600)

No contact-period sites have been excavated, and the terminal date is purely arbitrary. The initial Spanish *entradas* were superficial, with people traveling primarily through northwestern Costa Rica rather than settling there. Many native communities and customs remained unchanged, and attempts to pacify various groups continued at least as late as 1578 (Fernandez 1976:277). The ethnohistorical data for the area are potentially very useful but have not been seriously exploited since the work of Lothrop (1926) and that of Stone (1966).

Almost all sites identified for this period are concentrated on the northern Pacific coast. In contrast, the Nosara Valley on the southern Pacific coast of the peninsula (with minimal resources for marine mollusks) has no Late Polychrome component at any of the 28 sites located thus far in the valley. The most obvious factor in determining this settlement distribution is the presence of large molluscan colonies along the northern coast, although factors such as lack of large embayments sufficient to receive ocean-going trade were probably important as well. The reasons for a lack of a Late Polychrome component at the site of Matapalo on Tamarindo Bay (Sweeney 1975:43–45) following an extensive Middle Polychrome occupation are more difficult to explain and not readily apparent.

Sites during this period tend to be fewer but large (the Vidor site is one of six sites with a Late Polychrome component in excess of 10 ha on the Bay of Culebra), a trend paralleled in southern Nicaragua (Healy 1974:525–526). Willey (personal communication in Healy 1974:514) also reported that the only site located on the Bay of San Juan del Sur on the south coast of Nicaragua appeared to be from this period. Finch (1977) reported no materials from this period from the survey of Hacienda Jerico.

Middens found inland (2–4 hr walk) that had begun to be inhabited at the end of the preceding period reached their fullest occupation at this time. Some single-component Late Polychrome shell middens appear to be strategically placed either along small river valleys (and routes of travel between coastal and inland areas) draining into major coastal embayments or behind the headlands of the bays. The Ruiz site, located behind the first row of hills bordering the south side of the Bay of Culebra, is several hectares in size, shallow, and has only minimal evidence of Early and Middle Polychrome occupations. Material from the Late Polychrome component is considerably denser in concentration than material from any comparable components from sites on the shore of the Bay of Culebra. Surface collection at this Ruiz site recovered a lost-wax gold mold fragment (Figure 6.5), evidence that at least some gold-working was being carried out in northwestern as well as southern and eastern Costa Rica. Indirectly this also supports contact-period descriptions of gold manufacturing procedures and of ornaments collected from the Indians by the early Spanish (Lothrop 1966:184).

Both the small river valley and headland Late Polychrome sites are approximately equidistant between the marine resources of the bays and the

0   1   2   3   4   5 cm

Figure 6.5. Ceramic lost-wax mold fragment (interior and exterior), probably Late Polychrome Period, from the Ruiz site.

presumed agricultural resources of the interior plains. Marine molluscan and other exploitation patterns from one such site have been extensively analyzed by Moreau (1975).

In comparison with Middle Polychrome remains, most faunal material from the Late Polychrome Period at the Vidor site consists of fish bones. A similar decrease in bone from land animals is also recorded in the Late Polychrome component at Chahuite Escondido (Sweeney 1975:457). Some land animal bone, primarily deer, is still found, but people by this time had either hunted out the available game or driven it to less heavily occupied areas. Nutting stones are again more frequent at the Bay of Salinas than at the Bay of Culebra, and other lithic materials such as chipped stone vary widely in occurrence. In Nicaragua, Healy (1974:525–526) noted that "The . . . period was marked by more numerous and diversified stone tools. . . . There was also a quantum jump in sheer quantity of ceramic remains . . . there are strong impressions of a sizeable Nicarao population living in nucleated villages."

Healy's comment on the quantity of pottery is also an accurate reflection of Late Polychrome components in northwestern Costa Rica. It is significant that not only are there quantities of pottery but that almost all of it is culinary ware. In our Costa Rican Late Polychrome samples, decorated ceramics (very broadly defined to include painted, incised, appliqué, or punctate rims, body sherds, supports, or handles) comprise only 1.5 to 3.0% of ceramic inventories of 40,000 to 60,000 sherds.

Wyckoff (1973) suggested a major subsistence shift from heavy shellfish reliance in Middle Polychrome times to more hunting in Late Polychrome times, based on data from the site of San Francisco between Lake Managua and Lake Nicaragua and from Healy's site J-RI-4: Santa Isabel "A" (excavated by A. H. Norweb) about 4 km north of Puerto San Jorge on the shore of Lake Nicaragua. There is some doubt that faunal collection methods at either site were adequate to determine ecological trends. If so, there is a distinct and very interesting contrast to patterns observed on the Pacific coast of Costa Rica at the same time.

The ceramic unity of the preceding two periods dissolved in Late Polychrome times, reflecting population movements and political unrest to the north (Lothrop 1926:3; Haberland 1975). Ceramic types reflect northern, southern, and eastern stylistic influences, and distributions are highly variable. The area was fragmenting into the southern and northern spheres of influences described by the early Spanish explorers.

COMPARATIVE OVERVIEW

Coastal areas in northwestern Guanacaste were occupied throughout the presently known span of regional culture history. This is in distinct contrast with the Pacific side of Nicaragua, where populations were concentrated along the inland shore of Lake Nicaragua. In Costa Rica, the relationship between nearshore and more inland components of the same time period cannot be determined at present due to lack of both chronometric precision and preservation of comparable subsistence data which might indicate seasonality.

Both agriculture and exploitation of marine–estuary resources were practiced, with the latter being a late rather than an early development. Arboriculture was also important, and other forms of gathering and collecting were apparently practiced as well. Fishing and mollusk gathering became more important through time, but hunting less so. This may reflect reduction of game through hunting pressure and habitat reduction due to deforestation.

Numerically, deer are the most common fauna, although the overall count of individuals is small. Other mammals such as peccary, raccoon, opossum, and reptiles such as iguana are also represented in the inventories. Despite the modern seasonal presence of large numbers of Ridley turtle, turtle remains are very limited in archaeological contexts. Prehistoric peoples may have been exploiting turtle eggs rather than the turtles themselves, but this cannot be determined.

The role of agriculture in the area is enigmatic. Many coastal areas are not suitable for either intensive or extensive cultivation because of generally poor soil conditions. Even in the more fertile Nosara and Tempisque valleys we have neither strong artifactual nor any botanical evidence for agricultural activity. Agriculture was certainly practiced, but it is difficult to assess its importance in this area. Healy (1974) felt there was strong evidence for agriculture in southern Nicaragua (and farming is fully described in the Spanish documents), but the environmental potential was considerably lower in Guanacaste, and the alternatives apparently somewhat more abundant.

Linares, Sheets, and Rosenthal (1975:145) interpreted previous remarks I have made (Lange 1971b:51–57) about the lack of agriculture in the Rio Sapoa–Bay of Salinas area as a general regional conclusion. This was certainly not the case, but rather a local interpretation derived from artifactual and soils data, as well as observations regarding terrain and modern agricultural conditions in that specific area. Also, although it did not emerge as such, one point of emphasis was not to question the use of maize but to avoid the traditional assumption that the presence of maize was evidence for Mexican influence. Snarkis (1976:348) reported South American maize from a site on the Atlantic coast of Costa Rica, and given the relatively short distance involved (as well as emerging ceramic indicators of Atlantic–Pacific trade and sharing), there is no reason why maize farming could not have been derived from South America. Snarkis also pointed out that "some authorities suggest that the arrival of superior maize races from South America may have accelerated the development of civilization in Mesoamerica (Mangelsdorf, MacNeish, and Willey 1964:439)."

We have yet to locate clear-cut evidence of a particular habitation area, although lumps bearing pole impressions representing wattle-and-daub structures have been found at many sites. The lack of this type of data is partially a result of emphasis on shell midden contexts and partially a result of vertical rather than horizontal excavations. Most excavations in northwestern Costa Rica have been 4 m² or less, but Winter (1976:25) estimated that "cultural features comprising a single Early or Middle Formative household cluster at Tierra Largas may be scattered over an area of 300 sq. meters." Although household sizes from Mexico may not be directly applicable to Lower Central America, the point that horizontal rather than vertical excavations must be employed to develop data other than cultural chronologies is obvious and clearly demonstrated by the important data recovered from the extensive horizontal excavations in the cemetery area at the Vidor site in 1977.

Through time, one can identify South American, Caribbean, Mexican, and Mayan ceramic influences, adapted or reinterpreted to varying degrees, as well as strong local developments. Northwestern Costa Rican ceramics abound in varieties and subtypes, and Sweeney's rejection (1975:423–424) of the computer approach to analysis on the basis of prohibitive amounts of data to be accommodated is a reflection of the problems involved. Ceramics traditionally have been the underpinnings for sequence building in this and other ceramic culture area studies. It seems, however, that we are dealing with a geographical area where events in the ceramic sphere may not be inextricably correlated with events in other areas of behavior. The shift from nonmolluscan to molluscan-based subsistence was as important, if not more important to the majority of people, as was the shift from monochrome to polychrome pottery. Meaningful analysis must be based on entire cultural complexes to the extent that conditions of preservation and recovery permit.

The matter of data recovery presents its own problem, for at least in northwestern Costa Rica the sheer volume of data produced by shell midden excavations presents serious problems of field and analytical strategy. The richness of midden data we have been dealing with and the resources required to sample minimally one site (since excavation results indicate significant ceramic and ecological differences even between different midden areas of the same time period) require careful planning for the expenditure of limited human and financial resources. The study of coastal areas necessitates the development of regional research designs, and adequate control over an area's archaeological resources. In Costa Rica we are faced now with the rapid, and relatively uncontrolled, development of Pacific coastal areas in connection with tourist projects.

CONCLUSION

We have made considerable strides in reducing our dependence on Mesoamerican influence as a convenient explanatory device, and have come to recognize the complexity of this cultural frontier–buffer zone and the intricate nature of relationships between external forces and local traditions. We have turned the corner from, but not abandoned, traditional problems of chronometric alignment and ceramic sequences and typology, and we have developed the capacities to begin to take advantage of nonceramic data. With the important exception of finer chronometric control, we now possess a framework within which specific questions can be asked.

ACKNOWLEDGMENTS

This chapter has profited from discussions with Claude Baudez, Wolfgang Haberland, Jeanne Sweeney, and Carlos Aguilar at the First Congress of Central American Archaeology in San Jose, Costa Rica (30 June to 6 July 1975). In its later stages, I have benefited from consultations with my colleagues Michael J. Snarskis, Hector Gamboa P., and Luis Ferrero A. of the Museo Nacional de Costa Rica, with Richard Magnus, and with the editors of this volume. Field work has been conducted under permit from the Museo Nacional de Costa Rica during 1969, 1970, 1973, 1976, and 1977. During the first 2 years I was a graduate student at the University of Wisconsin—Madison, and was helped in various ways by Donald E. Thompson, David A. Baerreis, and William M. Denevan. During this period I also received two grants from the Organization for Tropical Studies, Inc., and assistance and student participation from the Associated Colleges of the Midwest; with respect to the latter institution I would like specifically to acknowledge the aid of Dr. J. Robert Hunter. During 1973 and 1976, work was conducted with student field school groups from Beloit College and the Associated Colleges of the Midwest and was greatly facilitated by Luis Diego Gomez P., Director of the Museo Nacional de Costa Rica, who also arranged for temporary export of study collections. The 1977 work at the Vidor and Ruiz sites was supported in part by a grant from the National Geographic Society. The greatest thanks goes to my wife Holley who, from the beginning, has assisted in the field work, laboratory analysis, and management of student groups and has read numerous report drafts.

REFERENCES

Balser, Carlos.
    1959   Los 'Baby Faces' Olmecas de Costa Rica. *Actas del 33 Congreso Internacional de Americanistas, San José, Costa Rica, 1958,* Vol. 2. Pp. 280–285.
    1969   A new style of Olmec jade with string sawing from Costa Rica. *Verhandlungen des 38 Internationalen Amerikanisten Kongresses, Stuttgart-München, 1968,* Vol. 1. Pp. 243–247.
Baudez, Claude F.
    1959   Nuevos aspectos de la escultura en territorio chorotega. *Actas del 33 Congreso Internacional de Americanistas, San José, Costa Rica, 1958,* Vol. 2. Pp. 286–295.
    1962   Rapport préliminaire sur les réchèrches archaeologiques enterprises dans la Vallée du Tempisque-Guanacaste-Costa Rica. *Akten des 34 Internationalen Amerikanisten Kongresses, Vienna, 1960.* Pp. 348–358.
    1967   Récherchès archaeologiques dans la Vallée du Tempisque, Guanacaste, Costa Rica. *Travaux et Memoires de l'Institut de Hautes Études de l'Amerique Latine,* Vol. 18. Paris.
Baudez, Claude F., and Michael D. Coe
    1962   Archaeological sequences in Northwestern Costa Rica. *Akten des 34 Internationalen Amerikanisten Kongresses, Vienna, 1960.* Pp. 366–373.
    1966   Incised slate disks from the Atlantic Watershed of Costa Rica: A commentary. *American Antiquity* **31:**441–43.
Brown, James A.
    1975   Deep-site excavation strategy as a sampling problem. In *Sampling in archaeology,* edited by James W. Mueller. Tucson: Univ. of Arizona Press. Pp. 155–159.
Coe, Michael D.
    1962a Preliminary report on archaeological investigations in Central Guanacaste, Costa Rica. In *Akten des 34 Internationalen Amerikanisten Kongresses, Vienna, 1960.* Pp. 358–365.
    1962b Costa Rican archaeology and Mesoamerica. *Southwestern Journal of Anthropology* **18:**170–183.
Coe, Michael D., and Claude F. Baudez
    1961   The Zoned Bichrome Period in Northwestern Costa Rica. *American Antiquity* **26:**505–515.
Fernandez, Leon
    1976   Conquista y Poblamiento en el Siglo XVI. In *Editorial Costa Rica, Vol. 2: Biblioteca Patria* San José, Costa Rica.
Finch, Will O.
    1977   Preliminary survey of the Hacienda Jérico, Guanacaste, Costa Rica. Manuscript on file, National Museum of Costa Rica.

Finch, Will O., and Deborah Swartz
 1976 Settlement and site survey of the Río Sardinal in Guanacaste, Costa Rica. Manuscript on file, National Museum of Costa Rica.
Frazier, Kendrick
 1970 Turning to the earth's smaller crustal plates. *Science News* **97**:153–155.
Haberland, Wolfgang
 1963 Ometepe 1962–63. *Archaeology* **16**:287–289.
 1966a El sur de Centroamérica. *Actas y Memorias del 36 Congreso Internacional de Americanistas, Seville, 1964*, Vol. 1. Pp. 193–200.
 1966b Early phases on Ometepe Island, Nicaragua. *Actas y Memorias del 36 Congreso Internacional de Americanistas, Seville, 1964*, Vol. 1. Pp. 399–403.
 1969 Early phases and their relationship in Southern Central America. *Verhandlungen des 38 Internationalen Amerikanisten Kongresses, Stuttgart-München, 1968*, Vol. 1. Pp. 229–242.
 1975 Further archaeological evidence for the Nicarao and Pipil migrations in Central America. *XMX Actas del 41st Congreso Internacional de Americanistas, Mexico, 1974*, Vol. 1. Pp. 551–559.
Hartman, Carl V.
 1901 *Archaeological researches in Costa Rica.* Stockholm: The Royal Ethnographical Museum.
 1907 Archaeological researches on the Pacific Coast of Costa Rica. *Memoirs of the Carnegie Museum.* Vol. 3. Pittsburg. Pp. 1–188.
Healy, Paul F.
 1974 The archaeology of Southwest Nicaragua. Ph.D. dissertation, Department of Anthropology, Harvard Univ.
Lange, Frederick W., ed.
 1969 An archaeological survey of the Río Sapoa Valley, Costa Rica. Chicago: Associated Colleges of the Midwest. Mimeograph
 1970 Archaeological research in the Río Sapoa Area. Chicago: Associated Colleges of the Midwest. Mimeograph.
Lange, Frederick W.
 1971a *Culture history of the Sapoa River Valley, Costa Rica.* In *Occasional Anthropological Papers, No. 4:* Beloit, Wisconsin: Beloit College, Logan Museum of Anthropology.
 1971b Northwestern Costa Rica: Pre-columbian circum-caribbean affiliations. *Folk* **13**:43–64.
 1972 *Historia Cultural en el Valle del Río Sapoa, Costa Rica.* Informe Semestral, Instituto Geográfico de Costa Rica. Pp. 61–76.
 1975 Excavaciones de salvamento en un cementerio del Período Bicromo en zonas, Guanacaste, Costa Rica. *Vínculos* **1**:92–98.
 1976a Costa Rica and subsistence archaeology. *Current Anthropology* **17**:305–307.
 1976b Bahías y valles de la costa de Guanacaste. *Vínculos* 2:45–66.
 1976c The Northern Central American buffer: A current perspective. *Latin American Research Review* **11**:177–183.
Lange, Frederick W., and Frederick M. Carty
 1975 Adaptation of the flotation technique to salt water. *Journal of Field Archaeology* **2**:119–123.
Lange, Frederick W., and Thomas A. Murray
 1972 The archaeology of the San Dimas Valley, Costa Rica. *Katunob* **7**:50–91.

Lange, Frederick W., and Charles R. Rydberg
  1972   Abandonment and post-abandonment behavior at a rural Central American house-site. *American Antiquity* **37**:419–432.
Lange, Frederick W., and Kristin K. Scheidenhelm
  1972   The salvage archaeology of a Zoned Bichrome cemetery, Costa Rica. *American Antiquity* **37**:240–245.
Lange, Frederick W., D. J. Bernstein, M. Siegel, and D. Tase
  1976   Preliminary archaeological research in the Nosara Valley. *Folk* **18**:47–60.
Linares, Olga F., P. D. Sheets, and E. J. Rosenthal
  1975   Prehistoric agriculture in Tropical Highlands. *Science* **187**:137–145.
Lothrop, Samuel K.
  1926   *The pottery of Costa Rica and Nicaragua.* 2 vols. Museum of the American Indian Contributions, No. 8. New York: Heye Foundation.
  1966   Archaeology of Lower Central America. In *Handbook of Middle American Indians, Vol. 4: Archaeological frontiers and external connections,* edited by G. F. Ekholm and G. R. Willey. Austin: Univ. of Texas Press. Pp. 180–208.
Mangelsdorf, P. C., R. S. MacNeish, and G. R. Willey
  1964   Origins of agriculture in Middle America. In *Handbook of Middle American Indians, Vol. 1: Natural environment and early cultures,* edited by Robert C. West. Austin: Univ. of Texas Press. Pp. 427–445.
Minelli, Laura Laurencich de
  1976   Informe sobre la investigacion arqueológica en Barrahonda (Costa Rica). Bologna: Universita di Bologna, Instituto de Antropologia. Mimeograph.
Moreau, Jean-Francois
  1975   Deux amas coquilliers Costaricains. Analyse conchyliologique. Master's thesis, Univ. of Montreal.
Murray, Thomas A., and Edward W. Jess
  1976   Preliminary report of the Río Sabalo Valley Survey. Manuscript on file, National Museum of Costa Rica.
Norweb, Albert H.
  1961   The archaeology of the Greater Nicoya Subarea. Seminar paper in anthropology, Harvard Univ.
  1964   Ceramic stratigraphy in Southwestern Nicaragua. *Actas del 35 Congreso Internacional de Americanistas, Mexico, 1962,* Vol. 1. Pp. 551–563.
Pohorilenko, Anatole
  1976   La prescencia Olmeca en Costa Rica. San José, Costa Rica: *Ancora* 234 (*La Nacion*), Sunday, November 2.
Rowe, John H.
  1959   Carl Hartman and his place in the history of archaeology. *Actas del 33 Congreso Internacional de Americanistas, San José, Costa Rica; 1958,* Vol. 1. Pp. 268–279.
Snarskis, Michael J.
  1976   Stratigraphic excavations in the Eastern Lowlands of Costa Rica. *American Antiquity* **41**:342–353.
Stone, Doris Z.
  1966   Synthesis of Lower Central American ethnohistory. In *Handbook of Middle American Indians,* Vol. 1: *Archaeological frontiers and external connections* edited by G. F. Ekholm and G. R. Willey. Austin: University of Texas Press. Pp. 209–233.
  1972   *Pre-columbian man finds Central America.* Cambridge, Massachusetts: Peabody Museum Press.

Sweeney, Jeanne W.
  1975   Guanacaste, Costa Rica: An analysis of PreColumbian ceramics from the Northwest
         Coast. Ph.D. Dissertation, Department of Anthropology, Univ. of Pennsylvania.
Winter, Marcus C.
  1976   The archaeological household cluster in the Valley of Oaxaca. In *The Early
         Mesoamerican village,* edited by Kent V. Flannery. New York: Academic Press. Pp.
         25–31.
Wyckoff, L.
  1973   An examination of Nicaraguan Late and Middle Polychrome assemblages. Manu-
         script, location unknown. Cited in Healy (1974).

chapter 7

Coastal Adaptations as Contact Phenomena among the Miskito and Cuna Indians of Lower Central America

MARY W. HELMS
Northwestern University

LATE PRECONTACT ADAPTATIONS

At present a significant proportion of two of the most populous enclaves of native peoples in lower Central America occupy coastal locales. Ten to fifteen thousand (out of a total of approximately 35,000–40,000) Miskito Indians reside in small villages located on the pine savannahs, lagoons, and sandy coast of eastern Honduras and Nicaragua (Figure 7.1). Riverine communities extend the range of Miskito settlement inland along several waterways, river settlement being most dense and extensive along the Río Coco, the boundary between Nicaragua and Honduras. Farther south the vast majority of the nearly 25,000 Cuna Indians of northeastern Panama live on approximately 50 of the offshore coral islands comprising the San Blas Archipelago (Figure 7.2). A few Cuna communities are located on the mainland, either along the rugged coast or in the mountainous interior of the *serranía* that rises abruptly from the very narrow Caribbean shore.

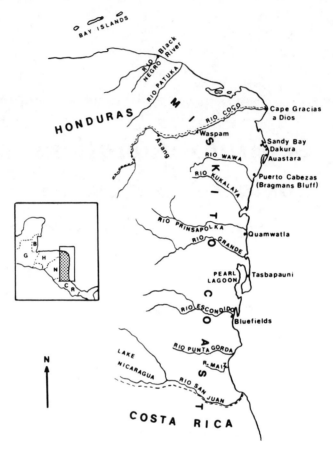

Figure 7.1. Miskito Coast place names.

At the time of European discovery the ancestral populations of both groups were differently distributed. In Panama the San Blas Archipelago was uninhabited. The native population resided on the mainland in dispersed communities situated in stretches of cultivated savannah and along the numerous rivers of the Panamanian isthmus. In eastern Nicaragua and Honduras (the Miskito Coast) riverine and savannah settlements also probably predominated. However, both in Panama and on the Miskito Coast the pre-Columbian native population utilized coastal resources, although in differing ways. Similarly, adjustments to Caribbean coastal settings by the postcontact descendants of these indigenous societies have not been identical, even though the Cuna and the Miskito shared a number of contact experiences.

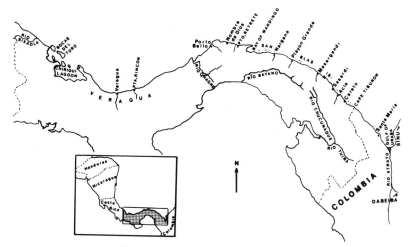

Figure 7.2. Panamanian place names.

It is my intent in this chapter briefly to compare and contrast the pre- and postcontact indigenous societies of Panama and the Miskito Coast with particular emphasis on the exploitation of that portion of the Caribbean coast which falls into their respective domains.[1] It will become apparent that coastal adaptations have developed in direct response to political or economic pressures from Europeans. Consequently, coastal associations must be studied not only in terms of local resource exploitation and settlement pattern but also within the context of larger sociopolitical milieus.

We shall also find that elements of traditional riverine adaptations have persisted over the contact centuries. Indeed, it will be argued that the coastal orientations encouraged by contact experiences have been feasible because adjacent riverine habitats have constantly permitted alternative behaviors that have ameliorated the often harsh environmental conditions characteristic of the coastal regions. Hence the coastal adaptations of the Miskito and Cuna must also be considered within a larger ecological perspective that includes interior or riverine adaptations.

Finally, the course of events detailed in the following pages indicates that coastal adaptations among the Miskito and Cuna have changed significantly over the centuries. Consequently adequate understanding of these

[1]Ancient Panamanian society also exploited Pacific shores, and some of these data will be mentioned. However, I shall emphasize the Caribbean versant of the isthmus in order to facilitate comparisons with the Miskito Coast. Furthermore, the postcontact focus of those descendants of ancient Panamanian society who escaped Hispanization has been directed toward the Caribbean.

adaptations necessitates diachronic as well as synchronic perspectives. As a corollary, this approach illustrates that great care must be exercised in extrapolating from present conditions to less adequately documented periods of the past.

Panama at the Time of Conquest

Much of the Caribbean shore of lower Central America first became known to Europeans in 1502 in the course of Christopher Columbus's fourth voyage, when the admiral's ships sailed from the Bay Islands of Honduras to a point approximately 30 miles beyond Puerto Retrete in Panama. Our initial information concerning the Panamanian lands still farther to the east derives from the *entradas* sent out by Vasco Núñez de Balboa from Santa María la Antigua, the first successful mainland Spanish colony. Spanish reports indicate that native Panamanians were organized into several dozen rank societies (chiefdoms) of modest size and complexity. Their ruling elites typically controlled an ecologically diverse territory that, in some cases, stretched from coastal (or interior) lowlands to the heights of the mountainous backbone extending the length of the isthmus. Similar regions sometimes were divided between two polities, one of which was located in the lowlands and the other in the mountains.[2]

The rugged headlands that mark the eastern Caribbean coast of Panama were divided among several chiefdoms. The coastal stretch from Cape Tiburón to Masargandi fell under the control of the *queví*, or high chief, Careta, whose *bohío* or chiefly compound was situated in the hills some 12–14 miles inland, in the Sierra del Darién. Careta's domain stretched from the summit of the *serranía* to the Caribbean, where it included at least one seaport, named Acla by the Spaniards. This port, also cited as a good turtling station (Oviedo y Valdés 1959:111), may have been under the administrative control of a brother of the *queví* and had been the site of a bitter contest between two rival elite siblings who were engaged in a bloody power struggle because "one of them desired to possess all [Andagoya 1865:9; Sauer 1966:238; see also Lothrop 1937:8]." Careta's coast is also reported to have been the sole source of brightly colored seashells which were traded

[2]The fullest account of the natives of pre-Columbian Panama at the time of conquest is provided by Gonzalo Fernández de Oviedo y Valdéz who lived at Santa María and later at the Spanish town of Panamá as a royal official (see Oviedo 1853:bk. 29, 1959). One hundred seventy years later the pirate–surgeon Lionel Wafer (1934) lived with the Cuna of eastern Panama for several months and recorded his observations. A number of secondary sources based on the accounts of Oviedo, Balboa, Andagoya, and other conquistadors are useful, too, including works by Anderson (1914), Romoli (1953), Sauer (1966), and Lothrop (1937:1–50).

into the interior and widely used as penis sheaths (Oviedo y Valdés 1853:bk. 29, p. 9; Andagoya 1865: 9; Sauer 1966:220, 259–260; Romoli 1953:93–94, 282).

The neighboring stretch of coast, approximately from Masargandi to Playon Grande (Romoli 1953:97), was part of the domain of the *quevi* Comogre, who appears to have been one of the most powerful isthmian chiefs. Comogre's large and richly decorated *bohío* was situated in the interior mountains (probably on a fork of the Río Bayano known as the Río Matumaganti). His coastal region contained one or two ports which were linked to the highland center by what seems to have been a broad, well-traveled route (Anghera 1912:I,218; Sauer 1966:253; Romoli 1953:97). Comogre's coastal ports probably were fishing sites, for fish fresh and smoked was the most important food staple according to Oviedo y Valdés (1959:29) and Ferdinand Columbus (Colón 1959:253, 254; see also Sauer 1966:244, 253). Salt apparently was not derived from the Caribbean coast in any quantity. It was obtained instead from Pacific shores and estuaries where, in contrast to the Caribbean, tremendous tides create extensive salt flats (Andagoya 1865:25; Oviedo y Valdés 1959:25; Wafer 1934:77, 104, note 1; Sauer 1966:274, 282; Lothrop 1937:16).

Both Comogre's and Careta's Caribbean ports also may have served as arrival and dispersal points for long-distance travelers and exchange goods. It is significant that Comogre's mountain *bohío* seems to have been strategically located between the headwaters of two major rivers, the Chucunaque and the Bayano (Figure 7.2). These rivers, which traverse much of eastern Panama, provide contact with Pacific lands and, via the Río Tuira, with southeastern Panama. Being so situated, Comogre's *bohío* was a collection point for scarce natural resources and valuable elite items from other regions of Panama. Balboa says that natives traveled by canoe to Comogre (probably by way of the Río Chucunaque, in Sauer's opinion) bringing pearls and gold nuggets, the latter found in large quantities in rivers of the Pacific coast. The pearls and gold were exchanged for cotton cloth and "good-looking men and women," probably war-captive slaves (Balboa, in Andagoya 1865:xii; Sauer 1966:229). It is likely that Comogre and other isthmian chiefs of comparable status were engaged in long-distance exchange with northern Colombia too. At least some of the pearls, gold grains, cotton cloth, and captives exchanged at Comogre's mountain center probably entered this exchange network. It is also likely that the easy passage connecting Comogre's *bohío* with his Caribbean port was part of the long-distance route and that the seaport itself was a way station for the ocean-going leg of such travels. Similar use may have been made of the fishing grounds near Playon Grande that fell under the control of Comogre's neighbor, Pocorosa. Pocorosa's *bohío* also was situated in the mountains near a tributary of the

Río Bayano (Romoli 1953:171), and his domain, like those of Comogre and Careta, extended across the *serranía* to a fishing harbor on the Caribbean (Anghera 1912:I, 350–351; Sauer 1966:253).

The native town of Darién (renamed Santa María by the Spaniards) is also associated with long-distance contacts. This community, the home of the *queví* of the chiefdom of Darién, was situated close to the Gulf of Urabá and to the Río Atrato, both of which give ready access to northern Colombia (Figure 7.2). Across the Gulf of Urabá on the lowlands of northern Colombia, the gold-crafting, temple-filled elite centers of Sinú were located (see Gordon 1957). In the interior mountains, readily accessible by tributaries of the Río Atrato, was another gold-crafting religious–political elite center, Dabeiba, where gold nuggets were processed into jewelry and figurines, some of which, Balboa tells us, came to Darién. Although the nature of the contacts that brought this gold to Darién is not specified, Balboa indicated generally that the Gulf of Urabá was a point of dispersal for the precious metal, saying that "all the gold that goes forth from this gulf comes from the house of the cacique Davaive [Andagoya 1865:viii]." The *queví* of coastal Darién surely played a significant role in effecting this distribution. In this context it is also noteworthy that the chiefdom of Darién, like that of Comogre, not only commanded a coastal position but also stood close to trails and waterways leading across the interior mountains to the Pacific via tributaries of the Río Tuira (Andagoya 1865:8; Anghera 1912:I, 202, 418; Casas 1927:bk 2, p. 351; Sauer 1966:228–252, 254; Trimborn 1948).

The importance of Caribbean coastal locations (particularly those conjoining important riverways or land trails) as nodes in exchange systems is also indicated by the limited evidence for a settlement of Mesoamericans at Nombre de Dios. This site stood close to the mouth of the Río Chagres, which provided ready access to Pacific regions. According to Andagoya, at this place lived a group known as Chuchures who spoke a strange language and had come by canoe from the direction of Honduras. The colony was dying off, purportedly from the effects of the climate, when Nombre de Dios was founded in 1519 (see Sauer 1966:239). A similar coastal settlement of nonisthmian peoples existed farther west, at the mouth of the Sigua (Sixaola) River in eastern Costa Rica. According to Lothrop (1942) this was also a Mesoamerican outpost which, like the settlement at Nombre de Dios, had a rather tenuous existence.

Between these two purportedly Mesoamerican settlements lay the deeply incised hills and craggy cliffs of the western Panamanian coast. This region, known to the Spaniards as Veragua, was divided into a number of chiefdoms about which we know little. However, the few data that are available, mainly from accounts of Columbus's fourth voyage, describe rich subsistence resources, including an abundance of river and ocean fish.

Certain anadromous varieties were moving upstream to spawning grounds at the time of Columbus's visit (Colón 1959:250, 253, 254). These fish were caught in great quantity and were roasted or dried "in an oven," after which they would keep "for a long time" (Colón 1959:254; see also Sauer 1966:132–133; Wafer 1934:74).

Columbus's party also found the entire coast from Almirante Bay to about Punta Rincón (that is, to the chiefdom of Cubiga) to be an area of active exchange (Colón 1959:241–244, 250, 252–253). At the islands and main shore of Almirante Bay and Chiriquí Lagoon some 80 canoes are said to have gathered about the Spanish ships as the natives exchanged their gold ornaments for hawks-bells and needles (Anderson 1914:93).[3] The accounts of the voyage also speak of "five towns of great trade [Colón 1959:243]," apparently in the chiefdom of Veragua.[4] One of these communities was the chief's residential settlement, which was situated on a river about a league and a half (that is, about 5 miles) from the sea. At this place golden plates or "mirrors" were made, probably by hammering raw metal derived from shallow pit mines located in the interior mountains (Colón 1959:252; Anderson 1914:99–100; Sauer 1966:133–134).[5] However, some of the gold pieces that the Spaniards acquired along this western coast were cast figures fashioned in various zoological forms. It is likely, in the absence of any evidence in the Spanish records for metallurgy in Panama other than hammering and *mise-en-couleur* gilding, that these cast pieces were obtained by long-distance exchange, probably with Colombia (see Sauer 1966:245–246). Almirante Bay and the "five towns of great trade" in the chiefdom of Veragua may have been contact points in this exchange system.

To summarize, in Panama at the time of conquest, Caribbean coastal lands were part of larger, ecologically diverse political units under the control of chiefs and their elite administrators. These lands contributed fish and probably other seafoods as major subsistence items. Although Spanish documents indicate that the Pacific coast also yielded pearls and salt, we find no such specializations for the more rugged Caribbean shores other than the collection of seashells along the coast of Careta. It does appear, however, that Caribbean coastal settlements (and probably also Pacific ones) may have been valuable adjuncts to chiefs' long-distance exchange activi-

[3]Elsewhere along the shore, however, the Indians brandished spears, blew horns, beat drums, and spat the juice of chewed herbs at the Europeans in an effort to dispel them before yielding to barter fish and gold ornaments for little bells (see Colón 1959:242; Anderson 1914:94,98).

[4]The use of the term *Veragua* as a name for a rank society should not be confused with the Spaniards' use of the same name to refer to this entire Caribbean section of western Panama.

[5]See the description of gold hammering in the region of Veragua as recorded in the report of Captain Diego de Sojo, who visited the region in 1587 (MacCurdy 1911:190–191).

ties, and the coastal ports probably were maintained in part to facilitate the oceangoing portion of such activity (see Helms 1977).

The Miskito Coast on the Eve of Discovery

It is difficult to reconstruct the conditions prevalent on the Miskito Coast prior to European contact. We have virtually no ethnohistoric data concerning this region until the 1630s, when records left by an ill-fated colony of Puritans on Providencia Island, some miles east of the Nicaraguan mainland, briefly describe trade with natives of Cape Gracias a Dios (Newton 1914:144–145, 166, 272–276). Our next information derives from accounts by British and French buccaneers who periodically used the isolated coast of eastern Nicaragua as a rest and rendezvous station during the last decades of the seventeenth century, when buccaneers and pirates were plundering ships and attacking settlements on the Spanish Main from Veracruz to Venezuela. The brief accounts by Esquemeling (1967, first published 1678), Lussan (1930, first published 1689), Dampier (1968, first published 1697), and the anonymous M. W. (1732) are the most useful of this genre. However, the information contained in these reports usually pertains to the Miskito Indians of Cape Gracias a Dios. This society, whose members included African and mulatto slaves and freedmen as well as local natives, emerged as a named ethnic group at this time as a direct result of European contact, and the customs and settlement pattern of this mixed population, although partly indigenous, were influenced significantly by European contact.

With these caveats in mind, a few general statements can be ventured concerning pre-Columbian conditions on the Miskito Coast. In contrast to the rank societies of Panama, the natives of eastern Nicaragua and Honduras traditionally lived as egalitarian tribesmen organized into small kinship units that also were differentiated by dialects. Approximately 10 kinship or linguistic groups can be identified in the seventeenth century (see Conzemius 1938). This population apparently lived in small settlements scattered along the gallery-forested rivers and the shores of lagoons. Women raised plantains and bananas (apparently already introduced by contact), maize, manioc, and other root crops on small plots of cleared land near river banks. Men hunted and fished for various forms of game including manatee and sea turtles (M.W. 1732; Lussan 1930:286; Dampier 1968:16, 32–33; Esquemeling 1967:250).

Esquemeling says that the Cape Gracias population (which was already mixed with Negroes; see Lussan 1930:285) was divided into two "provinces," one group cultivating the soil and apparently building shelters of some substance, the members of the other group being

> so lazy that they have not courage to build themselves huts, much less houses, to dwell in. They frequent chiefly the sea-coast, wandering disorderly up and down, without knowing or caring so much as to cover their bodies from the rain [Esquemeling 1967:250–251; Lussan 1930:287, see note 9].

M. W. indicates that these scattered coastal peoples were the contact-created, racially mixed, and newly emerging Miskito population, who preferred to settle near the sea or along lagoons in order to fish. In contrast, the "wild Indians" lived along the river banks, hunted game, avoided the Europeans, and hated the Miskito. However, in the dry season these "wild Indians" came to the coast to make salt. M. W. (1732) also reports that in the dry season the Miskito of Cape Gracias moved to nearby Sandy Key and lived on fish for a few months. Dampier (1968:16) indicates either riverine or coastal settlement that would facilitate fishing for the Miskito, although he also notes that when a couple married they first prepared a small agricultural plot or "plantation."

It is conceivable that European contact was responsible for some coastal settlements. For example, both M. W. and Lussan tell of a headman's village located at Sandy Bay, a coastal locality south of Cape Gracias, where the inhabitants conducted limited agriculture but lived mainly by fishing. Probably such coastal settlements were traditionally established for fishing advantages, but this particular community might also have been a response to the advantages of living near the Europeans, who resided at nearby Cape Gracias to the north and at Bragman's Bluff to the south. Lussan (1930:287) also implies that the Sandy Bay population had been displaced from Cape Gracias by the contact-created Miskito.[6] We read, too, of a savannah village a short distance inland from the coast inhabited by the newly appointed "Miskito king" and his relatives and other followers (M. W. 1732).[7] It is not possible to say whether savannah settlement was a traditional pattern or whether this, too, reflected contact influences.

[6]This interpretation rests on the meaning intended in the sentence "The *original inhabitants* of Moustique who entertained *these men* I have just mentioned, have settled ten or twelve leagues to windward of Cape Gracias a Dios, at places known as Sambey and Sanibey [Lussan 1930:287; my emphasis]." "These men" appears to refer to the population of Negroes and mulattoes who had settled at Cape Gracias and who had been succored by "the indians" (Lussan 1930:285). After some discussion of mulatto customs, Lussan records the movement of the "original inhabitants" to Sandy Bay. Thus I interpret these new residents of Sandy Bay to be native inhabitants of the Cape Gracias area displaced by more recently arrived Blacks.

[7]The "king" was a figurehead commissioned by the British government via the governor of Jamaica as a diplomatic ploy against the Spaniards. He had no prototype in traditional society.

It is difficult to arrive at firm conclusions regarding the nature of precontact settlement from these sources. However, I would venture to state that prior to European contact most native peoples on the Miskito Coast lived along rivers and in the savannahs that lie behind the coast proper. The seacoast was periodically visited (particularly near lagoons and river mouths) for dry-season salt-making and at periods favorable for turtling. Temporary dry-season camps set up on gravel river beaches and dry stream beds or on the seacoast are frequently reported in historical sources (Wickham 1872:213–214, 1895:208; Bell 1899:85–86, 160; Moravian Church 1849–1887, vol. 22:512; Sapper 1900:251, see note 9) and are used today by some riverine peoples to fish and enjoy a change from village life (Helms 1971:118). Thus, as in Panama, traditional coastal settlement and activities appear to have been largely adjunct to riverine-oriented habitations, the coast providing estuary and sea foods (fish, shellfish, turtle, manatee) and salt to diversify the river fish, savannah and forest game (deer, monkeys, peccaries), wild fruits, and agricultural produce obtained farther inland (see M. W. 1732).

The coast may also have been the scene of long-distance exchange activities. Roys (1943:56) notes the likelihood of a travel route extending from Maya territory along the Caribbean coast to Panama. Lothrop (1926:I, 9) mentions Torquemada's statement that a small Mesoamerican colony was located at the mouth of the San Juan River, whence gold was carried to Aztec rulers by way of Yucatan. We have no evidence, however, of the role that local populations may have played in such contacts and exchanges. Indeed it is possible that a San Juan Mesoamerican colony dealt primarily with Mesoamerican peoples in western Nicaragua, for the San Juan River offers easy access to Lake Nicaragua and Pacific lands and was frequently traveled for this convenience by Europeans.

CONSEQUENCES OF CONTACT

The European conquest of portions of lower Central America created significant changes in the distribution and cultural configurations of indigenous people. Probably among the first contact casualties were the systems of long-distance exchange. Although data are lacking, it can be assumed, in light of comparable situations elsewhere in Middle America, that after European contact Caribbean coastal ports lost their value as way stations or access points along native long-distance travel routes.

Contact experiences also forced population movements among native peoples. In Panama, for example, the focus of Spanish colonization soon shifted from the Caribbean town of Santa María to settlements on the Pacific coastal plain. The native population directly in the Spaniards' path was destroyed by overwork and disease or reduced to servitude under Spanish controls. Wherever possible, native peoples withdrew from the Hispanic territories, concentrating on the central cordilleras and on their Caribbean slopes (see Wafer 1934:89; Young 1971:51–52; Stout 1947:50). Gradually the elite stratum of native society was reduced (see Young 1971:45–46), although Wafer's description of eastern Panama some 170 years after initial European contact indicates that rank societies still endured. Particularly interesting is the buccaneer–surgeon's account of an influential chief, Lacenta, whose residence was located approximately where Comogre's domain formerly had been centered, that is, in the headwaters of the Río Bayano–Río Chucunaque, and who held a position of regional prestige similar to that of Comogre (Wafer 1934:18, 84, 96; see also Esquemeling 1967:280–281).

Colonial Impact on the Miskito Coast

By the late seventeenth century the buccaneers prowling the Spanish Main (see Bancroft 1886) had established pirate stations at various points along the isolated Caribbean mainland, including Cape Gracias a Dios, Bragman's Bluff (near the Río Wawa), and Bluefields (on Bluefields Lagoon at the mouth of the Río Escondido) in eastern Nicaragua. The buccaneers frequently enjoyed friendly relations with the native populations living in the vicinity of their stations. Among the most successful affiliations was that between the buccaneers and the population of Negroes, Indians, and mulattoes resident at Cape Gracias a Dios. This mixed group (identified as Zamboes or as Miskito Indians) assisted the pirates in various ways. Women provided domestic services to buccaneers ashore, and men accompanied them to sea as provisioners of fish, turtle, and manatee. Indeed, the Miskito men's skill in fishing and turtling and their ability as seamen put them in great demand among the buccaneers. Miskito men also guided pirate parties by land, up the numerous rivers leading inland from the Caribbean, to attack Spanish frontier settlements in the interior of Central America. In return the Miskito Indians received European manufactured goods, including guns and ammunition (Esquemeling 1967:249–250, 255, 341; Dampier 1968:15–16; Floyd 1967: chap 3; Helms 1971:15).

With these weapons the Miskito of Cape Gracias expanded their own range of influence and territorial control, driving other native peoples away from the lower river basins and the coast proper. These latter groups, now known by the collective term "Sumu," restricted their settlements to the middle and upper reaches of the river systems (Conzemius 1938; Anonymous 1885:422–423; Roberts 1827; Wickham 1895; Bell 1862, 1899). By the late eighteenth century, small settlements of Miskito appeared near the mouths of most of the major rivers of the Miskito Coast including the Río Coco (Cape Gracias), Río Wawa (Bragman's Bluff), Río Kukalaya, Río Prinsapolka (or Walpasiksa), Río Grande, Pearl Lagoon, Río Escondido (Bluefields), Río Punta Gorda, and Río San Juan. The Miskito also expanded along the coast of eastern Honduras from the Río Coco to the Río Patuca and the Río Negro (see Roberts 1827).

Concurrently an influx of English-speaking logwood cutters, sugar-plantation developers, cattle raisers, smugglers, and trading-post agents followed on the heels of the buccaneers, attesting to Britain's continued interest in the Miskito Coast. Bluefields, Cape Gracias, and Black River (at the Río Negro in eastern Honduras) became the largest European centers, with a mixed population of European, Indian, and Black residents. Numerous smaller European settlements sprang up elsewhere along the shore, where Englishmen "moved by the hundreds, putting up huts at virtually every cove and river mouth" between Cape Cameron in eastern Honduras and the Maiz river (south of Punta Gorda) in eastern Nicaragua (Floyd 1967:63). As these European colonists spread out, they were increasingly accompanied by Miskito who frequently established their settlements adjacent to those of the English (see Roberts 1827).

Although continuing their traditional subsistence occupations of horticulture, hunting, and fishing, the Miskito also exploited their association with the British by working as laborers (for example, as mahogany cutters or as suppliers of fish to European settlements) or as trade middlemen. In the latter role the Miskito encouraged (by force if necessary) the up-river Sumu to exchange forest resources, including rough-hewn dugout canoes and paddles, india rubber, sarsaparilla, game, and bark cloth for coastal foods (particularly turtle meat, turtle oil, and salt) and for European goods which the Miskito obtained from the traders. With the traders they exchanged Sumu goods and their own coastal products (such as tortoiseshell and deerskins) as well as craft goods (finished dugouts and paddles) which they prepared themselves (see Helms 1969). The Miskito also periodically raided interior settlements of Central America for captives, some of whom they sold as slaves to foreign vessels or to British colonists (Anonymous 1885: 422; Floyd 1967: chap. 5; Helms 1969, 1971:16–23).

The development of the Miskito as a distinct ethnic group after the late seventeenth century, the establishment of European settlements and trading posts at river mouth locations in succeeding decades, the spread of Miskito settlement in association with European communities, and the close cooperation of Miskito men with these Europeans initiated new native coastal adaptations, many of which, however, can be understood as variations on traditional themes. For example, certain traditional coastal resources probably were now exploited more intensely for foreign exchange. Although green sea turtle continued to be important as a subsistence item, as it probably had been for centuries, green turtle meat now provisioned foreigners, too. Hawksbill sea turtles, less desirable as food, now were avidly sought for their shells, which were valued in Europe. Since 2 months of successful turtling could yield enough shell to barter for goods to support a family for the greater part of a year (Moravian Church 1849–1887, vol. 22:243), Miskito men readily made annual trips to hawksbill nesting sites near Bluefields and on the beaches of Costa Rica, leaving children, women, and the elderly to fend for themselves for several months (Conzemius 1932:39; Roberts 1827:93–94, 101; Wickham 1872:278; Bell 1899:27, 40, 274, 276; Nietschmann 1973:34–39). Other coastal and savannah game, particularly manatee and deer, were probably hunted more vigorously to supply expanded subsistence (manatee) and exchange (deerskins) needs (see Roberts 1827:97–98, 127–128).

In like fashion, the newly emergent position of the Miskito as middlemen between foreign traders and interior natives may be interpreted as a readjustment of traditional coast–interior associations to fit new circumstances. In one sense, the Miskito simply gained more or less of a monopoly as middlemen over the ancient movement of coastal products to the interior, which in precontact times had been handled individually by the several kinship–linguistic groups inhabiting the various river systems of the territory. In the past, these small groups traveled their riverways availing themselves of coastal, estuary, and ocean resources as weather permitted and need required. Now most of these local river groups were encouraged to remain on the upper sections of the waterways, where they lived in small communities of two or three longhouses scattered at intervals on high banks along the rivers (Wickham 1869, 1872:213–214; Bell 1899:122; Moravian Church 1849–1887, vol. 27:253). The emerging Miskito established coastal and lower river settlements and assumed control of products available on the coast, both European trade goods and sea and estuary resources (see Wickham 1869; 1895).

The Miskito handled their middlemen roles in various ways. Sometimes, for example, they conducted their inland trade by traveling to Sumu villages. At other times, it appears, barter via "silent trade" occurred. In this context Bell (1899:266–267) describes how "river Indians" would plant a peeled and painted stick in a conspicuous position at the mouth of a tributary stream to attract the attention of "coast Indians" passing on the main river. Nearby, bunches of plantains, baskets of maize, and rolls of bark cloth and skins were tied to trees with a sample of the desired exchange item (for example, a fishhook, a few beads, a pinch of salt) attached to each article. After a while, however, if the bundles had not been touched, the "river Indians" would personally bring the articles to the coast for barter with Miskito villagers. Bell also notes (1899:127) that some groups of Sumu undertook annual trips to the coast to pay "tribute" in kind to the Miskito "king" and to barter canoes, india rubber, skins, cacao, and maize for hardware, cloth, beads, and salt from the "coastal Indians." Sometimes families of upriver Sumu came to the coast during the dry season for 8 to 10 days of salt-making (by the women) and settling of debts with Miskito traders (Martin 1894).[8]

Coastal settlement sometimes posed problems for the Miskito. Although fishing, turtling, and hunting savannah game were well rewarded, the sands and gravels of the coast and savannah made agriculture difficult (except for the cultivation of manioc), and observers frequently comment on the insufficiency of agricultural foods for coastal dwellers (Anonymous 1885:424; Porta Costas 1908; Roberts 1827:115, 127–128, 150–151; Bell 1899:274; Moravian Church 1849–1887: passim; see also Parsons 1955). Necessary horticultural produce and forest resources (for the Miskito could not live on fish, turtle, and deer alone) had to be acquired either by trade with interior natives (Roberts 1827:142, 150, 152) or by lengthy trips of several days to agricultural plots located (as in precontact times) upriver on the banks of streams (Roberts 1827:114, 115; Porta Costas 1908:262, 266; Moravian Church 1849–1887, vol. 31:509; but see Nietschmann 1973:130–138 regarding coastal agriculture). European traders and, after 1849, stores run by Moravian missionaries provided some foodstuffs, especially during periods of tropical storms and hurricanes. These spells of bad weather periodically flood extensive sections of the coastal lowlands, damage housing, and destroy fields (Moravian Church 1849–1887: passim; Porta Costas 1908:263–264; Bell 1862, 1899:297; see Nietschmann 1973:74–77 for a compilation of severe storms on the Miskito Coast since 1865).

Residential mobility also ameliorated these problems of food and weather, a pattern that accords generally with the riverine–coastal movements I have postulated as typical of precontact settlement. According to one late eighteenth-century source,

> during the season of fishing for Turtle the Mosquito Men, as they are generally called, dwell upon the Sea Coast; that is, from the beginning of May to the end of

[8]After the middle of the nineteenth century, when a mission program was initiated by the Moravian church, small groups of Sumu visited certain of the Moravian coastal trade and mission stations twice a year or so to exchange india rubber for European goods (Moravian Church 1849–1887, vol. 31:159–160, vol. 24:517, 1890–1956, vol. 1:434). The Moravians at this time frequently operated small trading stations at their missions to attract natives and to augment their own incomes. The missionaries also planted banana groves, dry rice, and other provisions for their own use and to assist natives in times of need (Moravian Church 1849–1887: passim; Helms 1971:22–23).

September, When they retire a considerable distance up the river and Lagoons, thinking themselves safer there from Floods and Gales of Wind; there they continue until the return of the Turtle season, shifting their abode According as they are led by the game and fruits in season [Anonymous 1885:419–420].

Similarly Brother Feurig, a Moravian missionary stationed in Bluefields, reported in 1858 that "the Indians erect small huts of bamboo covered with leaves, on the sea-shore for their abode during the dry season. But when the rains set in, they retire to somewhat more substantial dwellings, further up the river [Moravian Church 1849–1887, vol. 22:512]."[9] During the dry season, however, the able-bodied men usually were absent from their families for several weeks or months. At such times, Bell (1899:85–86) says, with reference to the settlement of Quamwatla (close to the mouth of the Río Prinzapolka), that women continued a mobile pattern by visiting neighbors or camping on the beach for a month or so making salt. The Moravian missionaries also complained bitterly about the "customary instability" of the coastal natives, for their teaching efforts were hindered by the frequency with which people tended to move about (Moravian Church 1849–1887, vol. 20:381, vol. 22:349, vol. 27:196, vol. 31:58; Hamilton 1901:141). According to their reports, population movement was attributable not only to turtling, to the weather, or to salt-making, but also to the belief that when a sudden death occurred in a village it was due to the malevolence of someone who had "buried poison" in the vicinity. The danger of buried poison could be avoided by abandonment of the settlement for at least a season and sometimes longer (see Moravian Church 1890–1956, vol. 1:90, 200, vol. 9:417).

For the furtherance of their work the missionaries were anxious to reduce population mobility and to encourage more permanent communities around the mission stations (see Moravian Church 1849–1887, vol. 22:347). In their opinion the establishment of a mission station and (especially) trade center did lead to somewhat more permanent coastal settlements and perhaps somewhat larger ones, for "the people like to build their houses near [the missions] (Moravian Church 1849–1887, vol. 27:34, 46, 196, vol. 28:53, 281, 282, vol. 32:576, vol. 33:175, 1903–1954, vol. 9:222)." It is somewhat difficult to know to what extent coastal villages did actually expand in size and permanence due to mission influence. Alexander Cotheal, who visited the coast sometime prior to 1848 (that is, prior to the

[9]This description continues: "In the morning the men go to fish, or fetch plantains from their provision ground, while the rest of the day is spent idly in their hammocks. All remaining work is performed by the women." This description of the division of labor at dry-season coastal camps seems to fit Esquemeling's description of the "lazy" coastal Indians some 175 years earlier. See page 129.

Moravians), comments that villages might contain a dozen or more huts. As a rough estimate, based on indications that a nuclear family tended to have its own residence, we can assume that a village with a dozen or more huts might have contained 75–100 persons. The few specific references to village size found in the reports of missionaries and other visitors to the coast during the latter half of the nineteenth century allow the generalization that by 1890, after half a century of missionary work, the average (coastal) village was composed of 10 to 20 houses with approximately 75–200 inhabitants (see Moravian Church 1890–1956, vol. 1:200, 400, 431, 1849–1887, vol. 25:183, vol. 28:281, vol. 33:175; Nicol 1898).[10]

It is likely, however, that the total number of coastal Miskito villages gradually grew during the contact centuries as population tended to cluster about the various trade stations and near the 10 to 12 mission stations that were established between 1849 and 1900[11] and as the Miskito population gradually grew in absolute numbers from perhaps 1000 persons in 1699 to around 5000–7500 in 1899 (see Nietschmann 1973:34). However, some of this population was expanding inland along the Río Coco.

The Cuna in the Colonial Era

The early stages of Miskito–European contacts were mirrored in Caribbean Panama. Once again buccaneers sought shelter, provisions, and rendezvous points in isolated ports at Boca del Toro (Almirante Bay) and on islands of the San Blas Archipelago as they plotted attacks on the Spanish isthmian settlements. Once again the pirates were frequently assisted in their depredations against the Spanish by native peoples, particularly by the residents of eastern Panama whom we can now identify as the Cuna (Wafer 1934:xviii–xix; Dampier 1968:8, 18–26, 129–130; Esquemeling 1967: 276–284; Wassen 1940:99–101, 113; Stout 1947:51; Bancroft 1886:519–524, 547).[12]

[10]Two exceptions to this statement must be noted. In the late nineteenth century, Auastara was reported to have 200–300 inhabitants, and Dakura, a mission station, held 300–400 persons (Siebörger 1890:41, 46). Regional administration centers such as Cape Gracias and Bluefields also were considerably larger. At the end of the nineteenth century, Cape Gracias included some 50 Miskito homes with perhaps 250–500 inhabitants in addition to the white population, while Bluefields contained 600–700 people (Moravian Church 1890–1956, vol. 3:46; Bell 1899:292; Moravian Church 1849–1887, vol. 23:208; Hamilton 1901:129).

[11]Until the turn of the twentieth century the Moravians concentrated solely on the coastal population of Nicaragua. About 1900 they began to extend their mission activities up the Río Coco and then into Honduras.

[12]In the territory of Veragua, on the Caribbean side of western Panama, the buccaneers were less successful in maintaining resource stations and in obtaining the assistance of the native Guaymí; see Dampier (1968:35).

Unlike the Miskito Coast inhabitants, however, the Cuna did not inter-mix with Negroes, although the mountains of eastern Panama, like Mosquitia, were a refuge for escaped slaves (see Stout 1947:50). Nor did the Caribbean shores of Panama become the site of permanent European settle-ments, trading posts, or mission stations (but see Roberts 1827:36–37, 50–51), although a few hardy settlers ventured briefly onto the islands of Bocas del Toro, and two colonies, one of Scots and the other of French settlers, were temporarily established on the San Blas Coast (see Bancroft 1886:570–579; Prebble 1968; Howe 1974:19–20). Nonetheless, during the eighteenth century the Cuna, like the Miskito, attacked frontier towns and gold mines settled by the Spaniards (see Bancroft 1886:581; Wassén 1940). Open Spanish–Cuna hostilities virtually ceased by 1800, however, as piracy waned and both Spain and England lost interest in the coast. Thus, by the turn of the nineteenth century, the Caribbean versant of Panama had be-come a peaceful hinterland.

The reduction of hostilities encouraged greater trade, particularly with North American ships that visited the San Blas Coast and with traders sailing from Cartagena, Caraçao, Jamaica, and Porta Bello (see Stout 1947:72–73). Orlando Roberts, a British trading agent who visited the coast of Panama in 1816–1817, gives a rare account of the nature of this exchange, which was conducted mainly on islands of the San Blas Archipelago. He notes, first, that the natives disliked strangers, "refusing to allow Europeans to settle on the mainland. Their trading intercourse is always carried on at one of the numerous kays or islands on the coast, selected at the time for that purpose [Roberts 1827:44]." On this particular trading trip, Roberts first stopped at one of the small keys off the entrance of the Bay of Mandingo and was investigated by two natives who recommended that he proceed to a specified harbor at Playon Grande. Roberts proceeded in that direction.

> In the evening, we came to an anchor off the river Daablo [Nargana]; and, according to custom, fired a gun as a signal to the Indians, whose chief settle-ments are situated on the banks of the rivers, a considerable way up from the sea . . . . On hearing this signal, canoes are immediately despatched, for the pur-pose of ascertaining the object of such a visit. Sometimes they arrive the same evening, but at all times not later than the next morning [Roberts 1827:35].

By the next morning quite a few Indians had arrived and suggested that Roberts take his brig to Needle Key, where he was shortly visited by chiefs and a shaman–priest. Several natives quickly erected a temporary shelter so that the trade goods could be displayed to better advantage. During the next 2 or 3 days, trade goods were arranged while the natives went off to collect stores of dye wood (fustic) which they had prepared. Shortly, natives with loads of wood began to arrive "from all parts of the coast," and bartering commenced (see Roberts 1827:35–36).

These contacts by sea also facilitated and encouraged ocean travel by Cuna men. A century earlier, during the decades of buccaneering, a number of Cuna men, like the Miskito, had sailed with the pirates. The peaceful trade conditions of the nineteenth century saw a continuation of this seafaring practice.

> By the middle of the 19th century some had sailed to Jamaica and the United States. Often they remained in foreign cities for many years before returning to the islands and some were educated by English and American ship captains [Stout 1947:57].

The seventeenth and eighteenth centuries also saw the gradual but persistent retreat of the indigenous inhabitants of the Pacific side of eastern Panama away from Spanish contacts onto the mountain fastnesses of the Río Bayano and Río Chucunaque headwaters (also the mountainous interior of the Río Tuira basin) and onto the Caribbean versant. These were the regions that chiefs of great reknown and influence, such as Comogre and Lacenta, had previously ruled.[13] The best determination from the rather sparse data indicates that most of this population continued to favor settlement along riverways some distance inland from the Caribbean (see Roberts quoted above; also Wassén 1940:106). It is likely, however, that the Cuna also exploited the Caribbean coast during this period. Wassén has collected population statistics "for the coast" from Spanish documents dated 1757 which indicate the number of families resident on some 14 rivers of the Caribbean slopes of eastern Panama. It is not clear, however, whether these population clusters were situated along the interior banks of the rivers or close to the coast proper.[14] A later source dating from the end of the eighteenth century notes that the Cuna who had fled from the South Sea to the area of the Gulf of Darién (Urabá) inhabited the river banks, "none living on the coast of the sea," and that those "who live along the same river consider themselves as of the same people, being distinguished according to the names of the rivers [Wassén 1949:24]."

In 1816 the trader Roberts, after completing his barter on Needle Key, took another short excursion along the coast and recorded native settlements on the banks of the "river Banana," at the "river Mosquito" (where appar-

---

[13]The approximate number of families in these locales is given in a publication dated 1741 and reviewed in Wassén (1949:22–23). At this time, over half of the population were said to be resident in the Río Bayano, Río Chucunaque, and Río Tuira regions combined, and under half the families were said to be residing on the "rios y quebradas de las bandas del Norte."

[14]These population clusters ranged in size in interesting increments from 3 or 4 families to 7–8, 10, 12, 15, 20, or 40 families. The size of a "family" is difficult to ascertain, but Wassén presents data from a 1741 source suggesting between 10 and 16 persons, although he feels 8 might be more appropriate (1949:23). The largest settlement of the region, one with 40 families, was located on the Acla river in association with a regional chief.

ently a trader lived some or all of the time), at "Sarsadee" (Sasardi), and at Careta (Roberts 1827:36–37, 50). Whether these settlements, most of which appear to have been at, or close to, river mouths, were temporary or permanent is hard to determine. Roberts mentions rather cryptically that the Indians at the Mosquito river settlement, being favorably inclined toward the British, had adopted the British flag, which they hoisted every morning regularly "from the month of April to October, which is the fishing season [1827:37]." Conceivably this was also the season when this coastal settlement was populated. It is also possible that the interest of British traders in bartering for tortoiseshell (supplies of which Roberts sought and found at the Banana River settlement, at the Mosquito River settlement, and at Sasardi) contributed to the maintenance of these coastal settlements during "fishing season" months, which also correspond to the hawksbill nesting season, when gravid females come to island and mainland beaches and can easily be captured (see Stier 1976:45 for information on sea turtles and turtling in eastern Panama). Yet Roberts (1827:37) also appreciatively describes the rich agricultural resources of the region and comments on the "abundance of plantains, bananas, maize, cassava" and other provisions raised by the natives of Sasardi, where, in addition, "abundance of the finest green turtle are caught close to the settlement." Thus Sasardi may have been a permanent settlement.

To a limited extent such coastal or lower-river Cuna also served as middlemen between European traders and those Cuna remaining in the mountainous interior, for they "trad[ed] cloth, beads, and domestic utensils for ivory nuts, cacao and rubber which the mountain Cuna brought to them at infrequent intervals [Stout 1947:72]." In this role the coastal or lower-river Cuna of eastern Panama resemble the Miskito of Nicaragua during the colonial era. However, this similarity and others that have been mentioned above were very limited. The Cuna of the Caribbean versant were themselves in retreat from Spanish contact and did not exercise political superiority over their confreres in the mountain headwater regions. The Miskito, in contrast, were not retreating from contact but were enjoying an expansion of territorial range and a growth of political influence as a direct result of colonial-era contact. As part of this process they did establish superior political status over the interior Sumu. In addition, the Miskito, whose numerous coastal settlements frequently adjoined those of the Europeans, seem to have had much closer and more constant ties with the foreigners than did the Cuna, since there were no permanent European colonists, missionaries, or traders in eastern Panama.

On the other hand, both the Cuna of the Caribbean versant and the Miskito appear to have frequently settled on the lower reaches of rivers rather than on the coast proper, although the Miskito did attempt to reside on the coast if it would yield contact benefits, and at least a few Cuna did the same. For the Cuna this decision was probably conditioned in large measure by the rugged character of the coast, which severely limits the amount of territory suitable for residence. The coastal plain of the Miskito Coast was of limited agricultural potential and was exposed to damaging storms. The Miskito, and probably also the Cuna, preferred riverine settlements for their access to interior agricultural grounds. In this respect it should be reemphasized that agriculture provided an important part of the subsistence diet of both groups, even though the skills of both Cuna and Miskito men as hunters and as fishermen are clearly recorded by European observers.

Finally, among both groups during the colonial centuries, significant change occurred in relationships between interior and coast. On the Miskito Coast, where it appears that riverine populations traditionally moved back and forth from coast to interior, the emergent Miskito Indians usurped most coastal contacts, resulting in a postcontact division between coastal–lower river inhabitants (Miskito) and upper river–mountain dwellers (Sumu). In Eastern Panama, where many pre-Columbian chiefdoms had been centered politically in the interior mountains, the Cuna now had begun to focus their settlements and activities more strongly on the Caribbean versant with respect to which the former mountain heartland gradually became an interior hinterland.

CONTEMPORARY ADAPTATIONS

The Cuna as Island-Dwellers

This process of Caribbean settlement accelerated during the second half of the nineteenth century when the Cuna population began a gradual migration onto the islands of the San Blas Archipelago.[15] The Archipelago contains some 360 small coral islets which rise a few feet above high-water level and stand a few 100 yards to a mile offshore. Today Cuna communities have been established on more than 50 of these islands.

In the absence of any data to the contrary, it can be assumed that these

[15]The Guaymí Indians of western Panama apparently favored residence on the rivers and in the interior mountains of the Caribbean versant of the isthmus, with the Valle Miranda or Valle del Guaymí as the focal region of their territory. They also inhabited the territory bordering Chiriqui Lagoon but did not extend to the islands, which were peopled by Talamancan Indians from neighboring regions of Costa Rica. This territory around Chiriquí Lagoon was then taken over by commercial banana companies for plantations, and the Guaymí retreated into the hills. Orlando Roberts spent several months with Guaymí families in the interior and provides a glimpse at the situation in the early nineteenth century (1827:83–89, 54–57, 69, 73). Pinart summarizes Guaymí ethnography in the late nineteenth century (1887:33–41).

islands were not usually inhabited by the native population during the pre-Columbian and colonial centuries, although they may have been visited during hunting and fishing expeditions (see Wassén 1949:23, 25). In the eighteenth century they are described as covered with trees—firs, palms, date, and citrus—all growing wild in the sandy soil; brush and mangrove swamps also might have been mentioned (Wassén 1940:140; Howe 1975:3). I have already noted how these sand and coral outcroppings served as rendezvous points for European buccaneers and traders after contact. It is probably accurate to say that it was on these islands that the native population experienced most of their more pleasant associations with Europeans during the seventeenth, eighteenth, and early nineteenth centuries.

By mid-nineteenth century, Cuna population movement to the islands had begun; it continued gradually during the latter half of that century (Stout 1947:54; Pinart 1887:51–52). In one sense, this movement can be seen as a continuation of the colonial-era coalescence of population on the Caribbean versant. As island populations grew, the Cuna villages in the mountain headwaters of the Bayano and Chucunaque rivers (and also on the Río Tuira) became progressively smaller until today their combined population totals only about 1400–1500 out of a total Cuna population of some 25,000 persons (see Howe 1974:3–5, 29).

The island move may also reflect, in part, the continued attraction of the islands as centers for profitable European contact, for they were particularly suitable for commercial coconut production. During the latter half of the nineteenth century, coconuts were becoming a major cash crop for the Cuna, as they are today. According to one source (McKim 1947:26), as the islands were gradually planted in coconuts, temporary shelters built there became permanent until entire villages had been established on some islands; other islands were turned entirely into coconut plantations (see Howe 1974:33). Ethnographic sources also mention the more salubrious living conditions on the islands, which are said to offer comparative freedom from mosquitos and other insect pests and parasites and therefore are less conducive to malaria and other illnesses that can plague mainland settlements (Howe, personal communication; see Stier 1976:59–61).[16]

Although the Cuna are now primarily an island-dwelling people, their traditional mainland, and especially riverine, focus has been maintained in many ways. Since some of the offshore islands completely lack fresh water, others supplying only brackish well water, water for drinking and cooking—and also firewood—must be procured from the mainland. Al-

---

[16]Also encouraging this island move were increasing encroachments from non-Cuna rubber collectors, turtlers, banana growers, and squatters moving into the Caribbean domain (Howe 1974:22–23). Thus the Cuna preference for the islands can also be interpreted as an attempt to continue to live apart from non-Cuna peoples.

though marine fish, including several varieties of sea turtle, are the major source of protein today, a number of subsistence staples including plantains and bananas, root crops, maize, and a variety of tree crops are grown on agricultural plots located on the mainland (see Howe 1974:33–34; Howe 1975a; Howe and Sherzer 1975).[17] Consequently, each morning men and women travel the few hundred yards separating their island homes from the mainland shore, heading for the particular mainland river with which their village is specifically associated. Here the women do the daily washing, bathe, and obtain fresh water while the men continue up the waterway or walk along the coast to their agricultural plots (see McKim 1947:46–49; Howe and Sherzer 1975; Stier 1976; Howe 1975a for fuller descriptions of all these activities).

Rivers also are accorded important symbolic significance by the Cuna. For example, many villages still take their names from their associated rivers (compare the historic custom mentioned above), and family or community burial grounds are situated by the river associated with a given island community (Howe 1976:162, note 8). The village as polity is metaphorically identified with (among other things) a river, too. Chiefs frequently allude metonymically to villages as rivers in admonishments, and the leadership of the community is metaphorically associated with rivers. To give one example, the action of a chief in "cleansing" the village of the "debris" (quarrels) that "soil" the social unity is likened to a river in active flood in the rainy season which scours clean the debris that has accumulated and "soiled" the riverbed during the dry season (see Howe 1975b:31–32).

Although most of the Cuna population is now resident on the islands, nine settlements are located on the mainland coast (two more lie a few miles inland on the Mandingo River) (see Howe 1974:3; Wassén 1949:71ff.). These communities are very small compared to the island settlements and have been difficult to maintain; each has a history of repeated problems (e.g., disease), abandoment, and efforts at resettlement. Significantly, most of these small settlements are located at sections of the coast lacking offshore islands and where coconut plantations have been established only on the mainland (Howe, personal communication).

The Miskito on Coast and Rivers

The coastal and lower-river settlement pattern that the Miskito gradually adopted during the first 200 years of European contact has continued into

---

[17]Note that reliance on marine fish is not entirely a new phenomenon since riverine and marine fish have traditionally been a major subsistence staple. River fish, however, now contribute less to the diet than do marine fish, although when bad weather precludes ocean fishing, upriver fishing is still practiced.

the twentieth century. Indeed, the Miskito villages that today dot the coastline from Pearl Lagoon to Plaplaya in Honduras appear to be firmly established. Under missionary influence (see Mueller 1932:137–138) shelters that traditionally were constructed of four or six support posts roofed with thatch have become fairly substantial houses built of lumber and/or bamboo slats with outside walls and interior partitions dividing the dwelling into several rooms and a porch. The house, now floored with wood or bamboo, is raised on pilings several feet above the ground. In many communities several rows of such homes create orderly streets. These substantial villages have also grown in population, and most coastal settlements now contain from 200–300 or even close to 500 persons (see Nietschmann 1972: fig. lb).[18]

This impression of fixed coastal settlement is, however, somewhat illusory. The Miskito are still a highly mobile people, and although their dwellings are more substantially and permanently constructed than in pre-mission days, a sizable segment of the population still moves about when possible or necessary. The major condition directing these moves is still the force of Western contact, which has entered a new phase since the late nineteenth century. Over approximately the last 100 years the Miskito Coast has witnessed a series of speculative "boom and bust" economic cycles based on North American and European exploitation of a number of tropical products including india rubber, mahogany lumber, bananas, gold, pine lumber, and, most recently, green sea turtles (see Parsons 1955; Helms 1971:chap. 1; Nietschmann 1973). These business ventures have provided wage labor jobs for Miskito men and have increased significantly the scope of the cash economy on the coast.

Over the last century, when work has been available most of the able-bodied men of many Miskito villages have once again left their homes for periods ranging from several weeks to several years. They have taken jobs as freight canoe paddlers (before the advent of motorboats and airplanes), as laborers in interior gold mines, as lumbermen, as rubber collectors, or as banana plantation laborers (see Moravian Church 1890-1956, vol. 8:54, vol. 11:266–267, vol. 6:671, 1903–1954, vol. 1:101, vol. 13:114–115; Sapper 1900:250; Helms 1971:150–152). When such jobs are available, subsistence hunting and fishing may be reduced significantly, with women and children conducting only a minimum of agricultural work, preferring the much easier task of buying food and other household and personal goods with the cash—or the credit—obtained by their men (see Helms 1971:113–114; Nietschmann 1973:188–193). Periodically, however, the foreign enterprises have petered out. At such times Miskito families,

---

[18]Tasbapauni, the largest Miskito community, now has more than 1000 Miskito residents.

lacking cash for essential purchases, have had to depend more heavily on agriculture, hunting, and fishing for subsistence (see Helms 1971:chap. 4). During these periods of depression in the cash economy, people may leave their coastal villages for a while to facilitate hunting and agricultural activities in the interior (Moravian Church 1890–1956, vol. 13:250).[19]

Nonetheless, coastal villages remain the primary homesites, largely because of the more permanent nature of housing today and because of the continued functioning of stores and mission stations in coastal or lower-river communities. The proximity of Miskito coastal villages to the coastal administrative centers of Bluefields, Puerto Cabezas (which originated as a lumber and banana port in the 1920s), and Waspam (largely replacing Cape Gracias as the administrative center of the low Río Coco and northern coast region) has also encouraged their continued viability. The recent (1969) appearance of foreign-owned turtle exporting companies has also given new impetus to certain coastal communities and has placed new emphasis on the coastal Miskitos' traditional expertise as turtlers and skilled oceanfarers (Nietschmann 1972, 1973:199–200). Green sea turtles are endangered, however, and this current wage labor fishing boom will not continue indefinitely. When the turtle boom turns to bust it can be predicted that the coastal Miskito will be forced to rely once more on traditional subsistence activities, including inland agriculture, for their livelihood.

Indeed, this inland, riverine focus may be already increasing. During the twentieth century the Miskito population has gradually expanded along the larger riverways, most significantly along the Río Coco. In fact, Miskito settlements have been expanding along this river since the early eighteenth century, and 14,000–15,000 of the approximately 35,000–40,000 Miskito currently resident in Nicaragua live along its banks today (Nietschmann 1972:44). But riverine moves are also occurring on a smaller scale along a number of other rivers (the Wawa, Kukalaya, Prinsapolka, Grande; see Nietschmann 1969). Continued population increase seems to be one of the major factors behind this expansion. It can also be understood as part of the riverine focus that the Miskito have always maintained. The native peoples of the coast traditionally were riverine people, and the contact-generated

[19]The considerable rearrangement of subsistence and cash activities during economic boom and in times of bust absolutely necessitates a diachronic approach in the study of the contemporary Miskito. Field work observations and other synchronic accounts made during *either* boom conditions *or* during depressions record only part of the adaptive process. To date, we have two comprehensive studies of Miskito communities, one dealing with a riverine village in depression conditions (Helms 1971), the other with a coastal community in partial economic recovery (Nietschmann 1973). The two together offer a fairly broad picture of adaptive circumstances; either alone presents only a partial picture of adaptive alternatives.

coastal and lower-river settlements characteristic of the Miskito during the last 250–300 years can be interpreted as a specialized response within the flexible range of adaptations open to river people who traditionally included the coast within their habitat range. However, the growing press of people on all forms of local resources, and particularly the limited agricultural potential of the coast proper, has encouraged some Miskito to intensify their traditional riverine orientation.

CONCLUSION

This chapter has focused on the coastal orientations of the Miskito and the Cuna in very general terms, ignoring the local variations in ecological adaptation that in fact exist among both groups. This approach was used to facilitate cross-cultural comparison and to highlight the fact that, regardless of local variations in ecological adaptation, the nature of the coastal associations developed by both groups must be viewed not only in terms of resource exploitation but also within the context of larger sociopolitical milieus. In addition, both economic and sociopolitical perspectives require a diachronic approach if the nature and degree of coastal orientation is to be adequately assessed.

In Panama the Caribbean coast proper has not been a focus of settlement at any time. Prior to European contact it was ancillary to interior, mountain-centered chiefdoms. Today, after centuries of defensive movement away from Pacific and mountain regions toward the Caribbean coast—movement conditioned directly by European conquest—the population has gone beyond the coast proper to offshore islands. In pre-Columbian times the coast was a way station connecting interior centers to marine products and long-distance contacts. Today it is a way station linking island centers to mainland agricultural and domestic resources. In Nicaragua the Miskito coastal focus of the last 300 years is again that of a middle ground between interior forest, riverine, and agricultural products and marine resources, some of which have been channeled toward the Euroamerican pirates, settlers, missionaries, and entrepreneurs whose presence has been the major catalyst in the development of a coastal population. Both the Cuna and the Miskito, in fact, have been basically riverine-oriented people who have always expanded their adaptive strategies to include coastal and marine resources. After European contact this ecological flexibility allowed both groups to effect successful readjustments to contact conditions by emphasizing coastal options and positions, and thus to continue a viable existence within a European–American-dominated world.

REFERENCES

Andagoya, Pascual de
  1865   *Narrative of the proceedings of Pedrarias Davila.* Clements R. Markham, trans.
          London: The Hakluyt Society. [Original: Relación de los sucesos de Pedrarias Dávila
          . . . In *Colección de los viages y descubrimientos* . . . Sec. 3. Madrid: Martin
          Fernández de Navarrete. 1825–1837.]
Anderson, C. L. G.
  1914   *Old Panama and Castilla del Oro.* Boston: The Page Company.
Anghera, Peter Martyr d'
  1912   *De orbe novo. The eight decades of Peter Martyr D'Anghera* (2 vols.). Francis
          Augustus MacNutt, trans. New York: G. P. Putnam's Sons. [Original: *Décadas del
          nuevo mundo.* . . Between 1493 and 1525. Many editions.]
Anonymous
  1885   Report on the Mosquito territory. The Kemble Papers, Vol. 2, 1780–1781. *Collections
          of the New York Historical Society for the Year 1884.* New York: New York Historical
          Society. Pp. 419–431.
Bancroft, Hubert H.
  1886   History of Central America, Vol. 2, 1530–1800. In *The works of Hubert Howe
          Bancroft,* Vol. 7. San Francisco: The History Company.
Bell, Charles N.
  1862   Remarks on the Mosquito territory, its climate, people, production, etc. *Journal of the
          Royal Geographical Society* **32:**242–268.
  1899   *Tangweera: Life and adventures among gentle savages.* London: E. Arnold.
Casas, Bartolomé de las
  1927   *Historia de las Indias,* edited by M. Aguilar, Madrid.
Colón, Fernando
  1959   *The life of the Admiral Christopher Columbus by his son, Ferdinand.* Benjamin Keen,
          trans. New Brunswick, New Jersey: Rutgers Univ. Press. [Original: *Historie del S.D.
          Fernando Colombo,* Venice, 1571]
Conzemius, Eduard
  1932   *Ethnographical survey of the Miskito and Sumu Indians of Honduras and Nicaragua.*
          Bureau of American Ethnology. Bulletin 106. Washington, D. C.: Smithsonian Institu-
          tion.
  1938   Les Tribus Indiennes de la Côte des Mosquitos. *Anthropos* **33:**910–943.
Cotheal, Alexander I.
  1848   A grammatical sketch of the languages spoken by the Indians of the Mosquito Shore.
          Transactions of the American Ethnological Society, Vol. 2. New York: Bartlett and
          Welford. Pp. 235–264.
Dampier, William
  1968   *A New Voyage round the world.* Republication of edition of 1729. New York: Dover
          Publications.
Esquemeling, John
  1967   *The buccaneers of America.* Republication of edition of 1893. New York: Dover
          Publications.
Floyd, Troy S.
  1967   *The Anglo-Spanish struggle for Mosquitia.* Albuquerque: Univ. of New Mexico
          Press.

Gordon, B. LeRoy
   1957   Human geography and ecology in the Sinú country of Colombia. *Ibero-American* No.
          39. Berkeley: Univ. of California Press.
Hamilton, J. Taylor
   1901   *A history of the missions of the Moravian Church during the eighteenth and
          nineteenth centuries.* Bethlehem, Pennsylvania: Times Publishing.
Helms, Mary W.
   1969   The cultural ecology of a colonial tribe. *Ethnology* **8:**76–84.
   1971   *Asang: Adaptations to culture contact in a Miskito community.* Gainesville: Univ. of
          Florida Press.
   1977   In search of power: Ideology and exchange in the chiefships of ancient Panama.
          Unpublished manuscript, files of the author.
Howe, James
   1974   Village political organization among the San Blas Cuna. Ph.D. dissertation,
          Department of Anthropology. Univ. of Pennsylvania.
   1975a Notes on the environment and subsistence practices of the San Blas Cuna, with
          comments and an addendum by Mac Chapin. *Working Papers on Peoples and
          Cultures of Central America* No. 1. Mimeograph.
   1975b Carrying the village: Cuna political metaphors. Unpublished manuscript, files of the
          author.
   1976   Communal land tenure and the origin of descent groups among the San Blas Cuna. In
          Frontier adaptations in Lower Central America, edited by M. W. Helms and F. O.
          Loveland. Philadelphia: Institute for the Study of Human Issues. Pp. 151–163.
Howe, James, and Joel Sherzer
   1975   Take and tell: A practical classification from the San Blas Cuna. *American Ethnologist*
          2:435–460.
Lothrop, Samuel K.
   1926   *Pottery of Costa Rica and Nicaragua* (2 vols.). *Contributions of the Museum of the
          American Indian* Vol. 8. *Heye Foundation.* New York: Heye Foundation.
   1937   *Coclé, An archaeological study of Central Panama, Part I. Memoirs of the Peabody
          Museum of Archaeology and Ethnology,* Vol. 7. Cambridge, Massachusetts: Peabody
          Museum of Archaeology and Ethnology, Harvard University.
   1942   The Sigua: Southernmost Aztec outpost. *Proceedings of the Eighth American Scien-
          tific Congress,* Vol. 2. Washington, D.C.: Department of State. Pp. 109–116.
Lussan, Raveneau de
   1930   *Raveneau de Lussan, buccaneer of the Spanish Main and early French filibuster of the
          Pacific; a translation into English of his journal of a voyage into the South Seas in
          1684 and the following years with the Filibusters.* M. E. Wilbur, trans. Cleveland:
          Arthur H. Clark.
MacCurdy, George G.
   1911   *A study of Chiriquian antiquities. Memoirs of the Connecticut Academy of Arts and
          Sciences,* Vol. 3. New Haven: Yale Univ.
Martin, A.
   1894   Handel und Kreditwesen der Moskito-Indianer. *Globus* **65:**100–101.
McKim, Fred
   1947   San Blas. *Etnologiska Studier,* No. 15. Göteborg: Etnografiska Museet.
Moravian Church
   1849–1887 *Periodical accounts relating to the missions of the Church of the United
              Brethren, established among the heathen, Vols. 19–34.* London.

1890–1956   Periodical accounts relating to the foreign missions of the Church of the United Brethren, Second Century, Vols. 1–17. London.
1903–1954   Moravian missions, Vols. 1–52. London: Moravian Mission Agency.
Mueller, Karl A.
1932   Among Creoles, Miskitos and Sumus: Eastern Nicaragua and its Moravian missions. Bethlehem, Pennsylvania: Comenius Press.
Newton, Arthur P.
1914   The colonizing activities of the English Puritans. New Haven: Yale Univ. Press.
Nicol, John M.
1898   Northeast Nicaragua. Geographical Journal 11:658–660.
Nietschmann, Bernard
1969   The distribution of Miskito, Sumu, and Rama Indians, Eastern Nicaragua. International Committee on Urgent Anthropological and Ethnological Research. Bulletin 11. Vienna: Institut fur Volkerkunde. Pp. 91–101.
1972   Hunting and fishing focus among the Miskito Indians, Eastern Nicaragua. Human Ecology 1:41–67.
1973   Between land and water. New York: Seminar Press.
Oviedo y Valdés, Gonzalo Fernández de
1853   Historia general y natural de las Indias, Vol. 3. Madrid: La Real Academia de la Historia.
1959   Natural History of the West Indies. Sterling A. Stoudemire, trans. Chapel Hill: The Univ. of North Carolina Press. [Original: Sumario de la natural historia de las Indias, Toledo, 1526.]
Parsons, James J.
1955   The Miskito pine savannah of Nicaragua and Honduras. Annals of the Association of American Geographers, Vol. 45. Pp. 36–63.
Pinart, M. Alphonse
1887   Les Indiens de l'etat de Panama. Revue d'Ethnographie 6:33–56.
Porta Costas, Don Antonio
1908   Relación del reconocimiento geométrico y politico de la Costa de Mosquitos. In Relaciones históricas y geográficas de América Central. Madrid: V. Súarez. Pp. 257–286.
Prebble, John
1968   The Darién disaster. London: Secker and Warburg.
Roberts, Orlando
1827   Narrative of voyages and excursions on the east coast and in the interior of Central America. Edinburgh: Constable.
Romoli, Kathleen
1953   Balboa of Darién. New York: Doubleday.
Roys, Ralph L.
1943   Indian background of colonial Yucatan. Carnegie Institution Publication No. 548. Washington, D.C.: Carnegie Institution of Washington.
Sapper, Karl
1900   Reise auf dem Río Coco (nördliches Nicaragua). Globus 78:249–252, 271–276.
Sauer, Carl Ortwin
1966   The early Spanish Main. Berkeley: Univ. of California Press.
Siebörger, W.
1890   Kaisa! Nach schriftlichen und münlichen Mitteilungen Missionary Siebörger's, edited by H. G. Schneider. Stuttgart: Missionsblattes der Brüdergemeine.

Stier, Fran
  1976   Bananas: An account of environment and subsistence on Playon Chico, San Blas.
          Working Papers on Peoples and Cultures of Central America No. 2. Mimeograph.
Stout, David B.
  1947   *San Blas Cuna acculturation: An introduction. Viking Fund Publications in An-
          thropology* No. 9. New York.
Trimborn, Hermann
  1948   *Vergessene Königreiche. Studien zur Völkerkunde und Altertumskunde Nordwest-
          Kolumbiens.* Kulturgeschichtliche Forschungen, Vol. 2. Braunschweig: Albert Lim-
          bach Verlag.
W., M.
  1732   The Mosquito Indian and his golden river. In *A collection of voyages and travels,* Vol.
          6, compiled by A. Churchill, London. Pp. 285–298.
Wafer, Lionel
  1934   *A new voyage and description of the Isthmus of America,* edited by L. E. Elliott Joyce,
          Oxford: The Hakluyt Society.
Wassén, Henry S.
  1940   Anonymous Spanish manuscript from 1739 on the Province Darien. *Etnologiska
          Studier* No. 10, Göteborg. Etnografiska Museet. Pp. 80–146.
  1949   Contributions to Cuna ethnography. *Etnologiska Studier* No. 16. Göteborg: Etno-
          grafiska Museet. Pp. 7–139.
Wickham, Henry A.
  1869   Notes of a journey among the Woolwa and Miskito Indians. *Proceedings of the Royal
          Geographical Society,* Vol. 13. Pp. 58–63.
  1872   A journey among the Woolwa or Soumoo Indians of Central America. In *Rough notes
          of a journey through the wilderness,* Part 2. London: W. H. J. Carter.
  1895   Notes on the Soumoo or Woolwa Indians of Blewfields River, Mosquito Territory.
          Journal of the Anthropological Institute of Great Britain and Ireland **24:**198–208.
Young, Philip D.
  1971   *Ngawbe: Tradition and change among the Western Guaymi of Panama. Illinois
          Studies in Anthropology* No. 7. Urbana: Univ. Illinois Press.

chapter 8

Changing Patterns of Resource Exploitation, Settlement Distribution, and Demography on the Southern Isthmus of Tehuantepec, Mexico

JUDITH FRANCIS ZEITLIN
Yale University

INTRODUCTION

The Pacific coastal plain of the Isthmus of Tehuantepec forms a distinctive environmental region among lowland areas of southern Middle America. Unlike the humid coast of neighboring Chiapas, the southern Isthmus is semiarid, with an annual rainfall of less than 1000 mm. The short summer rainy season defines the limits of the growing season for milpa agriculture, as the persistent *nortes* of the Tehuantepec region exaggerate the effects of a lengthy dry season. Northerly winds from the Gulf Coast gather strength as they funnel through the Isthmian break between the mountain ranges of the Sierra Madre de Oaxaca and the Sierra Madre de Chiapas. During the dry months, daily winds in excess of 60 km per hour are common. These natural conditions support two major vegetation types, the boundaries of which are often difficult to distinguish (Pennington and Sarukhán 1968:32). The first is a low, thornless tropical deciduous forest, dominated by resinous trees, with cactus and various succulents in the understory. The second vegetation type, a low, spiny, deciduous forest, prevails in much of the coastal plain presently under cultivation. Mesquite and other leguminous trees quickly overtake agricultural fields left to fallow.

Spanish missionaries and bureaucrats who traveled to Tehuantepec in the early colonial period found this dry climate "healthy," since the native population was not seen to suffer greatly from such diseases as yellow fever and malaria, which plagued many areas of lowland Middle America. The province was cited repeatedly as a prime location for the development of a major Pacific port, for the establishment of a Spanish *villa,* and for the bridging of trade and communications between the Atlantic and Pacific oceans. Until regional development accelerated in the postwar years of the twentieth century, bringing to Tehuantepec a federally controlled irrigation system, these schemes had little impact on maize agriculture, which remained the foundation of native economy.

Although the alluvial soils of much of the coastal plain are highly fertile, the short growing season and the threat of intermittent droughts have always made agricultural production somewhat precarious for the *milpero.* Only a few choice locations in the region are suitable for community-based canal irrigation, and there the regularized flow of water can maintain large fruit orchards and commercial crops of sugarcane. A well-developed, local exchange network brings to the average household a wide variety of regional products to supplement its own agricultural harvests. Specialized full-time fishermen supply Isthmian markets with an abundant variety of fresh seafood from the sheltered lagoons and estuaries of the coast. The sale of salted fish and shrimp both locally and in distant market centers is a major commercial enterprise for Zapotec businesswomen. Other sources of animal protein include a number of traditionally favored game animals as well as the ubiquitious chickens, pigs, goats, sheep, and cattle, which the Spaniards introduced to the region with great success. Iguana, armadillo, and rabbit are still found within reach of agricultural fields on the populous coastal plain, although deer and larger game have retreated to the protection of the deciduous forest and the uncultivated foothills.

This diversified resource base has fed large, concentrated populations from the earliest recorded history of the region. In the mid-sixteenth century, one detailed Spanish census for the province gave it a total population of nearly 17,000 inhabitants, 12,000 of whom resided in the *cabecera* of Tehuantepec alone (Paso y Troncoso 1905a:312n.). Before the arrival of Cortes's army, the Aztecs considered Tehuantepec to be one of the most populous and prosperous provinces of their realm, one whose subjugation to the military authority of the Triple Alliance was challenged continually. Intensive occupation of the southern Isthmus in earlier prehistoric times is indicated by numerous archaeological sites that dot the coastal plain, one of which shows the presence of nucleated population centers in the region as early as 1500 B.C.

Given the lengthy history of settled village life in this region, the archaeology of the southern Isthmus seemed a productive research area for an investigation of long-term cultural processes. Of immediate interest to the present study were changing cultural adaptations to the distinctive features of the regional environment. Environment was defined broadly so as to include not only the physical and biological features of the local landscape but a human component as well. My assumption was that social, economic, and political factors from this human environment exerted powerful influences on past cultural systems.

In my research greatest emphasis was placed on the reconstruction of subsistence practices and settlement patterns in a study area. These two classes of cultural information were considered to be reflective of the interaction between the members of a community and their natural and social environment. Moreover, good quantifiable data could readily be obtained for both, permitting a comparison of subsistence and settlement patterns across the chronological sequence as a whole. It was hoped that this temporal perspective might offer new insights into the dynamics of cultural change in the southern Isthmus.

ARCHAEOLOGICAL
RESEARCH DESIGN

The archaeological data were gathered in 1972 by Robert Zeitlin and myself during a 10-month field program in the Tehuantepec region (Figure 8.1). Preliminary excavations at three sites near the Río de los Perros yielded a refined ceramic chronology which extends from the Early Preclassic through the Late Postclassic periods (1500 B.C. to A.D. 1500). Abundant faunal remains associated in midden deposits with these ceramic phases formed the principal basis for inferring subsistence practices characteristic of each phase. Along with the excavation program, a settlement pattern survey was conducted. The purpose of this survey was the delineation of the location, spatial extent, and architectural complexity of all prehistoric sites within a sample area of the southern Isthmus region.

With the Río Perros as the focus of the settlement pattern study, three sample areas totaling 100 km² were selected for intensive survey from the

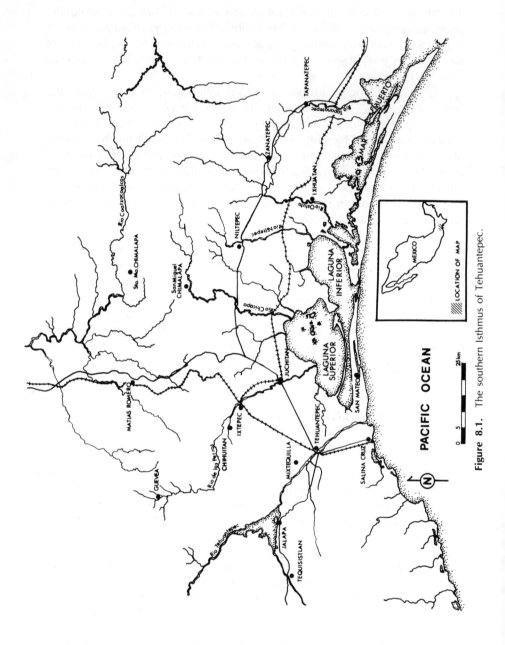

Figure 8.1. The southern Isthmus of Tehuantepec.

major environmental zones traversed by the river: (a) the piedmont zone; (b) the coastal plain; and (c) the lagoon–estuary zone. Each of these zones has a distinctive set of physical features and natural resources exploited by the modern inhabitants of the region, and presumably very similar economic activities were associated with them in the past.

The hills of the piedmont zone are the major locus of tropical deciduous forest within the limits of the study area, and the zone is valued by modern *istmeños* as a source of hardwood and economically important resins and dyes. With the high density of human population in the Isthmus at the present time, most of the larger game animals formerly found on the coastal plain are now restricted to less accessible parts of the piedmont. This sample area is, coincidentally, one of unique agricultral potential within the Río Perros subregion. Farther downstream the river has cut too deep a channel to permit the use of its waters for irrigation. In the piedmont zone, however, a community-maintained irrigation system diverts water to adjacent agricultural fields from a small tributary stream, the Río Mesquite. Sixteenth-century documents refer to native irrigation in Chihuitán, the principal piedmont village, and indicate a long history for such a system, one with probable prehistoric antecedents.

The second zone, that of the coastal plain, offers no special hydraulic resources, but it is an area of highly fertile alluvial soils that produce good corn yields on a short fallow agricultrual cycle. The third zone, that of the lagoon shore and estuaries, is significant principally for its aquatic animal resources. None of the important coastal salt-making sites used by modern commercial enterprises or known from colonial-period documents is located within the survey boundaries.

PREHISTORIC SUBSISTENCE

Evidence of the economic orientations prevalent during each of the cultural phases isolated by the 1972 excavations is limited to that provided by recovered animal bone and shell. Plant specimens survived too infrequently to permit interphase comparisons. This archaeological material is consistent with the modern flora and fauna of the southern Isthmus and indicates that no major environmental discontinuities are to be found between the start of the ceramic sequence (1500 B.C.) and the present.

In most cases the excavated faunal remains are significant for their presumed dietary contribution. Throughout the Preclassic era, however, there existed a sizable trade in shell ornaments that were transported outside the region. From native historical traditions and early colonial documents other Isthmian products are known to have figured importantly in interregional trade. Many of these products would have left only rare traces in the archaeological record, and their probable role in the development of the regional economy during earlier prehistoric times should not be overlooked. The Aztec rulers particularly prized wild animal skins from Tehuantepec and always included them in the bounty reaped from military victories in the province (Durán 1951:375; Alvarado Tezozomoc 1944:373). A more sustained trade with neighboring regions of Oaxaca in the protohistoric and early colonial periods was based on Isthmian salt, salted fish and shrimp, and cotton cloth (Paso y Troncoso 1905b).

Ethnohistorical evidence supplies native testimony on regional diet before the arrival of the Spaniards. Tehuantepec informants answered an inquiry of the 1580 *Relación Geográfica* with the statement that in pre-Columbian times they had eaten maize, chiles, beans, squash, sweet potatoes, fruits, and honey, as well as fish and the meat of deer, peccaries, rabbits, armadillos, iguanas, turkeys, and many kinds of birds and frogs (Caso 1928:171). Because of poor preservation of pollen and plant remains in our archaeological excavations, my reconstruction of diet in the more distant past must depend heavily on ethnographic analogy. Very likely, many of the same crops were planted by Preclassic and Classic Period farmers, who may have supplemented their harvest with wild herbs, seeds, and fruits of the coastal plain, as do their modern descendants. Abundant faunal remains from the excavations confirm the 1580 list of important animal species and add to it a number of other animals, including dog, opossum, various rodents, jaguar or mountain lion, raccoon, lizards, snakes, land and sea turtles, and crocodile or caiman.

Unmentioned by the informants of the *Relación Geográfica* are the various kinds of mollusks that contributed a large share of the animal protein in the prehistoric diet. Molluscan use by the modern Zapotec population is restricted mostly to a species of *Muricanthus*, which is a favored delicacy known locally as *abulón*. Prehistoric *istmeños* gathered a much larger variety of edible mollusks, the bulk of them from the tidal mud flats and estuaries of the lagoon shore, but including a few species of land snails and one freshwater clam as well. Not all of these mollusks are large, fleshy animals such as marsh clams and mussels. The tiny *Cerithidea mazatlanica* is often found unbroken in great numbers within a single stratigraphic deposit, suggesting that the local cuisine prized them as a flavoring for some shellfish broth.

In order to determine whether there were any significant temporal changes in patterns of animal resource procurement within the prehistoric sequence, quantified data on vertebrate and invertebrate faunal remains were compared for each phase. The mode of analysis used in this comparison employs an artifact index (Ziegler 1973:37) to approximate a measurement of the utilization intensity for different classes of animal resources. The measurement, which appears as a ratio between quantities of animal remains and quantities of a common artifact (in this case, numbers of potsherds), assumes that the artifact standard bears some constant relationship to the size of the prehistoric population responsible for the archaeological deposit. Although that relationship is admittedly imprecise, the measurement appears to be a reasonable approach to the problem of determining how important certain animals were in the diet, and how that role may have changed through time.

For purposes of illuminating major shifts in resource exploitation patterns, two broad classes of faunal remains were compared diachronically for variations in usage intensity: (a) terrestrial vertebrates, with a habitat centered in the coastal plain and piedmont zones; and (b) marine and estuarine mollusks, found within the lagoon-shore zone of the survey. To facilitate a comparison of the dietary importance of terrestrial vertebrates as a class, data on minimum numbers of individuals of each terrestrial species were converted to a measurement of quantities of edible meat provided by average individuals of the species. Guided by the volumetric scale presented by MacNeish (1967:296) in his analysis of changing subsistence practices in the Tehuacán Valley, I divided the Isthmian faunal species into eight general groups based on meat yield per individual. These groups are composed of the following animals:

1.	Deer	20 liters of edible meat
2.	Jaguar or mountain lion	10 liters
3.	Peccary	5 liters
4.	Dog	2 liters
5.	Raccoon	1.5 liters
6.	Opossum, armadillo, rabbit, iguana, turkey	1 liter
7.	Birds and turtles	.5 liter
8.	Rodents, lizards, snakes, frogs, and toads	.25 liter

For each phase the usage intensity for terrestrial fauna was calculated by totaling the edible volume of meat provided by all individuals and dividing that figure by the total number of potsherds found in components of the phase. The remaining class, molluscan resources from the lagoon and estuaries, did not require the use of a similar conversion factor. Total shell weight was used as the index for this class, since shell weight was thought to bear a closer relationship to the dietary contribution of mollusks. Terrestrial vertebrate usage intensity and marine–estuarine mollusk usage intensity are plotted on two separate graphs (Figure 8.2).

Comparison of the chronological trends from each graph reveals a large

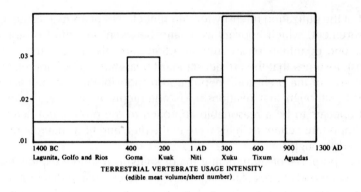

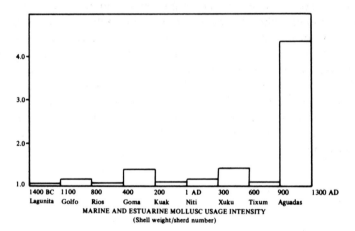

Figure 8.2. Chronological comparison of usage intensity for terrestrial and marine–estuarine fauna in the Río Perros excavations.

amount of variation in the usage intensity of both terrestrial and aquatic species. In all likelihood these fluctuations are due to random variations in the sample deposits examined from each phase. Phases with high terrestrial faunal counts also tend to be those with high mollusk counts; samples from these phases appear to have been richer in faunal remains than were others, a fact which I suspect represents differential patterns of trash deposition in the sites. A larger sample of components might have altered this picture of apparent temporal differences in the dietary importance of both aquatic and terrestrial animal protein. The final phase for which faunal comparisons could be made, the Aguadas Phase, does not conform to this pattern of variation. In this phase the vast increase in marine mollusk use, which is eight times that of the previous highest usage coincides with a relatively low level of land vertebrate consumption.

Use of the artifact index confirms the presence of a distinctive subsistence orientation during the Early Postclassic Period, an impression conveyed visually by the shell midden-like nature of components of the Aguadas Phase. This shift in resource procurement patterns did not involve simply an intensification of past shellfish-gathering practices. An increased reliance on one genus in particular marks the new dependence on resources available in the lagoon shore–estuary zone. Eighty-two percent of the shells found in components of the Aguadas Phase are marsh clams of the *Polymesoda* genus. In previous phases individuals of this genus had never constituted more than 16% of the mollusks.

Why such a shift in resource procurement patterns should take place is unclear. The Aguadas Phase is a period of maximum population density in the prehistoric Río Perros study area. It may be that wild game resources within the coastal plain diminished concurrent with increased clearing of deciduous forest for agricultural purposes or with shortening of fallow periods on cultivated lands as higher crop yields were needed to feed an expanded population.

PREHISTORIC SETTLEMENT PATTERNS

A diachronic study of settlement patterns in the Río Perros sample zone clarifies the picture of prehistoric subsistence practices and suggests other kinds of local cultural adaptations. Information obtained in the intensive surface survey on the size and distribution of communities during each chronological phase establishes several historical trends. These will be discussed in terms of three aspects of the regional settlement pattern: (a) population size; (b) the location of settlements with respect to major resource zones; and (c) differences of rank among contemporary communities.

An approximate indication of prehistoric population size was obtained from the areal extent of settlement during each phase. Because deposits of silt from periodic floodings of the Río Perros have deeply buried a few sites, which we discovered only through the chance location of road cuts, it is felt that the intensive survey techniques probably failed to record all prehistoric sites. Nonetheless, suggestions of relative population size can be made by calculating the total number of hectares occupied at known sites, if we assume that habitation density was fairly constant over time at these sites. By plotting settlement area for each phase in the prehistoric sequence, I have drawn a population growth curve, which can be divided into three stages of demographic change (Figure 8.3).

The first, spanning the Preclassic and Early Classic periods, is a stage of slow population growth in which great oscillations in population level result in a cumulative increase in area of settlement. This is followed by a shorter period of sustained growth through the Tixum and Aguadas phases, in which new population advances are not offset by prolonged periods of decline. The final precolonial phase of occupation, Ulam, witnessed a sudden, dramatic decrease in population within the Río Perros area. All the Late Postclassic population loss can be accounted for by the disappearance of any large,

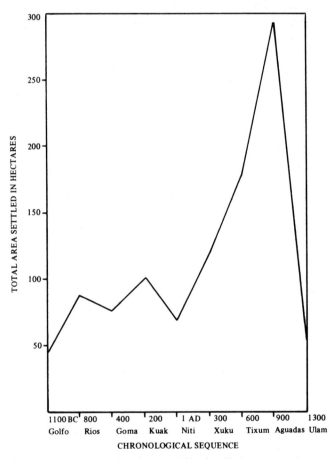

Figure 8.3. Demographic change within the Río Perros sample area.

nucleated population center. Although they did not expand sufficiently to absorb migrants from an urban center, rural communities actually increased in number at this time.

A general pattern of increasing settlement density in the study area shows different historical trends in each of the three major environmental zones. These differences in zonal growth patterns have interesting implications for the developing regional economic adaptation.

The coastal plain zone is one of continuous occupation and highest population density throughout the prehistoric sequence. All the large nucleated settlements of the subregion are located in this zone, within walking distance of the modern town of Juchitán. Higher soil fertility in the Río Perros floodplain may have attracted these prehistoric farming communities. Another economic advantage to settlement in this zone would have been the presence of localized rainy season waterholes. Juchitán farmers take advantage of the high water table of these *aguadas* by placing wells at their perimeters from which they water livestock. *Aguadas* are concentrated within the site boundaries of each of the three major prehistoric centers, and dense artifact scatters are often found at their edges.

The decision to locate settlement in the coastal plain zone necessarily made important resources in the other two zones more distant. That lagoon–estuary resources were important to prehistoric populations of the central area is demonstrated by abundant mollusks found in sites near Juchitán. Either an intensive local trade network delivered fresh aquatic products to these sites from small settlements located near the lagoon shore, or specialized fishermen made daily or seasonal trips from their homes on the coastal plain to the lagoons and estuaries, as fishermen from Juchitán do today.

In contrast to the central zone, the piedmont section was sparsely settled before the onset of the Classic Period. In the Early Classic a number of sites located in the vicinity of the piedmont were occupied for the first time, all of them situated on the margins of a Río Perros tributary, the Río Mesquite. Occupation at stream-bank sites continued through the Late Postclassic, although there was some decline in density during the intervening phases. Since the Río Mesquite is one of the few places in the Tehuantepec region known to have been used for primitive canal irrigation, the concentration of settlement along its margins during the Early Classic may have been associated with the development of a prehistoric irrigation system in the Río Perros area.

The third major environmental zone sampled is that of the lagoon shore and estuaries near the mouth of the Río Perros. Surprisingly little permanent occupation was found in this zone, despite the widespread use of its aquatic resources since the Preclassic Period. Only occasional surface scatters of artifacts from the Classic and Early Postclassic were spotted here, contrasting with contemporaneous, dense habitation sites of the adjacent coastal plain and piedmont zones. By the Late Postclassic Period, however, settlement in the lagoon shore–estuary zone came to resemble much more closely that of the plain and piedmont. Although no large, nucleated centers were present on the shore, dense occupation of the area is indicated through a more dispersed pattern of numerous hamlets and scattered houses dotting the length of the estuaries.

The cultural assemblages associated with these late lagoon sites are strikingly distinct. Contemporaneity with late sites of the coastal plain and piedmont zones can be demonstrated by shared ceramic traits, particularly by such diagnostic whole-vessel types as open, grey ware bowls with serpent-head feet, which represent a widespread Late Postclassic horizon marker for the southern Isthmus. Nonetheless, the bulk of the surface collections made at lagoon sites comprises a ceramic repertoire of plain and fancy wares, vessel shapes, and decorative modes completely different from pottery used by inhabitants of the coastal plain and piedmont zones. Equally strong differences exist between the lithic assemblages. In the Late Postclassic, surface collections from sites of the piedmont and coastal plain yield scattered finds of small, broken obsidian blades. By contrast, sites of the lagoon shore–estuary zone are littered with large blades, chunky flaked tools, and finely worked projectile points and earspools of obsidian. Cultural discontinuities indicated by these artifactual differences are reinforced by a discontinuity in the distribution of settlement in the study area. During this final pre-Columbian period of high rural population density, occupation shifted away from the southern sector of the coastal plain zone, leaving a virtually unoccupied buffer territory between that area and nearshore sites.

The combined evidence of differences in material culture and discontinuities in settlement distribution leads me to conclude that the Río Perros study area was inhabited by two distinct ethnic groups in the Late Postclassic Period. Their cultural dissimilarities may have been strengthened by differing economic orientations, as suggested by the selection of a previously underpopulated zone by the late lagoon shore–estuary settlers. Although quantified data are lacking from which to make a detailed comparison of subsistence orientations for the two groups, I suspect that the nearshore group relied more heavily on fishing and shellfish gathering than did their agricultural neighbors of the coastal plain and piedmont zones. At a later point in the discussion, my reasons for believing that this new ethnic diversity resulted from a Late Postclassic migration of non-Isthmian peoples will be examined at length.

The last settlement pattern topic I will discuss concerns structured differences of rank among contemporary communities and changes in ranking patterns over time. Evidence of variations in community size, function, or status is found from the earliest ceramic occupations of the Río Perros to the eve of the Spanish Conquest. Surface remains pertinent to intercommunity differences were most readily apparent as variations in site size and architectural complexity. Site size could be estimated by plotting the areal extent of the surface spread of cultural debris. While none of the sampled sites exhibited complex architectural plans, a simple division of sites according to the presence or absence of high mounds, 3 m in elevation or more, was useful in differentiating prehistoric communities. High mounds probably functioned as platforms, either for public buildings or for high-status residences.

Applying these two criteria, a four-class division of Río Perros settlements was derived which seemed to encompass discrete variations among the surveyed sites. The four classes are described by modern settlement types, partly out of convenience and partly from the assumption that the prehistoric site classes correspond roughly to the kinds of social units represented by the modern settlement types. Clearly this correspondence must remain hypothetical until extensive excavations at each class of site can ascertain the true structure and function of the prehistoric settlement categories.

The smallest class, that of the *homestead,* includes sites that are under 1 ha in size; such settlements probably represent occupations by single, extended-family households. *Hamlets* are larger sites, varying between 1–10 ha, but lacking clear architectural evidence of public buildings or marked status differences among residences. *Villages,* measuring 10–25 ha and dominated by the presence of one or more high mounds, must have been centers of some public functions as well as sites of larger residential units. The largest sites of the region are included in the final settlement category, that of *regional center.* These range in size from slightly under 50 ha to over 250 ha. Normally encompassing several large platform mounds, a site of this class is always unique among its contemporaries in the entire survey area, and, as will be seen in the discussion that follows, probably served important functions for the whole Río Perros subregion. Distribution maps of these classes of sites are provided for each phase in Figures 8.4–8.13.

The concept of settlement function used in this analysis is derived from the theoretical assumptions of economic geography, a discipline that is also concerned with the spatial distribution of human communities. Basing their conclusions on comparisons of regional settlement patterns from both Western and non-Western societies, geographers have demonstrated a general correlation between the relative size of a settlement and the number of economic functions that settlement provides for the local population (Haggett 1965:115ff.). Large, multifunction centers offer a range of goods

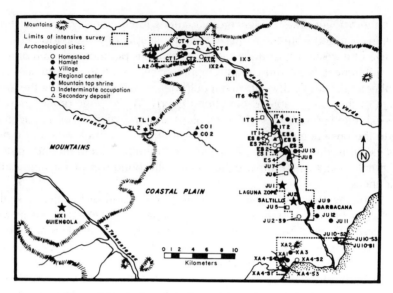

Figure 8.4. Archaeological sites of the Río de los Perros.

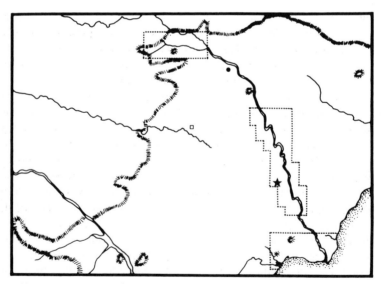

Figure 8.5. Golfo phase (1100–800 B.C.)

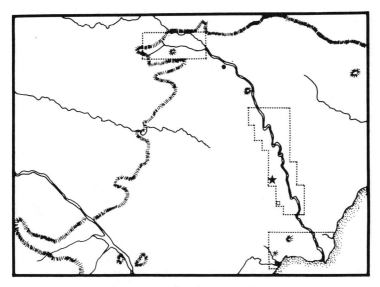

Figure 8.6. Ríos phase (800–400 B.C.)

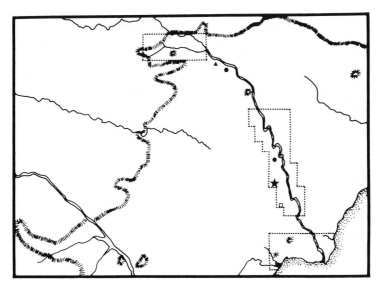

Figure 8.7. Goma phase (400–200 B.C.)

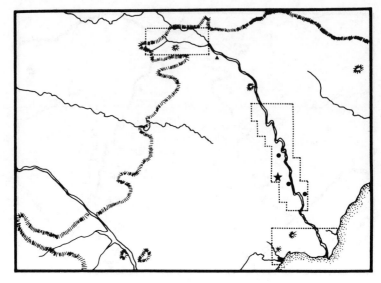

Figure 8.8. Kuak phase (200 B.C.–A.D. 1)

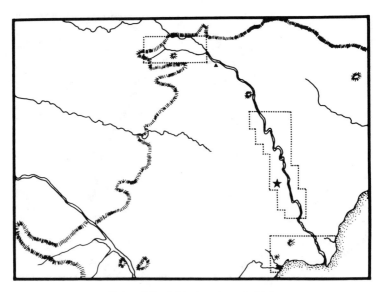

Figure 8.9. Niti phase (A.D. 1–300)

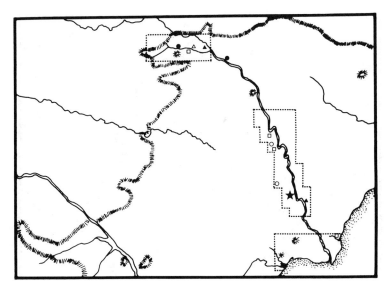

Figure 8.10. Xuku phase (A.D. 300–600)

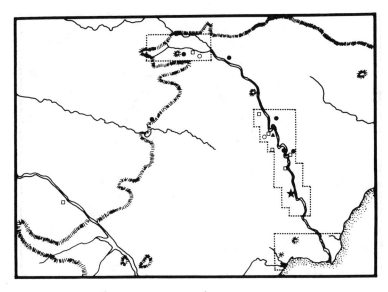

Figure 8.11. Tixum phase (A.D. 600–900)

167

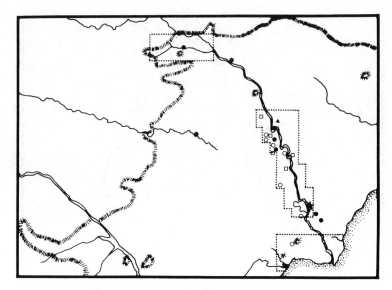

Figure 8.12. Aguadas phase (A.D. 900–1300)

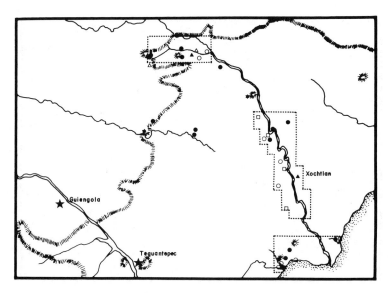

Figure 8.13. Ulam phase (A.D. 1300–1522)

168

and services not found in smaller centers; consequently, the populations of a number of smaller communities depend on the larger centers for some of their economic and social needs. In a densely occupied region, the classic models of economic geography posit the development of a complex hierarchy of settlements of different sizes, offering different ranges of goods and services.

From this analytical perspective, the broad outline of a prehistoric settlement hierarchy might be inferred from the site classification system established for the southern Isthmus. Villages and regional centers, the two classes that show physical evidence of having held some kinds of public functions, could be seen to have provided services for a number of lesser-rank homesteads and hamlets. Regional centers, by virtue of their special functions, should have served the populations of both villages and lower-order settlements on some occasions. Departing from the marketplace orientation of classic central-place theory, a more inclusive view of Mesoamerican settlement hierarchies would incorporate other classes of service function as well, functions such as the maintenance of political institutions and the provision of religious cult services. Morrill (1970:61) is one geographer who would automatically subsume such nonmarket services under his concept of central-place functions.

Although the outline of a central-place hierarchy can be sketched from the Río Perros settlement classes, the distribution of prehistoric sites does not conform fully with other implications of the theoretical model. Classic central-place theory portrays a densely settled landscape in which functionally equivalent centers are evenly spaced. Because of the pyramidal shape of the central-place hierarchy, lesser-rank centers should be tightly packed within the region, with higher-function centers distributed more thinly. In the Río Perros sample, neither an even density of settlement throughout the region nor a pyramidal shape in the settlement hierarchy appears until quite late in the prehistoric sequence.

As was pointed out earlier, settlement during the Preclassic Period was concentrated within the coastal plain of the survey area. Even as the piedmont and lagoon-shore areas came to be occupied in the Classic Period, population density continued to be highest within the coastal plain zone, rather than uniformly spread throughout the region. Some measure of this divergence from the ideal settlement pattern of the theoretical landscape must be seen as a consequence of the differential distribution of economic resources within the Tehuantepec region. The classical models presuppose a uniform plain, in which no natural barriers interfere with economic spacing principles. In reality, few regions are so uniform, and geographers have developed a number of techniques to account for the effect of uneven resource distribution on the settlement hierarchy.

A second major discrepancy between the Río Perros archaeological site distribution and the predictions of a central-place model appears when a pyramidal shape in the settlement hierarchy is sought. Even within the more densely settled zone the central-place hierarchy was weakly developed initially. Although the highest-level settlement, the regional center, was present from the earliest occupation of the zone, secondary and tertiary centers were not well represented until the Late Classic, when their appearance coincided with a stage of accelerated population growth. As rural population expanded, the lower levels of the hierarchy began to be filled with lesser-rank centers and isolated homesteads, slowly approximating the tiered shape required by central-place theory.

Perhaps a greater obstacle than localization of resources to the theoretical spacing of ranked centers is to be found in the low population levels that marked Preclassic and Early Classic agricultural settlement. The regular lattice distribution of central places dictated by locational models depends on an evenly settled rural hinterland to serve as a market for central-place services. Population density may have been too low in the earlier part of the prehistoric sequence to meet this requirement. Recently, a few economic geographers have attempted to adapt the rigid formulations of a central-place hierarchy in a manner that would incorporate changes in settlement pattern resulting from long-term population growth. I have discussed two of these population growth models at greater length elsewhere (Zeitlin, in preparation). I will summarize them briefly here and point out their applicability to the Río Perros archaeological data.

The first of these growth models is concerned with an evolving settlement hierarchy under prehistoric conditions of population growth in a neighboring region of Mesoamerica, the Oaxaca Valley. Kirkby (1973: 123ff.) developed a technique to predict the location of settlements and central places during successive phases of valley occupation, beginning with the Tierras Largas Phase at 1300 B.C. She based her expectations about the size and number of settlements in each arm of the Oaxaca Valley on a determination of the carrying capacity of maize agriculture; population size was related directly to the productivity of different land classes, applying indigenous cultivation techniques. Population growth was introduced into this carrying-capacity model by changes in maize productivity, changes resulting from the evolution of hybrid corn varieties, as evidenced in the Tehuacán Valley chronological sequence. In Kirkby's scheme, central places arose to serve fixed numbers of the farming population; as rural population density increased over time due to improved maize productivity, new service centers were created and existing ones expanded to meet economic, religious, and administrative needs.

Unfortunately, no test of Kirkby's model is possible with the current data on the Río Perros study area. Kirkby's success at predicting the actual distribution of prehistoric sites was dependent on an accurate assessment of carrying capacity, based on her thorough study of maize productivity among modern peasant farmers of the Oaxaca Valley. For the Tehuantepec region sufficient information is not available to permit a reconstruction of maize productivity within the survey area. Were such an analysis possible, the dietary importance of collected wild foods, particularly fish and shellfish, would have to be evaluated also before population carrying capacity could be calculated. These food sources are an important component of the present-day Isthmian diet, and archaeological evidence indicates that they were in prehistoric times as well. Marine and estuarine resources may have been an elastic calorie resource, capable of withstanding greater exploitation during the Preclassic Period, when maize productivity was lowest. Regardless of the dietary role these rich protein sources may have played, the extremely low rural population density for the fertile coastal plain zone suggests that population levels were well below carrying capacity at that time. Kirkby also found discrepancies between her predicted population density and archaeological estimates of population levels in the early part of the Oaxaca Valley sequence. She concluded that a small initial settlement of the valley by agricultural peoples may account for the existence of smaller Early Preclassic communities than maize cultivation would support. With slow, natural demographic increase, density gradually came to approach carrying capacity (Kirkby 1973:146). A similar situation may have prevailed in the Tehuantepec region.

A different type of predictive model was developed by Morrill (1962, 1965) to demonstrate the effect of population growth on the evolution of a regional settlement hierarchy. In Morrill's model, population density is not dependent on carrying capacity nor is population growth related to an expanding subsistence technology. Morrill treats demographic increase as an independent variable and constructs a model to simulate the effect of that increase on the expansion of settlement in a newly colonized region. As population grows, migrants move out of the original colonizing center to new frontiers within the region. Morrill employs a Monte Carlo simulation technique to predict where new settlements will be established and what hierarchical relationships will emerge among them.

Because the Monte Carlo simulation is based on the multiplying effect of random or unique initial choices, a different settlement distribution is created by the model each time the historical growth process is simulated. Morrill (1965:82) found several general characteristics to hold for the settlement patterns derived from his population growth simulation. These include (a) a functional hierarchy dominated at the top by the center which served as the point of origin for migration into the region; (b) the failure of the settlement system to produce as many service centers as the population base could accomodate theoretically; and (c) the radial patterning of new centers in the direction of early migration out from the center of origin, rather than an even distribution of settlements across the region as a whole.

Morrill's colonizing model appears to fit the special circumstances of prehistoric population growth in the Tehuantepec region better than a model in which settlement density is dependent on carrying capacity. To apply his model, we need not assume that the study area was unoccupied before 1500 B.C., when our ceramic sequence begins, nor that the pottery-bearing population was ethnically separate from its nonagriculturalist predecessor, thus representing new colonization. In an important sense, the agricultural subsistence orientation of these early villagers opened up settlement frontiers in much the same way as would actual physical migration into a new region. An examination of historical trends in the Río Perros settlement distribution shows growth characteristics similar to those generalized from the colonization model.

One center maintained dominance over the sample area throughout the prehistoric sequence. Although the exact location of this center shifted slightly twice between the Early Preclassic and the Early Postclassic periods, the move was a distance of less than 1 km in each case. Very likely these moves were prompted by natural disturbances, such as flooding or shifting of the Río de los Perros. Mention has already been made of the weak development of secondary- and tertiary-level settlements until the Late Classic, a phenomenon presumably related to the attractiveness of the primary center as a traditional multifunction central place. The third general feature of Morrill's growth simulation, a radial distribution of settlement frontiers, can been seen in the Río Perros sequence as well. Once population increase reached levels that spurred settlement proliferation, an increase in the number and diversity of settlements was concentrated in two particular areas of early colonization, the piedmont zone and the northern half of the coastal plain.

The position of the regional center in this sequence of prehistoric population growth is remarkable. Laguna Zope, which occupied the apex of the settlement hierarchy throughout the Preclassic, was a sizable community from very early in its history. Occupational debris was spread over an area of nearly 50 ha by the close of the Golfo Phase at 800 B.C. Without more detailed information on the internal structure of the site at this early date, it is difficult to determine on what basis such a large community was integrated. Robert Zeitlin (this volume) has suggested that Laguna Zope's role in long-distance commerce helped to attract a larger resident population than might be accounted for by central-place services provided for the local population. Congruent with this interpretation is the fact that rural settlement density was extremely low during the Early Preclassic.

Once established, the regional center increased in size as population grew and new settlements were founded. No rival center above the village level ever developed within the Río Perros study area. Even when important hydraulic resources came to be exploited in the piedmont zone, the coastal plain center continued to dominate. By the end of the Early Postclassic, the Barbacana site near Juchitán had spread over both banks of the river, covering an area of 264 ha. Given this long-standing stability of the local settlement hierarchy, a fact suggestive of strong regional political and economic integration, the sudden disappearance of a regional center in the Late Postclassic is quite dramatic. The lack of archaeological evidence for such a center is paralleled in ethnohistorical sources, which likewise do not suggest any Río Perros settlements larger than the village for that period. Without a densely populated, nucleated center at the top of the hierarchy, the truncated settlement hierarchy that remained was a dispersed distribution of homesteads and hamlets near the river, with a few smaller villages scattered among them.

CULTURAL CHANGE IN THE LATE POSTCLASSIC PERIOD

In summary, a diachronic analysis of settlement patterns prior to the Late Postclassic Period illustrated the following trends: (a) a prolonged period of demographic growth preceding Ulam Phase urban population decline; (b) an intensification of agricultural land use, with the development of localized canal irrigation, and (c) the persistence of a stable community hierarchy until the last period, probably reflecting economic and political integration of the entire river system.

In the Late Postclassic Period the archaeological record witnessed an abrupt transformation of the existing social order, a transformation that so violated the entrenched patterns of local development that preceded it as to suggest the intervention of extraregional processes and historical events. The placement of this transformation in a period dating just a few hundred years before the onset of recorded history provides an unusual opportunity for joint use of archaeological and historical evidence. Both sixteenth-century Spanish accounts of Isthmian society and culture and native oral histories relating preconquest events will be examined to search for probable causes of the prehistoric crisis.

Two major dislocations correspond to changes in the cultural integrity of the southern Isthmus as a whole and to changes in the sociopolitical integrity of the Río Perros subregion. Surface survey data produced strong evidence of a new ethnic discontinuity in the Late Postclassic Period by indicating a distinct separation between the material culture of the coastal

plain and piedmont residents on the one hand and that of the lagoon-shore
settlers on the other. At the time of the Conquest, three different ethnic
groups were known to inhabit the Tehuantepec region. Two of these groups,
the Zapotec and the Zoque, were primarily maize agriculturalists inhabiting
the coastal plain and piedmont zones. The third group, the Huave, were
fishermen and sweet potato farmers. By the time Burgoa (1934) described
the culture and distribution of these three groups in 1674, the expanding
Zapotec sphere of influence had pushed the Zoques to the extreme eastern
side of the region, where their numbers continued to shrink from disease and
economic disruption.

Huave villages were distributed along the perimeter of the lagoons and
on the barrier beaches between the lagoons and the open sea. Relative
physical isolation and a successful economic adaptation based principally
on the exploitation of marine resources permitted their cultural survival until
threatened by the advance of twentieth-century technology. Huave occupation of the lagoon shore–estuary zone of the Río Perros in particular is not
documented for the early colonial period, but such a location would be
consonant with what is known of Huave economy amd settlement distribution. Although an identification of the Late Postclassic lagoon shore archaeological culture with the protohistoric Huave must remain tentative
until more is known of the material culture of sixteenth-century Huave
villages, it seems a plausible hypothesis. In fact, the sudden intrusive appearance of this archaeological culture in the Río Perros zone, without clear
associations with the existing regional ceramic tradition, might find some
explanation in oral history should our hypothetical identification prove true.
Burgoa (1934:398) recorded that the Huave claimed not to be indigenous to
the southern Isthmus, but to have migrated there by sea at some time in the
prehistoric past.

Archaeological observations of a Late Postclassic breakdown of
sociopolitical integration in the Río Perros also find some clarification in
regional ethnohistory. During the middle of the fourteenth century, complex
political events in the neighboring Oaxaca Valley spurred the emigration of
a substantial population of Zapotec speakers to the southern Isthmus. Their
bloody entry into the region was described in Zapotec narrative history
(Burgoa 1934:328), and a legendary date of about A.D. 1350 is confirmed by
lexicostatistical evidence on the historical separation of Isthmus and Valley
Zapotec dialects (Fernández, Swadesh, and Weitlaner 1960). The intruders
established themselves at the site of Tehuantepec, which became a second
capital for the entire Zapotec realm. At the time of the Spanish Conquest all
the southern Isthmus was held tributary to Cosijopi, the Tehuantepec king,
although the effectiveness of Zapotec domination was strengthened by
Cortes's subjugation of their Mexican rivals. From the late fifteenth century,

Aztec military incursions frequently gnawed at the periphery of the kingdom, and the Zapotec *cacique* himself was obliged to pay tribute to the Triple Alliance from time to time.

In the early 1600s the town of Tehuantepec was so large and powerful among Isthmus communities that its population of almost 12,000 represented 70% of the total population of the province, including members of all three ethnic groups. Were any existing regional centers of the size of Barbacana, the 264-ha site near Juchitán, to have continued into the protohistoric period, their presence would have seriously threatened Zapotec hegemony. It seems likely that the apparent demise of primary rank communities in the Río Perros study area in the Late Postclassic represents military conquest and subversion of the local political organization by an intruding population, a population historically identified with fourteenth-century Zapotecs from the Oaxaca Valley.

CONCLUSION

Viewing culture change in the southern Isthmus from a developmental perspective has allowed us to discriminate between two kinds of patterns of change in prehistory. The use of a settlement pattern growth model identifies those patterns resultant from the internal dynamics of regional social and economic processes. By predicting patterns that should emerge at different stages of growth, the model also isolates those patterns which are inconsistent with established developmental trends.

In the Río Perros study area, a long prehistoric occupation was found in which local cultures were supported by an economy based on the exploitation of diverse regional resources. Specialized interregional exchange was very important in the earliest stages of cultural development, and may have figured significantly in later times as well. An integrated network of communities along the length of the river was established toward the middle of the sequence, and the hierarchical order basic to regional integration persisted until just prior to the Spanish Conquest and influenced the direction of settlement growth. The disruption of stable patterns of regional growth in the Late Postclassic Period can be explained best as a consequence of extraregional processes and events.

ACKNOWLEDGMENTS

My field project in the Tehuantepec region was generously supported by a fellowship for advanced study in Latin America from the Henry L. and Grace Doherty Charitable Foundations,

Inc. The research was authorized by the Instituto Nacional de Antropología e Historia of Mexico (archivo oficio no. 401-7 B/311.42(Z)/27-1).

Special thanks are due to Elizabeth S. Wing, Associate Curator in Zooarchaeology, and her students at the Florida State Museum for the identification and analysis of vertebrate fauna from the Río Perros excavations.

REFERENCES

Alvarado Tezozomoc, Hernando
1944   *Crónica mexicana*. México: Editorial Leyenda.
Burgoa, Fr. Francisco de
1934   *Geográfica descripción*. Tomo II. México: Publicaciones del Archivo General de la Nación.
Caso, Alfonso, ed.
1928   Descripción de Tehuantepec. *Revista mexicana de estudios históricos* **2** (suplemento): 164–75.
Durán, Fr. Diego
1951   *Historia de las Indias de Nueva-España y Islas de Tierra Firme*, Tomo I. México: Editora Nacional.
Fernández, M. T., M. Swadesh, and R. Weitlaner
1960   El panorama etnolingüístico de Oaxaca y del Istmo. Séptima mesa redonda de la Sociedad Mexicana de Antropología. *Revista mexicana de estudios antropológicos* **16:** 137–57.
Haggett, Peter
1965   *Locational analysis in human geography*. London: Edward Arnold.
Kirkby, Anne V. T.
1973   *The use of land and water resources in the past and present Valley of Oaxaca*. Memoirs of the Museum of Anthropology, University of Michigan, No. 5. Ann Arbor: Univ. of Michigan Press.
MacNeish, Richard S.
1967   A summary of the subsistence. In *Prehistory of the Tehuacán Valley, Vol. 1*, edited by D. S. Byers, Austin: Univ. of Texas Press. Pp. 290–309.
Morrill, Richard L.
1962   Simulation of central place patterns over time. *Lund Studies in Geography, Series B, Human Geography* **24:** 109–120. Lund, Sweden: C. W. K. Gleerup.
1965   Migration and the spread and growth of urban settlement. *Lund Studies in Geography, Series B, Human Geography* 26 (entire volume). Lund, Sweden: C. W. K. Gleerup.
1970   *The spatial organization of society*. Belmont, California: Wadsworth.
Paso y Troncoso, Francisco del
1905a   *Suma de visitas de pueblos por orden alfabético*. Papeles de Nueva España, segunda serie, geografía y estadística 1. Madrid: Establecimiento Tipográfico "Sucesores de Rivadeneyra."
1950b   *Relaciones geográficas de Oaxaca*. Papeles de Nueva España, segunda serie, geografia y estadística 4. Madrid: Establecimiento Tipográfico "Sucesores de Rivadeneyra."
Pennington, T. D., and José Sarukhán
1968   *Manual para la identificación de campo de los principales arboles tropicales de México*. México: Instituto Nacional de Investigaciones Forestales.

Zeitlin, Judith Francis
  1978 Community distribution and local economy on the southern Isthmus of Tehuantepec:
        An archaeological and ethnohistorical investigation. Ph.D. dissertation, Department of
        Anthropology, Yale Univ. In preparation.
Ziegler, Alan C.
  1973 *Inference from prehistoric faunal remains.* Addison-Wesley Module in Anthropology
        No. 43. Reading, Massachusetts: Addison-Wesley Publishing Co.

PART IV

Exchange Patterns

Symbiotic relationships among populations may be found in a variety of sociocultural realms. For example, these relationships can involve both exchanges of personnel and of resources. Both types of exchanges can be viewed as cultural mechanisms for adjusting populations and resources to one another. Most species of plants and animals have evolved means of adjusting populations to resources, but the reverse situation of the circulation of resources among populations has been uniquely stressed during the course of human evolution. In fact, this human system of a double balancing mechanism may be a paramount factor in the great biological success of humans.

Archaeologists in particular have recently become concerned with tracing the growth of exchange patterns through time. In general, the development of these patterns correlates with increased population sizes and organizational complexities. It seems apparent, then, that the study of human sociocultural evolution must consider the nature of the integrative networks that knit together local groups.

Archaeologists are better able to study resource exchanges than populational ones because at least some resources have the advantage of being readily assignable to their places of origin and are relatively indestructible. This is particularly true of commodities of mineralogical origin, but it is also true of some organic material with mineralogic properties. R. Zeitlin, in "Long-Distance Exchange and the Growth of a Regional Center: An Example from the Southern Isthmus of Tehuantepec, Mexico," concentrates on four key resources (obsidian, quartz, shell, and pottery) which he demonstrates were involved in interregional exchange networks. All of these resources have mineralogical properties (although the commodity shell is organic in origin, its physical characteristics are mineralogic) and are therefore durable and susceptible to sourcing studies. The author traces the diachronic frequency of occurrence and the nature of the key resources and correlates this information with data on settlement size at the site of Laguna Zope. He is able to demonstrate convincingly that the site's preeminence during Preclassic times is due to its commercial importance as a nexus in a trading network. R. Zeitlin also argues that the process of community development at Laguna Zope can be understood only by consideration of sociocultural events over a wide area rather than on a local scale.

One serious limitation that confronts the investigator seeking to reconstruct exchange systems from archaeological evidence is that many items of prehistoric exchange are not readily apparent in the archaeological record. Consequently, serious distortions can occur in the reconstructed network as compared with the prehistoric reality. This possibility of distortion may be especially great when coastal lowland populations are being considered, because it is probable that many of the resources exported from this habitat may be highly perishable ones. We will return to a discussion of this topic in the final chapter.

Stark's contribution, "An Ethnohistoric Model for Native Economy and Settlement Patterns in Southern Veracruz, Mexico" illustrates one method of confronting this archaeological situation. She develops a model of economic specialization and exchange within a coastal zone by analyzing ethnohistoric sources. One advantage of the ethnohistoric method is that economic commodities are more completely revealed than is the case when exclusively archaeologic remains are considered. After developing a model for settlement and economy in sixteenth-century southern Veracruz, Stark extrapolates the archaeological evidence that would be produced and then compares these expectations with available prehistoric evidence. By this means, the author proposes that a resource diversification and exchange model has some validity in terms of current evidence and warrants further investigation as an alternative to Rathje's (1972) core-buffer model.

Freidel, in "Maritime Adaptation and the Rise of Maya Civilization: The View from Cerros, Belize," provides evidence contravening the traditional view of the Southern Classic Maya as an inwardly oriented, isolated society. He bases his discussion primarily on evidence from the site of Cerros, which is located on the eastern coast of the Maya area. Evidence for the local preeminence of this site as early as the Late Preclassic Period indicates there was a stimulus to its growth beyomd local agricultural conditions. Freidel provides evidence that Cerros functioned in an interaction sphere as a nexus in a maritime transportation system that effectively linked populations in diversified habitats. Accordingly, Freidel's chapter contributes to the growing literature in which the Maya lowlands are viewed as internally differentiated rather than as uniform in resources; at the same time Maya communities are viewed as organically interdependent rather than as socioeconomic replicates of each other. Both Freidel's and R. Zeitlin's contributions document situations in which a local center must be understood within a much larger framework in which long-distance exchange figures prominently.

REFERENCES

Rathje, W. L.
    1972   Praise the gods and pass the metates: An hypothesis of the development of lowland rainforest civilizations in Mesoamerica. In *Contemporary archaeology: A guide to theory and contributions,* edited by Mark P. Leone. Carbondale: Southern Illinois Univ. Press. Pp. 365–392.

chapter 9

Long-Distance Exchange and the Growth of a Regional Center: An Example from the Southern Isthmus of Tehuantepec, Mexico

ROBERT N. ZEITLIN

Yale University

INTRODUCTION

There is a long-standing notion that in Mesoamerica environmental diversity and regional economic interdependence stimulated social and cultural development (Adams 1966:52–53; Sanders 1956; Wolf 1959:17–19). The Isthmus of Tehuantepec, in southern Mexico, has frequently been cited for its strategic location in this interactive network, linking as it does by just 200 km the vital Gulf and Pacific coast "channels of cultural transmission [Parsons and Price 1971:170]." Under these circumstances, can a strictly regional focus be adequate to an archaeological study of local social and cultural development? As an alternative, in a study of the southern Isthmus would there be more benefit in conceiving of that region as an open system, sensitive to distant events and to the activities of ethnically and politically disparate peoples?

One archaeologically feasible approach toward answering these questions might be first to demonstrate a correlation between long-distance exchange and the region's early political and economic growth. Tentatively it appears that on the southern Isthmus such an association can be found, suggesting that the precocious development of what was probably the major Preclassic settlement there might be traced, at least in part, to its inhabitants having availed themselves of opportunities for participation in an early interregional network through which goods and ideas moved in southern Mesoamerica. I will attempt to point out this correlation through archaeological evidence obtained from a series of test excavations conducted at Laguna Zope, site of the major settlement. Having demonstrated a mutual relationship between long-distance exchange and settlement growth, however, I would still need to determine how and why the exchange could have contributed to the Laguna Zope's development. Not without a wariness of oversimplified explanations, I will do so by drawing upon the ideas of James Vance (1970) and argue for the applicability of a mercantile model of settlement.

In support of this argument, six ceramically defined phases will illustrate, through commonalities in pottery form and decoration, that from the time of Laguna Zope's earliest occupation there was a well-articulated exchange of concepts operating between adjacent regions. Comparisons will be made with the pottery of four key geocultural localities surrounding the southern Isthmus: Soconusco to the southeast; the Valley of Oaxaca to the northwest; the northern Isthmus–Gulf Coast to the north; and the Central Depression of Chiapas to the northeast (Figure 9.1).

For each phase the results of a recently completed X-ray spectrochemical analysis will also be summarized to define the geologic sources from which Laguna Zope's inhabitants obtained obsidian, a highly valued tool and ornament material of restricted natural occurence in Mesoamerica.[1] With a knowledge of the distant sources, the likely interregional routes through which this material traveled to the southern Isthmus can be outlined.

The phase-by-phase exploitation of locally obtainable quartz will be examined as well, along with that of marine, estuary, and freshwater shells. This analysis is of particular relevance since there are indications that the use of quartz tools at Laguna Zope may have been related to an ornamental-shell export industry and that the causes and consequences of this and perhaps other interregional exchange enterprises were critical to the settlement's early growth.

If some of the data presented here seem superfluous to the subject of

---

[1]Details of the spectrochemical analytic procedure and complete results will be presented in Zeitlin (1978) and Zeitlin and Heimbuch (in press).

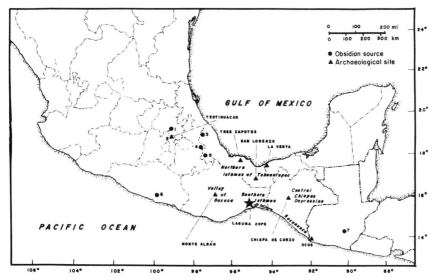

Figure 9.1. Archaeological regions and obsidian sources referred to in text. Key to obsidian sources shown on map: (1) Pachuca, (2) Teotihuacán, (3) Altotonga, (4) Guadalupe Victoria, (5) Pico de Orizaba, (6) El Ocotito, (7) El Chayal.

development at Laguna Zope, the excesses are at least partly by design. A secondary purpose of this chapter is to provide a preliminary description of the archaeological sequence at Laguna Zope for Mesoamericanists with an interest in the southern Isthmus.

LAGUNITA PHASE (1500–1100 B.C.)

The Settlement

The archaeological site of Laguna Zope, now reduced to a group of low mounds adjacent to the Pan American Highway, is situated about 1 km west of the modern town of Juchitán, Oaxaca (Figure 9.2). Throughout the entire Preclassic Period, it appears to have been the largest settlement on the southern Isthmus, a region extending about 150 km along the narrow Pacific coastal plain from the base of the Sierra Madre del Sur on the west to the Chiapas border on the east.

Accessibility to alluvial land and to water from the nearby Río de los Perros, one of the small rivers that bisect the plain, were undoubtedly crucial factors in the initial colonization of the settlement, sometime prior to 1500 B.C. As the site name suggests, the presence of some small ponds may have also figured in the location decision. These *aguadas* would have contributed

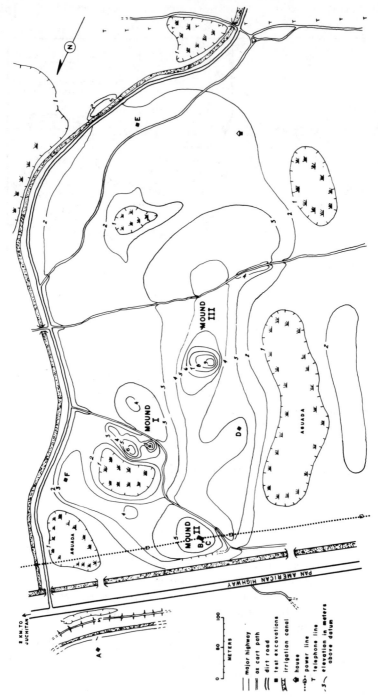

Figure 9.2. Laguna Zope site map, Juchitán, Oaxaca.

additional free-standing water and valuable humid land. On the southern Isthmus, erratic annual precipitation averaging less than 1000 mm, much of that lost through evaporation exacerbated by high temperatures and almost incessant winds, limits rainfall-dependent agriculture. About 5 km down-river from the site is the broad shallow Laguna Superior, sheltered by a barrier beach from the Pacific Ocean. Archaeological remains reveal that this resource for marine- and estuary-dwelling fauna was exploited by the inhabitants of Laguna Zope, just as it is today by the people of Juchitán.

Pottery

As might be expected, pottery of the earliest established ceramic phase at Laguna Zope closely resembles that of the Barra and Ocós phases from neighboring sites along the adjacent coast in Chiapas and Guatemala (Coe 1961; Ekholm 1969; Green and Lowe 1967; Lowe 1975). Most distinctive are several finely made categories of gloss-burnished buff-to-brown bottles, necked and neckless jars (*ollas* and *tecomates*), and flat-bottom bowls with vertical, outslanting, outflaring, or convex walls.

Many of these early vessels are simply burnished, some are white-slipped or black-smudged and others have rims and/or zones red or specular-red painted, usually in stripes and geometric designs. Plastic tech-niques of decoration are also used, notably stamping, cord marking, dentate punctation, gadrooning, indented-line burnishing, zoned toning, and ex-terior rim and body incision. Often, incised lines are used to mark off zones of red painted or plastic decoration. A few of the white-slipped examples have been differentially fired so that black clouds mark the exterior or, in some cases, a white rim effect is produced by blackening the entire exterior and/or interior surface below the rim zone. Along with a similar ware from the northern Isthmus (Coe 1970:25), this is one of the earlist manifestations of white-rim black pottery in Mesoamerica. The same buff-to-brown paste used to make these finely burnished types was also used to produce un-slipped *tecomates,* bowls and bottles with wiped or scraped surfaces or with rough, usually diagonal or cross-hatched striations. Where striations appear, they cover zones of the exterior or the entire exterior surface (cf. Lowe 1975:figs. 10–12).

Archaeological sites of the Pacific coast from Guatemala to Tehuan-tepec seem to produce the greatest elaboration and finest expression of this very sophisticated early pottery, but it is clear that all five regions, and others beyond, are encompassed within a single ceramic horizon. By this I do not imply that each region, or for that matter each site, participated completely and mechanically in the exchange of ceramic ideas. For instance, in the highland Oaxaca Valley frequencies of *tecomates* are much lower, perhaps a consequence of their special function; vessels with striated surfaces are also much less common, in this instance apparently a reflection of regional taste in design; and early production of white slipped and differentially fired black-and-white pottery is completely lacking, although occurring on occasion in even more northerly places such as Morelos (Grove 1974:30). Nevertheless, commonly shared vessel forms, plain or black smudged surface finishes with lustrous burnishing, and decorative modes such as red or specular-red rimming, striping and zoning, cord marking, and rocker stamping all indicate that underlying the regional adaptation and preference, there is an already established collective foundation of communication and interaction.

Obsidian

A single prismatic blade was recovered from Lagunita Phase deposits, a rare find at this time level in southern Mesoamerica. The other obsidian artifacts of the Lagunita Phase consist almost exclusively of small (under 3 cm maximum dimension) unretouched flakes, flake fragments, and flaking debris. Their function is puzzling, all the more so because similar forms also dominate the obsidian assemblages of numerous other contemporary lowland and highland archaeological sites.

Based on their high frequency in the Barra and Ocós phases at the Soconusco sites of Altamira and La Victoria, Lowe (1967:57–60; 1975:10–14) has proposed that such artifacts might have served as manioc-grater teeth in a lower Mesoamerican extension of an early South and Central American root-crop agricultural economy. Lowe's suggestion is particularly intriguing since southern Mexico and Guatemala are considered one of two New World centers of speciation for manioc (Rogers 1963:43). Recently, Davis (1974) advanced this hypothesis by constructing a model grater, set with obsidian flakes, with which he experimentally processed manioc tubers. Subsequent microscopic examination of the obsidian revealed a distinctive wear pattern identical to that found on a high percentage of the flakes from Altamira, La Victoria, and Laguna Zope.

Several ambiguities must be clarified, however, before the root-crop hypothesis can be accepted comfortably. Primarily—and perhaps due to poor preservability and low dispersion of pollen—no remains of manioc have yet been found in Mesoamerica prior to about 900 B.C., after which a single seed and some possible tissue fragments are seen at Tamaulipas and Tehuacán, much farther to the north (Callen 1967:272; MacNeish 1958:146), and two charred seeds are reported from highland Chiapas (Lauro González, personal communication in Lowe 1975:13). Parenthetically, there is no coeval tradition of small obsidain or other lithic flakes of the manioc-grating type associated with the scant northerly finds, nor is there any ethnographic or other evidence that such graters were ever used in Mesoamerica. In fact, there is not even any real requirement that manioc (*Manihot utilissima/esculenta*) be grated at all to make it edible since boiling or roasting alone is sufficient for removing or neutralizing its potential toxicity (Burkill 1966:1440; Hill 1952:364). Finally, small obsidian flakes are sometimes found in early Preclassic contexts at highland sites that are out of the frost-free environment manioc normally favors.

Although there are possible resolutions of every incongruity related to the manioc proposal and its implications, for the present I will rely on the more conservative conclusions of Davis's study: Based on wear patterns, the obsidian flakes found at Laguna Zope and other early Preclassic sites seem to have been utilized, either hand-held or hafted, for processing of animal, vegetal, or other soft substances whose consistency resembled manioc. With their extremely keen edges and sharp points, these irregular flakes, depending on form, make unexcelled cutting, scraping, or piercing tools, although the friability of obsidian precludes their use for the working of hard materials.

X-ray spectrochemical analysis of the Lagunita Phase obsidian indicates that it was being procured from at least three sources: Fifty percent of our sample came from Guadalupe Victoria, located about 400 km straight to the northwest in the Mexican state of Puebla; 25% came from El Chayal, a little over 500 km to the southeast in Guatemala; and 25% from a possible source about 500 km to the west near El Ocotito, Guerrero, Mexico (Figures 9.1 and 9.4). The sample size is quite small for this phase but the ratio of obsidian-to-pottery[2] suggests that these flakes, for whatever purpose, were already in common use (Figure 9.3a).

The geographic location of Guadalupe Victoria evidences interaction of the southern Isthmus with the northern Isthmus and/or Oaxaca Valley region(s) since either or both of the latter were likely intermediaries in the southward movement of obsidian to Laguna Zope. Similarly, interaction with Soconusco is seen through the use of El Chayal, Guatemala, obsidian. The eastward movement of obsidian from El Ocotito, Guerrero, may indicate another exchange linkage with the Valley of Oaxaca.

---

[2]Ratios of obsidian-to-pottery, quartz-to-pottery, and shell-to-pottery were used in this study as an estimate of relative (i.e., per capita) intensity of lithic and shell utilization for each phase. The required assumption is that per capita pottery remains were reasonably constant in quantity and friability over time. Lithic quantities were determined by multiplying summary counts of flakes and blades recovered for each phase by the calculated mean weight of each form. Numbers on the graph refer to total raw counts of flakes plus blades per phase. Ornamental shell quantities were measured by calculating the total weight of shell so designated for each phase. Numbers on the graph indicate total ornamental shell weight per phase in grams. Ceramic, lithic, and shell samples were obtained in the field by sifting all excavated material through ¼-in. screen.

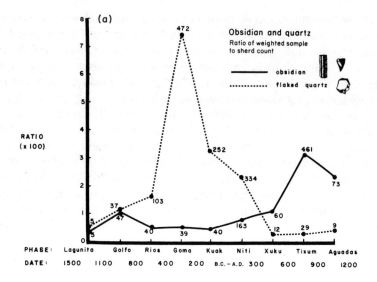

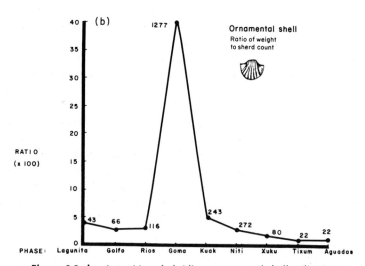

Figure 9.3a,b.   Intensities of obsidian, quartz, and shell utilization.

Locally Obtainable Quartz and Shells

The third category of Lagunita Phase artifacts to be considered includes the small irregular flakes and debitage of quartz, chert, agate and jasper.

These crystalline and cryptocrystalline materials are all obtainable in the low *sierras* which rise just behind the narrow Pacific coastal plain (Baker 1930:162–163). We personally encountered veins of high-quality prismatic quartz in the piedmont adjacent to Laollaga, about 25 km northwest of Laguna Zope.

A flake-to-pottery ratio for this phase indicates that about the same per capita amount of quartz was being utilized as was obsidian (Figure 9.3a). Since both materials were serving to produce flakes of only slightly different size and form (the quartz flakes of the early phases were generally smaller and more elongate than the obsidian ones), a question arises as to whether there were functional differences between the two categories of tools. Unfortunately we lack a microscopic wear-pattern analysis of the quartz tools equivalent to that carried out on the obsidian. Nevertheless, it is an interesting possibility that the quartz microflakes indicate a shell-working industry centered at Laguna Zope.

The superior hardness and durability of quartz make it an ideal material for cutting and engraving shell, and the specific pointed and sometimes burin-like forms of many flakes support the idea of such a function. Moreover, test excavations at Laguna Zope have produced a large quantity of worked, partially worked, and unworked marine, estuary, and freshwater bivalves and gastropods in association with these flakes.

In order to test this relationship, the total shell assemblage from Laguna Zope was divided into what I am calling ornamental and nonornamental species, the former having been utilized for the manufacture of beads, plaques, pendants, earplugs, and other nonutilitarian articles at the site or at a site in one of the surrounding highland regions. Those shells found at Laguna Zope and classified as ornamental include pearl oyster (*Pinctada mazatlanica*), chama (*Chama mexicana*), spondylus (*Spondylus princeps*), scallop (*Argopecten circularis*), nephronaias/sphenonaias (*Nephronaias/ Sphenonaias sp.*), olive (*Oliva polpasta, Olivella volutella,* and *Agaronia testacea),* cone (*Conus ximenes* and *Conus sp.*), neritina (*Neritina virginea*), trivia (*Trivia sp.*), and murex (*Muricanthus ambiguous*). By weight, ornamental species comprise 55% of the total shell assemblage from the Lagunita Phase. A correlation of their utilization through time with that of quartz flakes can be seen by comparing Figures 9.3a and 9.3b.

The possible social and cultural significance of ornamental shells in early Preclassic Mesoamerica was suggested by Flannery (1968) after he noted their association with high-status areas of archaeological sites in the Valley of Oaxaca. Flannery posited that among the emerging elites of regions such as the Valley of Oaxaca and the northern Isthmus, the exchange of such rare articles may have served to provide symbols indicating differential social status. At the same time these objects perhaps functioned as a form of stored wealth that could be utilized in time of need to obtain food from other regions.

The southern Isthmus of Tehuantepec was later pointed out by Flannery and Schoenwetter (1970:148) as a probable source for the pearl oyster, spondylus, marsh clams, and other shell recovered from elite provenances of Preclassic Oaxaca Valley sites. Subsequently, Pires-Ferreira (1975) developed the outlines of some early networks through which Atlantic and Pacific coast shell and other commodities may have moved and within which the site of Laguna Zope figures prominently as a "point of convergence."

I am not aware of any reports indicating Early Preclassic shell importation into the Central Depression of Chiapas. Thus, we can only conjecture whether this indicates that inhabitants of Laguna Zope's other neighboring highland region were not yet involved in the acquisition of shell or whether, for some reason, the data are simply lacking.

GOLFO PHASE (1100–800 B.C.)

The Settlement

No size estimate has been made of Laguna Zope for Lagunita times, but during the following Golfo Phase, surface survey suggests that it grew to an expanse of over 40 ha (nearly 100 acres). This impressive development would make Laguna Zope one of the spatially largest Mesoamerican settlements of the time. By means of comparison, San José Mogote, the largest of its contemporaries in the Valley of Oaxaca, covers only half the area (Flannery 1968:85).

Pottery

Ceramic changes from the Lagunita to the Golfo Phase are more quantitative than qualitative. Striated pottery decreases in popularity until by the end of the Golfo Phase, at about 800 B.C., it has all but disappeared. The practice of lustrous burnishing deteriorates, resulting in a duller, sloppier finish on most of the same forms as before. Black-smudging of the surfaces becomes more common, and there is also a marked increase in the use of white slip and of the differential black-and-white firing of these vessels. Many of the old decorative modes of red and specular-red rimming and zoning, rim and zone incising, and of punctation and rocker stamping continue, often in more standardized combinations. A few earlier techniques such as cord marking now seem to be absent or rare, replaced by others such as interior finger punching and appliqué nubbing.

The most striking parallel in ceramics continues to be with Soconusco to the southeast, whose Cuadros Phase Guamuchal Brushed, Méndez and Mapache Red Rimmed, Teófilo Punctate, Amatillo and Cuchilla Whites, Tilapa Red-on-White, and Pampas Black-and-White (Coe and Flannery 1967; Ekholm 1969; Lowe 1967) have close local paste homologues at Laguna Zope. Ceramic relationships with other regions neighboring the southern Isthmus are also strong. The slipped white ware tradition, as one example, has its equivalents in San José Phase Atoyac Yellow–White from the Valley of Oaxaca, the white monochromes of Cotorra Phase Chiapa de Corzo (Dixon 1959:7–12), and the white slipped wares of the North Isthmian San Lorenzo Phase (Coe 1970:25).

Similarly, differentially fired black-and-white pottery, red-on-white, red and specular-red rim painting and zoning, exterior rim incising, and black-smudging have their counterparts in all the regions under consideration. Their totality defines a ceramic cotradition in which much of Mesoamerica participates before the first millennium B.C.

Crosscutting many of these Golfo ceramic types on the attribute level are decorative modes that have come to be identified with the Olmec. Raspada-excised and sometimes red pigment-filled crossed bands, flame brows, paw wings, and opposed scrolls are motifs that occur at this time, and not only at Laguna Zope; they are time markers from the central highlands of Mexico to southern Guatemala and beyond. The innovative focus of this stylistic horizon is quite clearly the north Isthmian region, where San Lorenzo, La Venta, Laguna de los Cerros, and probably other as yet uninvestigated settlements appear to have grown rapidly into important centers of cultural development and probably of political and economic power. At Laguna Zope the fact that the Olmec style is simply superimposed on preexisting pottery forms and finishes seems more indicative of the settlement's heightened interaction with the northern Isthmus than of any submission–dominance relationship.

Obsidian

Our sample of Golfo Phase obsidian from Laguna Zope is composed entirely of the same small flakes, fragments, and debris that characterize the previous Lagunita Phase. A little over half of this obsidian had been obtained from the Guadalupe Victoria source in Puebla and, as before, would in all probability have passed through the Olmec north Isthmus or Oaxaca Valley region on its way to the southern Isthmus. El Chayal in Guatemala continued

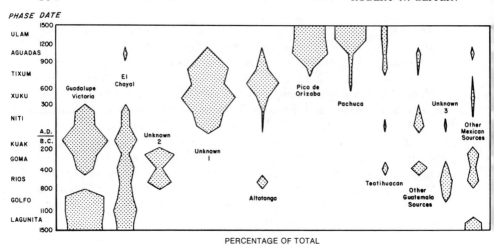

Figure 9.4. Geologic sources of obsidian supply for the southern Isthmus of Tehuantepec (1500 B.C.–A.D. 1500)

to be the other main source of obsidian, accounting for somewhat over 30% of the Laguna Zope supply (Figure 9.4).

It is noteworthy that Guadalupe Victoria and El Chayal were also the most important obsidian sources at this time for Olmec San Lorenzo (Cobean et al. 1971:669; Hester, Heizer, and Jack 1971:136). El Chayal obsidian might well have reached San Lorenzo by passing up the Pacific coast to the southern Isthmus via Soconusco, for which it was probably the primary Early and Middle Preclassic source (Pires-Ferreira 1975: table 2). From the southern Isthmus it would have been moved north to the Olmec center. Laguna Zope itself may well have been a transshipment point in this linkage.

At the same time, San José Phase sites in the Valley of Oaxaca appear to have been utilizing El Chayal and Guadalupe Victoria as well as other obsidian sources in Mexico and Guatemala (Pires-Ferreira 1975: table 2). Almost certainly the Guatemala obsidian would have traveled through the southern Isthmus on its way to highland Oaxaca, and conceivably some of the Mexico obsidian may have moved down the Gulf Coast and up to the Valley of Oaxaca via the Isthmian route.

Unfortunately, at present we do not have source information for the obsidian found in the Central Depression of Chiapas. On the bases of proximity and other kinds of interaction it seems likely that El Chayal or some alternative Guatemala source(s) were primary to this region.

The ratio of obsidian-to-pottery (Figure 9.3a) indicates only a slight intensification of per capita utilization at Laguna Zope relative to the preceding phase. The considerable growth of the site, however, connotes a much-increased absolute quantity being imported.

Locally Obtainable Quartz and Shells

The occurrence of small quartz flakes, fragments, and debris in the Golfo Phase closely parallels that of obsidian: An only slightly altered quartz-to-pottery ratio indicates at most a small per-person increase in utilization (Figure 9.3a). But again, considering the probable population growth at the settlement, this implies a much-expanded total exploitation, roughly equal to that of obsidian.

The hypothesis that quartz tools were being employed for shell-working is supported by the continuing correlation of their ratio to pottery with the similarly stable ratio of ornamental shell-to-pottery (Figure 9.3b). The projected increase in total quartz flake use would likewise have been matched by a greater overall procurement of ornamental shells. Going out on a limb, I propose that we might be dealing with a situation at Laguna Zope where more farmers who were part-time artisans were beginning to find it increasingly worthwhile, indeed profitable, to devote some of their efforts to interregional activities such as shell export.

I am unable, at the present time, to relate this directly to the evolution of social class differentiation, but it may well have been the case, as it was in the Valley of Oaxaca, that participation in long-distance exchange was limited to emerging elite segments ("big men") of the society. At any rate, the developing centrality of Laguna Zope would have been reenforced as it became a convenient focus for procurement, bulking, and export of local products—shell being the one for which we have evidence—and perhaps for receipt, interregional forwarding, and intraregional distribution of foreign goods such as obsidian. The consequences would have been a positive feedback between entrepreneurial activities and settlement growth.

RIOS PHASE (800–400 B.C.)

The Settlement

During the succeeding Ríos Phase there was continued rapid growth at Laguna Zope. Ríos pottery covers a surface area of almost 90 ha (over 200 acres), the maximum expanse ever achieved. San José Mogote, again as a basis for comparison, was still the largest settlement in the Valley of Oaxaca but, at somewhat over 40 ha (Flannery 1968:94), remained less than half the size of coeval Laguna Zope.

Pottery

Arriving with the Ríos Phase at Laguna Zope is a distinctive new ceramic complex. Most diagnostic is a silty-paste, silky-burnished, unslipped white monochrome whose commonest form is a flat-bottom, outflaring-wall bowl. The bowls are decorated, usually on the interior rim surface, by double (but sometimes one or three) sgraffito scored lines, many examples of which are some variation of the familiar "double-line-break" motif. Sgraffito incising also occurs, although less frequently, on the rim exterior below which there may be incised diagonals, scrolls, and/or a double line just above the base.

Other fine-white burnished forms are tall vertical-neck *ollas*, exterior-bolstered rim bowls, convex-wall bowls, and *tecomates*. The bolstered rims are often incised on top, and the *tecomates* commonly have a sgraffito or deeply incised exterior rim line.

Similar to the fine-white burnished ware in form as well as decoration is a light-tan colored ware whose paste is infused with small mica particles so that when burnished a specular gold surface effect is created. Additional gold-specular forms not having fine-white burnished counterparts are large, incised or plain, heavy-wall *tecomates*, a variety of high-neck *ollas*, open-mouth, convex-wall bowls, and shallow convex or flat-bottom plates. Finish and decorative techniques rare in the fine-white burnished are black-smudging and stick or fingernail jabs on the exterior body, particularly on the thinner-wall *tecomates*. The jabs are sometimes enclosed on top by an incised rim line and below by a scalloped line reminiscent of Jocotal Phase Tocanaque Red-unburnished pottery at Izapa (Ekholm 1969:fig. 50).

The new Ríos pottery at Laguna Zope is tied to much of Mesoamerica by a distinctive horizon style of which the fine-white burnished and gold-specular wares are regional representatives. Perhaps the best known single attribute of this horizon is the previously mentioned interior-rim sgraffito incising of bowls with double-line-breaks. This motif seems to be most often associated with slipped or unslipped white wares such as Guadalupe Phase Atoyac Yellow–White in the Valley of Oaxaca (Flannery 1968:fig. 8), Dili Phase White Monochrome (Dixon 1959:fig. 28) and Mirador II Smudged White (Peterson 1963:8) both from the Chiapas Central Depression, Nacaste Phase Camalote White and Tacamichapa Hard on the northern Isthmus (Coe 1970:28), and Conchas Phase White-to-Buff in the Soconusco region (Coe 1961:65–66; Coe and Flannery 1967:42–43).

Obsidian

Our sample for Ríos Phase is again small, but suggests an absence of obsidian at Laguna Zope from the Guadalupe Victoria source (Figure 9.4), an absence which may be related to the destruction of Olmec San Lorenzo across the Isthmus. Perhaps the problems at San Lorenzo also relate to the concomitant decrease from 28% to 19% of Guadalupe Victoria's contribution to the overall Oaxaca Valley supply (Pires-Ferreira 1975:table 2). I am not proposing (nor denying) that the San Lorenzo Olmec directly controlled Guadalupe Victoria obsidian; however, they did use it heavily, and their sudden political demise may have temporarily disrupted the network through which it was distributed in southern Mesoamerica.

Obsidian from Altotonga, Veracruz, the major source for Olmec La Venta (Hester, Jack, and Benfer 1973:167), appeared for the first time at Laguna Zope during the Ríos Phase. Comprising 16% of the total sample, perhaps it served as a partial, albeit temporary, replacement for Guadalupe Victoria. At the same time, El Chayal's contribution remained relatively unchanged at 16%. Another 33% of the obsidian was derived from Unknown Source 2 (possibly located in central Mexico), 16% came from El Ocotito, and the remainder from other unidentified proveniences.

The use of Ríos Phase obsidian continued to be primarily for the production of small unretouched flakes. A reasonably stable ratio of obsidian-to-pottery (Figure 9.3a) indicates that use per person had not changed significantly from earlier phases. Continued growth of population at the settlement, however, would mean that greater total amounts of obsidian were being brought in.

Locally Obtainable Quartz and Shell

It is during the Ríos Phase that the use of small crystalline and cryptocrystalline quartz flakes, in contrast to obsidian, began to grow substantially. This is noted not only as a result of population expansion at Laguna Zope but in terms of more intensive utilization as well (Figure 9.3a). If these flakes were being employed for shell-working the higher quartz-to-pottery ratio in our test excavations means that inhabitants of Laguna Zope were devoting more and more of their time to an expanding industry involving the procurement and export of whole shells, blanks, or finished ornaments to adjacent noncoastal regions.

GOMA PHASE (400–200 B.C.)

The Settlement

No expansion of Laguna Zope's dimensions was noted for the Goma Phase; in fact, the site may have decreased slightly in overall size. The significance, if any, of this possible contraction is unknown. Perhaps it denotes a denser, more nucleated population. If it reflects a cessation of growth or negative growth at Laguna Zope, what relationship might this have to the total abandonment of San Lorenzo just across the Isthmus on the Gulf Coast? These provoking questions await further investigation.

Pottery

Ceramic remains from Goma Phase deposits at Laguna Zope reveal another major change in forms and decoration. Although many shared attributes of the new pottery indicate continued interaction among regions surrounding the southern Isthmus, political upheavals and developments in Mesoamerica were altering the sources and distribution of the commonalities.

At Chiapa de Corzo, in the Chiapas Central Depression, corresponding roughly in time with the waning of Olmec culture on the northern Isthmus and preceding by a century or so what would be the Goma Phase on the southern Isthmus, a radical and possibly intrusive culture change has been noted (Lowe and Mason 1965:212). This event was marked by the introduction of a tradition of hard, lustrous-slipped, usually brown, orange, or red pottery whose locus of derivation seems to have been farther to the east. Its diffusion is seen in the appearance of such regional variants as the Conchas Orange and Streaky Black-Brown of Soconusco (Coe and Flannery 1967:48–55), the cream wares of Monte Albán I of the Oaxaca Valley (Caso and Bernal 1965:875), and somewhat later in the North Isthmian "brilliantly polished" red wares of Middle Tres Zapotes A (Weiant 1943:18).

The sudden popularity of lustrous-brown and waxy orange-slipped wares during the Goma Phase at Laguna Zope implies strong ties to this purportedly eastward-originating horizon. Particularly distinctive among its new attributes are bowls with inflected or composite silhouettes, spouts, wide-everted rims, labial or medial flanges and ribbing, and a great variety of rim-modeling techniques. On these forms there is an enormous elaboration of groove and sgraffito incising and punctation, most frequently on exterior walls and on the tops of flattened, bolstered, or everted rims. Pendant triangles, hatching and cross-hatching, hanging loops, zones of parallel straight, curvilinear, and zig-zag lines, and the so-called *xochitl* design abound in all sorts of combinations. Usulután clouding on Laguna Zope gloss-orange pottery is, to the best of my knowledge, the most northerly manifestation of this unusual decorative technique yet uncovered. Painted decoration, much less common than incision, is employed nevertheless to produce red and specular-red rims, interior body designs, and bichrome combinations of the orange and brown slips.

Along with the highly polished wares there is also a more prosaic development of unslipped, coarse orange–brown paste *ollas* with scalloped appliqué lug handles. Most of these large vessels are crudely burnished on the interior and exterior below the rim and lack any kind of decoration. Similar utilitarian *ollas* are found among the Monte Albán I coarse brown wares (Caso and Bernal 1965:875), the coarse unslipped pottery of the Chiapas Central Depression (Peterson 1963:58–63), and brown wares of lower Tres Zapotes (Drucker 1943:53–55).

Obsidian

Obsidian utilization during the Goma Phase at Laguna Zope witnessed the reappearance of Guadalupe Victoria as an important source of supply, accounting for 33% of the total (Figure 9.4). This could signify a reestablishment of the network through which Guadalupe Victoria obsidian was distributed. El Chayal, with about 9%, and the Unknown Source 2, now contributing 42% of the total, also continued to be utilized, as in the previous phase, along with several minor sources such as Teotihuacán, Tequila, and a possible Unknown Source 3.

The ratio of obsidian-to-pottery (Figure 9.3a) remains virtually unchanged from the preceding phase which, assuming stable population, would indicate not only a constant intensity of use but a roughly equal total quantity imported. From the continued preponderance of small flakes in the assemblage it is reasonable to assume that the obsidian was serving the same functions as before.

Locally Obtainable Quartz and Shell

An enormous increment in the frequency of small quartz flakes occurs during the Goma Phase, matched by a similar intesification of ornamental shell exploitation (Figures 9.3a and 3b). Obviously the importance of ornamental shell at Laguna Zope had increased dramatically over the last phase. Without going so far as to propose that some inhabitants of Laguna Zope were now specializing in a shell industry, I feel there is strong evidence that they were at least devoting much more of their time to its procurement, probably to its working, and possibly to its interregional distribution.

Comparative data are sparse, but available descriptions of late Preclassic artifact assemblages in highland regions surrounding the southern Isthmus (e.g., Lee 1969:169–183;Winter 1974:982) intimate that the total importation of shell and shell ornaments was, if anything, greater than during earlier phases. Moreover, the association of spondylus and other ornamental species with high-status burials (Mason 1960:17) and with elite areas of highland ceremonial centers (Blanton 1975:38) suggests that shell remained a valued commodity, perhaps an even more important symbol of differential social status than before. As such, demand for it would have intensified considerably with the accelerating development of class-structured settlements.

In the Valley of Oaxaca, as one nearby example, at least 40 elite sites with monumental architecture are found by the end of Monte Albán I, some very densely populated and extending over 400 ha in area (Flannery 1968:98). In light of all this potential new demand, an intensification of the ornamental shell industry seems a reasonable response for a place like Laguna Zope where the source of supply was readily at hand and a prior tradition of exploitation existed.

KUAK AND NITI PHASES (200 B.C.–A.D. 1 and A.D. 1–300)

The Settlement

During the last two phases of occupation the size of Laguna Zope persisted more or less as before at somewhere between 70 and 80 ha. The momentum of spatial expansion appears to have been lost, although the settlement continued to be the central place for the southern Isthmus. No other community in the region challenged its size and, judging by the quantity and quality of artifactual remains, it seems to have remained a dynamic, healthy, and perhaps even more densely occupied entity. Sometime around A.D. 300, however, Laguna Zope was permanently abandoned for reasons unknown, apparently in favor of what was to become the even larger Classic and Early Postclassic center of Saltillo, located about 1 km to the southeast.

Pottery

The most remarkable characteristic of certain Kuak and Niti phase pottery at Laguna Zope is an unmistakably close resemblance to its contemporaries at Monte Albán. Burnished grey, previously a very minor component of the ceramic assemblage, becomes by about 200 B.C. one of the most dominant wares in terms of popularity and is without rival in its elaboration of forms and decoration. Animal effigy vessels, bowls with concentric-line incised interior bottoms, and large ladles are among the silty-paste local equivalents of diagnostic Monte Albán I and II greywares (e.g., Caso, Bernal, and Acosta 1967:figs. 5, 115, 165, 171).

On the other hand, most of the Laguna Zope grey composite and inflected bowl forms, modeling techniques, and incised decorative motifs can be traced to styles introduced through the earlier lustrous brown and orange wares that themselves continue in attenuated number during the Kuak Phase. Still other attributes such as bridge spouts and hollow mammiform tripod or tetrapod vessel supports are common to much of southern Mesoamerica at this time and denote the continued ceramic relationships between regions.

Along with their greywares, Kuak and Niti Phases are characterized by a renaissance of black-and-white pottery. With its hard, well-burnished surface, this new differentially fired ware conforms to Wallrath's (1967:44ff.) Guizi varieties defined for the western edge of the southern Isthmus. In contrast to the polymorphic grey pottery, the black-and-white appears to be a standardized (albeit high quality) ware, mass-produced in a limited range of vessel forms and almost devoid of incised decoration. Its common shapes are open mouth convex, vertical, outslanted, composite, or inflected wall bowls. Rims are usually direct but are sometimes interior- or exterior-stepped. Plastic decoration is limited almost exclusively to the occasional application of small fillets, usually three in a row, at points along the exterior midlines of some vessels. Interregionally, the black-and-white pottery seems related to Guanacaste Phase white-rim black of the Chiapas Central Depression (Peterson 1963:9–10). The additional coincidence at this time of grey as well as stucco polychrome pottery in central Chiapas, the southern Isthmus of Tehuantepec, and the Valley of Oaxaca serves as confirmation that communication between regions continued to be active.

During the final Niti Phase at Laguna Zope, red or specular-red painted decoration becomes increasingly popular on black-and-white pottery, frequently along with, but often in place of, the differential firing. The painting consists of rim lines and a variety of wavy lines, hanging loops, zigzags, and lattices on interior and exterior surfaces. A contemporaneous, multiple wavy-line tradition evolves in the Central Depression of Chiapas in its Protoclassic Horcones Phase (Lowe 1962:figs. 12a and b).

Plain utilitarian *ollas,* noted for the previous Goma Phase, persist in abundance throughout the Late Preclassic and Protoclassic on the southern Isthmus and adjacent regions. At Laguna Zope, Protoclassic Niti Phase *ollas* are distinguished from their predecessors by the application of a thin dull-orange exterior wash below the rim.

Along with the intensification of ceramic affiliations with Monte Albán there is, during the final two phases at Laguna Zope, a marked and steady weakening of the Mayoid relationships previously observed in the highly polished brown and orange wares. It is interesting that the same cutting of ties with regions to the east and northeast has been observed at Chiapa de

Corzo in the Chiapas Central Depression (Lowe and Mason 1965:218) but not at Pacific coastal Soconusco. In the latter region, Izapa and apparently other centers such as Abaj Takalik grew to considerable size and importance during the Late Preclassic–Protoclassic, maintaining close affiliations with the ascending Maya civilization in lowland eastern Mexico and the Petén of Guatemala. These complex changes in ceramic affiliations appear to reflect the realignment of political and economic power that was taking place in southern Mesoamerica with the emergence of dynamic new polities such as Monte Albán, Chiapa de Corzo, and the Soconusco centers.

Obsidian

Our sample of obsidian artifacts from Laguna Zope indicates that the ceramic shifts of the terminal Preclassic on the southern Isthmus were matched by a drastic alteration in patterns of obsidian procurement (Figure 9.4). By the end of the Niti phase at A.D. 300, the two most important Preclassic sources—Guadalupe Victoria in Mexico and El Chayal in Guatemala—were no longer being used. The decline in El Chayal obsidian is particularly significant since thereafter Guatemalan sources never again figured substantially in obsidian purveyance for the southern Isthmus. Perhaps this is another indication of intensifying political and economic affiliations with the north during the final centuries of Laguna Zope. Perhaps also it reflects the diversion of El Chayal and other Guatemalan obsidian to Lowland Maya centers during the Classic Period (Hammond 1972).

Two major replacement sources appeared toward the end of the Laguna Zope sequence. The first, Unknown 1, I suspect from chemical analysis, might be the one identified by Stross et al. (n.d.:19) as Zaragoza, Puebla. The second is more securely identified as Altotonga, Veracruz. Both sources are located within 100 km south of the Classic center of El Tajín. During the Protoclassic Niti Phase, Unknown 1 was supplying 34% of Laguna Zope's needs; but, as obsidian recovered from later sites reveals, by the Early Classic, Unknown 1 usage on the southern Isthmus had risen to 78%. Similarly, the minor 3% contribution of Altotonga during the Protoclassic increased to 17% in the Early Classic and 48% by the Late Classic (Figure 9.4).

The total quantity of Kuak Phase obsidian imported to Laguna Zope remained about the same as before; but during the final Niti Phase an increasing obsidian-to-pottery ratio (Figure 9.3a) implies more intensive utilization. This expansion of per capita usage continued throughout the Classic Period. It is related to the rapid decline of microflakes in the obsidian assemblage and their replacement by large, skillfully made prismatic blades.

Locally Obtainable Quartz and Shell

Kuak and Niti phases are also a time of great change in the use of flaked quartz tools at Laguna Zope (Figure 9.3a). Having reached a peak between about 400 and 200 B.C., their production declined precipitously thereafter. By the Early Classic, utilization had dwindled to the point where, for the first time, the total quantity of obsidian imported exceeded that of locally obtainable quartz.

As anticipated, the drop in flaked quartz usage was accompanied by an equally sharp decline in the exploitation of ornamental shell (Figure 9.3b). Apparently the shell industry, while still important, was becoming decreasingly so toward the end of Laguna Zope.

SUMMARY AND CONCLUSIONS

Modern and ethnohistoric accounts invariably describe the southern Isthmus of Tehuantepec as a place of great enterprise in the exchange of local and nonlocal commodities. How far back in time does that characterize the region, and what role, if any, would interregional exchange have played in the development of its earliest major center, Laguna Zope? What I offer in answer is meant only as a working hypothesis, subject to revision when more extensive investigations have been carried out on the southern Isthmus.

The initial settlement of Laguna Zope, sometime prior to 1500 B.C., was probably dictated not by any extraregional factors but simply by its proximity to water and good agricultural land. In terms of Blouet's (1973) evolutionary scheme of settlement patterns, it would have been one of a number of small "limited function settlements" distributed over the landscape to make efficient use of resources.

During the Lagunita Phase, between 1500 and 1100 B.C., however, I have attempted to show that Laguna Zope had become part of an interregional network through which sophisticated ideas about pottery-making were being communicated, obsidian was being procured, and ornamental shell exported. In such a situation there are obvious transaction, distribution, and transport efficiencies in having one centrally placed settlement within a region serve as what geographers have called a "nexus of economic interchange [Zelinsky 1966:35–37]."

Why Laguna Zope assumed this role for the southern Isthmus may, to some extent, have been initially influenced by its central location in the region and its convenience to natural long-distance trade routes. Adjacent Juchitán has grown to become the current commercial nexus for the southern Isthmus primarily because of its placement near the intersection of two interregional highways, the Pan American and Trans-Isthmus. Other chance or opportunistic circumstances may have been equally decisive for commencement of the settlement's singular development. I have focused my attention on the possibility of a desire by at least some of Laguna Zope's residents to take advantage of the growing long-distance demand for ornamental shells.

Once established as a center of exchange, expanding interregional movement of products and cultural ideas during the following Golfo, Ríos, and Goma phases would have further stimulated Laguna Zope's growth. As it developed and became better known, even more exchange would have been drawn to it and more demand created for its export goods. Settlement nucleation might have facilitated part-time participation of its inhabitants in a shell export industry (and perhaps other exchange-oriented activities) through centralization while enabling these early entrepreneurs to continue cultivating outlying fields. There is, I might note, a long tradition of nucleation on the southern Isthmus, continuing into the present, in which modern town-dwelling *istmeño* farmers and fishermen walk several kilometers daily to their fields or the lagoons, while women run small, in-town market businesses, often selling their husbands' or foreign produce. Along with its collection, dissemination, and transport advantages of location and nucleation, Laguna Zope may have also assumed a role as the administrative, social, and ritual center for the southern Isthmus, enhancing still further its attractiveness as a locus of exchange and communication. The remains of large platform mounds support this possibility, although excavation of considerably larger scale than our preliminary testing is needed to provide more definite answers about the full range of activities at Laguna Zope.

I am hardly prepared to do more than guess about reasons for the precipitous decline in the importance of ornamental shell procurement that seems to have occurred at Laguna Zope after 200 B.C. The answer may lie in a shift of the industry to another nearby site or sites. Beyond the southern Isthmus, perhaps the growing political powers of Monte Albán and Chiapa de Corzo were beginning to exact seashells as tribute from other coastal localities in western Oaxaca and Chiapas over which they had more direct control.

My stress on a possible shell industry at Laguna Zope must also be considered in proper context. Perishability may have eliminated from archaeological consideration many other items that, if historical and ethnohistorical evidence can be projected backward, might more accurately represent south Isthmian participation in Preclassic exchange. We know, for example, that shortly after the Spanish Conquest, Hernan Cortés, as *Marqués del Valle*, was obtaining sizable tribute from the southern Isthmus in salted and dried fish and shrimp, fruits, vegetables, cotton, sea salt, and other local products (Anonymous 1952:372–377). It is not farfetched to presume that these same items may have figured in earlier Prehispanic trade or tribute. Other current exports to highland regions with known or possible pre-Conquest antecedents are turtle eggs, hard-baked tortillas, and decorated gourds (Chiñas 1976;Malinowski and de la Fuente 1957;Navarrete 1966). The list of possible export items could be much expanded and does not include subsistence, ritual, and ornamental items from other regions that are now or may previously have been transshipped through the southern Isthmus nor does it include those imported for local use. If some or all of them were being exchanged early in Mesoamerican prehistory, the importance of a central-place settlement on the southern Isthmus would have been even greater.

The inordinately large size of Preclassic Laguna Zope relative to its local contemporaries is also hard to explain, but again I think it profitable to look beyond the immediate region. Implicit or explicit in most models of growth derived from classic central-place theory (e.g., Berry 1967) is the concept that larger centers evolve through a competitive process of consumer servicing. In this primarily endogenous regional process, the formation of major centers is seen as an efficient response to the increasing consumer needs of an expanding local population. Such does not appear to have happened on the southern Isthmus, where the apparent primate development of Laguna Zope preceded rather than grew out of lower-order centers. Based on our survey data, only later in time does there seem to have been a filling in of secondary and lesser centers as regional population expansion created greater demand for goods and services.

A better explanation for the growth of Laguna Zope might be found in Vance's (1970) mercantile model. The model, although derived from more modern Western examples, could with some modification be applied to the development of early regional centers in Mesoamerica and perhaps elsewhere in the prehistoric world. According to Vance, externalized economics—and particularly expanded opportunities for long-distance commerce—play a critical role in the formation of many nucleated (and ultimately urban) centers. The entrepreneur becomes a key figure in the development of communities that grow into depots and eventually into entrepots for the collection, exchange, and distribution of nonlocal goods.

Although Vance focuses on the capitalistic impulse for trade which characterizes postmedieval Europe and the United States, other motivations might be adduced to widen the applicability of his model so that it serves beyond market-integrated situations. Certainly one motivation could have been the expanding interregional demand during the Preclassic Period for utilitarian resources specific to each of Mesoamerica's environmentally diverse zones. To meet this demand, interregional exchange would likely have been transacted in egalitarian and ranked societies through the institution of balanced reciprocity (Sahlins 1965), in the former case between trade partners, in the latter between tribal chiefs. Another motivation for exchange might have been an increasing appetite for esoteric knowledge and rare items such as ornamental shell. Conceivably, the desire for status derived from the acquisition and controlled distribution of these exotic commodities made trade partners out of developing elite segments of Early Preclassic societies.

At this point we can only speculate about whether south Isthmian traders were actually traveling to distant regions, whether more sophisticated peoples from other regions were journeying to Laguna Zope, or both. In any event, I suspect that over and above some "down-the line" (Renfrew 1972:465–466) utilitarian exchange between adjacent minor communities, exotic goods were being transported directly by traders who actually traveled from one major regional center to another. With status-related demand for such items restricted to emerging ranked societies, it would be unlikely that every small hamlet and village between regional centers participated directly in this network.

As a proposed variant on Vance's mercantile model of growth, Laguna Zope would thus be designated an early depot where local items such as shell were collected and prepared for shipment to exchange partners in adjoining regions. Eventually Laguna Zope might have taken on some aspects of an entrepôt in the symbiotic system through which regionally specialized goods began to move in southern Mesoamerica.

I conclude by reemphasizing that with only preliminary excavations carried out to date at Laguna Zope and none at other Early Preclassic sites on the southern Isthmus, the implications of my hypothesis remain to be fully tested. If, however, these prove to have been the circumstances underlying Preclassic development on the southern Isthmus they will further serve to illustrate, in a prehistoric context, one of Vance's central contentions: that attempts at understanding regional growth in a parochial framework, limited by local boundaries, may often be inadequate.

ACKNOWLEDGMENTS

Excavations and subsequent laboratory analyses were supported by research grants from the National Science Foundation (GS-83475), the Sigma Xi Society, and the Concilium on International and Area Studies, Yale University. Fieldwork on the southern Isthmus was conducted under a permit granted by the Instituto Nacional de Antropología e Historia (archivo oficio no. 401-7 B/311.42(Z)/27-1). Many thanks are due Prof. Michael D. Coe who, as my dissertation advisor, first introduced me to the southern Isthmus and made me aware of its fertility as a place for study. My gratitude also goes to Professor Kent V. Flannery whose friendship, guidance and kind offer of laboratory space in Oaxaca contributed immeasurably to the project. I am indebted to Professor Karl K. Turekian for his generosity and confidence in allowing me to use the X-ray fluorescence spectrographic system at the Department of Geology and Geophysics, Yale University, to carry out my obsidian analysis. Special thanks are owed my wife and fellow archaeologist, Judith Francis Zeitlin, for the identifications of shell remains. Helpful suggestions for the improvement of this paper were provided by Professor Irving Rouse who read it in an earlier version. None of these people, of course, are responsible for any errors, omissions, or misinterpretations of fact. Ms. Lois Martin contributed her skills in drawing Figures 9.1, 9.2, and 9.3.

REFERENCES

Adams, R. Mc.
  1966 *The evolution of urban society.* Chicago:Aldine
Anonymous
  1952 *El libro de las tasaciones de pueblos de la Nueva España, siglo XVI.* México:Archivo General de la Nación.
Baker, C. L.
  1930 Geological cross section of the Isthmus of Tehuantepec. *American Geologist* **53**(3):161–174.
Berry, B. J. L.
  1967 *Geography of market centers and retail distribution.* Englewood Cliffs, New Jersey: Prentice-Hall.
Blanton, R. E.
  1975 The Valley of Oaxaca settlement pattern project. Progress report to the National Science Foundation, the Instituto Nacional de Antropología e Historia, and the Research Foundation of the City University of New York. Manuscript.
Blouet, B. W.
  1972 Factors influencing the evolution of settlement patterns. In *Man, settlement and urbanism,* edited by P. J. Ucko, R. Tringham and G. W. Dimbleby, London: Gerald Duckworth. Pp. 3–15.
Burkill, I. H.
  1966 *A dictionary of the economic products of the Malay Peninsula,* Vol. II. Kuala Lampur: Ministry of Agriculture and Co-Operatives.
Callen, E. O.
  1967 *Analysis of the Tehuacan coprolites.* In *The prehistory of the Tehuacan Valley,* Vol. 1, edited by D. S. Byers. Austin: University of Texas Press. Pp. 261–289.
Caso, A., and I. Bernal
  1965 Ceramics of Oaxaca, In *Handbook of Middle American Indians, Vol. 3, Part 2: Archaeology of Southern Mesoamerica,* edited by G. R. Willey. (R. Wanchope, gen. ed.) Austin: University of Texas Press. Pp. 871–895.
Caso, A., I. Bernal, and J. R. Acosta
  1967 *La cerámica de Monte Albán.* México: Memorias del Instituto Nacional de Antropología e Historia, Vol. XIII.
Chiñas, B.
  1976 Zapotec Viajeras. In *Markets in Oaxaca,* edited by S. Cook and M. Diskin. Austin: University of Texas Press. Pp. 169–188.

Cobean, R. H., M. D. Coe, E. A. Perry, Jr., K. K. Turekian, and D. P. Kharkar
   1971   Obsidian trade at San Lorenzo Tenochtitlan, Mexico. *Science* **174:**666–671.
Coe, M. D.
   1961   La Victoria. *An early site on the Pacific Coast of Guatemala. Papers of the Peabody
           Museum of Archaeology and Ethnology*, Vol. 53. Cambridge, Massachusetts: Pea-
           body Museum of Archaeology and Ethnology, Harvard University.
   1970   The archaeological sequence at San Lorenzo Tenochtitlan, Veracruz, Mexico. *Con-
           tributions of the University of California Archaeological Research Facility* **8:**21–34.
Coe, M. D. and K. V. Flannery
   1967   *Early cultures and human ecology in South Coastal Guatemala. Smithsonian Con-
           tributions to Anthropology*, Vol. 3. Washington, D.C.: Smithsonian Institution.
Davis, D. D.
   1974   Patterns of Early Formative subsistence in Southern Mesoamerica, 1500–1100 B.C.
           Man (N. S.) **10:**41–59.
Dixon, K. A.
   1959   Ceramics from two Preclassic periods at Chiapa de Corzo, Chiapas, Mexico. *Papers of
           the New World Archaeological Foundation* No. 5. Provo, Utah: Brigham
           Young University.
Drucker, P.
   1943   *Ceramic sequences at Tres Zapotes, Veracruz, Mexico. Smithsonian Institution
           Bureau of American Ethnology* Bulletin 140. Washington, D.C.: Smithsonian Institu-
           tion.
Ekholm, S. M.
   1969   Mound 30a and the Early Preclassic ceramic sequence of Izapa, Chiapas, Mexico.
           Papers of the New World Archaeological Foundation No. 25. Provo, Utah: Brigham
           Young University.
Flannery, K. V.
   1968   The Olmec and the Valley of Oaxaca: A model for inter-regional interaction in
           Formative times. In *Dumbarton Oaks conference on the Olmec*, edited by E. P.
           Benson. Washington: Dumbarton Oaks Research Library and Collection. Pp. 79–
           110.
Flannery, K. V., and J. Schoenwetter
   1970   Climate and man in Formative Oaxaca. *Archaeology* **23**(2):144–152.
Green, D. F., and G. W. Lowe
   1967   *Altamira and Padre Piedra, Early Preclassic sites in Chiapas*, Mexico. *Papers of the
           New World Archaeological Foundation* No. 20. Provo, Utah:Brigham Young
           University.
Grove, D. C.
   1974   *San Pablo, Nexpa, and the Early Formative Archaeology of Morelos, Mexico*. Van-
           derbilt Univ. Publications in Anthropology, No. 12, Nashville:Vanderbilt
           University Press.
Hammond, N.
   1972   Obsidian trade routes in the Mayan area. *Science* **178:**1092–1093.
Hester, T. R., R. F. Heizer and R. N. Jack
   1971   Technology and geologic sources of obsidian artifacts from Cerro de las Mesas,
           Veracruz, Mexico with observations on Olmec trade. *Contributions of the University
           of California Archaeological Research Facility* **13:**133–141.
Hester, T. R., R. N. Jack and A. Benfer
   1973   Trace element analysis of obsidian from Michoacan, Mexico: Preliminary results.
           Contributions of the University of California Archaeological Research Facility
           18:167–176.

Hill, A. F.
  1952 *Economic botany,* 2nd ed. New York: McGraw-Hill.
Lee, T. A., Jr.
  1969 *The artifacts of Chiapa de Corzo, Chiapas, Mexico. Papers of the New World Archaeological Foundation,* No. 26. Provo, Utah: Brigham Young University.
Lowe, G. W.
  1962 *Mound 5 and minor excavations, Chiapa de Corzo, Chiapas, Mexico. Papers of the New World Archaeological Foundation,* No. 12. Provo, Utah: Brigham Young University.
  1967 Discussion and appendix. In Altamira and Padre Piedra, Early Preclassic sites in Chiapas, Mexico. *Papers of the New World Archaeological Foundation* No. 20. Provo, Utah: Brigham Young University.
  1975 The Early Preclassic Barra Phase of Altamira, Chiapas. A review with new data. *Papers of the New World Archaeological Foundation* No. 38. Provo, Utah: Brigham Young University.
Lowe, G. W., and J. A. Mason
  1965 Archaeological survey of the Chiapas coast, highlands, and upper Grijalva basin. In Handbook of Middle American Indians, Vol. 2, Part 1: *Archaeology of Southern Mesoamerica,* edited by G. R. Willey. (R. Wauchope, gen. ed.) Austin: University of Texas Press. Pp. 195–236.
MacNeish, R. S.
  1958 *Preliminary archaeological investigations in the Sierra de Tamaulipas, Mexico. Transactions of the American Philosophical Society (N.S.)* Vol. 48(6).
Malinowski, B., and J. de la Fuente
  1957 *La economí de un sistema de mercados en México.* Acta Antropológica, Epoca 2, Vol. 1(2). México.
Mason, J. A.
  1960 *Mound 12, Chiapa de Corzo, Chiapas, Mexico.* Papers of the New World Archaeological Foundation, No. 9. Provo, Utah: Brigham Young University.
Navarrete, C.
  1966 *The Chiapanec history and culture.* Papers of the New World Archaeological Foundation, No. 21. Provo, Utah: Brigham Young University.
Parsons, L. A., and B. J. Price
  1971 Mesoamerican trade and its role in the emergence of civilization. *Contributions of the University of California Archaeological Research Facility* **11**:169–195.
Peterson, F. A.
  1963 *Some ceramics from Mirador, Chiapas, Mexico.* Papers of the New World Archaeological Foundation, No. 15. Provo, Utah: Brigham Young University.
Pires-Ferreira, J. W.
  1975 *Formative Mesoamerican exchange networks with special reference to the Valley of Oaxaca.* Memoirs of the Museum of Anthropology No. 7. Ann Arbor: University of Michigan Press.
Rogers, D. J.
  1963 Studies of *Manihot esculenta* Crantz and related species. *Bulletin of the Torrey Botanical Club* **90**(1):43–54.
Renfrew, C.
  1972 *The emergence of civilization. The Cyclades and the Aegean in the third millennium B. C.* London:Methuen
Sahlins, M. D.
  1965 Exchange–value and the diplomacy of primitive trade. In *Essays in economic an-*

thropology. *Proceedings of the 1965 Annual Spring Meeting of the American Ethnological Society*, edited by J. Helm. Seattle: University of Washington Press. Pp. 95–129.

Sanders, W. T.
  1956   The central Mexican symbiotic region. In *Prehistoric settlement patterns in the New World.* edited by G. R. Willey. Viking Fund Publications in Anthropology, No. 23. Pp. 115–127.

Stross, F. H., T. R. Hester, R. F. Heizer, and R. N. Jack
  n.d.   Chemical and archaeological studies of Mesoamerican and Californian obsidians. In *Advances in obsidian glass studies: Archaeological and geochemical perspectives*, edited by R. E. Taylor. In press.

Vance, J. E., Jr.
  1970   *The merchant's world: The geography of wholesaling.* Englewood Cliffs, New Jersey: Prentice-Hall.

Wallrath, M.
  1967   *Excavations in the Tehuantepec region, Mexico.* Transactions of the American Philosophical Society (N.S.), Vol. 57(2).

Weiant, C. W.
  1943   *An introduction to the ceramics of Tres Zapotes, Veracruz, Mexico.* Smithsonian Institution Bureau of American Ethnology, Bulletin 139. Washington, D. C.: Smithsonian Institution.

Winter, M. C.
  1974   Residential patterns at Monte Albán, Oaxaca, Mexico. *Science* **186**:981–987.

Wolf, E. R.
  1959   *Sons of the shaking earth.* Chicago: University of Chicago Press.

Zeitlin, R. N.
  1978   Preclassic exchange on the southern Isthmus of Tehuantepec, Mexico. Ph.D. Dissertation, Department of Anthropology, Yale University. In preparation.

Zeitlin, R. N. and R. C. Heimbuch
          Trace element analysis and the archaeological study of obsidian procurement in Precolumbian Mesoamerica. In *Lithics and subsistence.* edited by D. D. Davis. Vanderbilt University. Publications in Anthropology. In Press.

Zelinsky, W.
  1966   *A prologue to population geography.* Englewood Cliffs, New Jersey: Prentice-Hall.

chapter 10

An Ethnohistoric Model for Native Economy and Settlement Patterns in Southern Veracruz, Mexico

BARBARA L. STARK

Arizona State University

INTRODUCTION

Ecological diversity, economic specialization, and intergroup exchanges have been singled out as important to the development and maintenance of complex sociopolitical organizations (Steward 1955:70; Service 1971:134–143; Flannery 1968:105–108; Sanders 1968; Sahlins 1972:140). To the extent that these factors are correlated with complex societies, we would expect to observe them in such contrasting environments as lowland and highland Mesoamerica. However, there are differing interpretations of prehistoric subsistence and economic practices in the Mesoamerican tropical lowlands. The position that environmental redundancy was a salient factor for socioeconomic organization in the southern Maya lowlands (Coe 1961b) has been amplified and extended to include the Olmec heartland in Southern Veracruz and Tabasco (Rathje 1972). On the other hand, Sanders and Price (1968:159, 171) conclude that environmental differentiation, especially notable in the highlands, contributed to the development of civilization throughout Mesoamerica (cf. Coe 1974).

Elsewhere I have examined ethnohistoric data pertaining to sixteenth-century communities in the Lower Papaloapan Basin, Veracruz, Mexico (Stark 1974). Economic specialization within and among these communities correlates with locally available natural resources. These community specializations figured in subsistence, trade, and tribute and have prompted me to argue against environmental redundancy as a major factor in late prehispanic economy. Two environmental patterns were described which seem to have affected sixteenth-century economy (Figures 10.1, 10.2). First, from the coast inland along river drainages, there is a contrast between estuarine deltas, which have plentiful aquatic foods, and interior areas with plentiful farming land on higher levees and terraces. Second, large segments of the Gulf coastal plain differ environmentally. For example, Central Veracruz is drier than Southern Veracruz, and there are marked rainfall differences within Southern Veracruz. The Lower Papaloapan receives greater rainfall than Central Veracruz and has renewed levee soils. The Tuxtla Mountains receive the greatest rainfall, but at the same time create a rain shadow; soils are well drained and fertile. Southern Veracruz from the Coatzacoalcos drainage eastward to the Tonalá is rainier than the Lower Papaloapan, though not receiving the maximum of the Tuxtlas; again, flooding and alluviation create rich soils along rivers (Coe 1970b; 1974). Clearly the

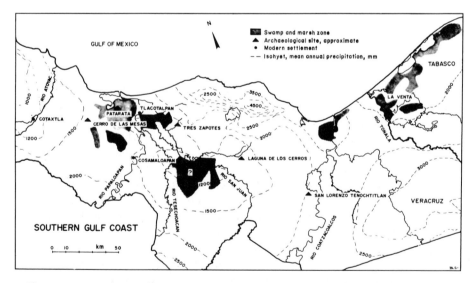

Figure 10.1. Southern Gulf Coast. Base map by Comisión Intersecretarial Coordinadora del Levantamiento de la Carta Geográfica de la República Mexicana (1957:14Q-VI, 15Q-V, 15Q-VII) and CETENAL (1970:14Q-VI, 15Q-V).

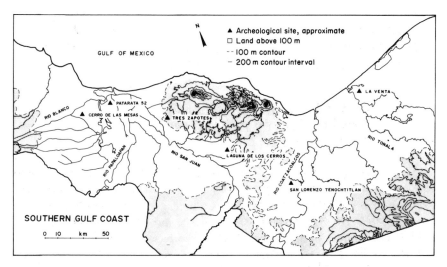

Figure 10.2. Southern Gulf Coast showing contour intervals. Base map and 200-m contour intervals from Comisión Intersecretarial Coordinadora del Levantamiento de la Carta Geográfica de la República Mexicana (1957:14Q-VI, 15Q-V, 15Q-VII); 100-m contour line from American Geographical Society of New York (1957); hydrography of Papaloapan Basin from Papaloapan Commission map, "Cuenca del Río Papaloapan, 1972." Note the difference in hydrography near Laguna de los Cerros compared to Figure 10.1.

variation outlined above could affect aboriginal farming, fishing, shellfishing, and gathering.[1]

With environmental data and sixteenth-century documents, it is possible to develop an ethnohistoric model for native economy and settlement. In this chapter I will review the evidence and formulate this model, which contrasts with Rathje's (1972) core–buffer model predicated on the importance of environmental redundancy. I will defer a synopsis of Rathje's model to the section of this chapter that compares some aspects of the ethnohistoric model with the archaeological record. The insufficiency of current archaeological data precludes rigorous testing of either approach. However, I

[1]In addition, differences in natural vegetation could have been important with respect to feral economic species. Gomez-Pompa (1973) summarizes current information on the distribution and ecology of natural vegetation in Veracruz. High evergreen and semievergreen *selvas* in parts of Veracruz include vegetation types in which *Brosimum alicastrum* Sw., *ramon*, is a dominant. Recently this species has received attention as a possible prehistoric food source for the Maya (Puleston 1968; 1971; Puleston and Puleston 1971). The lower slopes of the Tuxtla Mountains below 700 m are one locality where *ramon* occurs as one of the dominants in an evergreen *selva* (Gomez-Pompa 1973:110–111). In contrast, the frequency of *ramon* is less in evergreen *selvas* elsewhere in Southern Veracruz, where variation in microtopography and soils produces a complex vegetation mosaic (Gomez-Pompa 1973:106–110).

will discuss two statements derived from the ethnohistoric model along with test implications. The discussion of test implications and archaeological data will direct attention to the current lack of satisfactory information for prehistoric economic interpretations of the Gulf Coast.

ETHNOHISTORIC DATA BASE
FOR THE LOWER PAPALOAPAN
AND VICINITY

Data pertinent to the Lower Papaloapan Basin comprise sixteenth- and early seventeenth-century maps, geographic relations, descriptive accounts (sometimes incorporated into other documents), and tribute and taxation records (Stark 1974:200–201). Map analysis and placement of sixteenth-century communities will not be discussed here (see Stark 1974:206–208). Those near the Lower Papaloapan have received more intensive analysis and are more securely located than those to the west along the Atoyac River or to the east in the Tuxtla Mountains. Sixteenth-century communities in the Lower Papaloapan and vicinity included Tlacotalpan, Amatlán, Cosamaloapan, Puctla, Tlalixcoyan, Cotaxtla, Medellín, and Tuxtla (Figure 10.3). These were political communities, usually with a head settlement and subject settlements; I will refer to these as towns and hamlets (or villages), respectively.

Near the Papaloapan, towns and hamlets were distributed along the river, its tributaries, distributaries, and associated lagoons. Tlacotalpan was nearest the coast; it controlled the Papaloapan at its mouth and much of the eastern estuarine zone, including tracts of mangrove swamp and some low levee farmland. Its territory encompassed the junctures of the Papaloapan with the San Juan and Tesechoacán rivers. Puctla has disappeared but was located near a lower-activity distributary, the Acula River, and probably controlled a range of environments similar to those of Tlacotalpan; because it was farther inland (south), it probably held proportionately more farmland. Amatlán and Cosamaloapan were situated along the Papaloapan south of Tlacotalpan, holding areas with considerable levee farmland. Tlalixcoyan, on the western edge of the Papaloapan Basin, was near higher land on a tributary of the Blanco River; there are two major east–west trending ridges in that area, which are farmed and ranched today (Large, in press). Cotaxtla, on the next drainage west, the Atoyac, was inland with elevated land suitable for farming. Medellín was near the mouth of the Atoyac. The town of Tuxtla, located in the western Tuxtla Mountains, enjoyed a territory with well-drained fertile soils, a freshwater lake (Catemaco), and a stretch of coastline.

Economic information in descriptive accounts and geographic relations

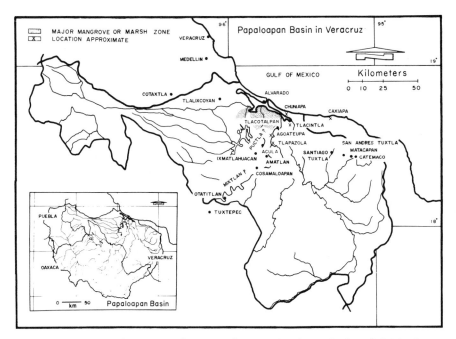

Figure 10.3. Sixteenth-century settlements in the Lower Papaloapan Basin and vicinity. Base maps were Comisión Intersecretarial Coordinadora del Levantamiento de la Carta Geográfica de la República Mexicana (1957:14Q-VI, 15Q-V) and Papaloapan Commission map, "Cuenca del Río Papaloapan, 1972."

pertinent to these communities is summarized in Table 10.1. Data from the geographic relations are particularly valuable because the list of questions differentiates characteristic foodstuffs from enterprises, trade, or commerce (question 33). Many other accounts do not distinguish between subsistence and other aspects of the economy. Usually, native commerce received little direct comment by Spaniards. Patterns of economic specialization may involve subsistence, manufacture, or commerce, but the latter two are of particular importance because they could form a basis for interdependent exchanges among communities.

According to community descriptions, economies varied with environmental characteristics. From the mouth of the Papaloapan inland, there is a progressive shift from greater reliance on fishing in the estuarine zone to a greater emphasis on farming where levees are higher and broader. This can be seen in the contrasts among Tlacotalpan, Amatlán, and Cosamaloapan. In addition, manufactures change from pottery and salt to cotton cloth from the estuarine zone inland. On interior levee lands cacao, a crop of wide commercial value, was also commonly grown. Immediately west of the

Table 10.1
SUMMARY OF DESCRIPTIVE ACCOUNTS

Town/hamlet	Local environment	Manufactures	Commerce	Subsistence	Pursuits of uncertain importance	Sources
Tlacotalpan	Low levee and swamp	See Commerce	Made pottery (2); made local salt, also imported it from Campeche (1); fishing (1) GR	Fishing (2); farmed corn, beans, chile, sweet potato, used tree fruits, kept fowl (1); raised bananas (1)		del Paso y Troncoso 1905:5:1–11; Trens 1947:239ff.; Mota y Escobar 1945:210–214
Atlacintla (Alvarado)	Sandy dune ridge			Several crops either sold or produced there (1)		
Tlacintla	Low levee					
Agoateupa	Low levee or levee					
Tlapazola	Low levee or levee			Fishing (1)		
Chuniapa	Sandy dune ridge					
Amatlan	Levee	Cotton cloth (1)		Farmed (1 + 1?); farmed corn, cotton (1); fishing (2)	Logging (3); transported provisions by canoes and boats (1)	Trens 1947:239ff.; Mota y Escobar 1945:210–214; AGN, Ramo de Tierras 1604: 2736, exp. 21
Quaguacan	Levee					
Quyuapa	Levee					
Tulancingo	Levee					
Achilcoatlitlan	Levee					

Cosamaloapan	Levee	Cotton clothing (1)	Sold produce in Veracruz (1)	Farmed corn, cotton, and cacao (1); farmed corn and cacao (1); farmed corn and cotton (1); fishing (1)	Logging? (1)	del Paso y Troncoso 1905:1:232; AGN, Ramo de Tierras 1590: 2692, exp. 10; Trens 1947:239ff.; Mota y Escobar 1945:210–214; AGN, Ramo de Tierras 1604:2736, exp. 21
Puctla	Swamps or low levee			Fishing (1); farmed corn and vegetables (1); farmed corn, beans, and vegetables (1)		AGN, Ramo de Tierras 1588:2695, exp. 7; Trens 1947:239 ff.; AGN, Ramo de Tierras 1604:2736, exp. 21; Mota y Escobar 1945:210–214
Ismatlaoacan	Low levee or levee	Cotton cloth (1)		Farmed corn and vegetables (1); farmed corn, beans, and vegetables (1)		
Acula	Levee	Cotton cloth (1)		Fishing (1)		
Tlatayan	?					
Tlalixcoyan	Levee and elevated ridge		Sold produce (1)	Farming and fishing (1)	Rowing travelers to Alvarado (1)	Mota y Escobar 1945:210–214
Cuatla	?					
Amayaca	?					
Cotaxtla	Levee or terrace		Imported Campeche salt (1); fishing (1) GR	Farmed corn, beans, chile, used tree fruits, ate dogs (1)		del Paso y Troncoso 1905:5:1–11

Table 10.1 (Continued)

Town/hamlet	Local environment	Manufactures	Commerce	Subsistence	Pursuits of uncertain importance	Sources
Medellín	Levee or low levee			Fishing (2)		del Paso y Troncoso 1905:5:197; Mota y Escobar 1945:215
Tuxtla	Tuxtlas Mountains	See Commerce	Made local salt, also imported it from Campeche (1); sold corn, cotton, cotton clothing (1) GR	Farmed corn, beans, chile, jicama, and other roots, had pimienta, fruit trees (1)		del Paso y Troncoso 1905:5:1–11; AGN, Ramo de Tierras 1604:2736, exp. 21
Conchihca	Tuxtlas					
Sant Andres Zacualco	Tuxtlas	Cotton clothing (1)		Farmed cotton and corn (1)		
Matlacapa	Tuxtlas	Cotton clothing (1)				
Caxiapa	Coast or lagoon or low levee			Farmed corn and fished (1)		
Chuniapa	Tuxtlas	Cotton clothing (1)				
Catemaco	Catemaco lake shore			Fishing (2)		

Note: References to the head town do not necessarily exclude subject villages. Tuxtla Mountain settlements are usually in mountain valley locations. Commerce information from a geographic relation is marked "GR." The numbers in parentheses are the number of source references.

Papaloapan along the Acula River, Puctla and its hamlets may have spanned the same environmental transition, although the exact location of Puctla itself is unknown. Along the Atoyac, Cotaxtla and Medellín offer a similar contrast; the latter is described as a fishing community, whereas the former combined farming and fishing. In the Tuxtlas, agriculture predominated in subsistence and commerce, although two specialized subject villages emphasized fishing. One of these was situated near the coast; the other, beside Lake Catemaco. Although we do not know where salt was produced in the Tuxtlas, it is possible that the coastal settlement was responsible. Food, cotton, and cotton cloth were principal commercial products in the Tuxtla district; there is no mention of cacao growing.

Tribute assessments from the sixteenth century do not contravene the patterns indicated by descriptions, but neither do they support them strongly (Stark 1974:213–215). Tax records pose special problems in interpretation. Much of the tribute consisted of less perishable, more widely marketable goods, although foods were sometimes required. Tribute assessments do not guarantee that goods were produced locally if a community was active commercially, a problem that arises with Tlacotalpan. Finally, in three cases of communities described as having economically diversified subject settlements (Puctla, Tlacotalpan, and Tuxtla), either tribute masked these differences or the descriptions are inaccurate. Tribute lists do seem to corroborate the production of surplus cotton and cotton clothing in Tuxtla and upriver towns (Amatlan, Cosamaloapan, and Puctla). Excepting Tuxtla, this is also true for cacao.

A final measure of the importance of economic specialization relies on relative population estimates (Stark 1974:215–217). I have used relative estimates given by individual authors in lieu of absolute figures because of the difficulties of evaluating the latter. Comparative estimates of numbers of tributaries, that is, heads of households, consistently judge Tlacotalpan to be the largest of the riverine communities; Tuxtla was possibly even larger, but this estimate derives from a different author. The relative size of Tlacotalpan suggests that its partly aquatic oriented economy could support a sizeable town relative to farming areas. Assuming Tuxtla was at least as large as Tlacotalpan, we find that two of the three economically diversified communities were among the largest in the area, again suggesting that economic specializations contributed to community size.

AN ETHNOHISTORIC MODEL

To develop an ethnohistoric model, my use of early sources attempts to build on patterns of agreement, but a degree of extrapolation is still required.

I find it useful to divide discussion of the model into several topics: geographic patterns of specialization, settlement patterns, economic strategies, and exchange. The first two topics consider the distribution of human settlements and economic activities in different environmental zones. Using distributional data, I posit economic strategies and exchange patterns. There are thus two levels on which I have developed the model: the first, a more empirical one for which economic activities and settlement patterns are outlined; the second, a more abstract level for which economic strategies and exchange patterns are hypothesized.

Indigenous economy, as reflected by postconquest documents, can be expected to differ somewhat from its prehispanic counterpart. Therefore, I will attempt to modify some aspects of the ethnohistoric model to make it more relevant to preconquest times. Specifically, I will suggest modifications concerning settlement patterns and exchange.

Geographic Patterns of Specialization

The Lower Papaloapan demonstrates only a degree of environmental and economic redundancy; patterns of specialization are also clearly evident. The Tuxtla montane environment is unique on the Gulf Coast, but the Papaloapan drainage, which juxtaposes inland farming with estuarine fishing and salt- and pottery-making may be replicated partly in other areas. The Atoyac provides a similar example. A diagram of the Papaloapan pattern of riverine specialization appears in Figure 10.4.

Data from Coatzacoalcos, Agualulcos, and Central Veracruz suggest some larger-scale patterns of specialization, although I have not subjected these areas to the same degree of scrutiny as the Lower Papaloapan. Eastward in the rainier Coatzacoalcos province, enormous quantities of cacao and corn were levied in 1554 (González de Cossío 1952:18–19, 62–63, 145, 203–204, 207–208, 242, 247–248, 257–258, 289–290, 311–312, 346, 483, 532–533, 570, 611). As a rule, however, less cotton cloth was

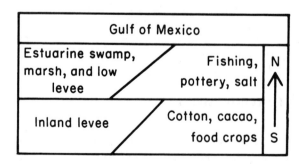

Figure 10.4. Coast–inland economic zonation in the Lower Papaloapan drainage.

required than in the Lower Papaloapan and Tuxtla areas. The higher rainfall requirement of cacao compared to cotton probably accounts for this difference; cotton is also more tolerant of drought compared to cacao (Purseglove 1968:348, 575–576).[2] Farther eastward, in western Tabasco, the production of plant fibers ("pita," probably agave or henequen) was of considerable importance in the Agualulcos district in addition to cacao and corn (de Solís 1945a,b). Environmental reasons for "pita" specialization are unclear. To the west, in drier Central Veracruz, cotton and cotton products seem to have been proportionately more important for many communities if we use Aztec tribute as a general guide to production (Barlow 1949:87–97). However, cacao was also important in the Guetlaxtlan province adjacent to Tochtepec (the latter included the Lower Papaloapan). A summary diagram of these major Gulf Coast sectors and their specializations appears in Figure 10.5.

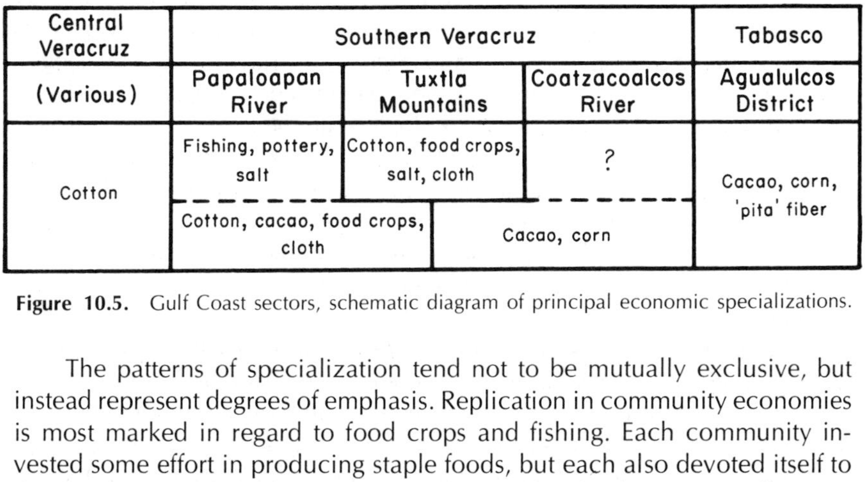

Central Veracruz	Southern Veracruz			Tabasco
(Various)	Papaloapan River	Tuxtla Mountains	Coatzacoalcos River	Agualulcos District
Cotton	Fishing, pottery, salt	Cotton, food crops, salt, cloth	?	Cacao, corn, 'pita' fiber
	Cotton, cacao, food crops, cloth		Cacao, corn	

Figure 10.5. Gulf Coast sectors, schematic diagram of principal economic specializations.

The patterns of specialization tend not to be mutually exclusive, but instead represent degrees of emphasis. Replication in community economies is most marked in regard to food crops and fishing. Each community invested some effort in producing staple foods, but each also devoted itself to the production of marketable goods or tribute. The latter specializations reflect both wider demand and the productive capabilities of community lands or resources. However, the fact that cacao was apparently not grown in the Tuxtla district is perplexing. Environmentally, parts of the Tuxtlas would not seem to preclude cacao orchards. Lower Papaloapan farming communities may have invested in cacao partly because this crop can withstand flooding (Purseglove 1968:575).

In summary, economic contrasts between these segments of the coast suggest zonation that differentiates coastal sectors. These segments can be designated (a) Central Veracruz; (b) the Lower Papaloapan; (c) the

---

[2]Without irrigation cotton is usually grown in areas with a 1016–1524 mm annual rainfall.

Tuxtlas; (d) the Lower Coatzacoalcos; and (e) Western Tabasco (cf. Coe 1961b:82). In the case of the Papaloapan River, there is another pattern involving a contrast between the estuarine zone and inland riverine–farming areas. To an extent this is true of any river reaching the coast, but the Papaloapan and Coatzacoalcos are noteworthy for their size and the corresponding extent of their estuarine deltas. The Tuxtlas present a more complex pattern of variation but still include fishing and farming localities.[3]

Native Settlement Patterns

With the possible exception of a few settlements in the Tuxtlas, settlements in the Lower Papaloapan and vicinity were located on the banks of rivers, lagoons, and lakes. Drier levee land, rich alluvial soils, water supply, and access to transport routes could all contribute to this pattern.

In cases where adequate records are available, communities exhibited two, possibly three, types of settlement patterns. There were two kinds of multisettlement communities, and there may have been one single-settlement community. Although Cosamaloapan seems to have lacked subject villages and thus constitutes a single-settlement community, it is a unique case and may be the result of incomplete description. Amatlán appears to have been a multisettlement community in which subject hamlets did not differ markedly from the head town in their economies. In contrast, Puctla, Tlacotalpan, and Tuxtla represent multisettlement communities with differentiation among subject settlements in resources, subsistence, and economy.

Settlement pattern is one of the topics for which I will suggest prehispanic alterations in the ethnohistoric model. More elaborate local social and settlement hierarchies may have prevailed in some pre-Columbian periods, as compared with the sixteenth century. Aztec suzerainty seems to have truncated social and settlement hierarchies, producing a situation somewhat similar to the Spanish case, in which a number of relatively small communities were of more or less equal stature. However, during periods without outside domination, one or a few local centers may have achieved preeminence over neighboring towns and may have incorporated a number of these smaller settlements into large multisettlement political and economic organizations. In such a situation, we could expect to see at least three tiers in the settlement hierarchy: hamlets, towns, and primary centers.

What guidelines does ethnohistory suggest for such large multisettlement organizations? I would expect successful ones to exemplify the eco-

---

[3]Rainfall also varies considerably within the Tuxtlas, and I wonder if the irrigated fields mentioned in the tax lists were located in the drier rain shadow.

nomic diversification strategy because this pattern was associated with the largest of the sixteenth-century communities and because it would provide strategic control of trade. In addition, some environmental circumstances may have selected for economically diversified organizations. For example, along the Lower Papaloapan, severe floods periodically create considerable destruction (Secretaria de Recursos Hidráulicos 1971:34). The effects of floods could be alleviated through multicommunity organizations uniting flood-prone and flood-safe areas. The Lower Papaloapan drainage includes the western slopes of the Tuxtlas to the east and two elevated ridges to the west, which may have been important as flood-safe, farming areas.

Assuming, then, some degree of economic diversification and exchange in large, multisettlement societies, we might expect the associated settlement pattern to be one in which primary centers occupy locations that provide for maximum efficiency in the acquisition and distribution of diverse goods and in administration and communication (cf. Haggett 1966:87–182). In an area with uniform environment and uniform transport facility, a spatially central position minimizes transport and travel costs for a rural population traveling to the center for goods and services. For the area in question, we must contend with distortions of uniform conditions in several relevant factors: the landscape and resources, economic production, and possibly demography. For example, river versus land transport, population density differences among localities, and discrepancies in the values of products from specialized zones would produce distortions. In such cases, a centralized position for minimizing costs might not coincide with a spatially central location in the territory.

Native Economic Strategies

The economically specialized, multisettlement communities bridge estuarine–farmland areas (Puctla and Tlacotalpan) or, in the Tuxtla case, bridge estuarine–freshwater–farmland localities. These specialized multisettlement communities suggest an economic strategy that attempted to control areas with diverse resources and/or those with advantageous spatial location. For diversified communities coastal or estuarine lands may have played two major roles that warrant further discussion. These zones offer optimal locations for (a) their faunal and salt resources; and (b) control of and participation in trade. With respect to the latter possibility, ethnohistory is disappointingly silent on the nature and extent of native commerce, but Aztec and early Spanish documents together imply that native trade along the Veracruz coast was active (Scholes and Warren 1965:784–785; Stark 1974:204–206). To the extent that this was the case, community location close to coastal and riverine trade routes would have been advantageous.

Estuarine resources were undoubtedly important in local subsistence, but they also may have entered into patterns of exchange. There is considerable likelihood that dried and salted fish constituted an exportable commodity (Stark 1974:212). Communities upriver along the Papaloapan could and did pursue fishing, but the delta is much richer in this fauna, and it can be obtained more readily in greater quantities (Stark, in press). However, in the sixteenth century, pottery and salt are the only recorded native estuarine products. Whether or not corn or other agricultural foods were imported, in turn, to estuarine settlements is unknown.

Not all communities had diversified settlements, however. In such cases there is evidence for a more general strategy: reduction of dependency on other towns for basic foodstuffs combined with emphasis on production of some economically strategic goods for which there was an appropriate local environment. On a larger scale, this strategy appears in the contrasting product emphases of different farming sectors (e.g., cotton in Central Veracruz and the Tuxtlas versus cacao in the Coatzacoalcos drainage).

Native Exchange

In discussing native exchange, I will deal only with environmental zones and their associated products or services. These specializations can be incorporated into an exchange model. Following the preceding discussion of the "diversification" strategy, I suggest that estuarine mangrove swamps were specialized environments (a) with populations at least partly subsisting on local fauna and possibly using fauna along with salt as exports, and/or (b) with people partly engaged in trade as "middlemen" for inland groups and/or as coastal traders. Inland along drainages, farming populations produced varying amounts of foodstuffs, cacao, cotton, and cotton clothing; they would have been suppliers of many commodities for long-distance trade and consumers of imported products. In Figure 10.6 a model for exchange is proposed with possible prehispanic products (asphalt, ritual marine products, and hard stone) and trade services noted.

The degree of economic specialization and the amount of exchange are difficult to document. Most of the ethnohistoric specializations are not mutually exclusive; rather, they create a more subtle pattern of degrees of emphasis and, hence, variations in the capacity for volume export of commodities. Comparisons with the Mesoamerican highlands underscore the problem of judging the significance of specialization. According to Nash (1967:91), the Guatemala highlands today exhibit generalized production of food combined with some crop specializations. Particularly in the case of corn, some towns are net exporters and others, net importers. In addition, many of the communities specialize in nonagricultural products (Nash

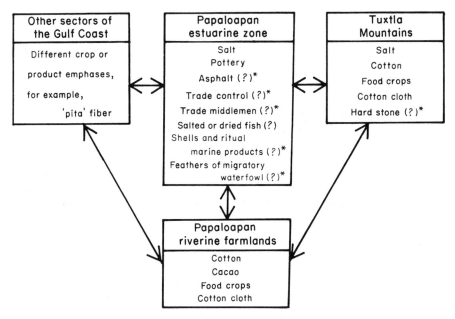

Other sectors of the Gulf Coast	Papaloapan estuarine zone	Tuxtla Mountains
Different crop or product emphases, for example, 'pita' fiber	Salt Pottery Asphalt (?)* Trade control (?)* Trade middlemen (?)* Salted or dried fish (?) Shells and ritual marine products (?)* Feathers of migratory waterfowl (?)*	Salt Cotton Food crops Cotton cloth Hard stone (?)*

Papaloapan riverine farmlands

Cotton
Cacao
Food crops
Cotton cloth

Figure 10.6. Ethnohistoric exchange model for the Lower Papaloapan Basin. Both overland and water travel are incorporated. Possible additional pre-Columbian trade items are marked with an asterisk.

1966:64–67). Sanders (1956;1968) characterizes the prehispanic Central Mexican highlands as economically interdependent. He argues that specializations responsive to environmental variations were essential for maintaining large populations.

There are no assurances, however, that the same degree of specialization obtained in Southern Veracruz. It is unclear, for example, whether any of the Veracruzano communities were net importers of basic foodstuffs; some of the recorded commerce in food was destined for Spanish populations. Unfortunately, many native exchange patterns would have been sensitive to population decline and economic changes attendant on the Spanish Conquest. Smith (1974:176–177) notes the possibility that Spanish colonialism tended to reduce native regional marketing and specialization and to foster Indian–Spanish trade favorable to the latter.

In fact, crops and crafts of inland farming communities in Southern Veracruz may have resembled a prehistoric variant of what Nash (1967:88) has termed the modern, adjunct export economy, in which communities produce chiefly for home and local consumption, but tend to have one or a few commodities produced for cash and market exchange. As noted before, sixteenth-century Southern Veracruz farming communities produced food but concentrated in part on cacao and cotton, which were widely traded items and/or required in tribute. I do not wish to downplay the role of interregional or pan-Mesoamerican exchange in the proposed model, but to highlight the potentials for intraregional exchange.

A COMPARISON WITH THE ARCHAEOLOGICAL RECORD

In order to determine the validity of the ethnohistoric model during various prehistoric periods, we would need to identify archaeologically testable implications. In addition to paleoenvironmental information, two major classes of archaeological data can be used, quantified distributions of artifactual, structural, and spatial indicators of economic activities, and settlement ranks and locations. Unfortunately there is no area in Southern Veracruz nor any prehistoric period there for which the necessary kind and amount of data are available. In lieu of a realistic test of the model, I will concentrate on two statements based on some aspects of it. For each I will discuss archaeological test implications that are tailored to the limitations of current archaeological information. It is not argued that the test implications are the only possible indexes of agreement between the statements and the archaeological record. By thus restricting myself, I can also discuss some of the scattered data presently available. Since some of the settlement pattern data have been argued by Rathje (1972) to fit the core–buffer zone model, such a discussion will be useful to contrast the two models. A further goal in this discussion of test implications and current data is to call attention to some research needs in Southern Veracruz.

The location of paleoenvironmental zones is important for testing the ethnohistoric model, but there is insufficient information to reconstruct the zones. For the ceramic periods I will examine, the most problematic factor in paleoenvironmental reconstruction is sea level. To facilitate my discussion, a substantial degree of similarity between modern and prehistoric sea level stands will be assumed; ancient and modern environmental zones should, therefore, be similarly distributed.[4] We can now examine archaeologically some propositions from the ethnohistoric model.

---

[4]Slightly lower sea levels would shift estuarine zones shoreward, but would not eradicate them. Scholl and Stuiver (1967:445) suggest that stable coasts have witnessed eustatic sea level rises of about 1.6 m since 1500 B.C. This generalization might not be applicable to the Veracruz littoral because of alluviation, subsidence, and possible tectonic activity. In the case of Patarata 52, archaeological data permit reconstruction of the Classic Period paleoenvironment, which appears to have been similar to the estuarine environment where the site is located today.

1. There were large, economically and environmentally diversified multisettlement social organizations in prehistoric times.

What I am interested in examining here is whether or not economic and environmental diversification was present. I will assume that large, public centers indicate multisettlement social organizations, ones in which economic and political ties unified a number of lesser social and political units probably centered in towns and hamlets. In Southern Veracruz several sites with substantial civic–ceremonial architecture and monuments are good candidates for such primary centers. In the absence of detailed survey to establish a system of site classification and ranking, I will confine my attention principally to the Preclassic Period and the set of primary centers analyzed by Rathje (1972).

There are two locational characteristics of primary centers that can be examined to test for economic and environmental diversification. According to the modified ethnohistoric model, we would expect, first of all, to find such centers located on lowland transport routes for participation in trade and communication with different areas. In Southern Veracruz these routes seem to have been waterways. But this criterion is weak, for sites might also be near water routes because of the attractions of floodplain farmlands and drinking water.

Second, I suggested that primary centers would, under certain conditions, be found near the boundary of contrasting environmental zones. This settlement location would be appropriate for a centrally located site serving, and supported by, a hinterland of diverse environments of comparable economic and demographic importance. Without knowledge of the size of the support area and some of its economic and demographic characteristics, it is difficult to specify how near a center must be to environmental transitions for the location to indicate a diversified economy. For the sake of argument, those primary centers lying at least within 6–7 km of an environmental transition will be taken to indicate agreement with the model. I would expect primary centers to have had a large territory, at least 20 km in radius and possibly more (cf. Hodder 1972:904–905). Figures 10.1 and 10.2 show boundaries of major swamp and marsh zones and land above the 100-m countour interval, which I am using as an arbitrary indicator of the piedmont transition to mountain elevations.

The use of proximity to environmental transitions by no means constitutes a definitive test of the model. If centers are not located near transition zones, they still may have had economically centralized locations for diversified sectors, but distortions in uniform conditions may prevent spatial location from serving as a straightforward diagnostic. On the other hand, we have no reason to expect sites to be near environmental boundaries if control over different resources was not important.

An alternative economic model with different settlement pattern implications has been proposed by Rathje (1972). This core–buffer model attempts to account for the development and demise of Olmec centers in the Southern Gulf Coast. In Rathje's view, the earliest lowland centers pertained to a resource-deficient, isolated, interior core area. Later centers were in buffer zones adjacent to resource-rich regions (especially the highlands) and to transport routes. Rathje (1972:372) views environmental redundancy, transportation difficulties, and dispersed settlement as promoting more integrated, complex sociopolitical groupings in lowland core areas. Suprahousehold units had to mobilize local resources to conduct long-distance trade for basic products (hard stone, obsidian, salt) that they lacked. "Community ceremonial interaction and luxury paraphernalia are equally necessary to maintain stratification and organization [Rathje 1972:372]." Core exports were ceremonial and stratification by-products, various kinds of cult and status goods. Eventually the core area declined because buffer-zone sites became self-sufficient in cult and status objects, removing the incentive for trade with core areas.

A detailed comparison of the two models will not be undertaken here. Minimally it should be noted that in addition to their contrasting views of the role of intralowland economic and environmental diversity, they differ in their perspective on lowland transport. Southern Veracruz, rather than suffering from transportation difficulties, enjoyed the benefits of two large river systems, the Papaloapan and the Coatzacoalcos, as well as the Gulf coastline. Potentially more important differences concern developmental factors. One model focuses on long-distance trade; the other, on local exchange between different lowland zones. However, in discussing native exchange I cautioned that long-distance and lowland–highland trade may have significantly enhanced lowland specializations. Ethnohistoric data from Southern Veracruz are insufficient to weight the two factors. It could be argued on theoretical grounds that preeminence of long-distance trade in economic development would result in a dendritic hierarchy of settlements situated along transport routes (cf. Smith 1974:177–179). This would contrast with the location near environmental boundaries for primary centers, which I have suggested. Development of a long-distance economic and settlement pattern model will not be attempted here. Ethnohistory does suggest that long-distance models should be entertained that accommodate a volume of lowland–highland trade sufficient to require participation of both buffer and core lowland areas.

In summary, one expectation from the modified ethnohistoric model is that primary centers will be located near the boundaries of diverse environmental zones along transport routes. In contrast, the core–buffer model suggests that the earliest centers will be found in the least accessible and most undifferentiated areas; later centers will be located near mountains or on the coast (buffer zones).

Despite the extremely limited settlement pattern data from Southern Veracruz, the location of known primary centers (Laguna de los Cerros, San Lorenzo Tenochtitlán, La Venta, Tres Zapotes, and Cerro de las Mesas) partly conforms to the model for economically diversified multisettlement organizations.

Laguna de los Cerros and San Lorenzo Tenochtitlán appear to be the two earliest Olmec centers (Coe 1968:62–63; Coe et al. 1967). Laguna de los Cerros is located in the southern foothills of the Tuxtlas near a stream tributary to the San Juan River (Figures 10.1, 10.2). The alluvial plain and the Tuxtlas are adjacent (Medellín 1960b:85–97; Comisión Intersecretarial Coordinadora del Levantamiento de la Carta Geográfica de la República Mexicana 1957:15Q-V). This site is not in the core area as defined by Rathje.

San Lorenzo is situated beside the Coatzacoalcos and Chiquito rivers, but it is not close to the estuarine zone and does not fit the multiple-environment model unless it can be demonstrated that its support area included estuarine localities in addition to farmland. Most scholars assume that basalt for the San Lorenzo monuments was transported to the site by coast and river routes, which would suggest that the Coatzacoalcos delta may have been part of the territory controlled by San Lorenzo. This does not, however, guarantee that the estuarine zone was inhabited or exploited.

La Venta, a slightly later Olmec site, is located on an island within an estuarine swamp about 29 km from the mouth of the Tonalá River (Heizer 1960:218). Again, a large support area is expected in this case. Heizer (1960) and Drucker (1961) have argued for the suitability of adjacent farmlands to the west, which lie between the Tonalá and Coatzacoalcos rivers; Sisson (1970:46) suggests the river levees. Both San Lorenzo and La Venta are well situated for water transport.

Tres Zapotes, a late Olmec and post-Olmec site, is situated similarly to Laguna de los Cerros; it lies between Tuxtla farming areas and the Papaloapan floodplains, near a tributary stream. It is also close to the Papaloapan estuarine delta (Stirling 1943:8; Large in press). Cerro de las Mesas, a large post-Olmec site, lies in farmland not far from the transition between extensive Central Veracruz farming areas and the estuarine zone of the Papaloapan (Drucker 1943b:1–2; Large in press). Although it is not far from rivers, I have not been able to determine the distance to the nearest channel. The environs of Cerro de las Mesas contain other large sites which make it difficult to define the functional boundaries of the center.

In summary, if the site of Laguna de los Cerros is as early as San Lorenzo, some of the propositions of the ethnohistoric model warrant consideration as alternatives to Rathje's core–buffer model. Laguna de los Cerros is not in the core as Rathje defines it because the site is adjacent to an area with hard stone resources. Four of the major centers considered are located close to different environments, which would be a reasonable expectation for large centers relying on diversified hinterlands. Although San Lorenzo does not conform to the ethnohistoric model with respect to its location, we cannot yet rule out a support area encompassing both riverine and estuarine environments. Nevertheless, environmental transition areas are extensive in Southern Veracruz, and positioning of centers near them is only approximate in any case. Furthermore, there is considerable variation in center locations. Available maps permit only a relatively gross characterization of environmental factors. Biotope analysis has already proved useful in identifying farmland ecological factors that are not incorporated in the modified ethnohistoric model (Coe 1974).

2. *There were economically and environmentally specialized settlements.*

In order to demonstrate this proposition archaeologically, identification of prehistoric habitation in contrasting environments will be necessary, along with specialized economic behavior appropriate to each environment. According to the model, we would expect fishing and shellfish gathering to be important in subsistence at estuarine sites, but less so inland. Asphalt, a coastal resource, should be concentrated in at least some estuarine and coastline sites in such a manner as to indicate its collection and use.

Farmlands are difficult to appraise archaeologically because many of their expected products are perishable. Among farmland products I will discuss only cotton and cotton cloth. Concentrations of appropriately sized spindle whorls may document the spinning of cotton yarn (Parsons 1972), but cotton growing and weaving would not be directly substantiated. Prior to the technological development of specially made whorls, perforated sherds may have served such a purpose (Kent 1957:473; Large 1975), although some perforated sherd disks may have been used as spindle rests (Kent 1957:475; Coe 1961a:101, 105). Because whorls also could have been made of perishable materials, lack of pottery or stone whorls does not definitively preclude spinning. However, in prehispanic Mesoamerica, durable whorls apparently were used as early as Preclassic times (ca. 1500–300 B.C.).

Judging from the ethnohistoric accounts, I assume cotton was spun primarily in the areas where it was grown and woven. Therefore, farmlands that produced cotton should exhibit much higher frequencies of spindle whorls or disks per capita than areas that produced very little cotton or that imported raw cotton. Similarly, the Coatzacoalcos farmlands should produce less cotton and hence fewer whorls or disks per capita than Tuxtla and the Papaloapan farmlands, and they, in turn, should produce less than Central Veracruz.

In Southern Veracruz only a few scattered sites have been investigated, and most of them have not been analyzed from an economic and environmental viewpoint. Therefore, we are in no position to reach definitive conclusions about whether or not there were economically and environmentally specialized settlements. In my discussion of archaeological remains, I will deal with only two topics: first, whether there were estuarine settlements and, if so, what economic specialization they indicate, and second, whether there were farmland settlements that produced cotton. For both the Preclassic and Postclassic Periods the presence of specialized estuarine sites has not yet been demonstrated, but there are indications of specialized, permanent habitation in estuarine localities near the mouth of the Papaloapan during the Classic Period, A.D. 300–900 (Stark 1972; in press). At Patarata 52, an excavated site, subsistence depended partly on estuarine fauna, although some gardening or levee farming may have been practiced as well. The prehistoric inhabitants used materials (household and luxury hard stones) obtained through long-distance exchange. Scattered small pieces of asphalt occurred in the midden deposits; one large utility jar was covered with asphalt over much of its interior, indicating that a large quantity had been heated or mixed. Thus, Patarata 52 conforms to two expectations from the ethnohistoric model. It demonstrates a marked subsistence orientation to estuarine aquatic fauna along with the collection and use of asphalt.

Some economic data at Patarata 52 are ambiguous. Five spindle whorls with all the attributes Parsons (1972) suggests were associated with spinning cotton were recovered from the deposits (Stark in press). Only limited cotton could be grown in the estuarine zone. Corn is also represented, but land for farming is scarce. Some of these crops might have been obtained from inland areas. However, until the density of estuarine occupation and the potential for localized low-levee and on-site farming can be assessed, importation of corn and cotton from inland farming areas cannot be assumed.

Farmland sites are predicted by the ethnohistoric model. Of course, inland Preclassic, Classic, and Postclassic sites have been reported for montane and riverine areas in Southern Veracruz, but data about subsistence are not available (Medellín 1960a; Coe 1965; García 1971).

The ethnohistoric model also suggests cotton and cotton cloth would be produced in farming localities. Archaeological data do not permit us to determine if relative whorl or disk frequencies match expectations from the model. Not only do we lack quantified distributional data from a number of sites, but we also cannot apply an index that could suggest frequencies per capita (for example, based on sherd counts). At several sites, durable spindle whorls and, possibly, perforated sherd disks do indicate the production of yarns. Hole diameters suggest use with cotton fibers on the basis of Parsons' (1972) and Large's (1975) criteria (but cf. Charlton 1975:163). Large has argued from lowland Maya data that perforated sherd disks may have been used for spinning cotton throughout the Classic Period; for both disks and specially-made whorls, most Maya examples had hole diameters of 4–8 mm. This range for hole diameters falls approximately between the ranges proposed by Parsons (1972) for late, Mexican highland cotton and maguey whorls. In Table 10.2 are listed Southern Veracruz sites for which whorls and perforated sherd disks have been reported. Where possible, I have scaled hole diameters from illustrations.

It should be cautioned that the Torres and Cerro del Encanto sites near La Venta raise the same question about the source of estuarine cotton as did Patarata 52: Was raw cotton imported or grown on limited site and levee lands? Trade in raw cotton and some domestic weaving for local household use might have been widespread in the lowlands, but cotton farming and volume weaving for export may have been more localized. The frequencies of spindle whorls against some index of population constitute the critical data, rather than their presence or absence. Such data are also critical for deciding if Coatzacoalcos farmlands were less active in cotton spinning than were the Papaloapan and Tuxtla areas, as the ethnohistoric model would suggest. Present information is insuffiencient in this respect.

Preclassic data, however, raise the possibility of a change in fiber processing in the southern Gulf Coast. Neither ceramic spindle whorls nor perforated sherd disks occur in Early Preclassic deposits at San Lorenzo, nor are they present in the Preclassic at La Venta (Coe, personal communication; Drucker 1952:143–144).[5] Only one perforated sherd disk is listed from Lower Tres Zapotes in the Middle to Late Preclassic (Drucker 1943a:87, 97, 101). If disks and whorls were absent in the Early Preclassic and scarce in the remainder of the Preclassic in Southern Veracruz, then farmlands there may not have produced cotton. In contrast, all Middle and Late Preclassic levels at El Trapiche in Central Veracruz produced worked sherd disks, some of which were perforated (García 1966:180).

According to ethnohistoric patterns the Coatzacoalcos and Tonalá areas would not be expected to emphasize cotton production as much as would the Papaloapan, Tuxtla, and (especially) Central Veracruz farmlands. However, the Preclassic evidence raises the question of whether there was once an even greater contrast in fiber production between Central and Southern Veracruz than is suggested by the ethnohistoric model. Only with better

---

[5]Although La Venta is in swampy terrain rather than farmlands, its role as a major center might lead to craft specialization there in spinning and weaving if cotton were grown nearby.

Table 10.2
WHORLS AND PERFORATED SHERD DISKS

Site	Cultural placement	Artifacts	Hole diameter	Source
San Lorenzo Tenochtitlán	Villa Alta Phase, ca. A.D. 900 Nacaste Phase, 900–700 B.C. and Palangana Phase, 600–400 B.C.	Mold-made whorls Perforated sherd disks	— —	Coe 1970a:31 Coe, personal communication, 1975; 1970a:28–29
Tres Zapotes	Middle Tres Zapotes B and Upper T.Z. material from Ranchito Grp. Middle and Upper Tres Zapotes	Spindle whorls (frequent) Perforated sherd disks Mold-made whorls	most approx. 4 mm — —	Weiant 1943: 19, 117 Drucker 1943a:87, 92, 95, 99 Drucker 1943a:86, 95, 99, 104
	Upper Tres Zapotes and Soncautla complex Upper Tres Zapotes	4 perforated sherd disks	2.5 mm	Drucker 1943a:109–114, pl. 50
Cerro de las Mesas	Lower II and Upper I (associated with Early Classic material in Teotihuacán style)	Spindle whorls Spindle whorls, probably mold-made	— —	Drucker 1943b:66, 76 Valenzuela 1945:88, fig. 6
Matacapan, Tuxtla Mountains, Mound 4	Postclassic	1 whorl	—	As above
Cerro del Encanto, near La Venta	Uncertain	Mold-made whorl	—	Drucker, Heizer, and Squier 1959:238, 239, 245
Torres site, near La Venta	Uncertain	Handmade whorl	5.6 mm	As above
Patarata 52	Limón Phase, A.D. 600–900	5 spindle whorls	4, 4, 3.5, 5, 3–4 mm	Stark, in press
	Camarón 1–3 Subphases, A.D. 250–550	3 spindle whorls	5, 6 mm	As above
El Trapiche	Middle to Late Preclassic	Perforated sherd disks	—	García 1966:180

distributional data from a larger sample of Preclassic sites in Veracruz can the apparent contrast be verified. In addition, further functional analyses of whorl and perforated disk attributes should clarify problems surrounding the evolution of fiber-processing industries.

SUMMARY

An ethnohistoric model for native geographic patterns of specialization, settlement patterns, economic strategies, and exchange was developed from sixteenth-century data and modified for prehistoric periods. Two statements based on the model were compared with archaeological data to explore their prehistoric validity. The results provide some support for the ethnohistoric model. The location of several primary centers near contrasting resource zones suggests economic diversification in their supporting hinterlands. Particularly during the Classic Period, there is evidence of occupation in estuarine, riverine, and Tuxtla montane environments. Estuarine habitation appears to have been specialized according to expectations from the model. During the Preclassic Period, the distribution of fiber-processing industries may have differed from that predicted by the model. The difference seems to imply even greater contrasts in economic specialization between coastal sectors. However, the severely limited data on prehistoric ecology and economics in Southern Veracruz impedes any detailed evaluation of settlement patterns, specialization, and exchange. One primary contribution of the ethnohistoric model is to call attention to the need for research designs, analytic procedures, and reporting more adequate to the task of evaluating contrasting economic models such as have been proposed for Southern Veracruz.

ACKNOWLEDGMENTS

This research has been supported by the Wenner-Gren Foundation for Anthropological Research, Inc., Grant 2894. I am also indebted to Michael D. Coe, who sponsored the project while I was a graduate student. Susana Berdecio, Geoffrey A. Clark, Elinor Large, John Martin, Timothy O'Leary, and Barbara Voorhies provided either much appreciated assistance or editorial comments, but are not responsible for statements in this chapter. Honorio Mendoza M. provided transcriptions of archival documents.

REFERENCES

American Geographical Society of New York
  1957   International map of the world. Series 1301: NE14, NE15.

Archivo general de la Nación (AGN)
 1588   Guaspáltepec, diligencias sobre dos sitios de ganado mayor. . . . Archivo General de la
        Nación, Ramo de Tierras 2695, expediente 7. México, D. F.
 1590   Guaspáltepec, diligencias sobre un sitio para potrero . . . . Archivo General de la
        Nación, Ramo de Tierras 2692, expediente 10. México, D. F.
 1604   Avisa del estado de las congregaciones de su cargo . . . Archivo General de la
        Nación, Ramo de Tierras 2736, expediente 21. México, D. F.
Barlow, R. H.
 1949   The extent of the empire of the Culhua-Mexica. Ibero-Americana, Vol. 28.
CETENAL (Comisión de Estudios del Territorio Nacional y Planeación)
 1970   Carta de Climas, Veracruz 14Q-VI, Coatzacoalcos 15Q-V, Tuxtla Gutierrez 15Q-VII.
        México: Talleres Gráficos de la Nación.
Charlton, Thomas H.
 1975   Review of Miscellaneous Studies in Mexican Prehistory, by M. W. Spence, J. R.
        Parsons, and M. H. Parsons. American Anthropologist 77(1):162–164.
Coe, M. D.
 1961a La Victoria, an early site on the Pacific Coast of Guatemala. Papers of the Peabody
        Museum of Archaeology and Ethnology, Vol. 53. Cambridge, Massachusetts: Pea-
        body Museum of Archaeology and Ethnology, Harvard Univ.
 1961b Social typology and the tropical forest civilization. Comparative Studies in Society
        and History 4(1):65–85.
 1965   Archaeological synthesis of Southern Veracruz and Tabasco. In Handbook of Middle
        American Indians, Vol. 3, Part 2: Archaeology of Southern Mesoamerica, edited by
        G. R. Willey. (R. Wauchope, gen. ed.) Austin: Univ. of Texas Press. Pp. 679–715.
 1968   San Lorenzo and the Olmec civilization. In Dumbarton Oaks Conference on the
        Olmec, edited by E. P. Benson. Washington, D.C.: Dumbarton Oaks Research Library
        and Collection, Trustees for Harvard University. Pp. 41–71.
 1970a The Archaeological sequence at San Lorenzo Tenochtitlán, Veracruz, Mexico. Con-
        tributions of the University of California Archaeological Research Facility 8:21–34.
 1970b San Lorenzo Tenochtitlán, archaeological and ecological maps. New Haven.
        (Mimeographed text, three printed maps.)
 1974   Photogrammetry and the ecology of Olmec civilization. In Aerial photography in
        anthropological research, edited by E. Z. Vogt, Cambridge, Massachusetts: Harvard
        Univ. Press. Pp. 1–13.
Coe, M. D., R. A. Diehl, and M. Stuiver
 1967   Olmec civilization, Veracruz, Mexico: Dating the San Lorenzo Phase. Science
        155:1399–1401.
Comisión Intersecretarial Coordinadora del Levantamiento de la Carta Geográfica de la República Mexicana
 1957   Veracruz 14Q-VI, Coatzacoalcos 15Q-V, Tuxtla Gutierrez 15Q-VII. México.
Drucker, P.
 1943a Ceramic sequences at Tres Zapotes, Veracruz, Mexico. Bureau of American Ethnol-
        ogy, Bulletin 140. Washington, D.C.: U.S. Government Printing Office.
 1943b Ceramic stratigraphy at Cerro de las Mesas, Veracruz, Mexico. Bureau of American
        Ethnology, Bulletin 141. Washington, D.C.: U.S. Government Printing Office.
 1952   La Venta, Tabasco: A study of Olmec ceramics and art. Bureau of American Ethnol-
        ogy, Bulletin 153. Washington, D.C.: U.S. Government Printing Office.
 1961   The La Venta Olmec support area. Kroeber Anthropological Society Papers 25:59–
        72.
Drucker, P., R. F. Heizer, and R. J. Squier
 1959   Excavations at La Venta, Tabasco, 1955. Bureau of American Ethnology, Bulletin 170.
        Washington, D.C.: U.S. Government Printing Office.

236 BARBARA L. STARK

Flannery, K. V.
1968   The Olmec and the Valley of Oaxaca: A model for inter-regional interaction in
Formative times. In *Dumbarton Oaks Conference on the Olmec*, edited by E. P.
Benson. Washington, D.C.: Dumbarton Oaks Research Library and Collection, Trus-
tees for Harvard University. Pp. 79–110.
García Payon, José
1966   *Prehistoria de Mesoamérica: Excavaciones en Trapiche y Chalahuite, Veracruz,*
México. 1942, 1951, y 1959. Cuadernos de la Facultad de Filosofía, Letras y Ciencias,
Universidad Veracruzana, Vol. 31. Jalapa.
1971   Archaeology of Central Veracruz. In *Handbook of Middle American Indians, Vol. 12,*
Part 2, Archaeology of Northern Mesoamerica, edited by G. F. Ekholm and I. Bernal.
(R. Wauchope, gen ed.) Austin: Univ. of Texas Press. Pp. 505–542.
Gomez-Pompa, Arturo
1973   Ecology of the vegetation of Veracruz. In *Vegetation and vegetational history of*
Northern Latin America, edited by A. Graham. New York: Elsevier Scientific Publish-
ing Co. Pp. 73–148.
González de Cossío, F.
1952   *El libro de las tasaciones de pueblos de la Nueva España, siglo XVI.* México:Archivo
General de la Nación.
Haggett, Petter
1966   Locational analysis in human geography. New York: St. Martin's Press.
Heizer, R. F.
1960   Agriculture and the theocratic state in lowland southeastern Mexico. *American*
Antiquity **26**(2):215–222.
Hodder, I. R.
1972   Locational models and the study of Romano-British settlement. In *Models in ar-*
chaeology, edited by D. L. Clarke, London: Methuen. Pp. 887–909.
Kent, K. P.
1957   *The cultivation and weaving of cotton in the prehistoric southwestern United States.*
Transactions of the American Philosophical Society, Vol. 47, Part 3.
Large, E. G.
1975   Cotton: A basic resource for the Classic Maya of the Southern Lowlands? Paper
presented at the 74th annual meeting of the American Anthropological Association,
San Francisco, California, December 2–6, 1975.
In press Photointerpretation and mapping. In *Prehistoric ecology at Patarata 52, Veracruz,*
Mexico: Adaptation to the mangrove swamp, by B. L. Stark. Vanderbilt University
Publications in Anthropology No. 18. Nashville: Vanderbilt Univ. Press.
Leopold, S. A.
1959   *Wildlife of Mexico.* Berkeley: Univ. of California Press.
Medellín Zenil, Alfonso
1960a   *Cerámicas del Totonacapan, exploraciones arqueológicas en el centro de Veracruz.*
Jalapa, Veracruz: Instituto de Antropología, Universidad Veracruzana.
1960b   Monolitos inéditos Olmecas. *La Palabra y el Hombre* **4**(16):75–98.
Mota y Escobar, Alonso de la
1945   Memoriales del obispo de Tlaxcala. *Anales del Instituto Nacional de Antropología e*
Historia **1**:191–306. México.
Nash, Manning
1966   *Primitive and peasant economic systems.* San Francisco: Chandler.
1967   Indian economies. In *Handbook of Middle American Indians, Vol. 6: Social an-*
thropology, edited by M. Nash. (R. Wauchope, gen. ed.) Austin: Univ. of Texas Press.
Pp. 87–102.

Parsons, M. H.
  1972   Spindle whorls from the Teotihuacán Valley, Mexico. In *Miscellaneous studies in Mexican prehistory*. Museum of Anthropology, University of Michigan, Anthropological Papers, No. 45. Pp. 45–79.
Paso y Troncoso, F. del, ed.
  1905   *Papeles de Nueva España*. Madrid.
Puleston, D. E.
  1968   *Brosimum alicastrum* as a subsistence alternative for the Classic Maya of the Central Southern Lowlands. M. A. thesis, University of Pennsylvania. Ann Arbor: University Microfilms.
  1971   An experimental approach to the function of Classic Maya chultuns. *American Antiquity* **36**(3):322–335.
Puleston, D. E., and O. S. Puleston
  1971   An ecological approach to the origins of Maya civilization. *Archaeology* **24**(4):330–337.
Purseglove, J. W.
  1968   *Tropical crops, dicotyledons 2*. London: Longmans, Green.
Rathje, W. L.
  1972   Praise the gods and pass the metates: A hypothesis of the development of lowland rainforest civilizations in Mesoamerica. In *Contemporary archaeology: A guide to theory and contributions*, edited by M. P. Leone. Carbondale: Southern Illinois Univ. Press. Pp. 365–392.
Sahlins, Marshall
  1972   *Stone age economics*. Chicago: Aldine-Atherton.
Sanders, W. T.
  1956   The Central Mexican symbiotic region: A study of prehistoric settlement patterns. In *Prehistoric settlement patterns in the New World*, edited by G. R. Willey. Viking Fund Publications in Anthropology, Vol. 23. Pp. 115–127.
  1968   Hydraulic agriculture, economic symbiosis and the evolution of states in Central Mexico. In *Anthropological archeology in the americas*. Washington, D.C.: The Anthropological Society of Washington. Pp. 88–107.
Sanders, W. T., and B. J. Price
  1968   *Mesoamerica: The evolution of a civilization*. New York: Random House.
Scholes, F. V., and D. Warren
  1965   The Olmec region at Spanish contact. In *Handbook of Middle American Indians, Vol. 3, Part 2: Archaeology of southern Mesoamerica*, edited by G. R. Willey. (R. Wauchope, gen. ed.) Austin: University of Texas Press. Pp. 776–787.
Scholl, D. W., and M. Stuiver
  1967   Recent submergence of Southern Florida: A comparison with adjacent coasts and other eustatic data. *Geological Society of America, Bulletin* **78**:437–454.
Secretaria de Recursos Hidráulicos
  1971   *Planificación integral de la Cuenca del Papaloapan*. México: Comisión del Papaloapan, Secretaria de Recursos Hidráulicos.
Service, E. R.
  1971   *Primitive social organization: An evolutionary perspective*. New York: Random House. (First edition, 1962.)
Sisson, Edward B.
  1970   Settlement patterns and land use in the Northwestern Chontalpa, Tabasco, Mexico: A progress report. *Cerámica de Cultura Maya* **6**:41–54.
Smith, C. A.
  1974   Economics of marketing systems: Models from economic geography, *Annual Review*

of *Anthropology*, Vol. 3, edited by B. J. Siegel, A. R. Beals, and S. A. Tyler, Palo Alto, California: Annual Reviews. Pp. 167–201.

Solís, José de
   1945a   Congregación de los pueblos de los Agualulcos y Provincia de Guazaqualco, 1599. *Boletín del Archivo General de la Nación* **16**(2):215–246.
   1945b   Estado en que se hallaba la Provincia de Coatzacoalcos en el año de 1599. *Boletín del Archivo General de la Nación* **16**(3):429–479.

Stark, B. L.
   1974   Geography and economic specialization in the Lower Papaloapan, Veracruz, Mexico. *Ethnohistory* **21**(3):199–221.
   1975   Prehistoric occupation in the Lower Papaloapan, Veracruz, Mexico: Habitation, subsistence, and economy in the mangrove swamp. In *XLI Congreso Internacional de Americanistas, September 2–7, Actas*, Vol. 1. Pp. 338–346. Mexico.
   In Press   *Prehistoric ecology at Patarata 52, Veracruz, Mexico: Adaptation to the mangrove swamp*. Vanderbilt University Publications in Anthropology, No. 18. Nashville: Vanderbilt Univ. Press.

Steward, J. H.
   1955   Some implications of the symposium. In *Irrigation civilizations: A comparative study*. Washington, D.C.: Pan American Union. Pp. 58–78.

Stirling, M. W.
   1943   *Stone monuments of Southern Mexico*. Bureau of American Ethnology, Bulletin 138. Washington, D.C.: U.S. Government Printing Office.

Trens, M. B.
   1947   *Historia de Veracruz*. Tomo II. Jalapa, Veracruz: Enriquez.

Valenzuela, J.
   1945   Las exploraciones efectuadas en los Tuxtlas, Veracruz. *Anales del Museo Nacional de Arqueología, Historia, y Etnografía* **3**:83–109. México.

Weiant, C. W.
   1943   *An introduction to the ceramics of Tres Zapotes, Veracruz, Mexico*. Bureau of American Ethnology, Bulletin 139. Washington, D.C.: U.S. Government Printing Office.

chapter 11

Maritime Adaptation and the Rise of Maya Civilization: The View from Cerros, Belize

DAVID A. FREIDEL

Southern Methodist University

INTRODUCTION

Students of the ancient Maya generally recognize the importance of marine resources and coastal canoe trade to the economy of the Yucatán Peninsula during the Postclassic Period (A.D. 1000–1520). Following the collapse of the southern lowland centers around A.D. 900, it is reasonable to view the thriving development of maritime Maya as an outcome of declining land-based economic networks in the interior and the migration of people to coastal regions (Thompson 1970; Sabloff and Rathje 1975). Some Mayanists presume that adaptation to coastal regions played a relatively minor role during the inception of Maya civilization and its Classic florescence (Ball 1977; Sanders 1973; Ball and Eaton 1972). The preponderance of great Maya centers is unquestionably in the interior jungles of Guatemala, Mexico, and Belize. Thus it is no wonder that attempts to explain the Maya rise to power focus on conditions there, such as competition over arable land (Ball 1977; Webster 1977) or an absence of vital resources (Rathje 1971; 1972). If one believes that localized environmental conditions are paramount in the development of complex society, then these archaeologists are justified in such emphasis.

The point of view taken in this chapter is that Maya civilization was not the product of local conditions, but rather resulted from the interaction of lowland communities undergoing distinctive adaptation to varying environments found on the peninsula. Rather than viewing the southern Maya lowlands as a "culture area" with an innovative nexus and radiating diffusion sphere, I see the lowlands as characterized by an interaction sphere with various subregional participants contributing to the totality by means of communication and exchange. To this end, adaptation to coastal regions is discussed as an integral part of Maya civilization from its inception.

The contribution of the coastal Maya is currently obscure because research has largely focused on the interior. Nevertheless, there are some data available on the subject, and some new evidence from Cerros, a coastal Maya center in northern Belize, substantiates trends seen at other sites.

MARITIME MAYA:
THE EASTERN LITTORAL

Archaeologists working in Belize have provided the bulk of available information on coastal Maya developments. David Pendergast's research at the center of Altun Ha, situated some 10 km from coastal lagoons, yielded an astonishing wealth of jade artifacts in Late Classic contexts. This exotic material originated in highland areas to the south. A cache dating prior to A.D. 500 containing a *tumbaga* bead and another cache dating to Late Preclassic–Early Classic times containing green obsidian eccentrics presumably from highland Mexico support the long-enduring commercial importance of this "peripheral" center (Pendergast 1967; 1971).

The agricultural land in the vicinity of Altun Ha is mediocre, but excavations revealed a heavy exploitation of marine–estuary resources evincing a stable and varied subsistence base. Whether the exotics cited above arrived at Altun Ha via the great centers of the interior or by sea up the coast is in one sense a moot question. On the one hand, Altun Ha must be seen as controlling local resources worthy of exchange for commodities imported over long distances and subjected to labor-intensive preparation. On the other hand, the center must have maintained sufficient control of importation and commerce to afford to bury substantial quantities of movable wealth. In either case, and a combination of both seems likely, the elite of this relatively small center must have been viewed as a power to be reckoned with by Maya of the interior lowlands. Whether the coastal Maya controlled local resources of great importance, commerce in exotics, or both, the concentration of wealth objects of the finest-quality Maya craftsmanship at Altun Ha reflects an independence of this center from the great interior communities and suggests that the adaptation of coastal Maya to marine resources and the sea was of vital importance to the interior communities.

Coastal Canoe Trade

Aside from the cosmopolitan quality of valued materials at Altun Ha and their concentration, other evidence for coastal trade along the eastern littoral comes from diverse sources. Hammond (1973) has offered data that obsidian from the Ixtepeque source in Guatemala was distributed along the eastern coast in Classic times, and obsidian from El Chayal, Guatemala follows interior routes into the lowlands. Ixtepeque obsidian is found on the bay islands off the coast of Belize, demonstrating along with other material evidence (fish remains, ceramics) the viability of Classic Maya canoe transport. Preclassic ceramics on Cozumel Island, Mexico, demonstrate that prior to the Classic florescence, coastal Maya were able to traverse the 10 miles of dangerous water separating this island from the mainland (Connor 1975). Andrews (1972) has observed the presence of Preclassic and Classic ceramics in abundance at Xcaret on the coast of Mexico, belying the notion of primarily Late Postclassic occupation of this section of the eastern littoral. The means (in terms of technology and expertise) and the motive (as seen in deposited exotics) were present for coastal occupation and trade from Preclassic times onward. Further support for this assertion comes from Cerros, a coastal Maya center that was evidently constructed, occupied, and abandoned prior to the Early Classic period.

Cerros

The site of Cerros is located directly on the coast of Chetumal Bay opposite Corozal Town, Belize (Latitude 18° 21′ 00″; Longitude 88° 21′ 10″; Figure 11.1). The commanding view of the New River's mouth offered by this location led to an early characterization of the site as a coastal lookout station (Gann in Hammond 1973). The immediate sustaining area of the center consists of a narrow peninsula, Lowry's Bight, characterized by mediocre soils (Wright et al. 1959:63) and seasonally inundated swamp.

Monumental architecture at Cerros is concentrated in a compact zone covering roughly 5.5 ha. This zone presently juts out into the shallow waters of the bay due to localized, recent erosion of the coast. Presumably the center was not originally constructed directly on the coast. Nevertheless, the

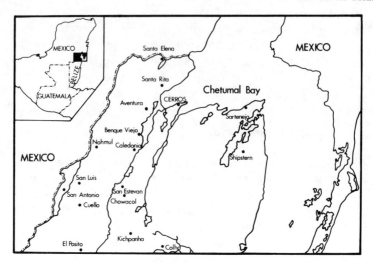

Figure 11.1.   Sites exhibiting Late Preclassic occupation in northern Belize (after Pring 1976).

presence of dark grey clays diagnostic of lagoonal deposits directly underlying midden deposits along the northeastern edge of the center indicates that the coast was not far from the center at any time.

In contrast to the typical arrangement of pyramidal mounds enclosing plaza areas found at such sites as San Estevan (Bullard 1965), Posito (Neivens 1976), Nohmul (Hammond 1976), and Altun Ha in northern Belize, Cerros has three major plaza–pyramid complexes with the major pyramids bordering one side of the plazas. These pyramids are further concentrated in the center of the precinct with the plazas radiating out from them (Figure 11.2). Such organization indicates planning in the total design of the center (with the concomitant implication of continuous construction over a relatively short period of time); this planning strongly emphasizes accessibility to the center's plaza–pyramid areas. In contrast, known Late Postclassic Maya centers found directly on the eastern coast and definitely involved in long-distance canoe trade show a strong tendency to defensive fortification and controlled access (e.g., Tulum, Ichapaatun; Lothrop 1924; Escalona-Ramos 1946).

To date, only some 30 ha in the vicinity of the center have been thoroughly surveyed, but evidence so far indicates that the surrounding community was dispersed in clusters of household groups in a fashion typical of Maya communities. Excavation in the sustaining area, discussed in detail below, yielded primary midden deposits at a distance of more than 50 m from the nearest visible mound, suggesting the possibility of "invisible" occupation at ground level between mapped mound groups. Exploration

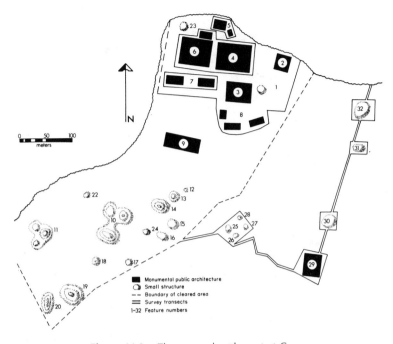

Figure 11.2.   The mapped settlement at Cerros.

outside the immediate environs of the center yielded remains of extensive occupation of Lowry's Bight.

Excavations at Cerros

Given the compact organization of the center, testing for Late Preclassic abandonment concentrated on the three large acropolises (Features 3, 4, 6, Figure 11.2) and on the summits of the largest secondary substructures in particular (3B, 4B, 6B, Figure 11.3). The premise here was that the final construction phases found in these locales would reflect the final prominent occupations of Cerros. Operation 17, a 2- by 3-m trench along the medial axis of structure 6B exposed a cache of seven Late Preclassic vessels deposited directly in construction fill 1.5 m below the surface (13.5 m above plaza level). Remains of a single fragmentary plaster floor were discovered 10 cm below the surface above which were a few Late Postclassic censerware sherds. Below this floor, ceramics in construction fill dated exclusively to Late Preclassic times. There were no intervening floors between the surface and the cache, and as the trench was cut to the southern edge of the mound,

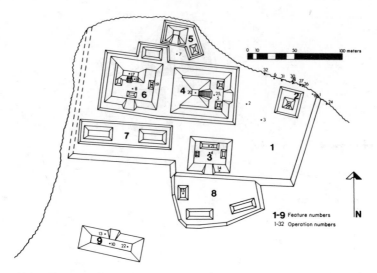

Figure 11.3. The central precinct at Cerros, Maler convention rendering from theodolite topographic survey.

the possibility of horizontal modification of the mound subsequent to the deposition of the cache was eliminated. This cache thus dates the final construction phase on Structure 6B to the Late Preclassic Period.

Further confirmation for this termination of construction on Structure 6B came with extensive exposure of the southern side of the mound, that is, the side facing the small raised plaza area on the acropolis. Late Preclassic sherds exclusively were found incorporated into the plaster melt of the stucco facade on this substructure, beneath a surface scatter of Late Postclassic censerware. Such sherds were found lying on the horizontal steps of this three-tiered pyramid under large fragments of fallen stucco. Half of a typical Late Preclassic, wide everted-rim dish was found smashed in situ directly under the final tread of the central staircase on the southern side of 6B.

It is possible that construction continued on the truncated pyramid 6A for many centuries following cessation of construction on 6B, but this seems less reasonable than the inference that cessation of construction on 6B reflects a general termination of construction activity on the acropolis as a whole. Test excavations in the raised plaza area and on another secondary substructure, 6C, bordering this plaza also yielded pure samples of Late Preclassic ceramics in construction fill, supporting the latter inference. This acropolis is the second largest feature in the center (60 by 60 m, 14 m high).

Excavations on Feature 4, the largest acropolis in the center (60 by 60 by 22 m), proved more equivocal, but they generally support the hypothesized abandonment. The final construction phase on 4B is a Late

Postclassic perishable superstructure and central staircase. The casual nature of this modification and its long separation in time from the construction phase immediately underlying it are easily demonstrated. The superstructure is built over roof collapse of a buried vaulted chamber, the slump of which was merely filled in and leveled off to provide a foundation. The Late Postclassic stairway consists of crude slab risers rammed into the humus and fall overlying the final major construction phase, with slab treads laid behind them. No further preparation of the surface was in evidence. This stairway is dated by a cache of Tulum Redware deposited at its base on the central axis.

Excavation of the buried vaulted chamber at the summit of 4B, 4B-sub-1, yielded a pure sample of Late Preclassic sherds in the single plaster floor and underlying construction fill. Above the floor was a deposit of trash, ash, and charcoal varying from 20 to 40 cm in thickness. The trash included large fragments of striated, necked jars, red-on-buff dishes with burned interiors, lumps of copal incense, fragments of jade, and plainware cylinders with lateral flanges decorated with appliqué rosettes and cutout designs. The sherds were uniformly unweathered and flat-bedded. A hearth area was discovered lying 10 cm above floor level. Finally, a single red-on-orange basal flange bowl fragment was found in this trash deposit. I interpret this deposit as evidence that the chamber was reused on a casual basis as a place of worship subsequent to its construction and initial sealing. The basal flange bowl fragment indicates a possible Early Classic date for the deposit.

Further excavation in 4B-sub-1 exposed a bench zone covering the northern third of the chamber. This bench was covered with a layer of censerware fragments identical to those found on the floor, sherds of Petén Gloss ware, and more copal and ash. The central section of the otherwise sealed plaster surface of this bench was absent, and directly under this disturbed area was a basal flanged bowl surrounded by a heavy concentration of Late Preclassic and Protoclassic sherds. Sherds from sealed sectors of the bench were uniformly Late Preclassic waxy wares. Full analysis of this complex deposit must await complete examination of the ceramic inventory, but I infer that the cache is associated with the reuse rather than initial construction of the chamber.

Excavation in the northern end of 4B-sub-1 revealed that the entire northern wall of the chamber had collapsed outward in antiquity. The density of censerware sherds increased dramatically in the doorway thus formed.

A cache of nine vessels on the third step from the top of the staircase associated with construction of 4B-sub-1 contained waxy ware plates and straight-necked subglobular jars with semigloss orange–red finish. Although the latter form and finish are diagnostic of both Protoclassic and Early Classic ceramics, the association of these jars with waxy ware plates leads me to believe that this cache is Protoclassic. Insofar as the cache can be dated, it provided a terminus post quem for the staircase. The fact that the cache is located well to the north of the central axis of the staircase, just around the corner from the improvised doorway into 4B-sub-1, suggests its association with the reuse of the chamber.

Although excavation on Structure 4B did not yield a primary Late Preclassic deposit in association with the final major construction phase, it did yield evidence of postconstructional reuse of the pyramid in its final form that dates to Protoclassic and Early Classic times. The possibility that the final pyramid was built, abandoned, and reused all during the period when Protoclassic ceramics were being made can only be eliminated by discovery of a primary Late Preclassic deposit in association with the major construction phase. Nevertheless, the weight of evidence renders a Late Preclassic construction followed by subsequent casual reuse in later times a more useful working hypothesis.

The chronological results of excavations elsewhere in the center and in the settlement zone are in concert with the hypothesized abandonment: superficial Late Postclassic deposits overlying substantial Late Preclassic ones. Aside from Structure 4B, nowhere in the center or settlement zone have Classic Period ceramics been located either on the surface or in excavated contexts (cf. Freidel 1976). A barrel of sherds collected by previous owners of the plantation on which the site is located did contain some Classic sherd material, so presumably Cerros was not entirely avoided during the long centuries separating Late Preclassic from Late Postclassic occupancy, but two facts are certain: (a) Cerros was a major center during the Late Preclassic Period; and (b) the community suffered a drastic decline at the close of that period.

The Late Preclassic Settlement

Test excavations in Feature 11, a housemound cluster in the settlement zone, produced a large, pure sample of Late Preclassic ceramics below sealed plaster flooring at surface level. Other operations, in Features 9 and 18, yielded similar trash deposits without sealed contexts. One outlying mound, Feature 22, contained mixed Late Preclassic and Late Postclassic debris. There is some evidence, then, that raised artificial areas were being constructed during Late Preclassic times in the settlement zone, but that some of the observable mounds may date in their entirety to the Late Postclassic Period.

A flat area test well away from any mounds exposed a dense layer of primary Late Preclassic midden at a depth of 40 cm below surface. Incorporated into this layer were pits containing large nested fragments of vessels, thin lenses of white marl, and a possible postmold. Only further exposure in this locale can ascertain the presence or absence of structural features, but the mere presence of primary trash more than 40 m from the nearest mound indicates the strong possibility of domestic structures at ground level in the vicinity. The rubble overburden on top of this midden contained Late Preclassic ceramics as well. Clearly this rubble is an artificial deposit reflecting intentional raising of the land surface in the vicinity. As the midden is deposited in a grey clay with flecks of white marl diagnostic of chronically inundated swamp or lagoon areas, the desirability of raising the area is understandable. Given the substantial effort involved in such an undertaking, however, it is noteworthy that low areas south of the center and away from the coast are not built up in this fashion, but that the area in question, directly next to the present coastline, is.

Excavation in trash deposits underlying the plaza east of the largest acropolis (Feature 1) turned out to be pertinent to settlement pattern analysis at Cerros. Erosion along the northern edge of this plaza revealed a rich midden and burials dating to Late Preclassic times. An initial 2- by 2-m test pit in this midden (Operation 1) exposed six interments, fragments of plaster flooring, and a rock-filled hearth area, in addition to primary trash lenses of marine shell, pottery, lithics, and fishbone. A 50-m² exposure around this initial pit was accomplished during the 1976 season by removing rubble construction fill associated with the latest expansion of the main plaza to the east (a 90-m stratigraphic profile of the plaza was conveniently provided by erosion, showing the sequential expansion of the plaza from west to east).

Extensive horizontal exposure of the midden confirmed that much of the deposit consists of lenses of primary trash and construction debris from small perishable structures built successively upon each other. Posthole patterns for two perishable structures with white marl (sascab) floorings were partially exposed in addition to partial outlines of structures with plaster floors. The complex overlapping of excavated structures with little intervening deposition demonstrates that secondary fill played a minor role in the formation processes. Rock-filled hearth areas, trash-filled pits, and burials found in the immediate vicinity of these structures and underneath them suggest activities associated with dwellings.

The midden deposit appears to represent the slow accumulation of construction debris and trash from residential compounds. There is good reason to believe that this formation process can be extrapolated to the midden as a whole. The stratigraphic profile bordering the excavated area is not different from the complex layering of trash lenses, marl floors, and plaster floors observed elsewhere along the face exposed by sea erosion. Interments like those associated with structures in Operation 1 occur throughout the deposit along the erosion profile (17 burials have been located and excavated in this area). Finally, the entire deposit dates exclusively to the Late Preclassic Period, which means that events determining the accumulation of debris in one sector of the midden are roughly contemporaneous with the events determining accumulation elsewhere. Consequently the entire deposit can be identified as the gradual accumulation of habitation debris.

The existence of such a nucleated residential zone has ramifications that must be viewed in light of other pertinent data. The sea-erosion profile shows that the deposit was accumulating on the eastern edge of the open plaza areas. As successive rebuildings of the rubble-filled plaza areas were pushed to the east, the residential zone was removed farther east as well. There is stratigraphic evidence that the habitation zone subsequently impinged on open plaza areas as it moved back toward the monumental structures of the center, only to be pushed back again to the east at a later time. The details of this complex stratigraphic record remain to be resolved, but it is certain that the residential area on the edge of the plaza was actively occupied while public monumental facilities were being built in the center.

Further support for this immediate juxtaposition of a residential area with ongoing construction of pyramid–plaza complexes is provided by ceramics. The vessels found in the summit cache on Structure 6B are identical to vessels found in burials associated with structures in the residential zone. As might be expected, the vessels in the cache match the burial vessels in the eastern sector of the residential zone, which was the last to be covered by open plaza. It seems that the residential zone was never entirely covered by public plaza, as it extends at least 40 m beyond the last plaza to the east. Nonetheless, the lack of midden buildup along the eastern edge of the final plaza may indicate a cessation of domestic occupation in the immediate vicinity of the center as Cerros neared the height of its development.

These findings document a "temple–town" organization at Cerros rather than an "empty center" pattern during the Late Preclassic Period. Although there is no way to tell how many people or buildings may have occupied the area under the last major plaza at Cerros, the mere presence of a residential district directly contiguous with public architecture is not characteristic of the Maya lowlands. Primary midden is commonly found underlying plaza areas in centers, but it has been attributed to domestic occupation preceding the initial raising of pyramids and open plazas (e.g., Ricketson and Ricketson 1937: 136–139). A reassessment of data from other Maya centers may reveal that the situation at Cerros is not unique, but for the present I must presume that this particular "temple–town" organization is unusual and specifically relates to the conditions under which Cerros developed as a center of regional importance.

Proximity to marine–estuary environments has been cited as a factor in the initial development of Formative communities in Mesoamerica (Coe and Flannery 1964). The relatively compact Formative settlement of La Victoria on the coast of Guatemala shows the more typical Maya pattern of individual household compounds located on discrete mounds (Coe 1961:fig. 3) rather than the contiguous mound accumulation or tell–mound formation found at Cerros. Dependence on marine resources might theoretically release inhabitants from the "centrifugal" effects of swidden agriculture. Moreover, the cooperative labor of some fishing technology might actually encourage compact settlement organization. Nevertheless, there is no reason to expect the combination of dispersed and nucleated settlement found at Late Preclassic Cerros as an outgrowth of adaptation to marine–estuary environments, for here nucleation is an aspect of the total pattern rather than an all-encompassing characterization of it.

Ethnohistorical documents (e.g., Landa, in Tozzer 1941) contend that Maya upper classes lived closer to the public architecture of communities than did commoners. The palace structures of the Classic Maya have been interpreted as elite residences (Harrison 1970; Adams 1974a). It is possible that the residential area next to the pyramids at Cerros represents the community's elite. The perishable structures excavated to date do not bespeak exceptional affluence, nor do the burials contain exceptionally fine furniture (although they all contain ceramic vessels). Control over the disposition of structures in this deposit, however, is still minimal; and it is quite possible that the structures excavated to date represent outbuildings associated with more substantial dwellings nearby. At least one building platform for a superstructure is visible in the erosion cut, suggesting the presence of more elaborate structures than those discovered so far in this district. In short, spatial differentiation of the community may reflect social distinctions.

Nucleation of residential areas around public facilities in fortified Maya sites has long been recognized for the Late Postclassic Period (for Tulum, see Lothrop 1924; for Mayapan, see Pollock et al. 1962). Recent research in northern Yucatán (Kurjack and Andrews 1976) suggests that defensive nucleation may have been a well-established practice by Late Classic times. Furthermore, the site of Becán in the central peninsular region appears to have been nucleated and fortified as early as Late Preclassic times (Webster 1977). Defensibility therefore, is a factor in settlement nucleation in the Maya lowlands and may yet prove to have been significant at Cerros. As discussed above, however, the general design of the center stresses greater accessibility than is found at other centers in Belize, which were evidently not fortified. Moreover, no evidence for fortification has been discovered at Cerros to date.

Since the residential area associated with public architecture at Cerros is spatially distinct from the rest of the settlement, it is possible that it formed some type of special precinct with functions beyond that of housing an elite. A special precinct has been identified at the Middle Formative site of San José Mogote in Oaxaca that was evidently associated with craft manufacture and long-distance trade (Flannery 1968). This precinct apparently also housed members of an incipient elite. At Chalcatzingo, another Formative center in highland Mexico, Grove has noted the presence of substantial structures (60 m²) which he identifies as dwellings within the confines of the ceremonial precinct. Given the identification of Chalcatzingo as a trading center (Grove 1968; Hirth 1976), such structures may have served purposes beyond that of elite residence.

Discriminating between dwellings and structures used for other purposes, such as storage and craft production, is a formidable task in the Maya lowlands. Nevertheless, the association of primary trash with structures in the plaza midden at Cerros may eventually allow identification of trade-related facilities. Quantities of obsidian, as well as fragmentary jade axes, basalt, and granite have been found in these trash deposits, reflecting trade of some sort at Late Preclassic Cerros.

Late Preclassic Subsistence Economy at Cerros

As might be anticipated from the community's location, substantial amounts of fish and shellfish remains were retrieved from the Late Preclassic midden. Notched sherds that might have been used as net-weights (Eaton 1976) and pumice spheres that may have served as floats are potential support for a fishing technology. Grinding stones reflect the probable presence of agriculture, and a wide variety of terrestrial animals including deer and peccary are well represented. In general, the inhabitants of the site seem to have enjoyed a mixed subsistence base derived from a variety of available resources.

Although agriculture may have been an essential supplement to the subsistence economy at Cerros, the severely limited amount of arable land on the narrow peninsula of Lowry's Bight, the mediocre quality of the soils there, and the location of the site on the coastal edge of this small landform all point to a dependence on fishing over cropping. It seems unlikely, however, that direct access to aquatic resources is sufficient to explain the development of Cerros into a major center. Several sites in northern Belize, some well inland, show heavy exploitation of marine–estuary resources (Rice 1974). Altun Ha, for example, with its purported reliance on such resources, is located some 10 km from the coastal lagoons. What is noteworthy at Cerros is not its access to these resources but its commanding position on Chetumal Bay at the mouth of the New River.

Dennis and Olga Puleston (1971) have theorized that pioneers moving into the Maya lowlands followed rivers into the interior, initially relying on marine and riverine food sources and using the rivers as a transportation system. Should further research reveal that Cerros was established in Early or Middle Preclassic times, it might be argued that it was a parent community with its offspring communities strung out along the New River. However, present evidence on the regional settlement patterns in the area does not support this scenario. The best established Early Preclassic occupation is at the site of Cuello (Hammond et al. 1976), which is several kilometers from the New River on the interriverine ridge bordered by the New and Hondo rivers. Other identified Early and Middle Preclassic occupations occur near these rivers as well as elsewhere on the ridges (Pring 1976:Fig. 11.2). Furthermore, the midden deposits in the central precinct at Cerros indicate that the major occupation dates to the Late rather than the Early or Middle Preclassic Period.

The information on regional settlement development through time is sketchy at best, as it is based on limited test excavation and surface collections. Nonetheless, it may be significant that the site of Sarteneja also shows initial occupation on the coast in the Late Preclassic Period (Pring 1976:Figs. 11.2, 11.3). If one presumes that a shift toward the coast is taking place between Middle and Late Preclassic times, then the pattern in northern Belize would match the one described by Ball and Eaton (1972) on the northern coast of Yucatán. They contend that the coastal areas were marginal and were occupied by groups of Maya who had been pushed off more favorable agricultural land in a time of population pressure during the Late Preclassic Period. It hardly seems appropriate, however, to have the "losers" in this contest over land establish the largest center in the region at Cerros while centers of venerable antiquity such as Cuello remain relatively small during this period. On the other hand, these coastal Maya may have been developing an alternative source of economic and political power, namely, coastal canoe trade and the commercial exploitation of marine resources.

The notion that the commercial exploitation of marine products coupled with coastal trade could provide a successful socioeconomic niche in the Late Preclassic world is in concert with the observed covariation of population increase and complex society during this period in the lowlands. It is reasonable to believe that a general intensification of sociopolitical interaction within and between groups accompanied such population increase. Granted that this is the case, some general premises exist derived from the observations of social scientists on culture change and material culture that I believe relate population increase to increased manufacture and exchange of commodities:

> Given: Social relationships are dependent on knowledge of the participants' socioeconomic status (Goodenough 1963; Goffman 1959).
>
> Then: Increasing population is accompanied by an increased number of social encounters in which knowledge of social status is not based on personal familiarity and hence in which social status must be symbolized (Goffman 1959; Merton 1957).
>
> Given: Material culture provides an essential symbolic medium for the expression of social-status distinctions (Mauss 1967; Renfrew 1975; Binford 1972).
>
> Then: Increasing population is accompanied by an increase in the number and complexity of material symbols capable of expressing social-status distinctions.

Increase in the complexity of material symbols can be qualified as an increase in labor investment and a decrease in accessibility to the techniques and materials needed for production. The rarer or more labor-intensive a commodity is, the greater its potential value and hence the greater its potential for expressing social-status distinctions related to power and authority. Exotic materials are, by definition, limited in access and labor-intensive. Therefore, as a society increases in population and in social complexity, there is a concomitant increase in the demand for exotic materials.

If the above calculus holds, then the development of complex society in the Maya lowlands should have been accompanied by a concomitant increase in labor-intensive local products and exotics. A glance at the archaeological record demonstrates that this is manifestly the case. Not only are there exotics present in the earliest known lowland contexts (Hammond 1976; Pring 1976), but there is a clear increase in both exotics and labor-intensive artifacts through time. Public monumental architecture, the hallmark of complex society in the lowlands, although certainly not "exchanged," constitutes a product of status-related exchanges and is an example of the manipulation of material culture to further define status relationships.

In the Late Preclassic Period, characterized as a time of endemic warfare by Ball (1977), jade, rare marine products, obsidian, crystalline hematite, and serpentine, among other materials, are broadly distributed in the lowlands. These materials reflect a demand for exotic materials and the presence of a commercial network to satisfy it. It is interesting that the Late Preclassic–Early Classic transition is marked primarily by the innovation of new labor-intensive local products denoting status, such as carved stone stelae, elaborate polychrome pottery, and chert eccentrics. Such innovation is, in my opinion, indicative of a strain on established material media for expressing social relationships brought on by the increasing, and uncontrolled, proliferation of status distinctions. It follows from this argument that local and long-distance commerce are necessary, if not sufficient, factors in the rise of the Maya, not because exotics were necessary to subsistence technology as argued by Rathje (1971, 1972), but rather because they provided a vital medium for the expression of complex social relationships.

If one assumes that the Late Preclassic Period witnessed the development of incipient elites throughout the lowlands, one can deduce a concomitant increase in the demand for exotic material and in traffic on long-distance trade routes as well as the emergence of specialists in trade. The strategic location of Cerros on water transport routes connecting the coast to the interior and its orientation to marine resources provide plausible explanatory factors for the rise of this center within its social environment.

In the last analysis, this schema places Cerros in an "open" system where the factors promoting its development lie outside local ecological conditions. It is supported by the untimely demise of the center at the end of the Late Preclassic. If strictly local conditions had been crucial, one might reasonably expect continued occupation through the Classic Period, as is typical of other centers in northern Belize.

LATE PRECLASSIC
COMMUNICATION–TRANSPORTATION
NETWORKS

The trade situation is an exchange situation, and an exchange situation is an information flow situation [Renfrew 1975:24].

Culture areas during the Classic era in the Maya lowlands have been defined traditionally by the geographic distribution of characteristic material traits so technically unusual or complex as to preclude the probability of independent innovation (e.g., corbel vaulted architecture, stelae, hieroglyphic writing, iconographic themes, portable art, and ceramics). In recent years there have been many attempts to replace such purely descriptive definitions with analytic models outlining the social processes manifested in these traits (Willey and Shimkin 1973; Willey 1977). Clearly the bulk of such traits constitute the labor-intensive and exotic artifacts that form the essential medium for expressing social relationships characteristic of civilization. It follows that comparisons of formal similarities and differences in this inventory of material culture are aimed at gauging the common roots of within-polity organization through an examination of between-polity ties, that is, the degree to which the innovation of complex society in any one part of the lowlands is due to localized conditions and the degree to which such innovation must be viewed as a regional, pan-peninsular phenomenon. In the last analysis, this is an inquiry into the organization and magnitude of communication networks both within and between polities.

Despite differences of opinion concerning the importance and organization of trade during the Classic Period in the lowlands, there seems to be a consensus that communication networks during this period were also trade networks (Willey 1977; Tourtellot and Sabloff 1972; Rathje 1972; Voorhies 1973). The correlation of trade, communication, and the geographic patterns of similarity in material culture has a definite bearing on Late Preclassic developments.

In a detailed and cogent exposition, Ball (1974) has argued that population pressure and consequent conflict over arable land were primary factors in the initiation of complex society in the northern lowlands. Central to his case is the observation that Dzibilchaltún, a major center in Late Preclassic times, shows no strong affinities to major centers in the southern lowlands in terms of architecture and ceramics. Consequently, the development of complex society in the north cannot be considered a result of diffusion from the south.

The dissimilarities cited by Ball in these contemporaneous expressions of complex society might be taken to reflect a distinct lack of communication between the southern and northern lowlands. Yet Ball also grants the presence of exotics such as jade in some abundance at Dzibilchaltún and specifically points to them as evidence of complex social organization because of their distribution. Clearly trade and the communication that accompanies trade are present between northern Yucatán and regions to the south. It follows that the elite of such centers as Dzibilchaltún in the north were not ignorant of their counterparts with different styles in the south, but rather that they chose not to emulate or otherwise identify themselves with southern leadership. The expression and assimilation of information are not mechanical phenomena, for they are guided by intentionality which may ultimately be isolated and qualified precisely through such distinct contemporaneous patterns.

I find Ball's reasoning persuasive that neither trade with the southern lowlands nor emulation of southern elites can be considered prime causes initiating complex society in the north. I would question, however, the notion that hostile social interaction as a mechanism inducing complexity follows more directly from a state of population pressure than does positive interaction in the form of trade. These are two interdependent aspects of systemically intensified interaction in the lowlands during the Late Preclassic Period.

Furthermore, Dzibilchaltún's proximity to the northern coast, with its salt, other marine resources, and transportation potential, should be seriously considered in any discussion of the site's Late Preclassic development. For if population on the peninsula was indeed so dense, massive quantities of salt must have been imported into interior regions, both in the north and in the south.

Despite the similarities between Dzibilchaltún and Cerros—proximity to the coast, peripheral location relative to the central interior regions, and precocity in the development of a complex society—these sites stand in marked contrast in terms of comparisons with central Petén sites. Dzibilchaltún does not share the attributes that link Cerros to central interior Maya sites. Structure 6B at Cerros exhibits massive modeled stucco masks flanking a central staircase, comparable in general construction and design to the famous masks on Structure E-VII-sub at Uaxactún and the fragmentary masks on Structure 5D-sub.3-3rd at Tikál (Ricketson and Ricketson 1937; Coe 1965a:fig. 17). A more precise correlation exists between a profile serpentine grotesque preserved on the lower stucco facade of this Cerros structure (Figure. 11.4) and a virtually identical carved stone grotesque at Tikál (miscellaneous stone 69, Coe 1965a:fig. 19). Although the Tikál carving is of problematical age, Coe notes its general stylistic affinities with Late Preclassic art in the highlands of Guatemala. As at Late Preclassic Tikal, polychrome fresco is a well-developed art at Cerros: The stucco facading on Structure 6B is elaborately painted. Other shared architectural traits present in Late Preclassic times at Cerros include apron moldings (definite) and corbel vaulting (probable).

In portable art, the five jade head pendants found in the Late Preclassic cache atop Structure 6B (Figure 11.5) not only show definite affinities with Late Preclassic jades from the nearby site of Nohmul in Northern Belize (Hammond 1974) but also with shell pendants and jades from Late Preclassic Tikál (Coe 1965:fig. 11; Coe 1965b:23). Iconographically similar jade pieces were found in the *cenote* of sacrifice at Chichen Itzá (Prouskouriakoff 1974:p1. 53), and a similar shell pendant was found in a Late Preclassic context in Veracruz (Stirling 1957:pl. 65). In short, the portable Late Preclassic art at Cerros correlates well with specimens found in the central Petén and other peripheral areas.

The Late Preclassic ceramics at Cerros are firmly within the Chicanel sphere, although due to the relatively large sample (about 40,000 sherds) variability is considerably greater than that noted elsewhere.

The similarities between Cerros and contemporaneous sites in the central Petén region, then, are both strong and manifold. It follows that communication between these areas was definitely positive. The question arises

Figure 11.4. Detail of polychrome stucco facading from lower terrace of Structure 6B, a serpentine grotesque.

as to whether the similarities in material symbol systems between Cerros and Petén sites and their organizational concomitants can be attributed to diffusion from the Petén to Belize. It can be argued that such is not the case. In the first place, Cerros does not exhibit crude, provincial expressions of more sophisticated material symbols found in contemporaneous Petén centers. On the contrary, the artistic quality of the stucco facade on Structure 6B is as fine as anything in the Petén and technically surpasses some known examples there (e.g., the facade on Uaxactún's E-VII-sub is not painted). Moreover, despite the shared presence of massive monster masks flanking a central stairway and of such minor motives as serpentine grotesques, knots, and twisted bands, the compositions at Cerros are distinctive. The large masks at Cerros are incorporated into facades that run the length of the vertical risers on the structure. This is unlike E-VII-sub or what is known of Late Preclassic substructures at Tikál. Rather it is a form of architectural design well represented in later periods in the Maya area. Furthermore, the central stairway on Structure 6B is outset, unlike the known Late Preclassic Petén examples but like those found on Late Preclassic pyramids at Dzibilchaltún in Yucatán and Chalchuapa in El Salvador (Sharer 1969); this form is typical of Early Classic architecture in the southern lowlands. Finally, the characteristic architectural complex at Cerros is a massive pyramidal sub-

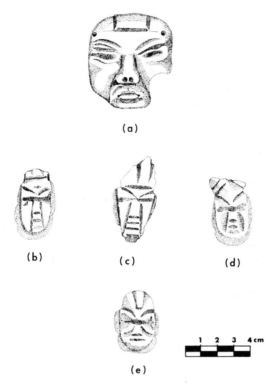

Figure 11.5.   Stone head pendants from the cache on Structure 6B. Key: (a) carved on a sawed-off fragment of a larger piece of stone, notch in cheek is smoothed but not polished, facial features ground smooth and highly polished, color is uniformly light green; (b) carved on a pebble, facial features defined by sawed grooves, highly polished but not modeled, color is mottled light green, grey, and dark green; (c) carved on a pebble, facial features same as (b), color, light green and white; (d) carved on a pebble, facial features same as (b) and (c), color is light green and mottled grey-green; (e) carved on a pebble, facial features same as (b), (c), and (d), color is light mottled grey-green.

structure bordering an open plaza area, forming an essentially asymmetrical and linear design. The four-sided E-VII-sub and the earlier versions of the North Acropolis at Tikál with three structures bordering on plazas point to a concentric, symmetrical design.

Variability in architectural design of Late Preclassic monuments is so poorly understood at the moment that few inferences can be drawn concerning the directional movement of artistic or ideological innovations, but clearly Cerros is not a carbon copy of central Petén conventions. In the end, unilateral flow of information and material concomitants in either direction is less likely than bilateral flow. Of significance is the fact that the elite of

Cerros and the elites of the central Petén region chose to ally themselves in a fashion that is reflected in their material symbols. There is no reason to believe that the people of Cerros were any more ignorant of alternative symbols, iconographic motives, and architectural designs than were the people of Dzibilchaltún.

One plausible motivation for long-distance communication and alliance between northern Belize and the central Petén region is mutually beneficial commerce. The coastal location of Cerros, its abundant exotics, and its settlement pattern suggest to me that the potentialities of commerce were no doubt instrumental in the florescence of this community. There is no need, however, to attribute motivation for long-distance trade solely to the central Petén region (with a resulting core–buffer zone schema, e.g., Rathje 1971; 1972). Demand for exotics is found throughout the lowlands, at Dzibilchaltún in the north, and in Belize in the Late Preclassic Period. The key to the Late Preclassic florescence at Cerros lies in its macrogeographical position relative to the northern and southern lowland interaction spheres as documented by Ball (1974), Rovner (1975), and Adams (1974). Cerros lies on a cultural boundary running east–west across the peninsula that persists, with modifications, throughout Maya history (Figure 11.6). In terms of land-

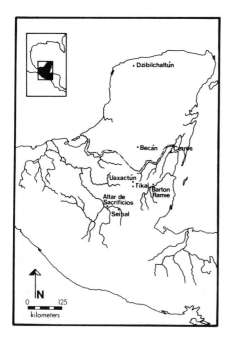

Figure 11.6. Major Late Preclassic sites in the Maya lowlands and the traditional north –south cultural boundary.

based interior routes, Cerros is entirely peripheral to any interface between north and south, but in terms of water transportation, the site is centrally located.

The northern interaction sphere is still largely defined by ceramic similarities in the Late Preclassic Period. Given present knowledge, however, it is fairly certain that the major centers in this sphere are located in the far north and are characterized by a "high culture" that is distinctive from that found in the southern lowlands. With the discovery of Cerros, the extent of the southern lowland Late Preclassic interaction sphere can be documented from the central Petén region to the coast of Belize. Land-based interior networks were sufficiently developed to make affiliation between Cerros and the centers of the Petén both feasible and desirable. I believe such long-distance affiliations had an economic motivation. In simplistic terms, the northern interaction sphere controlled a resource vital to the south: salt. The southern interaction sphere controlled exotic resources vital to the development of the material symbol systems in the north. Demographic pressure may well have provided the initial impetus for the development of various kinds of interactions, but long-distance trade was crucial to their realization and their ramifications. Presumably the Maya of the southern interior and those on the northern coast could have traded directly through the interior, but this would have entailed either the penetration of one interaction sphere by the other or the establishment of centers on the frontier, which in the long run would have been in a good position to usurp power from both north and south by controlling the means of distribution. Although the interior frontier between the north and south may have been characterized by tension and conflict in Late Preclassic times, as argued by Ball (1974), economic symbiosis between north and south was maintained by the maritime Maya of the eastern littoral who flourished through their commercial enterprises—maritime Maya who lacked the territorial control to threaten either land-based confederation. Hence, the rise of Cerros as a major center can be seen as an aspect of panpeninsular developments. At the end of the Late Preclassic Period, the interior frontier was successfully penetrated by the southern lowland interaction sphere, and access to northern resources through land-based routes was achieved. The collapse of the interior frontier signaled the collapse of maritime trade between the north and south and the subsequent abandonment of Cerros.

This historical scenario is supported by a number of empirical data. The florescence of Late Preclassic Dzibilchaltún and of Cerros parallel each other. In terms of regional settlement patterns, neither center is centrally located with regard to its potential sustaining area or land-based sphere of influence. Both sites are peripheral in their location near the coast. Furthermore, both sites are, on present evidence, considerably larger than contemporaneous centers in their regions, reflecting their probable political and economic dominion over neighboring communities.

These settlement patterns are more amenable to dendritic models in which the crucial variable is monopolized access to traded commodities and transport routes than they are to central-place models in which the crucial variable is management of local resources (Vance 1970; Hirth 1976). Moreover, the settlement patterns compare well with the Late Postclassic (A.D. 1200–1520) political dominance of northern Belize by the coastal center of Chetumal, control of Canpech province by the coastal center of Campeche, and control of Chi Kin Chel province by the center of Chauaca. In all these cases, canoe transportation was the primary medium of long-distance trade (Roys 1957).

Similarly the collapse of Late Preclassic Dzibilchaltún and Cerros parallel each other. In both cases, the abandonment seems to be site-specific, for occupation and development continue at neighboring centers located farther from the coast and on better land. These collapses are also accompanied by the development of the nucleated and fortified center of Becán on the interior north–south frontier (Figure 11.6). Becán signals the development of organized conflict in the frontier area and an attempt by communities traditionally affiliated with the north to stave off incorporation into the southern interaction sphere. As documented by Ball (1977), this attempt failed in the long run as the south eventually was successful in penetrating the north.

In this schema, the collapse of Dzibilchaltún can be attributed to the undermining of its monopolized control of exotics from the south via coastal transport routes. As the southern centers established interior routes into the north and supplied Dzibilchaltún's affiliates with these commodities, the economic underpinning of its interaction sphere was destroyed.

Force of arms no doubt played a role in the southern penetration of the northern interaction sphere, as witnessed by the rise of Becán. Yet focusing on warfare as a condition engendering complex society obscures the essential objective of these interaction spheres, which was the establishment of economic and political coordination and cooperation between polities. But the interaction-sphere scenario begs an important question. Why didn't the coastal Maya of the north establish alliances with the coastal Maya of Belize? Such an alliance would have allowed the north to circumvent the southern interior as a source of exotics and would have maintained northern control of the salt beds. That the southern centers of the interior maintained the allegiance of the coastal Maya of Belize, even when they were undermining coastal commerce, points to the essential superiority of the social institutions integrating the southern interaction sphere. Such superiority can be documented by the greater elaboration of southern material symbol systems. In the last analysis, ideology, rather than economic clout or military prowess, provided the southern interaction sphere with its competitive edge.

MARITIME ADAPTATION AND THE PRECLASSIC MAYA

During the Preclassic era, when interior communication–transportation networks were relatively weak and uncertain, long-distance trade between the northern and southern lowlands was initially predominantly coastal, a condition paralleling the strong development of coastal trade in the Postclassic era. The establishment of long-distance trade along the coasts encouraged the development of two distinct land-based interaction spheres in the lowlands, one in the far north and a second in the southern region of the Petén and coastal Belize. As long as trade for salt and exotics remained predominantly coastal, a relatively stable and symbiotic relationship was maintained between the two interaction spheres. The economic impetus of the northern sphere, however, was to expand southward in order to supply interior centers with exotics, whereas that of the south was to expand northward to supply interior sites with salt. Clearly the central peninsular region was a tension zone, as both interaction spheres could attempt better access to each other's monopoly. Conflict ensued when economic coercion could not succeed, and the southern sphere prevailed, establishing interior transportation–communication networks to the north. The north–south dichotomy was never really overcome, however, and the cultural distinctions established in the Preclassic remained throughout Maya culture history. In terms of access to desirable exotic resources, rationally one might have expected to see the initial and most advanced developments in the Río Bec region. A hypothesized initial dependence on coastal transportation–communication routes explains how the north–south dichotomy became established in the first place.

ACKNOWLEDGMENTS

The research at Cerros has been carried out under permit from the Belizean government. I am grateful to Archaeological Commissioner Joseph O. Palacio for his support and encouragement and to Mr. Santiago Perdomo, Minister of Trade and Industry, for many kindnesses. Support for research has been provided by citizens of Dallas, Texas, through the Cerro Maya Foundation based in that city. I am particularly grateful to Mr. Stanley Marcus and Mr. Lee Fikes for soliciting the support of the Dallas community. Mr. T. Tim Cullum and Mr. Richard Sandow, officers of the Cerro Maya Foundation, through untiring effort launched the project off the drawing board and into the field. The staff of the project, Maynard B. Cliff, Robin Robertson-Freidel, James Belew, Vernon Scarborough, and James Garber are responsible for the orderly retrieval of the data discussed in this chapter, as are the many American and Belizean volunteers who have worked with the project. I thank T. Patrick Culbert, William Rathje, Joseph Ball, and Gordon R. Willey for making unpublished materials available to me and for discussions of the Cerros material. The author is soley responsible for conclusions drawn from such discussions. Finally, I thank Robin Robertson-Freidel for editing the manuscript and for offering many cogent comments and criticisms of the arguments presented here. Mary Coleman carried out the arduous task of typing and retyping the manuscript.

REFERENCES

Adams, Richard E. W.
    1974a   A trial estimation of Classic Maya palace populations at Uaxactún. In *Mesoamerican archaeology: New perspectives,* edited by Norman Hammond, Austin: Univ. of Texas press. Pp. 285–296.
    1974b   *Preliminary reports on archaeological investigations in the Río Bec Area, Campeche, Mexico.* Middle America Research Institute, Publication 31. Pp. 103–106.
Andrews, Anthony P.
    1972   *A preliminary study of the ruins of Xcaret and a reconnaissance of other archaeological sites on the central coast of Quintana Roo, Mexico.* Atti del XL Congreso Internazionale degli Americanisti, Rome–Genova.
Ball, Joseph W.
    1977   The rise of the Northern Maya chiefdoms: A socioprocessual analysis. In *The Origins of Maya civilization,* edited by R. E. W. Adams. Albuquerque: Univ. of New Mexico Press. Pp. 101–131.
Ball, Joseph W., and J. D. Eaton
    1972   Marine resources and the prehistoric lowland Maya: A comment. *American Antiquity* **74**(3):773–776.
Binford, Lewis R.
    1972   Mortuary practices: Their study and potential. In *An archaeological perspective.* New York: Seminar Press. Pp. 208–243.
Bullard, William R., Jr.
    1965   *Stratigraphic excavations at San Estevan, Northen British Honduras.* Art and Archaeology Occasional Paper. No. 9. Royal Ontario Museum.
Coe, Michael D.
    1961   *La Victoria: An early site on the Pacific Coast of Guatemala.* Papers of the Peabody Museum of Archaeology and Ethnology, Vol. 52. Cambridge Massachusetts: Peabody Museum of Archaeology and Ethnology, Harvard Univ.
Coe, Michael D., and Kent V. Flannery
    1964   Microenvironments and Mesoamerican prehistory. *Science* **143**:650–654.
Coe, William R.
    1965a   Tikal, Guatemala, and emergent Maya civilization, *Science* **147**(3664):1401–1423.
    1965b   Tikal: Ten years of study of a Maya ruin in the lowlands of Guatemala. *Expedition* **8**(1):5–56.
Connor, Judith G.
    1975   Ceramics and artifacts. In *A study of changing pre-Columbian commercial systems:*

The 1972–1973 seasons at Cozumel, Mexico, edited by J. A. Sabloff and W. L. Rathje. Monographs of the Peabody Museum, No. 3. Cambridge, Massachusetts: Peabody Museum of Archaeology and Ethnology, Harvard Univ. Pp. 114–135.

Eaton, Jack D.
1976   Ancient fishing technology on the Gulf Coast of Yucatan, Mexico. *Bulletin of the Texas Archaeological Society* **47**:231–243.

Escalona-Ramos, A.
1946   Algunas ruinas prehispánicos en Quintana Roo. *Boletín de la Sociedad Mexicana de Geografía y Estadística* **61**(3):513–628.

Flannery, Kent V.
1968   The Olmec and the Valley of Oaxaca: A model for inter-regional interaction in Formative times. In *Dumbarton Oaks Conference on the Olmec,* edited by E. P. Benson. Washington, D.C.: Dumbarton Oaks Research Library and Collection. Pp. 79–110.

Freidel, David A.
1976   Cerro Maya: A Late Preclassic center in Corozal District. In *Recent archaeology in Belize,* edited by R. Buhler. Occasional Publication, No. 3 Belize City: Bisra (Belize Institute for Social Research and Action). Pp. 73–99.

Goodenough, Ward H.
1963   *Cooperation in change.* New York: Russell Sage Foundation.

Goffman, Erving
1959   *The presentation of self in everyday life.* New York: Doubleday Anchor Books.

Grove, David C.
1968   The preclassic Olmec in Central Mexico: Site distribution and inferences. In *Dumbarton Oaks Conference on the Olmec,* edited by E. P. Benson. Washington, D.C.: Dumbarton Oaks Research Library and Collection. Pp. 179–185.

Hammond, Norman
1973   Models for Maya trade. In *The explanation of culture change: Models in prehistory.* edited by C. Renfrew. Pittsburgh: Univ. of Pittsburgh Press. Pp. 601–607.
1974   Preclassic to postclassic in northern Belize, *Antiquity* **58**:177–187.
1976   *Archaeology in northen Belize: British Museum–Cambridge University Corozal Project 1974–75 Interim Report.* Cambridge, England: Centre of Latin American Studies.

Hammond, Norman, Duncan Pring, Rainer Berger, V. R. Sivitan, and A. P. Ward.
1976   Radiocarbon chronology for early Maya occupation at Cuello, Belize. *Nature* **260**(5552):574–581.

Harrison, Peter D.
1970   Form and function in a Maya 'palace' group. *Verhandlungen des XXXVIII Ameikanistenkingresses* **1**:165–172.

Hirth, Kenneth G.
1976   Inter-regional trade and the formation of prehistoric gateway communities. Paper presented at the 40th Annual Meeting, Society for American Archaeology, St. Louis.

Kurjack, Edward B., and E. W. Andrews V
1976   Early boundary maintenance in northwest Yucatan. *American Antiquity* **41**(3):319–325.

Lothrop, Samuel K.
1924   Tulum, an archaeological study of the east coast of Yucatan. Publication 335. Washington, D.C.: *Carnegie Institution of Washington.*

Mauss, Marcel
1967   *The Gift: Forms and functions of exchange in archaic societies.* I. Caunison, translator. New York: W. W. Norton.

Merton, Robert K.
    1957   Social theory and social structure. Glencoe, Illinois: The Free Press.
Neivens, Mary B.
    1976   El Posito, a late classic site. In *Recent archaeology in Belize,* edited by R. Buhler.
            Occasional Publication, No. 3. Belize City: Bisra (Belize Institute for Social Research
            and Action). Pp. 53–64.
Pendergast, David M.
    1967   Altun Ha, Honduras Britanica: Temporadas 1964 y 1965. *Estudios de Cultura Maya*
            6:149–169. Universidad Autónoma de México.
    1971   Evidence of early Teotihuacan–lowland Maya contact at Altun Ha. *American An-
            tiquity* **36**(4):455–460.
Pollock, Harry E., R. L. Roys, Tatiana Proskouriakoff, and A. Ledyard Smith
    1962   *Mayapan, Yucatan, Mexico.* Publication 619. Washington, D.C.: Carnegie Institution
            of Washington.
Pring, Duncan
    1976   Summary of the ceramic sequence in northern Belize. In *Archaeology in Northern
            Belize: British Museum–*Cambridge University Corozal Project, 1974–75 Interim
            Report. edited by N. Hammond. Cambridge, England: Center of Latin American
            Studies. Pp. 109–205.
Rovner, Irwin
    1975   Lithic sequences from the Maya lowlands. Ph.D. dissertation, Ann Arbor, University
            Microfilms.
Proskouriakoff, Tatiana
    1974   Jades from the cenote of sacrifice, Chichen Itza, Yucatan. *Peabody Museum Memoirs*
            10(1). Cambridge, Massachusetts: Harvard Univ.
Puleston, Dennis, and O. S. Puleston
    1971   An ecological approach to the origins of Maya civilization. *Archaeology* **24**(4):330–
            337.
Rathje, William L.
    1971   The origin and development of Lowland Classic Maya civilization. *American An-
            tiquity* **36**(3):275–285.
    1972   Praise the gods and pass the metates: An hypothesis of the development of Lowland
            Rainforest civilizations in mesoamerica. In *Contemporary archaeology,* edited by M.
            P. Leone. Carbondale: Southern Illinois Univ. Press. Pp. 359–392.
Renfrew, Colin
    1975   Trade as action at a distance: Questions of integration and communication. In
            Ancient civilization and trade, edited by J. A. Sabloff and C. C. Lamgerg-Karlovsky.
            Albuquerque: Univ. of New Mexico Press. Pp. 3–59.
Ricketson, Oliver G., and E. B. Ricketson
    1937   *Uaxactún, Guatemala: Group E. 1926–1937* Carnegie Institution of Washington
            Publication 477. Washington, D.C.
Rice, Don S.
    1974   The archaeology of British Honduras: A review and synthesis. Katunob. Occasional
            Publications in Mesoamerican Anthropology No. 6. Greely: Univ. of Northern Col-
            orado.
Roys, Ralph L.
    1957   *Political geography of the Yucatan peninsula.* Publication 613. Washington, D.C.:
            Carnegie Institution of Washington.
Sabloff, Jeremy A., and W. L. Rathje
    1975   Cozumel's place in Yucatecan culture history. In *Changing pre-Columbian commer-*

cial systems: The 1972–1973 seasons at Cozumel, Mexico, edited by J. A. Sabloff and W. Rathje. Monographs of the Peabody Museum No. 3. Peabody Museum of Archaeology and Ethnology, Harvard Univ. Pp. 21–28.

Sanders, William T.
   1973   The cultural ecology of the Lowland Maya: A re-evaluation. In *The Classic Maya collapse,* edited by T. P. Culbert. Albuquerque: Univ. of New Mexico Press. Pp. 325–365.

Sharer, Robert J.
   1969   A preliminary report of the 1969 archaeology research program at Chalchuapa, El Salvador. *Katunob* **7**:55–69.

Stirling, Mathew W.
   1957   *An archaeological reconnaissance in Southeastern Mexico.* Bulletin 164, Anthropological Paper 53. Washington, D.C.: Smithsonian Institution. Bureau of American Ethnology Pp. 213–240.

Thompson, J. Eric S.
   1970   *Maya history and religion.* Norman: Univ. of Oklahoma Press.

Tourtellot, Gair, and J. A. Sabloff
   1972   Exchange systems among the ancient Maya. *American Antiquity* **37**(1):126–135.

Tozzer, Alfred M.
   1941   *Landa's Relación de las Cosas de Yucatán,* edited by A. M. Tozzer with notes. Papers of the Peabody Museum of Archaeology and Ethnology, Vol. 18. Cambridge, Massachusetts: Harvard University.

Vance, James W.
   1970   *The merchant's world: The geography of wholesaling.* Englewood Cliffs, New Jersey: Prentice-Hall.

Voorhies, Barbara
   1973   Possible social factors in the exchange system of the Prehistoric Maya. *American Antiquity* **38**(4):486–489.

Webster, David L.
   1977   Warfare and the evolution of Maya civilization. In *The origins of Maya civilization,* edited by R. E. W. Adams. Albuquerque: Univ. of New Mexico Press. Pp. 335–372.
   1975   Warfare and the evolution of the state: A reconsideration. *American Antiquity* **40**(4):464–470.

Willey, Gordon R.
   1977   The rise of Maya Civilization: A summary view. In *The origins of Maya civilization,* edited by R. E. W. Adams. Albuquerque: Univ. of New Mexico Press. Pp. 383–423.

Willey, Gordon R., and D. B. Shimkin
   1973   The Maya collapse: A summary view. In *The Classic Maya collapse,* edited by T. P. Culbert. Albuquerque: Univ. of New Mexico Press. Pp. 457–501.

Wright, A. C. S., D. H. Romney, R. H. Arbuckle, and, V. E. Vidal.
   1959   Land in British Honduras. *Colonial Research Publications* Vol. 24. London.

PART **V**

Overview

chapter 12

Commentary

WILLIAM T. SANDERS
Pennsylvania State University

In her introductory chapter Voorhies has presented a detailed summary of research in coastal Mesoamerica. In the summary chapter, Voorhies and Stark have summarized the work of the contributors in terms of the major topics of subsistence, settlement patterns, and exchange networks. In the discussion that follows, I will therefore refrain from this type of synthesis and make observations on these themes only to illustrate the essentially methodological and theoretical points.

The purposes of the symposium, as Voorhies states, were to bring together available information on prehispanic adaptation to the coastal habitat of Mesoamerica that reflects the kind of research being done; to define the nature of the coastal ecosystem as a type; and, finally, to discuss the significance of the coastal ecotype in terms of the broader patterns of Mesoamerican civilization as a whole. By *coastal* the editors refer to those ecosystems in which a substantial component of the subsistence and technological resources of the group were obtained from an estuarine, lagunal, or marine source.

In my opinion, the editors have achieved the first objective. The data

269

base, although it is rather thin and spotty in time and space, is sufficient to allow at least a tentative statement with respect to the second objective. Furthermore, this tentative statement produces at least a number of major questions for future research that bear on the third objective. It is to this third objective that I will address most of my comments.

A major theoretical question in Mesoamerican literature is the suggested precocity of the coastal habitat in the early phase of the development of Mesoamerican civilization (i.e., the beginnings of agriculture and consequently of ranked society). Basically the argument is that the coastal resources are so rich, in terms of abundance and dependability, that an early preagricultural sedentism developed. These sedentary gatherers, under the influence of population growth and pressure, then invented agriculture. The data summarized in this volume do not seem to justify this theoretical argument at all. If anything, the coastal habitat seems marginal through the early phases of development, particularly when compared to the immediately adjacent lowland plains (in terms of population growth, permanent occupation, and location of major centers). In virtually all of the cases cited, coastal resources were used early, but by inland farmers who established seasonal camps to collect the wild resources. It is not until inland groups reach substantial levels of population and a degree of sociopolitical complexity that permanent, economically specialized or semispecialized communities emerge in the coastal zone, apparently closely aligned with inland centers in a pattern of economic symbiosis. This suggests to me a suspicion I have entertained for years: that we have grossly overestimated the productivity of the tropical coastal habitat, and that permanent settlement occurred there only when large agricultural surpluses could be generated by inland groups to underwrite the energetically more costly fishing and collecting economies of the coast.

The contrast in cultural evolution between the immediate coastal zone and the riverine plains of the adjacent lowlands is striking. The latter environment was clearly one of the early centers of Mesoamerican development—if not in the earliest stages of plant domestication, at least in the early development of ranked society, as the Olmec phenomenon demonstrates. Present evidence suggests that there was a virtually continuous band of tropical lowland, with variable rainfall, that extended from the western Guatemalan Pacific plain through the Chiapas Pacific plain, across the Isthmus of Tehuantepec to southern Veracruz and western Tabasco; that was the setting of the most complex Mesoamerican society during the Early and Middle Formative periods.

What little evidence we do have suggests that the earliest phase of this development was linked with a root-crop cultivation, and settlements may have been closely limited to riverine locations where fishing provided the protein complement. The maize–beans complex had replaced this subsistence system by 1100 to 1200 B.C., and the introduction of maize apparently was closely linked with the sudden appearance of ranked societies in the area. The set of events suggested here parallels very closely Reichel-Dolmotoff's (1965) reconstruction of the early developments on the northern coastal plain of Columbia, where an early root-crop-based ecosystem with a close relationship to riverine resources is replaced by a maize–bean complex that enabled the population to expand into nonriverine areas of the plain. Once the agricultural economy was released from its linkage to the riverine locale, the result was a considerable increase in population and evolution of more complex sociopolitical systems in both areas. In connection with this, it would have been highly productive to increase the geographic range of the data in this volume and compare the Mesoamerican sequences with those of Columbia and Ecuador.

One final qualifying note must be added to the developmental sequence I have suggested. It does not necessarily mean, as Coe, Bernal, and others have argued, that contemporary and later developments elsewhere in Mesoamerica were the product of colonization, conquests, and missionization from this core area. There is growing evidence of a parallel cultural development in terms of date and, in certain respects even in scale, in the Valley of Oaxaca and on the Central Plateau. In fact, some of the largest sites in the latter region, such as Tlatilco and Chalcatzingo, were comparable in residential areas to the major sites in the Gulf–Pacific Coastal Plain nuclear area.

A second topic that is approached in several chapters in the volume, and one that has considerable theoretical importance, is the analysis of settlement systems and their relationship to resource procurement and institutions. Unfortunately, the projects reported here suffer from two major defects: a deficient data base and the uncritical use of central-place models from geography.

With respect to the data base, one needs large-scale regional settlement surveys to make the kinds of reconstructions that are attempted in several chapters. The only study that comes close to a formal settlement survey is the one by the Zeitlins in the Isthmus of Tehuantepec, and even this involves only three small areas (on the piedmont, plain, and littoral) and a total of 100 km². We have been involved, since 1960, in a program of intensive settlement surveys of the Basin of Mexico, an area of 7000 km², which was completed in 1975 (in fact actual survey time amounted to about 500 man-months). If we were to select 100 km² of this region as a basis to write a settlement history of the Basin, the results would be meaningless.

For example, in J. Zeitlin's chapter the author is concerned with the problem of apparent population decline and the absence of a regional center for the Late Postclassic Period. As she herself points out, ethnohistoric data indicate that the town of Tehuantepec, outside of the survey region, was the major population center at the time of the Conquest, and the survey area was apparently a frontier tributary zone to that town. What conclusions would one draw without the ethnohistoric data? Our own surveys for the Basin of Mexico show dramatically the effects of unusually large centers on population distribution. If it were not for the fact that Eduardo Matos' Tula project has recently involved surveys around the city of Tula, we would not be able to explain our Mazapan Phase settlement profile for the Basin of Mexico. Even a survey area of 7000 km² may be, therefore, inadequate. Obviously the larger the area included in a survey, the better the possibility of offering explanations for the variation in settlement systems in the area through time; there is always the question of how much is enough, but 100 km² clearly is not.

I also object strenuously to the naive way in which many of my colleagues—and here I am not singling out any particular writer in this volume—have applied central-place theory from geography. The fact is that virtually none of the efforts to apply specific models used by geographers have been successful, and the reasons are clear. The geographers' models are based on societies much more complexly organized than those traditionally studied by anthropologists. Many of the central-place models are economic models, derived from economic systems and structures based on the market principle of profit. In a recent book on contemporary markets in Oaxaca (Cook and Diskin 1976), several chapters emphasize that although transactions in Oaxaca today take place in "market places" and money is almost always used as a mechanism of exchange, in fact, much of the exchange, in terms of its structure, is based on the principle of redistribution. In prehispanic times this was probably the most important principle governing the exchanges. There were exceptions, of course, one of which would be a professional merchant class like the Aztec *pochteca,* who apparently did operate on the basis of a profit kind of economy, but their contribution to the overall economy was relatively slight. What this means is that archaeologists must generate their own models from the much broader range of ethnographic data that anthropologists traditionally have produced. The basic principle of spatial modeling undoubtedly is sound and can be highly productive for anthropological research. By way of suggestion, one fact that emerges from our own Basin of Mexico survey is that settlement hierarchies tend to lack the neat pyramidal form of the published central-place models from geography; there tends to be unusual concentrations of population in the larger communities, a pattern also reported by J. Zeitlin in her Tehuantepec study. How this relates to a redistributive economy is not completely clear, but there undoubtedly is a close relationship.

A few final comments relate to the significance of exchange networks in the evolution of centralized or hierarchical sociopolitical institutions. Here my comments involve not only the coast but also any geographic habitat. In recent years there has been an increasing focus on energy studies in cultural ecology, calculations of costs of production and distribution. These studies seem to suggest that it would be more useful for archaeologists to concentrate on local exchange systems as a significant factor in the evolution of social stratification rather than on long-distance trade. The point is that preindustrial transportation technology was extremely primitive, and this was particularly true in Mesoamerica, and only low consumption, restricted use, and highly valued merchandise could be moved over considerable distances. In his recent book *Environment, Power and Society,* Howard Odum (1971) has argued that the quantity of energy that moves through points in an ecosystem has a powerful effect on the structure and the functioning of those points. What this means in terms of cultural evolution is that the control of production and distribution of high-consumption, general-use, and low-value goods—in the case of Mesoamerica, local regional production—is much more likely to have played a significant role in social stratification than the kinds of goods moved along the long-distance trade network. This basic point was made many years ago by people like Leslie White and Chapple and Coon, but archaeologists have not consistently used this principle in their own evolutionary theory.

From the point of view of the archaeologists, all of this means we should focus on regional surveys, either with 100% coverage or with some very judicious use of stratified sampling that captures the geographic variety of the area and is large enough in scale to solve some of the problems that are produced by a hierarchical sociopolitical organization. Our research should also include systematic excavation of sites that cover the range of ecological settings and sociopolitical levels; it should utilize both new techniques of collecting perishable materials and developments in laboratory techniques of analysis of sources and functions of artifacts. What this obviously means is that archaeologists must make long-range plans and commitments to research in particular geographic regions if the research that they do is going to produce major leads as to the nature of sociopolitical evolution.

REFERENCES

Cook, Scott, and Martin Diskin, eds.
1976 *Markets in Oaxaca*. Austin: Univ. of Texas Press.
Odum, Howard T.
1971 *Environment, power and society*. New York: Wiley, Interscience and Technology series.

Reichel-Dolmotoff, Gerardo
  1965   *Columbia*. New York: Praeger, Current Peoples and Places series.
White, Leslie
  1959   *The evolution of culture*. New York: McGraw-Hill.
Chapple, Eliot D., and Carleton J. Coon
  1942   *Principles of anthropology*. New York: Henry Holt.

chapter 13

Future Research Directions

BARBARA L. STARK
Arizona State University

BARBARA VOORHIES
University of California, Santa Barbara

INTRODUCTION

The study of Middle American coastal peoples is entering a phase in which we anticipate significant advances in the near future. Among the many problems remaining to be investigated concerning relationships between coastal populations and their biophysical environments and among coastal and other Middle American populations, we will consider some research directions that seem to us to have a high potential for scientific productivity. We will follow these research directions using the topics of procurement, settlement, and exchange, subjects that have particular importance for prehistoric ecological and economic analysis. For each topic we will comment on relevant variables, methods of analysis, and models.

A recurrent methodological consideration that has arisen in the discussion of each of the three topics is the scale of research. Our reflections have demonstrated to us the importance of research at the level of the local region. Sanders has recommended this research approach in his commentary, but perhaps the most persuasive argument for regional analysis comes

275

from a social anthropologist, Carol Smith (1976:II:3–20). Smith's two volumes of collected papers demonstrate that the regional scale of analysis is imperative for understanding the operation of social and economic systems. For archaeologists, practical implementation of the regional scale will probably remain somewhat more restricted than it would for social anthropologists and geographers. By a local region we mean an area sufficiently large to encompass a number of sites and biotopes but not so large as to entail whole sets of interrelated regions. Of necessity, the regional scale will be tailored to both research objectives and practical considerations. The local regional scale will permit us to identify variations in resources and their uses, the relations between settlements and the natural environment, and, lastly, exchange patterns among different economically specialized communities and zones.

At the conceptual level we have found it useful to think in terms of an ecological setting that is distinctively coastal. This is perhaps equivalent to Sanders' concept of a coastal ecotype. The formulation of such an analytical construct is based on the assumption that the coastal environment is in some ways distinctive compared to other types of environments. This conceptualization is necessary if we are to examine certain developmental issues from a comparative ecological perspective. Sanders has reviewed some of the current developmental debates, and we will return to the same topics in this chapter. We suspect, however, that our current notion of a coastal setting ultimately may be found to be too simplistic for the resolution of some processual problems and that considerable refinement may be required in the near future. In no sense do we wish to negate the variations in coastal environments. As Voorhies noted before, investigators have defined coastal populations both geographically and functionally; both senses are implied by our recognition of a coastal ecological setting.

PROCUREMENT PATTERNS

In the introduction to the section "Procurement Patterns" (Part II) we noted that local procurement activities encompass subsistence food-getting as well as extractive activities for raw materials such as minerals, shells, clay, etc. However, nonfood substances will not be treated in our discussion here because many of them apparently played significant roles in exchange networks, and accordingly we defer their discussion to the section on exchange, later in this chapter.

The archaeological emphasis on reconstruction of food resources is justified by the energetic relationship between available food supply and population size and activities. In the present discussion we consider two important aspects of the archaeological reconstruction of procurement patterns, particularly as they pertain to ancient coastal peoples: first, local resource characterization; second, prehistoric procurement behavior.

Local Resource Characterization

We are still painfully limited in detailed characterizations of Middle American coastal food resources. Discussions of coastal resources continue to be plagued by the fact that investigators do not always make clear what set(s) of coastal resources they are evaluating; coastal habitats and hence resources are actually quite varied. We will identify a number of variables that seem to us to be important in the assessment of coastal resources. These can be grouped into three sets of variables: (a) abiotic; (b) biotic; and (c) sociocultural. Among the abiotic variables would be ones relating to seasons, climatic fluctuations, geomorphology, soils, etc. But in many respects biotic variables are of more pressing, direct interest because of the importance of food species. (Clearly, food species are responsive to abiotic variables.) Biotic variables of particular interest for differentiation and comparison of food species include: size of organisms, amount of usable parts, nutritional characteristics of usable parts, spacing of species (individually and in terms of their habitats), density, and periodicity (e.g., seasonal). Finally, we cannot interpret the human behavioral implications of biotic variables without examination of certain sociocultural variables related to procurement. Particularly relevant are time and energetic effort (costs), probability of success, technological overhead, and preservation span (given certain processing and storage measures). Some of these biotic and sociocultural variables warrant elaboration here and will enter into a case example we will consider.

In order to bring home the importance of resource characterization, we will examine a case example concerning protein and calorie yields of fish in relation to labor investment in the Lower Papaloapan Basin, Veracruz, Mexico. Employing the results of this analysis, we can reopen some developmental debates of general interest about Middle American coastal peoples. In this manner we can give some teeth to our claim that resource characterization according to some of these variables affords a desirable research direction. Following this, we turn to the related topic of paleoenvironmental reconstruction and examine it from the point of view of identification of prehistoric resources and of mapping resources in a catchment area.

Resource Variables

Among the biotic variables, seasonality of resources is one important aspect of resource periodicity, in part because it is a key to understanding scheduling decisions of prehistoric populations (Flannery 1968). In most regions, following the establishment of a farming lifeway, seasonal variations regulate rainfall agricultural systems (Coe 1974). Coastal populations that draw on both aquatic and terrestrial biotopes for food are dependent on seasonal variations of both wild and domesticated foods. Consequently, coastal research must be concerned not only with environmental parameters of soils, temperatures, moisture, and light, which closely affect cultigens, but also with wild foods, especially fauna, and their seasonality. Seasonal rainfall and accumulated runoff bring marked changes in aquatic environments, principally in estuaries, where a delicate balance of currents, turbidity, salinity, and temperature affect survival and movements of various mollusks, crustaceans, and fish.

In addition to periodicity, we noted above that a number of other biotic variables are important in evaluating food species: size, density, spacing, amount of usable parts, and nutritional value. We have inadequate information about these variables. Although it is usually possible to obtain meager descriptions of the preferred habitats and habits of coastal organisms, data on species' size, density, and distribution are much more difficult to obtain. Therefore, we have little precise knowledge about wild coastal foods. In addition, we need to be able to convert organisms to usable parts and ultimately to caloric, protein, and other nutritional yields. Wing's chapter in this volume is a cornerstone of this type of research.

We also need to consider sociocultural variables such as labor costs required to obtain resources and process them into foods. For example, certain resources having high nutritional yields may also have high associated labor costs that have the effect of making them less desirable resource choices. One factor affecting cost is probability of resource capture. It is possible that high costs are associated with hunting some large aquatic mammals, such as manatee (Neitschmann 1973:161), because the prey is either elusive or rare. Humans confronting such a situation might exhibit greater use of small animals that are more abundant and hence associated with lower capture costs. Sessile mollusks, which may be locally plentiful, could provide a food source that is preferred to manatee even though the molluscan meat is inferior to that of manatee in both caloric and protein yield measured per unit of edible portion (Neitschmann 1973:151–152; Stark 1977b:215). The occurrence of mollusks in known local habitats, their ease of collection, and the low technological overhead required to obtain them may make them attractive food sources. Therefore, the use of mollusks in particular situations may indicate the employment of a rational economic strategy that is revealed by means of a cost–benefit analysis.

It seems clear to us that archaeological studies of prehistoric coastal populations must proceed in close interdependence with studies by natural scientists and ethnographers. Neitschmann's (1973) subsistence study of a Miskito village indicates one kind of project that is vital to our understanding of coastal procurement patterns. Neitschmann considers resource seasonality, abundance, and return for labor, and his analysis is particularly strong in the first and last areas. We will have occasion to draw on his data in our discussion of a case example of resource characterization.

Implications of Resource Variables

What may we anticipate as payoffs from the kinds of studies we are outlining in coastal resource characterization? We can illustrate some of them by reconsideration of traditional developmental debates surrounding coastal populations in Middle American prehistory. We will discuss some issues in prehistoric coastal development by drawing on modern resource information from the Lower Papaloapan Basin in order to evaluate the economic possibilities and limitations of aquatic resources there.

Certain debates about the role of coastal populations in Mesoamerican prehistory have already been considered by Voorhies and Sanders in this volume and have received some recent discussion by Stark (1977b:222–224). One developmental issue is whether coastal habitats fostered precocious preagricultural sedentarism because of their rich, dependable foods, or whether they were instead only seasonally exploited by early agriculturalists living inland. As stated, this is simply a question of fact, one provoked by a rather loose characterization of coastal resources (cf. Osborn 1977).

In the following example we illustrate how more accurate resource characterization in one local region can affect developmental debates such as the one concerning the nature of early coastal adaptation. In this example we attempt to answer the question: Could aquatic resources alone actually provide subsistence for a nonagricultural family? An answer to this question should help us better understand the subsistence potential of the Lower Papaloapan prior to the development of agriculture. The Lower Papaloapan is relatively rich in estuarine aquatic resources compared to many other regions and therefore should provide us with information on food potential in a highly productive coastal situation.

In the following hypothetical example we make certain simplifying assumptions. The first is that Lower Papaloapan fishing is pursued on a full-time basis and that therefore fish harvest as converted to nutritional return is nearly maximized within local environmental restraints. A second assumption is that present-day catches are sufficiently similar to those of the past as to be approximately representative of them. A third assumption is that Neitschmann's nutritional consumption data for a present-day, relatively

healthy coastal population can serve as a representation of nutritional requirements of ancient populations.

In order to estimate the amount of fish that potentially could have been
obtained in the past from the Lower Papaloapan, we will use data on fish
(plus some turtle) catches from the two modern towns Tlacotalpan and
Alvarado.[1] Data on fish catches for these towns for the years 1948 and 1949
(Attolini 1950:35–46) gives us a composite annual total of 1,771,710 kg of
fishes.[2] The reported catches are apparently only those of organized full-time
fishermen and do not include fish caught by other individuals for their own
private consumption or sale. Accordingly, these data in no way represent
environmental productivity but, rather, catches by one set of fishermen.

According to Wing's data, presented in this volume, most fish yield
90% usable meat. The total annual catch therefore represents approximately
1,594,539 kg of edible meat. This figure can be converted to average caloric
and protein yields by averaging published nutritional data on various fishes
(Woot-tsuen 1961:81–86).[3] Averages for these fish (and turtle) are 101.72
calories per 100 gm of raw edible portion, and 19.2 gm of protein per 100 gm
of raw edible portion. Dividing the total production of calories and protein[4]
by the reported number of fishermen (1087), we are able to calculate the
average amount of calories and protein produced per fisherman on an
annual basis: 1,491,854.8 calories and 281,648.1 gm of protein.

We would like to assess these production figures in terms of nutritional
needs. In order to do this we will adopt the information available for the
Tasbapauni Miskito. Using Neitschmann's figures, we calculate that an
average adult consumes 857,750 calories per year and 10,293 gm of protein

[1]Fishing technology at the time that these data on fish catches were assembled was not
greatly mechanized; 84% of the boats used were without motors, and 93% were under three
metric tons. Nonetheless, fishing may have been somewhat more productive for labor investment than fishing with aboriginal technology.

[2]Alvardo fishermen did some fishing in nearshore Gulf waters rather than in the estuarine
and fresh waters where Tlacotalpeños fished. The protected estuary waters would probably
have been favored aboriginally. Therefore, it will be desirable to scale the Alvarado catch in
terms of the Tlacotalpan catch to compensate for any increase per fisherman due to use of the
Gulf. A total of 1087 fishermen are recorded, 776 in Alvarado and 311 in Tlacotalpan (based
partly on a weighted proportion). The annual total of Tlacotalpan catches of various fish
(generally excluding mollusks and crustaceans) is 506,203 kg (includes a small amount of crab
and turtle that cannot be factored out). We will assume that Alvarado fishermen could catch fish
only proportionately to their numbers, which would add 1,265,507 kg for a combined total of
1,771,710 kg annually.

[3]Bagre, carp, flounder, an unspecified fat-poor fish, mullet, pejerrey, robalo, saw-fish,
snapper, turtle meat, and trout.

[4]Every kilogram of usable Papaloapan fish would therefore represent about 1017 calories
and 192 gm of protein. The total catch would represent an annual production of 1,621,646,163
calories and 306,151,488 gm of protein.

per year. According to Neitschmann, an average Miskito family of seven requires 4,380,000 calories and 50,370 gm of protein per year.[5]

Comparison of the average annual production of calories and protein by a single full-time fisherman with the consumption figures presented by Neitschmann reveals that a single fisherman would be unable to produce sufficient calories from fish alone to support the consumption requirements of himself and one other adult. In contrast, each Lower Papaloapan fisherman would produce on the average over five times the protein consumption of a Miskito family of seven. This finding does not inform us about the limits of productivity in the Lower Papaloapan, but fish yields do provide an important clue about faunal potential in terms of fulfilling the requirements of human nutrition. Fish tend to have a higher percentage of edible portion per live weight than other aquatic vertebrates according to Wing's data (this volume); they also have greater nutritional value compared with mollusks and crustaceans. Yet the Lower Papaloapan data indicate that a hypothetical adaptation based only on fishing would suffer from a calorie crunch.

On the basis of the exercise just completed, it seems to us that early coastal populations always must have exhibited mixed economies involving significant inputs of plant resources as important caloric sources. If we assume no intercommunity exchange of food resources, then food require-ments hypothetically could be met equally well by two separate strategies: (a) seasonal population movement between plant-rich locales and fish-rich locales; or (b) population localization at a single settlement where both plant and aquatic resources are conveniently accessible. We would predict that people would choose the latter alternative in coastal environments in which biotopes are closely spaced. The interfingering of levees and waterways in the Lower Papaloapan delta is an example of a coastal environment with these characteristics, but it is not yet possible to assess the productivity of wild plant resources on levees. In fact, most coastal habitats have not been properly assessed by archaeologists in terms of plant resource potential.

A related issue noted by Sanders is whether or not early sedentary coastal groups ever engaged in the domestication of plants. This is moot in view of the uncertainties we have outlined earlier. This issue has been more prominent in South American than in Middle American coastal literature (cf. Reichel-Dolmatoff 1965:61; Sauer 1952:23–24, 41–42). Middle American

[5]Tasbapauni Miskito have a relatively high annual protein consumption: Adults average 28.2 gm per day; an average family of seven (consisting of two adults, two adolescents, one older child, and two younger children, Neitschmann 1973:220) averages 138 gm per day. The average Miskito adult daily consumption is 2350 calories, and the average consumption for a family of seven is 12,000 calories. Therefore, an average adult would need 857,750 calories per year and 10,293 gm of protein per year; a family of seven would need 4,380,000 calories per year and 50,370 gm of protein per year.

coastal sedentarism has been discussed mainly as a form of preadaptation leading to a rapid adoption of agriculture developed elsewhere (Coe and Flannery 1967:104); coastal populations have also been posited as producers of excess population which would stress resources in poorer upland areas and promote plant domestication there (Binford 1968).

Sanders raises the possibility that coastal areas were marginal and used only seasonally pending the development of large populations of inland farmers. He suggests that permanent and specialized coastal communities grew up in symbiotic relationships to inland areas, which underwrote the energetically more costly coastal fishing–collecting activities. We are in partial disagreement with this notion.

First, the assumption is apparently made that coastal regions are not capable of producing plant foods adequate for the maintenance of permanent populations. We question, however, whether we are in a position to rule out the support capacity of wild plant resources (e.g., nuts) that might provide needed calories in some coastal areas. Furthermore, with the addition of agriculture, coastal regions with favorable juxtapositions of aquatic and terrestrial biotopes would have been excellent locations for people with mixed economies in which aquatic foods figured importantly in provisioning protein needs and locally produced plant foods provided caloric needs. Stark (1977b:222) has pointed out that hunting, fishing, and collecting plant foods seem to involve less labor than full-time agriculture. Hence, coastal localities where a combination of pursuits is possible might tend to attract an early permanent population.

Second, Sanders' suggestion apparently is based on the assumption that the effective carrying capacity of the inland-farmer adaptation is greater than that of possible coastal adaptations. Certainly we are not currently in a position to evaluate critically this proposition, but it seems plausible to us that some coastal regions might have underwritten large inland populations by providing them with protein (cf. Lange 1971) just as inland peoples could have underwritten coastal peoples in calories. In other words, the critical issue here concerns the relative weights of limiting factors in the coastal and inland environments.

Is an exchange of estuarine protein for farmland calories feasible according to food production capabilities in each case? To answer this question local regions must be evaluated separately. We can illustrate that for some regions such exchange appears to be feasible in the sense that an individual family could produce a sufficient surplus to supply the needed dietary element to a counterpart family. In order to illustrate this we will draw on fishing data from studies of the Lower Papaloapan and on crop data from studies of lowland farming systems.

To analyze the exchange potential between protein-producing fishermen and calorie-producing farmers, let us assume for simplicity's sake that maize will be the caloric source. Let us give the average farming family the same size and structure that we have used for fishermen. Maize production figures from ethnographic community studies in the lowlands vary according to local environments.[6] Coe (1974) analyzed farming around San Lorenzo Tenochtitlán, Veracruz, Mexico, and these data provide the best guidelines for slash-and-burn farmers along the Lower Papaloapan River because Coe's study treated farming on levees and adjacent upland terraces. Mean annual rainfall is somewhat higher along the Coatzacoalcos than along the Papaloapan, but, nevertheless, Coe's data are presently the most relevant for our purposes. We would like to know the degree of parity between fishermen's production of excess protein and farmers' production of excess calories. Would many or few farming families be needed to create a sufficient surplus of calories to maintain a fisherman and his family?

Before we attempt to explore this issue, let us note that our results cannot be conclusive. As we cautioned before, modern fishermen may be more productive than would have been possible aboriginally. Nor can our estimates of farm production be defended in detail for prehistoric periods. Earlier races of maize were less productive, and we will attempt here to scale production accordingly (but see Kirkby 1973). Moreover, excess production is notoriously an elastic factor. Exchange or demographic incentives may create marked variation in efforts undertaken to produce a surplus above subsistence needs (cf. Boserup 1965). Our purpose is simply to provide some guidelines as to what might transpire in the exchange of protein for calories.

According to Cowgill (1962:277), one farmer assisted by his family can care annually for up to 13 acres (5.26 ha) with a lowland slash-and-burn system. Coe (1974:10) reports that an annual average of 3.15 metric tons of shelled corn can be obtained from 1 ha of Coatzacoalcos levee land, which gives the highest yield in the San Lorenzo area. A lower yield of 2.25 metric tons is the average on neighboring upland soils. For a conservative estimate of corn production, we will use the upland figure. On this basis a farmer cultivating 5.26 ha could obtain 11,835 kilos of shelled corn annually. This would represent 15,267,150 calories annually (based on Woot-tsuen 1961:27). If the farmer must provide 4,380,000 calories for his own average family of seven, he will have 10,887,150 calories in excess.

Therefore, theoretically a farmer could support calorically more than three fishermen's families.[7] It may be recalled that an average fisherman

---

[6]For example, Reina (1967) studied the inhabitants of San Jośe, Petén, Guatemala, who suffer precarious subsistence corn production. Cowgill (1962) interviewed farmers around Lake Petén and presented data indicating surplus corn could be produced beyond family needs.

[7]The average fisherman's family has a caloric deficit of 2,888,145.2.

could produce over five times his family's annual protein needs. No doubt some of the apparently greater protein support potential is illusory because of the perishability of dried or salted fish compared to dried corn. Families could also have a higher protein consumption than the estimated one, although perhaps farmers could not cultivate as many hectares as we have assumed.

Nonetheless, we may conclude that there appears to be no great imbalance in the production and exchange potential of fishing-based protein and farming-based calories in the Lower Papaloapan. We do not expect this finding to be necessarily characteristic of all segments of the coast. In many cases, estuarine or marine production may be much less, or seasonally structured so that production is limited to part of the year; farming may be less productive. Adequate resource characterizations from various coastal areas will eventually help us decide the representativeness of the apparent Lower Papaloapan potential. The utility of studying caloric and protein procurement not just on the coast but in the tropical lowlands in general is illustrated by analyses of riverine ecology elsewhere (Gross 1975; Meggers 1971).

The purpose of the resource calculations we have undertaken is twofold. First, from the examples we see that resource data help us structure more explicit models about what we might expect and should look for in the coastal archaeological record. For example, localities with extensive, rich estuarine resources (e.g., Lower Papaloapan) and inland tropical forest fauna (e.g., those comparable to the Miskito Coast) may prove to be settings in which fishing–collecting will represent an attractive labor solution for faunal protein procurement both prior to and following the establishment of a farming lifeway. Following the initiation of farming, and particularly under conditions of population growth, we could expect exchanges of protein and calories between fishermen and farmers. Second, we have couched the analyses in terms of fish and maize yields from a particular area in order to emphasize the importance of local regional analysis. Both terrestrial and aquatic environments may exhibit important differences in critical subsistence variables. It may be, for example, that many estuarine environments offer a greater subsistence potential than many marine biotopes (cf. Osborn 1977).

Our preceding discussion of the implications of resource variables in developmental terms makes no pretense of completeness; we have devoted very little attention to other important ecological variables such as demography. Moreover, we are not convinced that procurement is the only key to understanding the course of coastal prehistory. Control of exchange networks may have been equally vital for many localities (see Freidel, R. Zeitlin, Helms, this volume).

Paleoenvironmental Reconstruction

Compounding the problems of resource characterization in coastal areas is the task of paleoenvironmental reconstruction. Because coastal environments involve the description of both terrestrial and aquatic biotopes, the effort appears more difficult than that facing researchers in most inland Middle American environments. Paleoenvironmental reconstruction in coastal areas is critical not so much because we anticipate marked contrasts in basic resources, but because we need to know *where* particular resources or biotopes are at different time periods. This "catchment area" information is important in understanding the labor investment for obtaining different resources (for people at a particular site), and Voorhies has already noted the tendency for coastal procurement to vary with the coastal biotope in which a site is situated.

The geomorphology of coastal zones is subject to accelerated processes of change compared to interior regions such as the Tehuacán Valley, the Basin of Mexico, or the Oaxaca Valley. Investigations at each of these highland localities indicate a substantial amount of similarity to modern conditions well back into Archaic times even though shifts in moisture and vegetation zones may still present problems (Flannery 1967:140–145; Kirkby 1973:127–128; Sanders 1965:28). True, some highland areas have suffered episodic changes due to tectonic or volcanic activity (Sharer 1974:172), but coasts pose the potential problem of pervasive shifts in critical environmental features and hence biotic resources.

Rising sea level, subsidence or uplift of land masses, volcanic activity (e.g., Tuxtla Mountains), shifts in river channels and shorelines, tides, currents, and winds interplay to create a landscape with both marked biotope variation and active change in biotope location. Although we can expect continuity with modern conditions, we cannot extend this to include stable locations. Hence, independent historical environmental studies are urgently needed by coastal archaeologists. In addition, the diversity of coastal biotopes represents a substantial strain on cross-disciplinary planning. Changing landscapes threaten not only our confidence in the details of paleoenvironmental interpretations, but also the archaeological record itself. Particularly if erosion or subsidence are indicated, extreme care must be exercised in any arguments based on lack of prehistoric occupation.

Prehistoric Procurement Behavior

There are many ways to categorize and study prehistoric procurement behavior. Here we will indicate briefly some important topics for investigation, but we will not attempt any extensive discussion of pertinent variables and models. The reason for our brevity is that we feel the subject is both too complex and too little advanced in coastal studies to be amenable to detailed exposition at the present time. There are numerous reasons why coastal research has not progressed far in identification of variables and elaboration of models. Despite the fact that theoretical persuasions and approaches to research design have contributed to this situation, there is also a mundane factor at work: insufficient opportunity to analyze a corpus of relevant archaeological data. Models provide a structure within which particular variables take on significance, and many models of prehistoric procurement behavior are tied to large-scale investigation. Previously Voorhies noted the lack of intensive regional settlement pattern studies in previous coastal research. The study of resource procurement ultimately requires a regional scale and cannot be documented in isolation from investigation of settlement and exchange patterns. This scale of study is required if we are to determine annual population movements in subsistence cycles (cf. Struever 1971 on reconstruction of settlement–subsistence systems). It is also necessary if prehistoric procurement was conducted in part for exchange purposes.

At best, we can attempt here to identify some variables useful for the study of procurement behaviors, many of which already have proved valuable in coastal archaelogical studies. These variables would include the following: choice of resources, relative emphasis on chosen resources, scheduling of resource use (including timing and duration, cf. Flannery 1968),[8] and intensity of resource use per capita (see J. Zeitlin and R. Zeitlin, this volume). There are additional variables of great interest, but for which archaeological methods are not yet well developed—for example, size, compositions, and organization of procurement task groups, which can be subdivided according to whether or not the groups engage in activities of resource acquisition, processing, or distribution to "consumers." At this point we can see that the study of procurement patterns intergrades with economic analysis.

We can illustrate by means of a case example the possibilities for analyzing procurement behavior with the variables we have listed. The example will illustrate the potential for descriptive models of strategies of prehistoric resource selection. This example is one that will combine use of a resource-characterization variable (amount of usable meat per organism) with data on a procurement-behavior variable (relative emphasis on chosen resources).

---

[8] Scheduling may closely correspond to periodicity in food species, but it also can be directly tied to abiotic factors connected with seasonal weather. Seasonal storms and currents impede boating and fishing on some coasts; see Neitschmann's (1973) study of a Miskito village in Nicaragua.

Following consideration of this case example, we will turn to some methodological topics that are important if we are to acquire data suited to development and verification of models for procurement behavior.

Modeling of prehistoric procurement strategies is an area that warrants
greater archaeological attention. Armed with adequate resource characterizations and archaeological information on resource use, we can begin to
describe some of the principles of this aspect of prehistoric behavior. This
type of analysis has been attempted ethnographically. Neitschmann (1973),
for example, presents information on subsistence strategies, a topic that
warrants additional research for prehistoric periods. Neitschmann was able
to demonstrate the Tasbapauni villagers placed greater reliance on aquatic
fauna, particularly turtles, than on land fauna (despite the greater caloric
yield per hour of labor expended for the latter compared to the former); this
pattern represents a lessening of risk of unsuccessful trips as well as a gain in
protein acquired (Neitschmann 1973:174–175). Neitschmann's comparison
of terrestrial hunting and aquatic exploitation provides a situation that con-
tradicts Osborn's (1977) generalization that marine resources are less attractive for subsistence than terrestrial fauna.

To provide an archaeological example of the possibilities for strategy
analysis, we will employ Wing's (this volume) data on vertebrate fauna from
four Veracruz sites. In performing this analysis we are ignoring some important uncertainties about how well the faunal data represent prehistoric diet
and procurement. Our information is poor concerning intrasettlement activity loci from which food remains derive and concerning what processes
have contributed to formation of the archaeological faunal record (cf. Binford and Bertram 1977). Nevertheless, we feel the example has some value
for illustrating the description of procurement strategies. The problem we are
interested in at these four sites is whether or not there is a tendency toward
selective use of animals that provided, on the average, more usable meat per
individual.

We have elected to examine separately the categories of fish, terrestrial
animals, and turtles on the grounds that these broad categories would have
commanded distinct procurement activities. Species can be grouped into
classes of large and small animals in average amount of usable meat per
individual within each category. These classes, rather than species, will be
the focus of our strategy analysis. Within these classes, prehistoric concentration on a particular species and neglect of other species within the same
category would undoubtedly be responsive to ease of capture, technology,
seasonality, tastiness of meat, etc. We wish to determine whether or not
there is a tendency toward selective use of classes of animals that provide
more usable meat per individual within each of the three categories studied.
Certainly procurement practices may be conditioned by a host of factors

besides the average amount of meat obtained from each animal. Nonetheless, this seems to be a likely variable affecting selection.

Frequencies of large and small animals in each of the three categories
can be compared to expected frequencies based on no preferential use. The χ^2
test can be applied using the formula

$$\chi^2 = \sum_{i=1}^{k} \frac{(O_i - E_i)^2}{E_i},$$

where O_i represents the observed frequency in the ith category and E_i
represents the expected frequency in the ith category (Siegel 1956). Unfortunately, we cannot define expected frequencies very satisfactorily. With no
preferential use, we might expect capture of food species to be proportionate
to their natural occurrence (if each could be obtained with the same
technology and effort). But quantifiable frequencies of natural occurrence
and means of capture are not known. To proceed with analysis here, we will
make an assumption: When species' sizes range from very large to small, we
assume larger animals will tend to be less frequent than smaller ones
because of food-chain requirements. Then, for the sake of example, we can
generate expected frequencies conservatively by assuming equal use of
large and small organisms. We ought to be able to detect selective use with
χ^2 and determine by inspection whether or not animals that gave more
usable meat per individual were favored. In using Wing's data, we will
combine all four Veracruz sites that she studied.[9]

Comparison of the frequencies of small and large fish (Table 13.1)
demonstrates that large fish were selectively favored over small ones. Wing's
data reveals that most large fish were snook. Comparison of frequencies of
small and large terrestrial fauna (excluding all birds except turkey) shows
that large animals were selected in preference to small animals (Table 13.2).
These large species were dog, deer, and peccary. In this case, we suspect
that domesticated dogs involved the least effort to obtain, and this helps
account for the great number of dogs among large animals. Comparison of
the frequencies of small and large turtles (Table 13.3) demonstrates that
small turtles were selectively favored, contrary to our expectations. This
raises the question of what factor could account for this food preference.
Perhaps small turtles were selected because of greater ease of capture and/or
much greater abundance compared with large turtles (a difference in abundance of greater magnitude than is the case with large and small terrestrial

[9]New means for usable meat per animal were calculated where necessary for all four sites
pooled. Animals were arranged in rank order within the three categories of terrestrial, fish, and
turtle. A division into large and small was made at the first instance of a major gap in mean
usable meat between species. For fish this was between the average for *Mugil* and *Caranx;* for
terrestrial animals, between *Dasyphus* and *Canis;* and for turtles, between *Geomyda* and
Dermatemys.

Table 13.1
COMPARISON OF FREQUENCIES OF SMALL AND LARGE FISH IN AVERAGE GRAMS
OF EDIBLE PORTION PER INDIVIDUAL AT FOUR VERACRUZ SITES

	Observed	Expected	$O - E$	$(O - E)^2$	$\dfrac{(O_i - E_i)^2}{E_i}$
Small	18	47	29	841	17.89
Large	76	47	29	841	17.89
Total	94				35.78

$\chi^2 = 35.78$; $df = 1$, alpha $= .01$, chi square $= 6.64$.
$H_0 =$ Observed frequencies show no selectivity at the .01 level (one change in 100 of Type 1 error, rejection of H_0 when it is true).
$H_1 =$ Observed frequencies show selectivity.
$\chi^2 > 6.64$, reject H_0.

Table 13.2
COMPARISON OF FREQUENCIES OF SMALL AND LARGE TERRESTRIAL FAUNA
(EXCLUDING BIRDS) IN AVERAGE GRAMS OF EDIBLE PORTION PER INDIVIDUAL AT
FOUR VERACRUZ SITES

	Observed	Expected	$O - E$	$(O - E)^2$	$\dfrac{(O_i - E_i)^2}{E_i}$
Small	26	41	15	225	5.487
Large	56	41	15	225	5.487
Total	82				10.974

$\chi^2 = 10.974$; $df = 1$, alpha $= .01$, chi square $= 6.64$.
H_0 and H_1 as in Table 13.1. $\chi^2 > 6.64$, reject H_0.

Table 13.3
COMPARISON OF FREQUENCIES OF SMALL AND LARGE TURTLES IN AVERAGE GRAMS
OF EDIBLE PORTION PER INDIVIDUAL AT FOUR VERACRUZ SITES

	Observed	Expected	$O - E$	$(O - E)^2$	$\dfrac{(O_i - E_i)^2}{E_i}$
Small	59	46	13	169	3.637
Large	33	46	13	169	3.637
Total	92				7.346

$\chi^2 = 7.346$; $df = 1$, alpha $= .01$, chi square $= 6.64$.
H_0 and H_1 as in Table 13.1. $\chi^2 > 6.64$, reject H_0.

animals or fish). Unfortunately, we are not able to pursue analysis of these other factors. This exercise has revealed an apparent difference in procurement strategies among three categories of fauna and points to topics warranting future investigation.

It is our expectation that pursuit of strategy analysis in coastal settings will allow us to determine whether people tended to optimize their economic behavior and, if so, in terms of what factors. If optimization incorrectly describes the behavior, alternative principles can also be examined.

In order to deal with variables relating to prehistoric procurement behaviors, we must adopt field and analytic methods that will give us appropriate data. At various points in this volume the need for greater technical standardization and sophistication has been noted, for example, use of flotation and screening, conversions to MNI and usable meat, etc. Collection of representative data is also tied to our sampling procedures, a topic which we discuss in the next section.

Not only regional but also intrasite variations in procurement data warrant our attention. Although we have tended to stress the importance of a regional scale of analysis, we include, nested within it, settlement and domestic area levels of study. We can only acknowledge the relevance of Flannery's (1976) charges that Mesoamericanists have paid insufficient attention to variations within sites. Lateral exposures of site and housemound areas can be expected to yield evidence of distinct activity loci, which in itself will help us understand resource processing and consumption. Neitschmann's (1973:153) subsistence data on the Tasbapauni Miskito warn us that we must expect differences among families within villages as well as among villages.[10]

SETTLEMENT PATTERNS

We will first discuss briefly selected issues concerning theoretical models for settlement patterns. Much current analysis of settlement patterns draws on models and ideas from economic geographers. As Sanders notes (this volume), not all of the experimentation has been successful. We wish to discuss some of the reasons behind this and to note some of the directions that may prove valuable to pursue. In part, our discussion will note settlement pattern variables of current interest. We caution that the rapidly

[10]For a variety of technologic, economic, and seasonal factors, Tasbapauni as a whole exhibit a mixed faunal strategy, with some men engaged principally in hunting (15%), others, hunting and turtling (20%), and still others, only turtling (65%). The distribution of meat among socially related families increases the benefit of this mixed strategy to the village as a whole.

changing and complex nature of spatial studies in archaeology does not allow firm claims about what will be or should be done. Following discussion of issues related to locational models, we will touch on some valuable methods for future settlement pattern efforts.

There are two effects of the current ferment in settlement studies. There is more conscious attention to spatial variables, in part as a descriptive aid, and a heightened concern with the causes of identifiable patterns. Spatial variables in settlement patterns include distance, area, and volume, which are one-, two-, and three-dimensional characteristics of things in space. Ratio scaling of these variables facilitates use of statistical methods for comparing and evaluating spatial distributions and characteristics, whether of sites, features, or artifacts. To give some examples drawn from Middle America, we can note that site area has been categorized into intervals for nominal and ordinal scaling of site types in surveys of the Basin of Mexico (e.g., Parsons 1971:21–24); population estimates have been generated from site areas and artifactual densities using modern population and settlement as a guide. Analyses of intersite distances have employed first-order areal and linear nearest-neighbor statistics for greater rigor in the description of spacing in terms of clustered, dispersed, and random point patterns (Hammond 1974; Earle 1976; Stark and Young 1977).

Unfortunately the use of spatial variables coupled with statistical techniques has not always proceeded with sufficient methodological rigor. We do not refer to problems of insufficient sample size and/or faulty data, which are frequent difficulties. Rather, we refer to incomplete attention to the limitations and requirements of the methods themselves. For example, Hammond (1974, see note 3) initially did not consider boundary effects on the areal nearest-neighbor statistic. Earle (1976) makes no use of confidence intervals in evaluation of nearest-neighbor values for a given sample size.

Partly spurring the growing interest in spatial variables is the fact that many ideal models in economic geography generate settlement distributions with measurable spatial characteristics. Statistical methods help evaluate whether real distributions are significantly close approximations to ideal ones. Central-place theory is one such ideal model, and flawed implementation of quantitative methods is one aspect of the lack of success to date in applications of it.

It has been pointed out that we should choose our ground carefully in the application of models like central-place theory (Webber 1971). This would include weighing how closely environmental parameters approximate the featureless plain that is assumed in the ideal model. Smith (1974:175) has noted that distortions of such environmental conditions will not necessarily prevent us from detecting agreement with, and systematic deviations from, the model. However, lack of concern by archaeologists for the probable applicability of central-place theory contributes to doubts about its relevance. Similarly, we must give careful consideration to temporal parameters. The ideal landscape of central-place theory represents a homeostatic "marketing" equilibrium. For periods prior to the establishment of such an equilibrium, we must turn to various developmental models (see J. Zeitlin, this volume).

The relevance of central-place theory to prehispanic Middle America hinges not only on temporal and environmental matters; behavioral processes that create settlement patterns are also a problem. Classical central-place theory is concerned with retail marketing in centers serving a rural hinterland. Sanders raises the interesting question of whether or not redistributive economies will prove immune to some of the effects of economic competition and distance on settlement patterns which are built into central-place theory. In part, Sanders seems to be pointing out that redistributive political organizations represent barriers to free exchange following purely economic motivations. This may well be the case, but the question remains: Do outlying "consumers" weigh distance–cost considerations in their political-economic arrangements? There is a converse question: To the extent that politically controlled redistributive networks confront population-management problems and must attempt to maintain organizational allegiances across increasing distances as well as absorb the costs of noneconomical supply and consumption patterns, do these organizations face some of the same cost constraints that operate in marketing situations? We do not know yet if redistributive economies will diverge so much in their settlement pattern effects from "market" economies that hierarchical settlement distributions will lack aspects of the least-cost features prescribed by a central-place lattice. It must be remembered that the mode of exchange must be addressed with different kinds of data and techniques than are strictly appropriate to settlement pattern analysis.

Partly at stake is the role of trade and exchange in the evolution of more complex societies. Renfrew (1975) has recently argued that early, small-scale states may grow up endogenously partly through economic interactions, including redistributive ones. Settlement patterns of small states that grew in part out of economic exchanges might be expected to reflect economic decisions to some extent in regard to distance–costs. We recognize that this possible line of evolution of early states leaves unanswered the question recently reiterated by Flannery (1977:760) of how certain families or groups came to seize and maintain advantageous control of exchange. Certainly organizational transactions have an important equivalent to economic ones.

In any event, it remains the archaeologist's task to determine the validity of central-place theory (or any other locational model) in some or any early societies, as well as to examine any systematic distortions to determine what social or environmental factors might account for them. Tests of explicit models such as central-place theory have the advantage exhibited by Smith's (1975) work in the Guatemala highlands: Systematic exceptions may reveal unanticipated relationships between economy, social organization, and settlement pattern. Certainly the settlement–spatial features of redistributive economies need to be developed as alternatives to, or modifications of, central-place theory. It seems premature to rule out either central place or other least-cost (distance or travel time) spatial models before we have pinned down what forms and patterns of exchange, as well as settlement patterns, characterize different periods. Ideally, our investigations should be directed at detecting the degree of fit between alternative models and observations within a probabilistic framework.

One suggestion we would offer for future locational research in the coastal lowlands is greater attention to linear models of various kinds. The reason for this suggestion is that several coastal localities exhibit linear settlement patterns, either along coasts (e.g., on Cozumel, see Sabloff and Rathje 1975b) or along rivers (e.g., in Belize, see Willey et al. 1965). Central-place theory can be cast into a linear framework (Dacey et al. 1974; Flannery 1976:174–175). Dendritic patterns also can have linear forms (Smith [1974:177–179] summarizes dendritic patterns and associated economic functions, specifically export–import). Although analysis of linear patterns is not yet as advanced as that of areal patterns, they would appear to be more relevant to many coastal situations.

A second suggestion for future settlement pattern research is more analysis of the relationship between settlement variables (e.g., size, distance, and function) and natural resources, such as farmland, clay deposits, and economic mineral and stone deposits (cf. Gumerman 1971). These resources warrant attention in the analysis of exchange patterns, and we expect that they will show systematic relationships to settlement patterns.

In the execution of field research, greater use of air photography to locate sites in some environments (e.g., wetlands, see Bruder, Large, and Stark 1975) and greater attention to probabilistic sampling surely will prove valuable (S. Plog 1976; Mueller 1975). In view of the scarcity of regional surveys on Middle American coasts, probabilistic sampling appears desirable as a means to broaden our data base while attempting to safeguard its representativeness.[11]

[11]Rice (1976) reports a survey project conducted around the Yaxhá and Sacnab lakes in the Petén, Guatemala, that combined air photography and ground survey using a sampling procedure. Although his is not a coastal study, it does apply some of the methods we feel will prove worthwhile in coastal research, where vegetation is often similarly dense.

EXCHANGE PATTERNS

We are confident that future studies of ancient Middle American coastal peoples will emphasize the reconstruction of exchange systems as long as the present trend in American archaeology continues on its current course. This trend has been explained by Renfrew (1975) as the dual result of a pragmatic and a historic factor. The pragmatic reason cited by Renfrew is that trade can be studied, whereas the historic reason is that many archaeologists have viewed the development of human society in material terms. This latter point is reiterated by Flannery's (1976:283) Skeptical Graduate Student who insists that "trade is the King Kong of all prime movers."

From a theoretical standpoint the burgeoning interest in exchange is appropriate. Exchange is simply a particularly human mechanism for resource sharing and is concerned on a fundamental level with energy capture and cycling. The amount of energy available to a population correlates with the population's size and social complexity. When we look at human sociocultural evolution we can see a trend in the development of exchange mechanisms, which began in a simple way at the interpersonal level (probably between a woman and her offspring) but which ultimately interlink large numbers of communities in a single complex system. Exchange, then, insofar as circulation of basic resources is involved, appears to be a cement uniting social units.

Although archaeology is not yet armed with alternative models defining circumstances under which different exchange systems develop, we are beginning to establish descriptive models suited to defining specific exchange systems. These models aid conceptualization of ancient exchange on a two-dimensional plane; they particularly involve the identification of exchanged items (i.e., commodities), loci, and directionality (cf. F. Plog 1977). Some models are designed to describe the points of origin of particular raw materials and the points of human use (i.e., sites); directionality is inferred to have been from source points to utilization points. Other two-dimensional models deal with utilization points exclusively. In these models the emphasis is placed on human exchange transactions. These either describe transactions between communities by means of intersite analysis, or within communities by means of intrasettlement analysis. Certain other models, in addition to arraying data spatially, comprise an organizational dimension. This property is produced by network analysis, for example (cf. F. Plog 1977).

The application of models is possible only in situations in which the existence of exchange networks has been established. This occurs only when relatively complete sets of data are available and sophisticated techniques of data collection have been applied by field investigators (F. Plog 1977:132). Plog emphasizes that the major prerequisite for the modeling of exchange systems is the employment of intrasite and intersite sampling techniques coupled with a regional approach to research design. Sanders, in his commentary to this volume, also stresses these prerequisites. Previous research concerning Middle American coasts (cf. Voorhies this volume) strikingly demonstrates that these criteria have not been met.

Accordingly, the immediate and pressing research requirement confronting investigators of coastal sites is the collection of basic data pertinent to the reconstruction of ancient exchange systems. We restrict the remainder of this discussion to the identification of data collection problems facing investigators in coastal habitats and to methods available for their solutions.

Problems of Data Collection

In archaeological situations in which the existence of an exchange system is not previously known but must be established empirically, the necessary precondition for its study is the identification of the inventory of commodities once involved in exchange transactions. This is the first-order task of the field archaeologist, because without the identification of commodities, definition of the structure and function of ancient exchange systems is stalled. One of the most knotty problems confronting coastal field investigators is that potential commodities in prehistoric exchange systems are difficult to identify. It seems to us that this circumstance is due to a combination of certain factors which are not restricted to the coastal lowlands but are particularly characteristic of them.

One of these factors is extrinsic and pertains to the fact that most of the Middle American coastal environment is climatically hot and humid (Vivó Escoto 1964; West 1964b:375–381) and subject to particularly rapid rates of biodegradation. The result is impoverishment of the archaeological record. We would like to point out that this circumstance is not uniformly true of the American tropical coasts; in other culture areas coastal settings are arid, and preservation is excellent (e.g. Moseley 1975). In the Middle American coastal setting, arid conditions are approximated only along a small portion of the northwestern coast of the Yucatan Peninsula and on the Pacific coast bordering the Gulf of California (Vivó Escoto 1964:fig. 14).

The second factor leading to difficulties in recognizing commodities in the archaeological record is intrinsic to the commodities themselves. It seems possible that the inventory of coastal commodities would tend to have less archaeologic visibility than commodity inventories of other regions because of the relative proportions of mineral resources, which tend to have good archaeological survival, and organic resources, with low frequencies of survival.

Mineral resources have a tendency to be scarce in many coastal environments. This is because the surfaces of much of the Middle American coastal lowlands are alluvial plains (West 1964a) and consequently are underlain by unconsolidated sediments rather than by bedrock formations. In regions where coastal landforms are formed by recent river-deposited alluvium or by uplifted marine sediments, prehistoric inhabitants may have lacked ready access to hard stone of the size and/or quality desirable for masonry architecture or the manufacture of lithic tools (cf. Rathje 1972). These environments also would tend to be lacking in precious minerals.

Scarcity of stone is not uniformly true of the Middle American coasts; the alluvial plains are interrupted by ranges of hills of varying geologic origin. In situations where the coastal lowlands are formed by metamorphic or igneous formations, bedrock outcrops could have provided ancient coastal inhabitants with some lithic resources. Although the possibility has not been systematically examined, prehistoric peoples may have concentrated on the plains rather than in coastal regions underlain by bedrock (West 1964a).

This socioenvironmental characteristic may be responsible in part for certain current assumptions about the role of coastal peoples in sociocultural development. If the major archaeological indicators of exchange happen to be mineralogic, and this type of resource is notably scarce within occupied coastal habitats, then the assumption can easily arise that coastal peoples were not active in prehistoric exchange systems.

Compared to mineral resources, biotic resources of many coastal environments are proportionately abundant. Most nearshore marine environments of the American tropics have a high diversity of fauna, and most adjacent land areas have high diversities of both faunal and floral resources. Apparently a wide spectrum of these biotic resources are potential food sources for humans, and the Middle American coasts cannot be considered biotically depauperate. Potentially these resources could have figured importantly in ancient exchange systems, particularly at the local level. However, there is a difficulty in the perception of these patterns because of the high probability of total degradation of physical remains and hence erasure of direct archaeological indicators of former exchange patterns.

Methods of Data Collection and Interpretation

How can investigators at coastal sites maximize their data collection and interpretation so that it will be possible to use available evidence in order to reconstruct ancient exchange systems? One answer is that investigators are encouraged to be more imaginative, systematic, and scientific in their efforts, and we will discuss below some specific methods for meeting these objectives.

Although many minerals are absent from coastal habitats, there are some that commonly occur, and these could be used to good advantage in identifying ancient coastal exchange systems. One of these is asphalt, a petroleum product especially present on the Gulf Coast lowlands and other portions of the Middle American eastern seaboard as well as in the lower Central American western coast (Encyclopaedia Britannica 1974, Vol. 14:165,173). Asphalt formed the basis for a black paint used in prehistoric times (see Stark, this volume) and was probably also used to caulk boats and as an adhesive. The significance of this resource in ancient Middle American exchange systems remains to be assessed. This assessment will be greatly aided by the good preservability of the commodity.

A second common coastal mineral, salt, must have figured regularly in ancient exchange systems, but analysis is obviously hampered by the fact that this item dissolves readily in water. Because direct remains of this commodity cannot be expected to occur, archaeologists must look for positive evidence of extraction processes and for archaeological correlates of transactions in order to reconstruct salt trade. An example of this strategy is the current research of Eaton and Adams (see Stark 1977a:276–277).

A third resource is high quality clay and tempering additives for ceramic manufacture. Because the deposition of clay depends in part on the presence of water as a sorting agent and because some of the finest clay beds are of recent marine origin, we would expect at least some portions of the Middle American coasts to be rich in argillaceous sediments. This possibility, to our knowledge, has not been systematically examined, but it may be significant that two widely traded ceramic types, Fine Orange (Sayre, Chan, and Sabloff 1971) and plumbate (Diehl, Lomas, and Wynn 1974), sometimes have been cited as possible coastal goods. In addition, we are beginning to see source and exchange analyses of ceramics both on the local regional and long-distance scales (Rands 1967; Sayre, Chan, and Sabloff 1971). These studies demonstrate that ceramics, although not as restricted environmentally as some other commodities, do exhibit localized production and do enter into exchange networks.

Although the restricted nature of mineral resources poses problems for reconstructing exchange at the local level, ironically this situation is an asset in the study of interregional exchange. When nonlocal mineral resources are found at coastal sites, they are so obviously exotic that even the most abstruse investigator must recognize that some form of ancient exchange was responsible for their presence. Thus, even without sophisticated data analysis, it is sometimes possible to paint in the broad outlines of long-distance exchange systems by tracing the direction of commodity flow from source areas to points of lowland consumption. However, this type of reconstruction is deficient because (a) it uses the unidirectional movement of a restricted set of resources as the basis for reconstructing a system that, in all probability, consisted of a two-way flow of multiple resources; (b) it involves sources of raw materials and points of consumption rather than establishing human behavior patterns; and (c) it provides data on an interregional basis but not within particular regions.

We believe that remains recovered from coastal sites can produce more evidence bearing on ancient exchange than is currently the case in Middle American coastal research. This contention is partially in response to Earle and Ericson's (1977:4) observation that "quantitative research based on the chemical characterization of raw materials is rapidly becoming *the* primary approach used to identify prehistoric exchange [emphasis ours]." The current emphasis on chemical characterization of raw materials is a research technique of tremendous potential but, as we have explained earlier, one of limited relevance for pinpointing possible coastal exports.

There are steps that can be taken to maximize the archaeological information on biotic resources in order to improve our reconstructions of coastal exchange systems, especially on a local level. One productive approach is to tap into ethnographic and/or ethnohistoric information on coastal commodities and to use these sources to formulate specific test implications for the archaeological record. For example, Voorhies has observed a number of specific techniques that are used by present-day peoples in the coastal village of La Palma, Chiapas, to preserve local resources and permit the extension of exchange beyond the range of the local group.

One simple technique is the capture of live animals and their transportation to consumption sites where they are killed just before use. This occurs particularly with reptiles such as turtles and iguanas. Other techniques include slow, thorough roasting over an open fire (meat), cooking and sun-drying (shrimp), baking (maize, in order to make *totopos*, a kind of crisp bread), and sun-drying (fish). All of these last methods involve the heating of organic substances in order to remove water. The techniques involved are very simple and the results are effective. It is probable that these techniques were developed long ago in coastal habitats. It is the archaeologist's task to demonstrate whether or not this actually was the case. If it were, the possibility of coastal peoples' full participation in exchange systems, even interregional ones, would be enhanced enormously.

Archaeological tests designed to establish the time depth of the techniques mentioned above fall into two categories. One is the identification of archaeological indicators of processing and manufacturing techniques;

these indicators can provide us with evidence of production, although not circulation, of particular commodities. For example, the discovery of large pottery jars embedded into raised-platform hearths would suggest prehistoric production of *totopos,* but it would not be positive proof that this food item figured in an exchange system. In order to develop unequivocal archaeological diagnostics of processing activities, detailed ethnoarchaeological studies are required, and if direct diagnostics of exchange are unavailable, then exchange can be inferred only.

The second kind of test is direct and can be used to yield information establishing prehistoric direction and extent of commodity transactions. If we are correct in suspecting that many coastal commodities are biotic rather than geologic in origin, we need to consider ways to identify these possible commodities in archaeological deposits. Zeigler (1973) has discussed this particular topic in detail in reference to vertebrate faunal remains and has pointed out how improved methods in data collection and analysis can provide information concerning prior existence of trade routes (Ziegler 1973:49–50). The faunal evidence bearing on exchange interpretation can be considered to fall into two groups.

The first involves faunal remains that are found at archaeological sites outside of the organism's natural habitat. Such an occurrence suggests that human exchange may have been responsible for the finding, but the investigator must also be able to demonstrate that the paleohabitat at the time of deposition was not congenial to the species under consideration. We have wondered above whether dried fish once formed export commodities from particular coastal habitats. If this were the case, and if prehistoric peoples utilized the same technique of gutting and splaying the nonskeletonized fish, we would expect to discover fishbones at inland sites as confirmation of this exchange pattern.

This type of analysis has already proved quite successful with hard parts (such as shells, fish spines, shark's teeth) from other marine animals found in inland archaeological deposits (e.g., Flannery 1976:341–344; Pires-Ferreira 1976). In these examples marine remains found in the Valley of Oaxaca clearly were exotic and hence were interpreted as imports from the coasts. The sources of resources such as these cannot be pinpointed as narrowly as some minerals, and hence only zones, rather than points of origin, can be established for the commodities.

The second kind of evidence regarding exchange in faunal resources depends on especially careful methods of data recovery and analysis. It requires the detection of frequency of occurrence of individual bones for each species represented in the archaeological deposits. When relative bone frequencies are found to differ significantly from those calculated on the basis of occurrence in a single organism of a particular species, some form of exchange in specific body parts may have been extant. As an illustration Flannery (1976:340) has interpreted the high frequency of macaw wing bones as compared with other macaw bones at Oaxacan sites as evidence for trade in macaw wing feathers.

An additional suggestion for coming to grips with the low preservation potential of coastal resources is to interpret some resources as *suites* of commodities rather than individually. Pires-Ferreira (1976) has demonstrated unequivocally the value of treating each commodity separately when direct remains are available; in instances in which some suspected commodities are expected not to have left recoverable remains, other analytic approaches are required. Voorhies (1976) has suggested that three littoral resources (shrimp, clam, and fish) can be interpreted best as a suite of possible coastal exports. The proposition is that shrimp remains might not survive in deposits, and that clams could have been shucked before export (an idea consistent with the presence of large shell middens within the littoral zone), but if fish were dried and exported their bones should occur at consumption sites. The test of the export proposition of the three items would rest on the recovery of fishbones in the inland archaeological remains. The justification for this procedure of dealing with suites rather than individual commodities derives from ethnographic observation. The results cannot be taken as final proof of the existence of exchange transactions in each of the items for which remains are lacking. Rather, they provide a means for producing an interpretation that is tied as closely as possible to the archaeological data base but at the same time provides a means to counterweight bias in interpretations based on easily preserved commodities.

If more complete archaeological accounts of exchange patterns are out of reach until we make a considerable effort to trace commodities, this does not mean that we are at a standstill in our attempts to determine the role of coastal populations in Middle American exchange systems, and the role of exchange in sociocultural development. Many investigators (see Helms, R. Zeitlin, Freidel, this volume) have used composites of various kinds of data in order to block out ideas about the relative importance of exchange for particular centers, societies, and periods of time in Middle American coastal prehistory.

In general, however, we feel that coastal peoples have been neglected somewhat by theorists ascribing an important role to long-distance exchange, and this may be an unintended result of the emphasis that previously has been placed on mineral commodities. It is also due to the fact that the human history of the Middle American coastal plains has been inadequately studied and therefore remains largely conjectural. Recently some developmental theories have emphasized the importance of maritime trading systems (Freidel, this volume; Sabloff and Rathje 1975a), and the possibility of this activity requires examination for different coastal peoples through time. We should expect significant alterations over time in the nature of coastal societies in view of the fact that they have been determined as much by the costeños' social environment as by their biophysical environment. The unraveling of these developmental patterns largely remains an endeavor for the future.

REFERENCES

Attolini, J.
  1950 *Economía de la Cuenca del Papaloapan. Bosques, fauna, pesca, ganadería e industria.* México, D. F.; Instituto de Investigaciones Económicas.
Binford, L.
  1968 Post-pleistocene adaptations. In *New perspectives in archaeology,* edited by S. R. Binford and L. R. Binford. Chicago: Aldine. Pp. 313–341.
Binford, Lewis R., and Jack B. Bertram
  1977 Bone frequencies—and attritional processes. In *For theory building in archaeology,* edited by Lewis R. Binford. New York: Academic Press. Pp. 77–153.
Boserup, E.
  1965 The conditions of agricultural growth. Chicago: Aldine.
Bruder, J. S., E. Large, and B. Stark
  1975 Aerial photography as an aid to archaeological survey in estuarine mangrove swamps: A field test in Veracruz, Mexico. *American Antiquity* **40**(3):330–337.
Coe, M. D.
  1974 Photogrammetry and the ecology of Olmec civilization. In *Aerial photography in anthropological field research,* edited by E. Z. Vogt. Cambridge, Massachusetts: Harvard Univ. Press. Pp. 1–13.
Coe, M. D., and Kent V. Flannery
  1967 *Early cultures and human ecology in south coastal Guatemala.* Smithsonian Contributions to Anthropology. Vol. 3. Washington, D. C.: Smithsonian Institution.
Cowgill, U.
  1962 An agricultural study of the southern Maya lowlands. *American Anthropologist* **64**:273–286.
Dacey, M. F., O. Davies, R. Flowerdew, J. Huff, A. Ko, and J. Pipkin
  1974 *One-dimensional central place theory.* Northwestern University, Studies in Geography, Vol. 21. Evanston, Illinois: Northwestern Univ. Press.
Diehl, R. A., R. Lomas, and J. T. Wynn
  1974 Toltec trade with Central America: New light and evidence. *Archaeology* **27**:182–187.
Earle, T. K.
  1976 A nearest-neighbor analysis of two formative settlement systems. In *The Early Mesoamerican village,* edited by K. V. Flannery. New York: Academic Press. Pp. 196–223.
Earle, T. K., and J. E. Ericson
  1977 Exchange systems in archaeological perspective. In *Exchange systems in prehistory,* edited by T. K. Earle and J. E. Ericson. New York: Academic Press. Pp. 3–12.
Encyclopaedia Britannica (15th ed.)
  1974 *Petroleum* Vol. 14. Pp. 164–189. Helen Hemingway Benton, Publisher.

Flannery, K. V.
   1967   Vertebrate fauna and hunting patterns. In *Prehistory of the Tehuacan Valley, Vol. 1: Environment and subsistence,* edited by D. S. Byers. Austin: Univ. of Texas Press. Pp. 132–177.
   1968   Archeological systems theory and Early Mesoamerica. In *Anthropological archeology in the Americas,* edited by B. J. Meggers. Washington, D. C.: The Anthropological Society of Washington. Pp. 67–87.
   1977   A setting for cultural evolution. *Science* **196:**759–761.
Flannery, K. V., ed.
   1976   *The Early Mesoamerican village.* New York: Academic Press.
Gross, D. R.
   1975   Protein capture and cultural development in the Amazon Basin. *American Anthropologist* **77:**526–549.
Gumerman, G. J., ed.
   1971   *The distribution of prehistoric population aggregates.* Prescott College Anthropological Reports No. 1. Prescott, Arizona: Prescott College Press.
Hammond, N.
   1974   The distribution of Late Classic Maya major ceremonial centres in the central area. In *Mesoamerican archaeology: New approaches,* edited by N. Hammond. Austin: Univ. of Texas Press. Pp. 313–334.
Kirkby, A. V. T.
   1973   *The use of land and water resources in the past and present Valley of Oaxaca, Mexico.* Memoirs of the Museum of Anthropology, University of Michigan. Vol. 5. Ann Arbor: Univ. of Michigan Press.
Lange, F.
   1971   Marine resources, a viable subsistence alternative for the prehistoric Lowland Maya. *American Antiquity* **73**(3):619–639.
Meggers, B. J.
   1971   *Amazonia: Man and culture in a counterfeit paradise.* Chicago: Aldine.
Moseley, M. E.
   1975   *The maritime foundations of Andean civilization.* Menlo Park, California: Cummings.
Mueller, James W., ed.
   1975   *Sampling in archaeology.* Tucson: Univ. of Arizona Press.
Neitschmann, B.
   1973   *Between land and water: The subsistence ecology of the Miskito Indians, Eastern Nicaragua.* New York: Seminar Press.
Osborn, A. J.
   1977   Strandloopers, mermaids, and other fairy tales: Ecological determinants of marine resource utilization—the Peruvian case. In *For theory building in archaeology: Essays on faunal remains, aquatic resources, spatial analysis, and systemic modeling,* edited by L. R. Binford. New York: Academic Press. Pp. 157–205.
Parsons, J. R.
   1971   *Prehistoric settlement patterns in the Texcoco Region, Mexico.* Memoirs of the Museum of Anthropology, University of Michigan, Vol. 3. Ann Arbor: Univ. of Michigan Press.
Pires-Ferreira, Jane W.
   1976   Shell and iron-ore mirror exchange in Formative Mesoamerica, with comments on other commodities. In *The Early Mesoamerican village,* edited by Kent V. Flannery. New York: Academic Press. Pp. 311–328.

Plog, Fred
    1977   Modeling economic exchange. In *Exchange systems in prehistory*, edited by T. K.
           Earle and J. E. Ericson. New York: Academic Press. Pp. 127–140.
Plog, Stephen
    1976   Relative efficiencies of sampling techniques for archeological surveys. In *The Early
           Mesoamerican village*, edited by K. V. Flannery, New York: Academic Press. Pp.
           136–158.
Rands, Robert L.
    1967   Ceramic technology and trade in the Palenque Region, Mexico. In *American histori-
           cal anthropology*, edited by C. L. Riley and W. W. Taylor. Carbondale: Southern
           Illinois Univ. Press. Pp. 137–151.
Rathje, W. L.
    1972   Praise the gods and pass the metates: An hypothesis of the development of Lowland
           Rainforest civilizations in Mesoamerica. In *Contemporary archaeology: A guide to
           theory and contributions*, edited by M. P. Leone. Carbondale: Southern Illinois Univ.
           Press. Pp. 365–392.
Reichel-Dolmatoff, G.
    1965   *Colombia*. New York: Prager.
Reina, R.
    1967   Milpas and milperos: Implications for prehistoric times. *American Anthropologist*
           69(1):1–20.
Renfrew, Colin
    1975   Trade as action at a distance: Questions of integration and communication. In
           Ancient civilization and trade, edited by J. A. Sabloff and C. C. Lamberg-Karlovsky.
           Albuquerque: Univ. of New Mexico Press. Pp. 3–59.
Rice, Don S.
    1976   Middle Preclassic Maya settlement in the Central Maya Lowlands. *Journal of Field
           Archaeology* **3**:425–445.
Sabloff, J. A., and W. L. Rathje
    1975a The rise of the Maya merchant class. *Scientific American* **233**(4):73–82.
    1975b *A study of changing pre-Columbian commercial systems*. Peabody Museum Mono-
           graphs, Vol. 3. Cambridge, Massachusetts: Peabody Museum of Archaeology and
           Ethnology, Harvard Univ.
Sanders, W. T.
    1965   *The cultural ecology of the Teotihuacan Valley*. University Park, Pennsylvania: De-
           partment of Sociology and Anthropology, Pennsylvania State Univ. Mimeo.
Sauer, Carl
    1952   *Agricultural origins and dispersals*. New York: The American Geographical Society.
Sayre, Edward V., Lui-Heung Chan, and Jeremy A. Sabloff
    1971   High-resolution gamma ray spectroscopic analyses of Mayan fine orange pottery. In
           Science in Archaeology, edited by R. Brill. Cambridge, Massachusetts: MIT Press. Pp.
           165–181.
Sharer, R. J.
    1974   The prehistory of the southeastern Maya periphery. *Current Anthropology*
           15(2):165–187.
Siegel, S.
    1956   *Nonparametric statistics for the behavioral sciences*. New York: McGraw-Hill.
Smith, Carol A.
    1974   Economics of marketing systems: Models from economic geography. In *Annual*

Review of Anthropology Vol. 3, edited by B. J. Siegel, A. R. Beals, and S. A. Tyler. Palo Alto, California: Annual Reviews. Pp. 167–201.

1975   Examining stratification systems through peasant marketing arrangements: An application of some models from economic geography. *Man* **10**(1):95–122.

1976   *Regional analysis.* 2 vol. New York: Academic Press.

Stark, B. L.

1977a   Mesoamerica. In Current research, edited by Thomas P. Myers. *American Antiquity* **42**(2):272–280.

1977b   *Prehistoric ecology at Patarata 52, Veracruz, Mexico: Adaptation to the Mangrove Swamp.* Vanderbilt Publications in Anthropology, No. 18. Nashville, Tennessee: Vanderbilt Univ. Press.

Stark, B. L., and D. Young

1977   Linear nearest neighbor analysis of Cabeza de la Vaca sites, Veracruz, Mexico. Paper presented at the 42nd Annual Meeting of the Society for American Archaeology, New Orleans, Louisiana.

Struever, S.

1971   Comments on archaeological data requirements and research strategy. *American Antiquity* **36**:9–19.

Vivó Escoto, Jorge A.

1964   Weather and climate of Mexico and Central America. In *Handbook of Middle American Indians, Vol. 1: Natural environment and early cultures,* edited by Robert C. West. (Robert Wauchope, gen. ed.). Austin: Univ. of Texas Press. Pp. 216–264.

Voorhies, B.

1976   *The Chantuto people: An Archaic Period society of the Chiapas littoral, Mexico.* Papers of the New World Archaeological Foundation No. 41.

Webber, M. J.

1971   Empirical verifiability of Classical Central Place theory. *Geographical Analysis* **3**:15–28.

West, Robert C.

1964a   Surface configuration and associated geology of Middle America. In *Handbook of Middle American Indians, Vol. 1: Natural environment and early cultures,* edited by Robert C. West. (Robert Wauchope, gen. ed.). Austin: Univ. of Texas Press. Pp. 33–82.

1964b   The natural regions of Middle America. In *Handbook of Middle American Indians, Vol. 1: Natural environment and early cultures,* edited by Robert C. West. (Robert Wauchope, gen. ed.). Austin: Univ. of Texas Press. Pp. 363–383.

Willey, G. R., W. R. Bullard, Jr., J. B. Glass, and J. C. Gifford

1965   *Prehistoric Maya settlements in the Belize Valley.* Papers of the Peabody Museum of Archaeology and Ethnology, Vol. 54. Cambridge, Massachusetts: Peabody Museum of Archaeology and Ethnology, Harvard Univ.

Woot-tsuen, Wu Leung

1961   *Food composition table for use in Latin America.* Bethesda, Maryland: Institute of Nutrition of Central America and Panama and Interdepartmental Committee on Nutrition for National Defense, National Institutes of Health.

Ziegler, Alan C.

1973   *Inference from prehistoric faunal remains.* Addison-Wesley Module in Anthropology, No. 43. Reading, Massachusetts.

Index

A
B
C 8
D 9
E 0
F 1
G 2
H 3
I 4
J 5

STUDIES IN ARCHEOLOGY

Consulting Editor: Stuart Struever

Department of Anthropology
Northwestern University
Evanston, Illinois